TOOLS AND TACTICS FOR THE MASTER DAY TRADER

TOOLS AND TACTICS FOR THE MASTER DAY TRADER

Battle-Tested Techniques for Day, Swing, and Position Traders

OLIVER VELEZ
GREG CAPRA

McGraw-Hill

New York   San Francisco   Washington, D.C.   Auckland   Bogotá
Caracas   Lisbon   London   Madrid   Mexico City   Milan
Montreal   New Delhi   San Juan   Singapore
Sydney   Tokyo   Toronto

Library of Congress Catalog-in-Publication Data

Author:	Velez, Oliver L.
Title:	Tools and tactics for the master day trader : battle-tested techniques for day, swing, and position traders / Oliver L. Velez and Greg Capra.
Published:	New York : McGraw-Hill, 2000.
Description:	p. cm.
LC Call No.:	HG4515.95.V45 2000
Dewey No.:	332.64/2/0285 21
ISBN:	ISBN 13: 978-1-265-80237-0 ISBN 10: 1-26-580237-8
Subjects:	Electronic trading of securities—Handbooks, manuals, etc.
	Day trading (Securities)—Handbooks, manuals, etc.
Other Authors:	Capra, Greg.
Control No.:	11881185

McGraw-Hill

A Division of The McGraw-Hill Companies

16 17 18 19 20 QFR/QFR 1 5 4 3 2

The sponsoring editor for this book was Stephen Isaacs, the editing supervisor was Paul R. Sobel, and the production supervisor was Elizabeth J. Strange. It was set in Palatino by Carol Barnstable / Carol Graphics.

This publication is designed to provide accurate and authoritative information in regard to the subject matter covered. It is sold with the understanding that neither the author nor the publisher is engaged in rendering legal, accounting, futures/securities trading, or other professional service. If legal advice or other expert assistance is required, the services of a competent professional person should be sought.

—From a declaration of principles jointly adopted by a committee of the American Bar Association and a committee of publishers.

McGraw-Hill books are available at special quantity discounts to use as premiums and sales promotions, or for use in corporate training programs. For more information, please write to the Director of Special Sales, Professional Publishing, McGraw-Hill, Two Penn Plaza, New York, NY 10121-2298. Or contact your local bookstore.

This book is dedicated to my beautiful, ever patient, and supportive wife Brenda, the very best investment I ever made, and to my daughter Rebecca and my son, Oliver Jr., the sweetest dividends I've ever received.

This book is also dedicated to my loving parents, Dwight Velez and Louise Velez, who taught me that mastery of life easily follows he who has mastered himself.

O.V.

To my wife Lori, for her love, support, and understanding through this exciting journey.

G.C.

CONTENTS

Chapter 3

Loss: The Prerequisite to Trading Power and Success   67

Chapter 7

Secrets of the Master Trader: 15 Things Every Trader Should Know, But Doesn't 133

Chapter 8

10 Lessons for the Master Trader 153

Chapter 9

Final Words of Wisdom from a True Master 163

ACKNOWLEDGMENTS

We would like to acknowledge all those who, through the years, have placed their financial independence in our hands. You have fueled our desire to write this book and ignited in us a lifelong purpose.

Most certainly we are thankful for the love, guidance, and wisdom of our parents. And for the never-ending sacrifices made by our wonderful wives. Brenda and Lori, we are eternally grateful for your love.

We wish to express our appreciation for Dave Bush's boundless energy and enhusiasm for this project. His tireless and passionate efforts in helping to organize and edit the material are evident throughout this book. We would also like to thank Mike Campion for lending his extensive knowledge of level II to this work.

Last, but far from least, we wish to give a special thanks to Jeffrey Krames and Stephen Isaacs of McGraw-Hill. Their patience and support during our many delays and setbacks demonstrated a tremendous faith in our ability. We truly would not have finished without their help.

PREFACE

There I was, nearly 6 years ago, sitting in front of what was then a sophisticated trading system, waiting for the market to open. I was anxious to make a trade. It would be my very first as a professional day trader. The opening bell rang. And, instantly, blinking red and green quotes, along with shifting NASDAQ market makers, battled for my attention. They seemed to be using my computer monitor as their terrain. In the midst of the chaotic price quotes, I saw what I *thought* was an ideal opportunity. I was nervous. The moment of truth had finally arrived, and for the briefest of moments, I doubted. But I was determined to make it as a day trader. With mounting credit card bills, a wife, and a brand new baby, I just *had* to make it. For an instant, fear wrestled with me, almost begging me to hold off. "No," I said to myself. I *had* to do it. I *had* to make the trade. I reached for my keyboard and, for a brief second, closed my eyes. Several key stokes later, I was the owner of 4000 shares of Microtouch, Inc. (MTSI), one of the faster moving over-the-counter (OTC) stocks of the day. I was amazed at how fast, how quickly I was able to buy $150,000 worth of stock. Moments later, I was up a whopping $4000. I couldn't believe my eyes. In several minutes, I was up more money than I could make in 2 full months at my prior job. It felt good, damn good in fact. And life, for the moment, was simply grand.

Then it happened. MTSI stalled. I battled with the idea of taking my swift gain. After all, a $4000 profit was an impressive way to start off the first day of my new life as a day trader. "Yes," I told myself. "I would sell. I would take the money and go home a hero." Once again, I reached for my keyboard. And before I could act, the bid in MTSI collapsed. My heart stopped. There was nothing but silence. In a flash, my $4000 gain went to breakeven, and at that moment, the fear I so arrogantly dismissed decided to pay me another visit. "How could this happen," I asked. I sat back in my chair for a moment. Stunned. Confused. Suddenly, MTSI's bid took another dive. "My god," I shouted. I was now *down* $4000. What was going on? I quickly looked to the right and left of me to see if any of the 70 or so surrounding traders were watching me. No one was. Judging by the few faces I saw, they had their *own* problems to deal with. I struggled to compose myself, to somehow regain my mental equilibrium. But MTSI was not finished with me yet. Another $1 drop increased my deficit to $8000. I could barely breath. My better judgment begged me to take the loss, but there was something stopping me. I couldn't move. I physically couldn't move. All I could do is watch, and watch I did.

Over the next 25 minutes, I watched in agony as MTSI took more than $16,000 away from me. Dejected, depressed, and depleted of all hope, I finally mustered up enough courage to kill the trade. It was over. *Everything* seemed to be over. One more time, I looked on both sides of me. I wanted to see if anyone had witnessed the atrocity that just happened to me. But no one seemed to notice. If they did, they didn't care. "What was I going to do," I silently asked myself. "What was I going to tell my wife, my family, and the partners who backed me?" Failing to come up with any coherent answers to those questions, I did the only thing I could do. I slowly lowered my head into my hands, and I wept.

*   *   *

My name is Oliver L. Velez, and this was my first experience as a so-called professional day trader. Many might be tempted to call it my inauguration day, but I have always referred to it as my graduation day. For it was on this painfully dark day that I abandoned the ranks of those starry-eyed day traders who naively think that fast money and easy riches in the market are the norm. I abandoned that novice-filled group forever, and graduated to the more intelligent group of realists who sees and appreciates the art of day trading for what it truly is: one of the most demanding endeavors on planet Earth. There is no doubt that a big part of me died that day, right there in front of that flashing monitor. But in its place, something more splendid, something more grand, came to life. It came in the form of a fierce new determination to make sense of it all. On that infamous day, I became a new man. Out of the ashes of a beaten trader, rose a driven man bent on finding a sensible method, an intelligent approach that went well beyond the fly-by-the-seat-of-your-pants style practiced by the majority of the crowd. On that day, a powerful thirst for *more* developed. I wanted *more* knowledge, *more* discipline, *more* skill, *more* direction, and I was determined to get it, at any cost. Fortunately, I did.

Over the ensuing 6 years, I managed to formulate a trading philosophy that made sense. Slowly a trading plan based on this philosophy began to take form, a step-by-step plan that not only sounded good in theory, but actually worked in the real world and made money. The book you now hold in your hands covers a good part of that trading philosophy and the trading plan I put together during those driven years.

*   *   *

I never did tell my wife what happened in the evening of that devastating first day. But it was quite apparent she knew. She simply allowed me to maintain a measure of self-worth by remaining silent on the issue. Many months passed before I was I was able to open up to her, to verbally explain what happened. By that time, my newfound determination was beginning to bear rich fruit. The account I was trading was up some $250,000, and, for once, my wife was no longer borrowing money from her uncles and charging baby pampers on our overextended credit card. Ten months after that, the account crossed the $1,000,000 mark, and I decided to cash out of the partnership, to go it alone.

Today I can honestly say, "I did it." I bagged the elephant, as they say. I beat the market. With great effort and countless hours of study each day and night, I had devised a trading philosophy and a plan that was sensible. More importantly, it made money. Despite the fact that almost all of that money I earned was not mine, I felt content. I felt comfortable. And everything stayed that way, until I met a trader who would help me forge forward into even more splendid levels of trading mastery. His name is Greg Capra, my partner, my brother, and my friend.

* * *

My name is Greg Capra, fellow trader, partner, and dear friend of Oliver L. Velez. It was only a little before the time Oliver was going through his life-changing experience that I had my first taste of serious market play. Prior to this, my market activity was limited to the boring arena of municipal bonds, and the slightly more exciting world of mutual funds. So it was only natural that when I decided to make my first foray into the dynamic world of trading, it was in the most volatile market on the planet: the index options market. To my novice way of thinking, equities didn't move fast enough for me. I needed action. I wanted something that could score mind-numbing gains all at once, *and* I wanted it fast. I did not respect the "make-a-few-dollars-here-and-a-few-dollars-there" approach that I saw so many others trying. That was all behind *me.* Or so I thought. Besides, I was already earning big money as a successful businessman for over 10 years. By this time in my life, I was well beyond the need to just survive. Nickels and dimes no longer appealed to me, and my thirst to simply do well was already thoroughly quenched. It was the gusto that I was after. Yes. That *megabuck.* And I wanted it to come to me by way of a rush, by way of a mighty thrill. Index options would provide me with just that, and a great deal more. Well, it was the "great deal more" that almost ruined my chances of ever becoming the day trader that I am today. With a high-tech satellite feed that spat out delayed quotes and an options account with a major Wall Street brokerage firm, I was armed. A fresh new subscription to one of those "get rich quick" options newsletters made me dangerous. I was ready. I picked up the phone, speed-dialed my broker, and shot out the command. "Buy 200 contracts of March XYZ!" There was silence on the other end. "Sir, are you sure?" "What do you mean am I sure," I blurted back. "Just do it, now!" At that point I hung up the phone and impatiently waited for the customary return phone call informing me of where I bought this sizable number of contracts. The phone rang, and the voice on the other end nervously revealed my entry point. I immediately started watching my delayed quotes. With each tick, my account swung wildly, and a rush of adrenaline gushed through my veins. I was so young at the game of trading that I did not realize that 200 index contracts was almost equivalent to owning 20,000 shares of a very volatile Internet stock, an unbelievable size for a novice. A customer walked through my front door wanting some service. I remember barely being able to pry myself away from my monitor. Ten minutes later I returned to the trading area I set up in the back of my office. And to my horror, I found my account down $26,000. My limbs went absolutely numb. With conflicting thoughts fighting each other to gain dominance in my mind, I managed to press the speed-dial button and immediately got my broker. The phone barely rang which told me that he too was glued to his monitor, watching my money evaporate into thin air. I was silent. "Hello! Hello!" the broker repeated. I answered his call with a deep moan. "Mr. Capra," he said solemnly. "Is that you?" Again I was silent. I couldn't speak. For the life of me, I simply couldn't speak. The voice on the other end of the phone was asking for Mr. Capra. And for the first time in my life, I did not want to *be* Mr. Capra. More important was the fact that I did not want to do what I knew had to be done. I did not want to make this large paper loss real by selling my position. But I had too. I had been in business long enough to know that cutting my losses was the only smart act possible at this point. My power of speech returned and I meekly mumbled two of the most painful words in a trader's vocabulary. "Dump it," I said. "Dump the whole god-forsaken thing!" "At the market," my broker asked. "Yeah" I said. "Whatever that means." I hung the phone up, closed the door to my office, and cut myself off from the rest of the world.

All in all, I lost over $30,000 on that trade. It was not enough money to hurt me financially, but money was not the thing at stake here. It was my pride and my sense of confidence that were on the line. I had succeeded at virtually everything I ever tried. This was supposed to be no different. I went home that night struggling with the notion of quitting. "I was making good money with my business," I told myself. "Why did I have to play the market?" But quitting was not in me. As much as I tried to convince myself that giving up the hope to become an astute market player wasn't the end of the world, I could not bring myself to quit. And I didn't. As unbelievable as it may seem, the very next day I boldly repeated my actions. I arbitrarily bought 200 contracts of the same option. Only this time, I hit pay dirt. In less than one hair-raising hour, I cashed out the trade with a $32,000 profit. Breathing heavily, I sat back in my chair trying to feel good about what had just happened. But the joyous feelings of a winner eluded me. Despite coming out ahead, I still felt depressed. That was because I knew in my heart that I was *not* a winner. Luck was the only thing on my side that day, and it was not enough to erase my feelings of inadequacy. There was no skill in my actions. Intelligence was nowhere near my approach, and it bothered me. That day, I closed my options account and made a vow to myself that changed the course of my life. I decided that I would take the gift of redemption that fortune seemed to be giving me, and throw myself into a much-needed learning process. That day I decided that, whatever the cost, I would become a professional trader *the right way*. When Oliver and I met, we found ourselves in similar situations. I am proud to say our ensuing years together brought about a very profitable philosophy of trading, much of which is presented in this book.

Oliver Velez
Greg Capra

INTRODUCTION

Make no mistake about it my friends. We are at the doorstep of a brand new era. If we had to give this era a name, we'd call it the *era of self-empowerment*, and the revolution that marked the dawn of this era is only in its infancy. A 20-year decline in commission rates, coupled with new order-handling rules, the Internet, and phenomenal technological advancements have helped level the playing field and open the hidden door to Wall Street forever. The old guarded ways, designed to keep the public from true access, are crumbling as we speak, the age-old profit centers once hidden are now being exposed, and a more sophisticated investor is demanding that it stay that way. Never before in history has the complete democratization of Wall Street been so near. And never before has so much opportunity been available to the average individual on Main Street. In the next few years, that opportunity will be even greater. Our question to you is, "Are you ready?"

We see a day, not too far in the future, when there will no longer be fragmented exchanges in America. The stage is being set right now for one giant, unified U.S. Stock Exchange. Shortly after that, we see a day when there will be one world-wide stock exchange, bringing true capitalism in its purest form to all four corners of the earth.

Shortly after that, or even before that, the day will come when every single computer sold on the planet will come with a preloaded trading platform that provides direct access to this world-wide market, giving individuals the ability to trade anything on earth that moves: stocks, bonds, options, futures, rocks, trees, in-laws. Well, may be not in-laws, but once again, we have to ask, "are you ready?"

The stage is being set for an incredible drama that will most definitely be played out over the next 5 to 10 years, and those who get prepared today, those who get trained and educated now, stand a good chance of becoming the new titans of the new game on Wall Street.

This is a new day, and those who don't like it had better get used to it because *self-empowered traders are here to stay.*

WHAT HAS BROUGHT ABOUT THIS NEW REVOLUTION?

Several significant developments have occurred over the past 10 years to ignite what is, in my opinion, a phenomenal revolution that is only in its infancy:

1. The precipitous drop in commission rates during the last decade has increased the potential profitability as well as the plausibility of short-term trading. Prior to this drop, only institutions and high-net-worth individuals enjoyed bargain-basement commission rates. Today, access to our equity market can be had for pennies.

2. A world-wide collapse in interest rates has made equity ownership participation an absolute must. This change, along with a runaway Bull attitude, lead to a higher level of sophistication and an increasing need for self-empowerment.

3. Mind-boggling technological advancements have helped to bring Wall Street to Main Street. As a result, big and small, rich and poor, novice and pros alike can, with the click of a mouse, directly access the largest markets in the world, right from the comfort of their very own living rooms. These technological marvels have helped level the playing field for the individual. They have removed the barriers to access and, in so doing, have removed much of the unfair advantage enjoyed by the elite members of "the club."

4. New order-handling rules have changed the way Wall Street works forever. Not only have recent changes in the way firms handle our orders provided for greater fairness and transparency, they have helped the user in the vehicle that will ultimately change the way the financial world does business: the ECN, better known as the Electronic Communication Network.

5. Last, but far from least, is the advent of the Internet. Not since Alexander Graham Bell's telephone has something caused such a radical change in the way we think and live our lives. Today, the information gap between source and recipient has been reduced to near zero. Because of the Internet, we have truly become a global society. A local consumer is now a global consumer. A sixth-grade student on Sycamore Drive in North Carolina is now a student of the world, and a business that once dominated its niche in the northeastern part of the United States can work to expand its niche to the world. The Internet will drive the way we think, walk, talk, live, and love in the next millennium, and those who do not embrace the changes it brings will become a part of prehistoric history in years to come.

WHAT IS PROPER TRADING?

Proper trading, in many respects, is a by-product of proper "thinking." One of the first things this book will do is create a revolution in your mind. It will change the way you see and think about the markets. For instance, one of the first lessons we teach is that "you do not trade stocks, you trade people." Far too many novice market players fail to realize that there is someone on the other side of every single trade they make. Each time you buy, someone is on the other side of the transaction selling the stock to you. Each time you sell, someone is on the other side buying the stock from you. The 64K question is, "who's smarter?" Is it you, or is it the person or entity on the other side of your trade? This book will make sure you are the smart one, by training you in the fine art of playing people.

We will show you that successful trading calls for the ability to find two sets of ill-formed individuals: those willing to give up their merchandise to you too inexpensively and those willing to buy your merchandise too expensively.

In other words, and I hope I don't sound too brash here, successful trading is the art of finding an idiot. This book will make sure you are not the idiot.

We believe that day trading is far broader in its scope than most people realize. Unfortunately, many individuals, in and out of the industry, have erroneously defined day trading as a frenzied, rapid-fire buy-and-sell approach that never calls for taking the position home over night. While that is a form of day trading, it is not the only form.

It is our view that if you are committed to your trades on a day-to-day basis and if you are applying attention and focus to the markets daily, you are, by definition, a day trader. On the other hand, if you practice what we call the Rip Van Winkle approach to the market, which is buying a stock, taking a nap for 5 years, and hoping everything is OK when you wake up, then you are not a day trader.

It is very important to understand that day trading is not investing. In many respects, the two activities are diametrically opposed to each other.

WHAT DOES THIS BOOK SET OUT TO ACCOMPLISH? WHAT WILL I GET FROM IT?

This book is designed to help active self-directed traders gain the knowledge and acquire the tools necessary to approach the markets with intelligence and a well-thought out trading plan. In other words, it will help you know what to do, but that is not where it ends, because knowing "what" to do is no guarantee that you'll do it. Because 85 percent of the trading game is psychological in nature, we also help traders deal with some of the psychological and emotional challenges that every active market participant must face.

WHAT METHOD DO YOU USE TO PICK YOUR STOCKS?

Our approach is a technical one. It is based on a number of very reliable chart patterns that represent key short-term shifts in market psychology. There are certain chart patterns that pinpoint when a change in the balance of power between the buyers and sellers have occurred. We will teach you not only how to identify these chart patterns, but also help you to build tactics and strategies that are designed to profitably exploit them.

Charts are the footprints of money. And let me tell you something, they don't lie. They are like a doctor's x-ray, which provides deeper insight into his patient. In the trader's case, the market is his patient.

For instance, we have found that stocks experiencing a great degree of momentum tend to correct (or rest) for 3 to 5 days before they resume their upward moves. This 3- to 5-day decline typically sets up a unique opportunity for the educated swing trader. We teach, through this book and a variety of services, *when* the trader should strike, *where* the traders should place his protective stop, and *what* the trader should look for in the trade.

SEEDS OF WISDOM FOR THE MASTER TRADER

Preparing the Trader's Mind for Greatness

Trading tactics and techniques will have little to no value if the mind behind those techniques has not been properly prepared. This section is specifically designed to pepper the trader's mind with bite-sized seeds of wisdom, which over time will germinate and give rise to a heightened state of awareness and a deeper level of understanding. We call this *depth*. One of the most undiscovered truths of the day is embedded in the fact that the greatest riches of a successful trader lie within his or her thinking, not within the methods used. Sound methods follow the trader who has a sound mind. To state this another way, "proper trading is proper thinking." We firmly believe that the trader who reads and digests the following sections will emerge from the experience a more seasoned individual. Each time these pearls of wisdom are digested, they will help bring into being a deeper sense of understanding, heightened mental awareness, and greater emotional mastery. Within these short essays are locked some of the most potent pearls of wisdom known to successful traders. These timeless gems have enriched the trading lives of individuals all over the world via our daily newsletter, *The Pristine Day Trader*. We are certain they will help provide you, as well, with a richer, fuller life in the markets.

* * *

You are certain to find repetition in many of the following themes, but we have always lent support to the notion that repetition has a great value. What won't penetrate the various barriers to understanding one way may do so when truth and wisdom is communicated another way. May you enjoy your first steps on the path to trading mastery.

C H A P T E R

INITIATION OF THE MASTER TRADER

Understanding the Master Trader's World

DO YOU UNDERSTAND HOW HIGH THE COST IS?

How high is the cost to be a master trader? While the actual price is difficult to quantify, we have been at the business of trading long enough to know that it's higher than most people think. And in most cases, it's higher than most people are willing to pay. Show me someone who wants to quit his or her job to become a day trader, and I'll show you someone who probably doesn't understand what it takes to be a day trader. Those who feel this is a game that can be conquered or mastered in a few short months are deluding themselves. Not only does it take many months to years of relentless effort to obtain market proficiency, but also excellence seems to emerge only after one has learned and experienced every conceivable way to lose. The truth of the matter is that the pains, the agony, the scars of an experienced trader run especially long and deep. If aspiring market mavens do not possess a great deal of fortitude, or if they lack resolve, are devoid of passion, and are unwilling to forsake all, they simply won't last. Individuals who truly desire market success will have to pay with their blood, their money, and a very big part of their lives. The tuition is high. There is no denying that. But the ultimate reward that goes to those willing to pay the price is immeasurable.

Successful traders enjoy an independence that can't even be imagined by most. With a notebook computer and a telephone line, they are free to trade, to book profits, from any place in the world. They can earn more money in 2 hours than most people earn in a month. With the click of a mouse and the stroke of a few keys, successful traders can bring into existence their every material desire and shield themselves from the day-to-day concerns that typically plague the mediocre and the average. By properly responding to the electronic impulses flashing on the computer screen, traders can create the world of their choice, live a lifestyle that supersedes the wildest of all dreams, and rest securely in the fact that no one on planet Earth can take it away. But in order to get there, *you must last!* To reach the lofty level of which I speak, *you must survive,* however difficult things get. And that, my friends, is no easy task. So if you are truly willing to pay the price, the best advice I can give you is this: Develop a plan, find a mentor who will teach you, and *never surrender!* Make up your mind this very day that you will either rise or perish. And then watch your unshakable resolve work out the details. You can do it. We *know* this to be true because we did it.

SEED OF WISDOM

Recognize that the cost of trading mastery is high. Then, provided you accept the cost, decide to make achieving a successful life your "magnificent obsession." Fan the flame of you passion until it ignites into a white-heat desire to attain that wonderful state we call *trading mastery.* Make your sole mission in life to overcome all obstacles to your success without any thought of ever giving up. This burning desire for trading mastery is the wind behind the sails of every profitable trader in existence. It is what gives the new trader the ability to survive that first booby-trapped filled year of his or her new life.

THE MASTER TRADER REQUIRES ONLY A FEW TOOLS

It has always been my belief that the mastery of a few trading tools is all that's necessary to become a highly successful trader. Most would-be successful traders are incapacitated by the false notion that in order to trade for a living, one must have accumulated a wealth of knowledge over countless years of experience. Not only is this not altogether true, the exact opposite is actually closer to the truth. In fact, it has been my experience that those who possess a limited amount of trading knowledge have a much better chance of becoming effective market players than their so-called overly experienced brethren. Why? Because varied market experiences, if not utilized and interpreted correctly, help to crystallize inaccurate beliefs. And inaccurate beliefs, which are allowed to exist over time, eventually flourish into full-blown, faulty ideologies that ultimately result in the trader's ruin. Knowledge *is* power, but only if it's the right knowledge. By mastering any two or three of the many trading techniques contained in the Tactics section of this book, you'll be well on your way to becoming a consistently profitable trader. It literally only takes two or three workable techniques to rise to the top of this game we call trading, and we are certain you will find more than enough of them in this book.

SEED OF WISDOM

The best traders are minimalists. They find two or three tactics or techniques that work consistently. Once they've found them, they simply implement them over and over and over. Repetition really does have value.

SEEKING SUCCESS IN THAT PLACE CALLED THE HERE AND NOW

Looking back to understand when and why the market has developed a cancer, so to speak, has its place. But there is nothing more valuable than knowing why it will develop cancer *before* the fact. If this is so, why are so many Wall Street analysts and market technicians more comfortable looking backward? Perhaps it's because looking forward requires that someone step up to the plate and put his or her hard-earned reputation at risk. It not only requires that someone study and perform a mountain of homework, it also calls for that someone to reveal the results of that study to the rest of the world. And we don't have to tell you that we are the inhabitants of a very critical world. Considering the risk, it is not surprising that the firms and services with the most to lose are the ones most reluctant to step out on the limb in a forward manner. However, if we may say so ourselves, this is where services like *The Pristine Day Trader* and many others have come in. For the past 6 years or so, the Internet has given rise to many additional firms and market services that are bold and willing enough to step up to the plate with that all-important forward-looking view. It is our opinion that the active market player in today's world is finding more value with these firms and services than the more established titans of Wall Street, who have more to lose by taking the same steps.

In the course of a few short years, our service has managed to attract a worldwide following that spans over 48 countries. Why? Why has our dominance been so complete? It's simple. Because we—and other firms that represent the new breed—have been willing to put our reputations on the line each day by doing our best to tell you what *will* occur. We spend very little time dwelling on what has *already* occurred, which only has a small academic value. The majority of our efforts are directed toward what we think is about to happen. And today's market player, who is a lot more sophisticated than his or her counterparts of the past, thrives on that.

There is, however, a flip side to all of this that is very important for us not to miss. While we feel it is extremely important to approach the markets with a forward-looking view, and less important to look back-ward, it is not always beneficial to project one's thoughts and/or market views too far into the future either. This is why we are not overly inter-ested in what will happen 8 months from now. That is actually a reverse cop-out behind which a tremendous lack of talent has historically hid from critical eyes and played it safe. As a former hedge-fund manager who was responsible for periodically reporting my market views, I quickly learned a *secret* rule of thumb that is so commonly used on Wall Street, it's a wonder why more of the general investing public is not aware of it. The rule was this: *When uncertain and crippled by doubt, give your 6- to 8-month market outlook.* It buys you a good deal of time during which you may get a clue. Should you fail to get a clue—and most do fail—you can always change your view (the public has a short memory) or just issue another view, which in turn buys you another 6- to 8-month outlook on the market. Needless to say, this is pathetic. Although rare, the real talent on the street doesn't need to hide behind a 6- to 12-month gap in time. They are not always right, for sure. But they are confident and willing to step up to the plate each day, if need be, and say, "this is what we feel you need to be aware of, and this is how we propose you can profit from it." Whenever I hear that type of gutsy action from an an-alyst, a newsletter, or trading service, the first thing I do is tip my hat to pay my respects. Second, I make it my business to get to know them, ei-ther through their service or even personally if possible.

Our whole point is this. As far as we are concerned, our domain, as traders, is the Here and Now. We do not live our lives drifting in the past, nor do we avoid the realities of the moment by lingering in some distant future. As active market players, our entire lives are perpetually spent in the next 2 to maybe 10 days. Have you got that? Write it down. In other words, we look forward by breaking up the market into a very digestible 2-day to 2-week period. Write that down too. If we get it right, we will tend to make a good deal of money. If we happen to get it wrong—and we do at times—we quickly regroup and move on. There is always the next 2- to 10-day period to get right. But even when we miss the mark in our 2- to 10-day projection, at least we haven't lost or wasted an entire 8 to 12 months of our trading lives being dead wrong. That would be a crime in our book: a crime that in this rapidly changing world may not be eligible for redemption. Why take that chance?

SEED OF WISDOM

Don't waste too much energy looking backward. Approach the market with a forward-looking view that extends over the next 2 days to 2 weeks. We, as traders, can't trade the past, and we certainly have not been endowed with the capacity to accurately see very far into the future. We have, however, been given dominion over the period of time that lies just beyond us. For lack of a better phrase, we call this period of time the Here and Now. It is in that place that we traders will find the comfort, success, and higher accuracy that we seek.

WHY THE MASTER TRADER TRADES WITH CHARTS

Most of our market work is based on technical analysis, which, in our view, provides the short-term trader with a more solid basis for making intelligent buy and sell decisions. As many traders know through personal experience, even the most fundamentally sound companies can decline $2 to $10 in a matter of days, hours even, while fundamentally poor companies can rise and do the exact opposite. Fundamentals, while useful at times, possess their greatest value when one is considering a stock over a period of 1½ to 5 years. Technicals, however, such as proven price patterns, support and resistance, volume characteristics, institutional accumulation/distribution, break-outs and break-downs, etc., are the tools of choice for short-term traders, because they are based on the Here and Now we spoke about earlier. But what must be realized above all else is the fact that technical setups and chart patterns are only guides, nothing more, nothing less. They help the trader to assess the odds of a particular play, to see its merits and its risks at the current moment. They are not guarantees. They are not foolproof. And they definitely can't deliver the comfort of absolute certainty. But then again, what can? But as far as a barometer of what the probability of a certain occurrence is, technicals and charts are unrivaled, in our view.

Now many ill-informed novices will witness a certain technical concept, such as price support, fail and erroneously assume that it is unreliable and useless. This is a very big mistake that should be avoided like the plague. The astute trader learns just as much, if not more, from a technical concept failing as he does from it working. If price support, which proved reliable four times in a row, suddenly failed, that would be very valuable and useful information. That, in our view, is not a concept that has failed. That is a technical concept that is revealing the strongest and most valuable message of all: the message of change. Let us take a look at an example. In the middle of October 1998, Intel Corporation broke a major 3-month support level at $90. No doubt there were those who saw that and said, "See how unreliable technical analysis is? Support failed!" Many of these same critics were the very same souls that got hurt by Intel Corporation's subsequent fall to $70. No, my dear friends, Intel's break of support at $90 was not a failed technical concept. It was a *message:* one that many wish they understood!

SEED OF WISDOM

Fundamentals, while important, do not help the trader assess risk and timing issues in the Here and Now. This is where technicals and charts outshine the fundamentals. It would be the height of naïveté to think or expect charting concepts to work all the time. They don't. At times they fail, but even when they do, they are serving the astute trader with valuable messages. The trader has only to learn how to listen.

CHARTS DON'T LIE!

There are far too many casual market players who don't have even a small grasp of what technical analysis or the art of chart reading is all about. That is not necessarily their crime; however, the sad part lies in the fact that many of these ill-informed individuals are amongst the most outspoken critics of this art. As mentioned before, price charts do nothing more than graphically display what we call the "footprints" of money. They show human psychology at work and the repetitive cycles of fear, greed, and uncertainty. What we have always liked about charts is that they are factual. You see, a large money manager can show his face on *CNBC, MSNBC,* or *MoneyLine* and lie about how much he or she loves a stock, when all the money manager really wants to do is generate enough buying to offset his or her major blocks of sell orders. But guess what? The chart won't lie. Each sell order issued will show up on the chart the instant it occurs, and the volume will reveal just how large the sell order is. It's because of charts we can say, "Gotcha!" A key analyst can issue a major brokerage report stating how XYZ is positioned to dominate its industry, yet you will be able to tell if this is really true. How? Because if the chart of the stock is rising faster than its industry group, you can confidently say, "that analyst is my friend." If the chart looks like a staircase leading to the lower depths of purgatory, you can say, "Gotcha pal. Either you are a fake, or you don't know what you are talking about!" Earnings reports can paint a false picture with the help of fancy accounting, but charts don't lie. A CEO can hold a conference and boldly issue inaccurate statements about a company, but the chart, my friends, won't ever lie. Investors and traders, both large and small, bet with their money, not with their mouths. Now the bet may not always be right, but at least you know that their bets (buys and sells), which make up the chart, are based on true convictions, on true beliefs. And just in case you've forgotten. Each bet is what actually makes up the chart. Charts don't lie.

SEED OF WISDOM

Every stock move is driven by one of three emotions: greed, uncertainty, and fear, uncertainty being the pit stop between greed and fear, the two most dominant emotions. When the most dominant group of players in a stock is being driven by *greed*, the stock will rise. We call this the *Bull phase*. When the most dominate group of players in a given stock are experiencing the pains of *fear*, the stock will head steadily lower. When the dominant group is *uncertain*, on the fence so to speak, prices will stabilize in a sideways pattern, as if for a brief period it had no home to go to or direction to travel in. Charts give us the power to be able to quickly assess what the *real* players in any given stocks are experiencing. Charts don't lie. They reveal what that all-important group is feeling and doing. Fail to use charts in your analysis and you run the risk of being one of the many naïve patsies commonly taken advantage of by those in the know. Simply put, the astute trader can't afford to be without charts.

TRACKING THE FOOTPRINTS OF MONEY

Many of our potential or newer subscribers tend to become somewhat concerned when they discover that we base most, if not all, of our analysis on chart patterns and other technical indications, as opposed to the more conventional fundamental information. Historically, the general investment public has been more comfortable with analysis that looks at things like the earnings of a company, its P/E (price to earnings) ratio, debt level, industry developments, etc. Technical items, such as frequently repeated chart patterns, price breakouts, increasing volume, reversal days, moving averages, etc., have not only been criticized, but also shunned and written off as hocus-pocus nonsense. But the truth of the matter is that technical analysis, or charting to be more specific, is nothing more than the art of following the flow of money. And just in case you didn't know, *money doesn't lie.* You see, investors, analysts, and Wall Street firms can and will say what they please. They will broadcast their opinions and advice very freely and generously. But after all is said and done, their true beliefs can only be found out by tracking how they place their bets, by monitoring how and where they spend their money. I cannot tell you how many times a major brokerage firm will upgrade or reiterate a stock as a "buy" when, in fact, their largest institutional clients, whom they advise, will be selling that same stock. Have you any idea how often a corporate director and other upper-level management in a firm will make glowing remarks about their company's future outlook, while every employee from the CEO to the janitor is dumping the stock on the secondary market? Money brings out the truth. Tracking its movement helps to remove the façade, the misleading exterior. It reveals the genuine intent of the major players. This is why astute traders use charts. Think about it. Isn't a price chart nothing more than the footprints that real money has left behind? Sure, earnings and those other things are important. But numbers and reports don't move stocks. Only money does. So we say don't show us reports. *Show us the money!*

SEED OF WISDOM

As active traders, we are not unlike medical internists who are only able to do their jobs properly after looking inside the patients, after seeing what is called an x-ray. Yes, medical internists can get full reports from their patients about how they feel and what they feel. But good doctors won't stop at the report. While they listen to the patients' verbal and sometimes written reports, they prepare the patients for x-rays, so that they can take their own "inside" views. If our doctors did not do this, we would label them quacks and fakes of the highest order. Short-term traders find themselves in similar situations. They are constantly being bombarded with both glowing news and horrible news, with *this* conflicting opinion versus *that* conflicting opinion. Everyone from personal friends to the chief executives of *Fortune 500* companies want to influence the way traders think, even what they see and believe. While the astute traders can take all of that in, they know that only after they take their own "inside" look, their own x-rays so to speak, can they ever hope to be free of outside influences. In this way, charts tell traders who is lying and who is being truthful. With their charts they can spot the flow of money, when and where the big investors are placing big bets, or when they are packing up to go home. People who have a vested interest in us believing and thinking a certain way have to be looked at with skeptical eyes, but charts are our true friends. They represent the footprints of money. And just in case you didn't know, money is the trader's ultimate friend. So why not have a map of it?

GIVE ME THE TECHNICALS, OR GIVE ME DEATH

Many traders find it quite amazing that we base our trading analysis almost entirely on technical factors (volume, price patterns, momentum, etc.) without deeply considering the *story* or fundamentals behind a stock. In fact, we rely so exclusively on the technicals that we rarely refer to news during the day, other than *CNBC*, which we watch for light market updates and an occasional laugh (*CNBC* does a great job at taking boring subject matter and making it entertaining). This is not to say that stories or fundamental information have no value. We are only insinuating that the value of these items is relatively small and, at times, irrelevant when it comes to short-term trading. How is that? Well, allow us to explain. Let's assume that we've bought an issue at $20. Our target price is $22.50, and our protective stop (mental or otherwise), our line in the sand, so to speak, is placed at $19. A negative news story of some sort is suddenly released and the stock declines enough to trigger our stop. What's the result? A $1 loss (commissions are omitted for the purpose of simplicity). Now, let's look at this scenario another way. The same issue we've bought at $20 declines to trigger our $19 stop, for no apparent reason at all. In other words, no news was the catalyst. Isn't the result, a $1 loss, the same? What is the real value of knowing what is *causing* a decline, if your well-thought out trading plan is to exit at your stop point anyway? In fact, being aware of the *cause* has a strong tendency to trip the trader up by making it difficult at times to act when the need arises. I cannot begin to tell you how many times I've allowed a news story, an overpaid Wall Street analyst, or some chat room rumor to shake me out of a trade, only to see it skyrocket. I've also been extremely guilty of the re-verse. But all my years of experience have convinced me that every one of our actions should be dictated by a well-thought out trading plan, not rumors or stories. This is how traders remain disciplined in the face of chaos. This is how the best traders keep their sanity when everyone else is paralyzed and confused. In short, this is how the master trader makes money, by listening to and focusing on the only thing that counts: The movement of the stock. Everything else is superfluous. Everything else is fluff. To our way of thinking, every trader should boldly make the fol-lowing affirmation, which is derived from Patrick Henry, the father of our Revolution, "I know not what course others may take, but as for me, give me the technicals, or give me death."

SEED OF WISDOM

News, stories, rumors, and tips can at times help to ignite abrupt moves in the underlying issues at which they are directed. But the astute traders will refrain from allowing such outside sources to alter the plan, espe-cially when dealing with the decision to sell. The reason behind a stock's decline should mean very little to the astute short-term traders. Once they establish where they will sell the stock based on the technicals, that's it. No news or rumor will alter that plan. Novice traders looking for justifications and reasons to hold on to losing trades often ask things like, "Why is XYZ falling like a stone?" "Is there any news on ABCD, be-cause it is tanking?" Often times, the news behind the drop will cause them to rationalize. "Oh, that news is not very bad at all. Perhaps if I hold on another hour or another day, it will come back." The master traders adhere to the technicals and their predetermined stop loss at all costs. They act when the technicals and their stops tell them to, and they ask questions later. It is our view that questions should be asked from the sidelines. Stated another way, questions should be asked before the bat-tle and after the battle, not during the battle. When in the trenches (when in the trade), your plan (trading strategy), based on your maps (charts), must be adhered to. Think about it. Would you feel safe in the trenches with someone who was nervously asking a slew of questions?

DON'T SHOW UP TO A GUNFIGHT WITH JUST A DULL A KNIFE

There I was, being thoroughly grilled by a Canadian reporter who wanted to know precisely why *The Pristine Day Trader* was so highly regarded in his native country. *"Are you a professional trader,"* he asked? "Yes" I responded. "How long have you been trading?" he asked me next. "Twelve years now: six as a professional, six as a novice." "Were you ever a loser?" "You bet I was. One of the best at it too." "Wait a minute. Let me get this straight," he said. *"You* were a loser?" "Yes, and a consistent one at that." "For how long?" he asked incredulously. "Oh for about 4 to 5 years." At this point in the interview I could tell that this Canadian reporter was thrown. Here he was talking to Oliver L. Velez, the chief editor of *The Pristine Day Trader*, the service that *Barron's* hailed as the best day-trading service on the Web, and he was listening to me flatly say that I was once a consistent losing trader. "But . . . but . . . *Barron's* ranked your service as the best," he continued. "So? My service is a winner, but that does not mean *I* was not a loser" I shot back with a light touch of attitude. A painfully long pause ensued, and I refused to be the one to break the silence. I was starting to enjoy his discomfort. "Well tell me this," he finally said. "Anything, sir." "Are you *now* a winner?" Now, I knew what this guy wanted to hear. He was not used to talking to someone who gave him the cold, hard, unadulterated truth. He was thrown off balance and was out of his element. And I must admit, I loved every second of it. The truth is, I dreaded having to comply. But I did. "Sometimes I win, sir" I answered. Another pause took place. "Most of the time?" he asked with a curiosity that was now at its peak. "Yeah. I now win more often than I lose." Another pause set in. It would be the last one from him. "One final question, Mr. Velez." "Shoot." "Can you prevent *others* from losing?" he asked forcefully. Now here was the trap. Here was where so many other producers, promoters, and marketers of their services might have failed. But not me. I was not about to go down by such an obvious attempt at entrapment. I knew that this guy would have loved for me to say that I am the true answer to every trader's prayers so that he could go out and find a horde of people who lost money with my service. "No! I cannot prevent others from losing." "Well what *can* you do, Mr. Velez? If you can't prevent others from losing, what *exactly* are people paying you for?" It was now *I* who delivered the pause. "To make sure they don't show up at a gun fight with just a dull knife, sir!" He roared with laughter.

Most traders who seek our instruction are shocked when we tell them that we cannot turn them into winners. As the editors of a popular advisory letter, they expect us to sell them the notion that we're miracle workers, deliverers of dreams, and guarantors of hope, fortune, and massive wealth. Those who know us better know that we will never promise or promote such things. You see, the truth of the matter is that no one is capable of transferring trading proficiency. We cannot, with the wave of a wand, hand over the mind-set, the mental attitude, the discipline, and the ways of a winner. Only *you* can do that. Only the individual can earn for himself the right to win. Each would-be trader possesses the capability to win, but that possibility lies dormant and can only be drawn out by the individual. It's a personal challenge that no one else can pull off for the trader. The only thing we, and other mentors like us, *can* do is help guide and direct the trader along the way. Even with our advanced knowledge, we can only point out the many pitfalls and booby traps that are designed to snuff out a trader's life. We can show the trader what works and what doesn't. We can even give up some of the hard-earned knowledge that we possess, and reveal some of the tactics and techniques that have proven very reliable for us. But no matter what we do, we *cannot* control what players do with those things. We *cannot* control the way traders think or the way they feel or react. And we *cannot* influence their fears or alter their psychological and emotional makeup. We can certainly make sure that they show up to the game with all that is necessary. But after we have packed their bags, so to speak, and after we have knelt down to whisper some words of faith and encouragement in their ears, the traders are on their own. We cannot take the test for them. We can only help them prepare. That is our mission. That is what this book is designed to do. That is what traders all over the world pay us for. And that is what we spend sleepless nights trying to accomplish. We have written this book with only one purpose in mind, and that is to make sure you never have to show up to a gunfight with just a dull knife!

SEED OF WISDOM

Trading mastery can never be achieved without first achieving some measure of *self*-mastery. The reality is that a teacher, whether he or she manifests in the form of an instructor or a trading service, is indefinably limited in ability to deliver or transfer success in trading. The only role a teacher can play is to make sure you are properly equipped and thoroughly prepared for the upcoming battle. But it must never be forgotten that the battle is all yours. No one can fight for you. No one can take your place or even alleviate inevitable hardships. Only you can bring about success. And with the proper guidance, you can, and you will.

SEEK KNOWLEDGE FIRST, PROFITS SECOND

Success is a very vague term, the true meaning of which must be determined by each individual. Why? Because each of us has his own unique definition of what success is and what it means. But failure, the very opposite end of the spectrum, is defined by only one thing, and that is *the act or habit of majoring in minor things*. Most people spend the bulk of their existence going after and focusing on the more minute things in life, the things that offer the smallest value. Let's quickly take a glimpse at an example of this. Our daily newsletter attempts to deliver two potential benefits: trading knowledge and trading profits. Now, while profits are likely to receive most of the attention, knowledge is by far the more important of the two. Isn't a $2 or $3 short-term trading gain, once taken, gone forever? We're afraid it is. But acquiring or having a grasp on the knowledge that produced that gain makes profiting a life-long possibility. A famous Chinese proverb says it the best. "Give a man a fish and you'll feed him for a day. Teach a man to fish and you'll feed him for a lifetime." We provide an educational element to our newsletter because we want traders to major in what matters. By all means, we want them to go after and get profits. But in all they're getting, we want them to make sure they get the knowledge that will ultimately determine not only how profitable they are at the moment, but also how profitable they *stay*.

SEED OF WISDOM

In terms of the degree of importance, knowledge must always come first. Astute traders must make sure that their desire to profit takes a back seat to their desire to know. The traders who seek knowledge, even at the temporary expense of profits, will discover that the biggest profits of all await them in the near future. When knowledge is secured first, profits in abundance almost have to follow, and when they do, they will be real, authentic, and very lasting. In every possible way you can, seek knowledge and understanding, and you will soon find that your cup is running over.

SHORT-TERM TIME FRAME: THE MASTER KEY TO HIGHER TRADING ACCURACY

As stated earlier, we are very much in the habit of keeping our students and subscribers abreast of how we feel about the market on a very short-term basis *(2 days to 2 weeks)*. However, there are times when our subscribers request that we give our intermediate-term to long-term views on the market to help them better determine what our approach will be in the many months to come.

By now you are fully aware of the fact that we place very little importance on market calls that go beyond a several-week focus. This is primarily due to our being short-term traders, but there is another important reason that deserves attention. It is quite apparent to us that accuracy dramatically breaks down as the analytical time frame expands. However, most academics and Wall Street analysts argue that the reverse is true, which doesn't even make sense on the most fundamental level. Isn't it true that the clarity of one's vision diminishes as the distance between the viewer and the object being *viewed* increases? Aren't we more likely to know our exact whereabouts 15 minutes from now as opposed to 1 year from now? Of course we are. So it is with the markets. One's accuracy can be extremely high on a short-term basis, but the innumerable circumstances that can, and will, change over a lengthier period of time will make being highly accurate infinitely harder. This is precisely why a 2- to 10-day period of time dominates our focus.

SEED OF WISDOM

The astute *swing* trader knows that the odds of being right over the next few days, as opposed to the next few years, are immeasurably greater. The astute *day* trader knows that the odds of being right over the next few hours, as opposed to the next few days, are far more favorable. And the astute *micro* trader understands fully that the odds of being right over the next few minutes are impressively better than they'd be over the next few hours. You should never lose sight of the fact that good traders, in their most basic form, are really masterful odds players. While it is true that absolute certainty can never be achieved, traders do have the power to skew the market's odds to a highly favorable condition by operating in a shortened time frame. The very best traders understand this, which is why the very best traders tend to be short-term oriented in their market view and in their market approach.

WHY THE SHORT-TERM TIME FRAME IS THE SAFEST TIME FRAME

It is during the market's most troublesome times that we feel exceptionally fortunate to be short-term traders. The long-term approach to the market, while forever viable, really gets tested to the limits when the market moves into a state of panic. And while the landscape for traders will also get a bit harder during periods of turmoil, the advantage during these times will always reside on the side of the short-term market player. Why? Because nimble traders can take things, as dark as they may become, day by day. The short-term traders have the luxury of turning on a dime. They can bob and weave, switch sides with the speed of light, change stances, and even position themselves to capitalize on the fear for a while. Then they can flip back just as quickly when the mood begins to improve. It is an undeniable fact that the in and out trader shines more brightly during times of darkness, while anything even suggesting the long-term gets hammered if not completely decimated. Consider the near collapse of the all-mighty hedge fund, "Long-Term Capital Management" in late 1998. If it were not for the mighty Federal Reserve and a slew of the nation's biggest banks, like Merrill Lynch and J. P. Morgan, one of the world's largest and most revered hedge funds would have been a memory. Now, I don't know if they would have fared much better had their name, and their approach, been "Short-Term Capital Management," instead of "Long-Term Capital Management." But given what happened to them, bet we could make them seriously ponder that thought. What's the point you ask? Just be glad to be a short-term trader. When things are not going well, and an angry market seems determined to make you feel its wrath it may hurt. But know that the long-term players almost always get hurt more. In today's new world, being short term is better.

SEED OF WISDOM

There was a time, not long ago, when being a nimble in and out trader used to be regarded as a nerve-racking, stress-filled activity that produced migraines and ulcers. It was also believed at the time that holding all stocks for the long term was the only safe approach that helped the market player stay sane. However, today's excessive market volatility, coupled with its frequent bouts of weakness that commonly produced 40 to 60 percent declines in certain stocks, has almost compelled market players to become more short term. Today, being a nimble, short-term trader means staying more stress-free. Watching a stock you own drop 40 percent in 2 weeks is a very stressful situation, while watching a stock drop 40 percent from the sidelines is not. Short-term traders can now boast that they practice the safer approach. To our way of thinking, there is no excuse for allowing a stock to move against you 40 percent. The best traders would never do such a thing. Why? Because they believe in the following points:

1. When in doubt, it is best to get out.

2. You can always get back in.

3. Clearing the slate (selling out) also clears the mind.

4. There are times when the market rewards the cowards.

5. A 5 percent loss on a stock that drops 20 percent is a win, not a loss.

6. A good defense is at times the best offense.

7. Stepping aside guarantees that you live to play another day.

Playing the market long term with mutual funds and carefully selected blue-chip stalwarts (see the section "Market Tool #5: Mighty Five Index" in Chapter 10) will always be a viable approach for retirement-type investing. But for money outside those vehicles, the short-term time frame rules.

MY THREE GREATEST DISCOVERIES

I would like to briefly share with you several discoveries that led me to a re-warding career as a professional trader. It is not often that an individual is able to pinpoint the one or two life-changing discoveries that dramatically altered his existence. Feeling that I have managed to be one of those who have, I can only hope that the following few statements of mine fall into the hands of those who will find them helpful and enlightening.

Trading for a living is no doubt the goal and burning aspiration of nearly every novice market player who experiences his or her first willing trade. Total independence, absolute freedom, and the potential for enormous financial rewards are but a few of the possibilities that capture their imaginations, give fire to new hopes, and invade their every dream. It was 13 years ago (I was 20 years old at the time) when the obsession to master the markets took me as its captive. At first, my style was that of a strict fundamentalist, believing that all knowledge of future stock prices lay in those highly manipulated financial reports generated by overpaid accountants and high-speed printing presses. After a very prolonged period of frustration as a ratio carrying, bean-counting fundamentalist, I finally realized that knowing all there is to know about a company *does not* tell you when and where to buy the *stock* of that company. After a multiyear losing streak, and a drastically reduced war chest, I made several life-changing discoveries. I present them now for your review:

1. My consistent losing record made it very apparent that a market player could buy *the right stock* at the *wrong time* and lose his shirt, and his or her pants. I paid a great deal to learn

this lesson, but when I did, it revolutionized the way I thought and approached the market.

2. Equally important was the discovery that a trader could buy the *wrong* stock at the *right time* and make a fortune. This discovery was the magic elixir that put my thinking over the top. It helped me fully realize that many of the generally accepted concepts and practices exposed by Wall Street are flawed.

3. Discovery 1 and 2 together forced me to truly understand an overwhelmingly basic truth that every market player *claims* to know already, but really doesn't. That fundamental principle is this. There is only one power on planet Earth that can make a stock rise, and that power, my friends, is simply, *MORE BUYING THAN SELLING!* That's it. Good fundamentals do lift stocks. Good management doesn't raise prices. Neither do good earnings. The direct power behind every possible up move in a stock is simply *more buying than selling.* There can be many reasons that ignite that power. Varying circumstances can kick it into action, but the direct power behind every move is none other than more buying then selling.

These discoveries contain some subtle points, the potency of which can be easily missed if you are not careful. The final point contains one of the rare master keys to trading success. So allow me to elaborate a bit by asking a question. If a company were to report robust earnings on a holiday in which nobody participated in the markets, would the stock go up? Of course it would not. If no one showed up to buy it, the report would be worthless, which clearly shows that reports don't lift stocks, heavy buying does. It is easy to think this is a play on words, but if you catch the subtlety, the quiet hint it contains, something in your thinking will radically change. After making these discoveries, it was quite obvious that I could use charts to monitor the level of "buying" going on in the underlying issue of my choice. If I used charts well enough to detect when the buying was beginning to overwhelm the selling, I could catch rapidly rising stocks long *before* they would be discovered by those market players who perpetually keep their heads stuck in yearly financial reports. This meant that through the use of charts I could consistently beat the crowd by being in earlier and out earlier. And guess what? I quickly found myself doing just that. From that point onward, I decided to buy everything in sight that my charts told me to buy, especially if my fundamental background told me *not* to buy. Why? Because the favorable chart with an unfavorable fundamental picture meant that I was likely getting in before the crowd, before the bean counters found out what was really happening. If a rising issue had a ridiculously high P/E ratio, and my charts said go, *I bought it.* No earnings? That was no problem for me. As long as the stock was rising (in essence, being bought), I dove in. High debt levels, absurd book-to-bill ratios, and negative cashflows became pleasing music to my ears *when they did not prevent the stock from advancing.* **Tip:** Read that statement again, for it contains an important key to charting success. Needless to say, these overlooked gems earned a very special place in my trading portfolio: at the very top.

So to make a long story short, after focusing on the stocks themselves, and not stories, statements, tips, rumors, and empty promises of future earnings made by super-rich CEOs, I found myself on the winning side of the market much more consistently. At the age of 26, I began deriving my entire livelihood from the markets. The rest, my friends, is history.

I want every reader of this book to know, beyond a shadow of a doubt, that chart reading is *real.* Despite what you may have heard from the old, conventional Wall Street crew, technical analysis works. My entire professional trading life, and the high degree of accuracy which our trading services enjoy, serve as daily proof of this. Fundamental analysis does have a certain value and it should command a place in your overall investment arsenal. But what every short-term market player needs to understand is that the fundamentals of a company fail to answer the most important question a trader can ask. And that is, "*When* do I buy?" "Now that I know that management is doing the right thing, the company has a good product, and quarterly earnings are accelerating, *when* do I buy it?" Short-term traders who concentrate only on the "what" (what company is good?) and not on the "when" (when do I strike?) will be trading on a very short term basis indeed.

SEED OF WISDOM

Astute traders understand that stock prices move before Wall Street's fundamental numbers do. That is because the market is a discounting mechanism. Collectively, the market attempts to anticipate events by 2 to 6 months. Traders who wait for the fundamental numbers to bear out what the stock price has been communicating all along will find themselves always a few months late and a few thousand dollars short. What's more, chart reading, combined with a few technical rules, is the only form of analysis, which answers the following question. "Now that

I know the company is good, *when* do I buy?" So, if someone dares to tell you that studying charts is a lot of bunk and does not work, just send them to us. In fact, hand them a copy of one of our newsletters and ask, "Well, how do you explain this? These guys are chart readers."

LOVE: THE TRADER'S GREATEST POWER

Thomas Edison, one of America's greatest inventors, was known for saying, "I never did a day's work in my life. It was all fun." When it comes to trading the market, I must admit, I feel exactly the same way. Despite the fact that trading delivers a never-ending mixture of delight and frustration, it is only when I am sitting in front of my real-time charts and my point-and-click execution system that I feel the most alive, and time seems to stand still. Even when the market environment becomes more difficult and favorable opportunities are in scarce supply, I still feel a thrill each morning I awake. My love for the game compels me to view any rocky periods of time as thorns that do not, in any way, take away from the beauty of the rose. This game we call trading is one of the most difficult endeavors an individual can ever attempt. But despite the hardships, I still love it with all my heart and soul. In fact, I love it for the very reason that it *is* hard. I love it because most people can't and won't last, and my survival provides me with a sense of accomplishment that I don't believe I could derive from any other endeavor. Like everyone else, I don't like to lose, but even when I do, the love for trading still flows out freely in a thousand ways. I truly believe that if more people loved trading just for the sake of trading, and not just for what trading can deliver, skill would replace greed, carelessness would give way to prudence, and intelligence would stand as the cornerstone of all actions. I honestly believe that I possess a secret weapon, one which forever keeps me ahead of the greedy crowd who would love to have my head on a platter and my spoils in their pockets if they could. My secret weapon is my sheer, unadulterated love for trading. And when I speak of this love, I do not refer to the weaker form of love that is often used in conjunction with things like pizza and sunny afternoons. No. When I use the term "love" here, I refer to that condition in the human spirit that is so profound that no power or presence on Earth can quell it or quench it. The love I speak of is that that deep love, that *agape* type of love. This is my secret weapon and I wouldn't give it up for the whole world. My love, my secret weapon, helps me survive. It guarantees that I outlast the crowd. It ensures that I overcome every obstacle in the way of my success, and it gives me the strength to endure every trail, every tribulation, and every dark moment the market and/or my personal stupidity can muster or conceive. Again, I say to you with the greatest pride that I love trading. And during especially trying times, I love the fact that I love trading, because if I didn't, I'd be history by now. If you try to love trading the way I do, it may just decide to love you back. And let me tell you something, when trading and the market decide to love you back, life truly becomes grand.

SEED OF WISDOM

Love is considered by many philosophers to be the most potent force known to humans. When love is lavished on our children, they grow strong and build noble characters that successfully and audaciously lead them into the arms of a welcoming future. When love is directed toward one's spouse and/or one's chosen field of work, each waking moment brings with it a warm welcome mat that leads eternally into the house of prosperity. There is no doubt in my mind that life and the world itself seems to completely yield to the power of love. And those who have it in abundance and generously spend it on something are richly rewarded. It is my belief that if the aspiring trader can truly learn to love this art we call trading, no obstacle will be able to withstand the potent force created by the mighty combination of love and the desire to succeed. When a trader loves trading, just for the sake of trading, losses won't even have the power to stand in the way. Hardships will more easily be endured. And setbacks and periods of crisis will be viewed as opportunities and compelling reasons to excel even higher. Love is a powerful thing indeed, even for traders. And just in case you think this point does not fit in the context of a trading book, I challenge you to conduct a test. Try to find a wildly profitable, successful trader who admits that he or she hates to trade. Try to find someone who commands the market with incredible acumen, yet despises the craft. You can search all four corners of the Earth, and I guarantee you won't be able to find one. This is no coincidence. Traders today, who are magnificently endowed with the ability to profit beyond most people's wildest dreams, will tell you that they love trading with all their heart. The question is, do they love trading because they are winners today? Or are they winners today because their love for the art of trading kept them alive when most individuals without that love would have fallen by the wayside? I'm willing to bet it's the latter. Try to love it.

TRADERS AND FORTUNE TELLERS

It is human nature to desire comfort and certainty. We are brought up to want it, worship it, and go after it. In fact, much of our lives are spent biting, scratching, and arduously striving for it, usually under the guise of something else. For instance, we think we want education for ourselves and our children, but a much closer look reveals nothing more than the desire to be secure. We do not typically look to education as a beneficial end. Rather, we approach it as a means to an end, and that end is safety, certainty, and security. Isn't the person who works long and hard hours at a job he or she hates doing so because of the desire for certainty? In some ways, almost everything we do is connected to the desire to feel secure, safe, and certain. Yet interestingly, certainty can never really be had in life. And when we turn our attention to the market, that near perfect mirror of life, we find that statement to be even truer. The truth is, certainty is predicated on a myth. Why is that, you ask? Because, certainty can only come into being when the future is fully known, and we're sure we don't have to tell you that we, as humans and traders, have not been afforded the benefit of knowing the future. Sure, we can guess what tomorrow holds, and at times be right. But we can never be sure of being right. So, in a sense, the search for certainty is a futile attempt that will invariably lead to frustration and disappointment. We find that far too many traders are looking for certainty in the markets, and that is why there is such a large number of them who are frustrated and disappointed as they move from one service to the next, from this guru to that one. Instead of wanting to be traders, these naive individuals secretly harbor the wish to be fortune-tellers and tea-leaf readers. They don't seem to recognize that all we can really hope for is a superb ability to assess the odds of being right. Good traders are really probability specialists. That's all. They don't ever *know*. But they've learned to live with that.

SEED OF WISDOM

The desire for certainty is a trap into which many traders continue to get caught. But it must be realized that certainty can never be found in life, nor can it be found in the stock market. Every trader must learn to accept the fact that we can never be certain of what the future holds. Once this truth is accepted, the trader will undoubtedly experience a great lift. Why is this? Simply because the search for certainty carries with it a heavy burden. It is a fruitless activity from which there can be no rest, for it will never end.

Oddly, it is believed that certainty, if achieved, would bring about clarity and peace of mind. But, paradoxically, peace and clarity of mind can only come into being when one realizes that certainty *cannot* be achieved. Certainty is an unattainable myth. Tomorrow can never be "known." The only thing we can do is acquire a few tools and techniques that are designed to help us assess the odds of what tomorrow may bring. That is our only course, and that is what we help you accomplish in the second half of this book. Those who learn to seek good odds will be well on their way to becoming professional traders. Those who seek certainty are inviting upon them a future that is wrought with failure, disappointment, and dismay. Seek better odds, not certainty.

2
C H A P T E R

DEVELOPING THE MASTER TRADER'S MIND

Keys to Correct Trading Behavior

ARE YOU GAMBLING OR TRADING?

Trading is one of the most exhilarating activities one can undertake. Each day, each hour, and even each price tick can dramatically increase, or diminish, the financial well being of the active market participant. The winnings can be swift and enormous, while the losses, if you are careless, can just as quickly take you out of the game, forever. The potential to acquire fast and enduring wealth, coupled with the strangely exciting possibility of economic ruin, makes professional trading one of the most desired activities in the financial world. However, most who make a go at this demanding profession fail. And they fail miserably. This hard, cold reality is due to several reasons, but I'd like to point out one of the most damaging of all those reasons. What has guaranteed the failure of countless trading novices is the inability to see the difference between a "gamble" and a "professional trade." Loading up on a stock just before the company releases what is "expected" to be positive earnings, and buying into issues that are crashing at the speed of light are just two of the actions that fit the criteria of senseless gambling. While these "shoot-from-the-hip" approaches can score big at times, their greatest value is in their fleeting entertainment, not in their intelligent approach. They have no place in an intelligent, well-planned trading program. If you want to

25

be entertained, it is better and cheaper to go to the movies. If you want to make consistent money in the market, your methods had better be professional and extremely disciplined. This is why each of the picks we provide to our *Pristine Day Trader* subscribers is accompanied by a very detailed, professional trading strategy. We leave very little to guess work and hunches, and focus entirely on making: (1) the proper entry, (2) the proper position management, and of course (3) the proper exit. When you approach the market this way, with intelligence and a well-thought-out plan, many of your plays may lack the excitement of the "gamble" and occasionally they won't live up to your dynamic expectations. But, as traders with a professional approach, you can be assured that you'll be around to trade another day, another year, and maybe even another decade. Smart trading involves executing a plan. Gambling is nothing more then buying and selling with little more than the *hope* that you are right. So it is of paramount importance that you trade smart. You can never lose sight of this fact: *in order to win, you must last.* Those who trade smartly *last,* and those who gamble don't last. Every trader must learn to recognize which is which.

SEED OF WISDOM

The desire for the big score, in other words the gamble, is one of the hallmarks of a truly novice trader. Professionals fully recognize that the entire art of short-term trading really boils down to a game of eighths and quarters, and at times quarters and halves. Think about it. Market makers and specialists represent the most astute players on Wall Street. At any given time, they can control tens of millions of dollars. The firms they represent are immense, influential, and very powerful. In a very real sense these master traders *are* Wall Street. They are the titans of the game, the kings of the hill, and as a result, they have etched out a permanent place at the very top of the financial food chain. Market makers and specialists are the true professionals, and their sole purpose is to do what? Do you know? *Their goal, in every moment of their trading lives, is simply to gain the spread or the difference between the bid and ask prices of the stocks they trade.* Reread this last statement for it contains one of the master keys to short-term trading success. The biggest and most powerful firms on the street, the financial gods who have amassed and control untold fortunes are after one thing and one thing only: *the spread.* They are not after a $40 gain in Amazon.com. They are not trying to capture a robust $4 advance in America Online, either. In short, they are not gamblers, they are processional traders of the highest order, and their sole objective is to gain the spread. There is a very powerful message here. Those who get it will have captured one of the most hidden, most protected truths of this game. While the novice may occasionally get lucky and hit pay dirt with a huge mouth-watering gain, the true professional is after the smaller but surer gain. They just grab it thousands upon thousands of time. The novice, lacking skill, is the one who feels as though his or her only course of action is to capture that one big score. Failing to formulate a plan, and missing the mark time and time again, the novice thinks the ticket to a better trading future is in the form of a financial lottery ticket. The most astute traders on Wall Street don't buy or even hope for lottery tickets. They sell them, to the novices. By all means, trade. Just don't gamble.

A WIN IS NOT ALWAYS A WIN AND A LOSS IS NOT ALWAYS A LOSS

Does a profit determine whether a trade was sound or correct? Should we automatically assume that we were wrong if a trade lost money? The answer to both of these questions is an emphatic *no!* The end result of any one particular trade does not determine the rightness or wrongness of your method, or your decision to make the trade. Many traders who don't grasp this truth find themselves tinkering with, and perpetually jumping from one technique to another, ultimately gaining no expertise in the process. Too many players fail to realize that even a rudimentary toss of a coin will be right at times. But a "heads you buy, tails you sell" strategy is certainly not a sound method, despite its occasional win. The point we are trying to make is this. In the real world, every trade, however sound and workable the strategy, is not going to be a winner. There will be times when your technique will be flawless, and the end result will still be a loss. Conversely, there will be times when you'll win despite a faulty approach. The professional knows that as long as he concentrates on making sure that the individual components of every trade are handled properly (the waiting, the execution timing, the entry, the money management, the exit, etc.), winning will eventually take care of itself. So instead of using the end result of one trade to determine if a particular trading tactic is sound, one should use the end result of, say, 10 trades. In fact, traders should perpetually remind themselves, before each transaction, that this is only one trade in a "lifetime" of trades. Therefore, a win here or a loss there will not make a major difference in the grand scheme of things. This should psychologically help the traders if they find themselves spending far too much time worrying about the end result of every single trade, an activity that breeds fear, lost opportunity, and eventually mental insanity.

SEED OF WISDOM

Becoming a professional trader should be regarded as a life-long process that never ends. The trader clothed in this mind-set looks at each play as just one tiny trade in a lifetime of trades. By itself, it is insignificant, whether it results in a win or a loss. Approaching each of your trading decisions in this way will remove much of the trade-by-trade pressure usually experienced by beginning market players. It will help create a peace and clarity of mind that further promote independence of action and intelligent decisions. But the central theme, one that must be thoroughly understood by all serious traders, is that one individual trade cannot—and will not—communicate where you are as a trader, or what level you are on. It is only after a significant block of trades that your true level is revealed. Losers hit the lottery at times and feel like kings for a day. Winners get whacked every now and then, and for a brief time do not show to the world their greatness. But after 10 or 12 trades, the *real* is usually separated from the *false*. It is only after a block of trades that the wheat is separated from the tares and the real winners emerge to take their rightful place on top of the hill as kings. You can never judge your success or failure by the result of any one trade. Take score after 10 trades. Trust us. After 10 or 12 consecutive trades, you will know all you need to know about who you are and where you are as a trader. The truth is revealed in sets of 10. Remember this.

THE MASSES CAN'T WIN FOR LONG

During times of market turmoil, many of our retail broker contacts reveal to us when their clients, individual investors, are dropping out of the market in droves. Whenever this happens, it is a strong indication that the bottom of the stock market's recent drop is close at hand. The stock market has an inherent tendency to shake out what we call the "weak hands" just before it takes back off to the upside. The intense level of frustration and the high level of euphoria among retail brokerage clients are, in fact, intriguing market barometers that some astute traders use to pinpoint market tops and bottoms. And we must admit that these barometers fare quite well. But when you think about it, it makes perfect sense. The financial markets were not designed to benefit the majority, which is why corrections tend to obliterate the typical investor (the majority), while the astute market players (obviously the minority) last long enough to pick up the pieces when the market finally does turn. Professionals are simply masters at keeping the average investor perpetually on the wrong side of the equation. When the novice wants to buy, the professional is willing to sell to him. When the novice wants to throw in the towel and sell, the professional is perfectly willing to relieve him of his pain by buying from him. Our question to you is, "Which character in this grand comedy are you?" Are you a part of that sad, manipulated group who surrender just when the game is about to shift in your favor? Only the able survive in this business, and obviously the survivors are the only ones who can succeed. Do your very best to be a survivor. Your success depends on it. When the going gets tough, the winners get tougher. In order to win in this game, you must last. The next time you find yourself thinking about quitting, ask yourself, "What role in this grand comedy am I playing right now?" That should help usher in a moment of clarity, in which the correct answer may emerge.

SEED OF WISDOM

The game of trading is a perpetual battle between the minority and the majority, the astute and the ignorant, the haves and the have-nots. And it must be thoroughly understood that the haves, the majority, those in the know, almost always win. The markets are designed that way. In order to be successful, one must become part of the winning group. But the reality is, very few wind up making the switch from the larger group of losers to that much envied, minority group of winners. As stated here, the markets are not designed to reward the majority. In fact, the very purpose of the majority, the reason the majority is even allowed to play, is to provide food (perpetual profits) for the gods, the winners. The following metaphor should clearly show you how the markets were designed to work.

THE BANDWAGON THEORY: A GLIMPSE AT HOW THE MARKET REALLY WORKS

Imagine a bandwagon that is rolling forward at a quickened pace. Music that is very pleasing to the ear is being played from speakers on each side of this bandwagon, and a few people currently on the back of the wagon are partying, having the time of their lives. The music, loud and clear, starts to attract many other onlookers that happen to be idly standing on the sidelines. These onlookers, unable to resist the sweet sounds being played, run to join the party that seems to be going on. Progressively, more and more onlookers jump on the back of this bandwagon, and those few who were initially enjoying the first phase of the party begin to leave. As the crowd of new party animals on this bandwagon grows larger, the bandwagon finds it harder and harder to move forward at the same pace. It slows, enabling more and more late onlookers, witnessing the great fun, the chance to jump on. The crowd grows even larger. Larger and larger this crowd grows, until the bandwagon, heavily laden with the bodies of drunken party animals, can no longer move forward. It finally comes to a complete stop. Now that the bandwagon is at a *complete* standstill, more people jump on. And why not? At this point, joining the fun is easy. Absolutely no work is required, for individuals wanting to join the crowd no longer have to run to jump on board. But the nature of the bandwagon is to move forward. Its motionless state is unnatural, and therefore cannot last. It tries to move forward again, but can't. The crowd, piled on back, is much too large. It must free itself of the heavy burden. And it does. It quickly shifts into reverse, and jolts backward, knocking a few of the party animals off the back. The music stops. Puzzled faces from the crowd begin to emerge. Before anyone figures out what's going on, another backward jerk takes place, only this one is more violent. Another large group of people gets thrown off the back. Now, reality sets in. The fun has turned into a nightmare of epic proportions, and panic begins to run rampant. Some decide to jump to their deaths. Another thrust backwards sends an even larger group of drunken, off-balance people, hurling to the muddy ground. It doesn't stop. The jolts backward continue, each successive one more violent than the last. At this point, only a few die-hard wagon dwellers are holding on, their very lives hanging in the balance by a very thin thread. Failing to be completely free, the bandwagon angrily puts the pedal to the metal, and this final thrust backward is so vicious that its front wheels lift high off the ground, momentarily suspending the wagon in a perpendicular position. The last of the hangers-on crash to the ground, broken and maimed to no end. At this point, a new group of onlookers emerge from the nearby woods. They are clean and serene. Each movement they make is deliberate and powerfully energetic, for they did not take part in the tragedy that just transpired. Or did they? A few of the dejected souls lying on the ground take a closer look, a look that reveals something very interesting. This seemingly new group is not new at all. It is the same group that was seen quietly exiting the party before it came to its violent end. An even closer examination by a few more beaten-down onlookers reveals something even more stunning. This group not only exited the party early, *they were the originators of it!* "My God," someone exclaims. Paralyzed, and unable to move freely, all these dejected souls can do is watch, as the masters of the game go to work, *again.* No sooner does the bandwagon's wheels hit the ground than this professional platoon bolts for the wagon. In a flash they are on board. Easy. The bandwagon, now free of the larger crowd, can move forward freely and gracefully, comfortably carrying the more astute group with it. Its pace quickens, and before long a smooth elegant stride is in place. After a few miles of uninterrupted movement, someone from this masterful group flips on a switch, and suddenly the loud sounds of entertaining music start again. Someone yells, "OK everyone. Here they come. Let's do it again." Within moments, those who were the former victims of the backward crash become interested again. The music almost calling them from the grave. And once more, the never-ending cycle repeats.

SEED OF WISDOM

The analogy you just read is worth many more times the price of this book, if you grasp all that it contains. If you truly hear its message and lay hold to the hidden wisdom embedded in its metaphors, you will find yourself laying claim to a higher level of understanding and mastery. With each read, you will discover a deeper insight into the inner workings of the market and how the financial sages of Wall Street manipulate it for profit. As we've stated earlier, the purpose of this book is to help you make the all-important transfer from the larger group of novices to that much smaller group, the invitations for which are very few. If you don't make the transfer, you will be nothing more than one of the many play toys for those who have. And when you can no longer entertain the gods with your willingness to play the game, they will send you on your way, broke, dejected, and depressed. Don't let this happen to you. The answers you seek are within the pages of this book. In fact, a very big clue to the whole game we call trading is contained in the bandwagon theory just explained. Why not read it again, right now? Your future may just depend on it.

MONEY ISN'T EVERYTHING

Oscar Wilde, whom I've quoted several times wrote, "When I was young, I used to think money was the most important thing in life. Now that I'm older, I know that it is." For the short-term–oriented trader, this statement couldn't be truer. Our ultimate success as market players is, and always will be, determined by our ability to make money. So in a very real sense, money *is* the most important thing. However, despite its ring of truth, it is still possible to take Mr. Wilde's facetious statement too far. For instance, a losing trade, in and of itself, doesn't necessarily indicate the execution of a faulty strategy. We must never lose sight of the fact that we live in the real world, and in the real world the best of intentions, even the soundest of strategies, don't work at times. A loss here and a loss there is simply not enough proof to determine the overall effectiveness of a particular approach. A single loss could be the result of poor market conditions, a sudden shift in the odds, an unexpected news item, a late entry, an early exit, a fumbled execution, etc. When we are testing the effectiveness of a particular strategy, we must look for the results after 10 trades. If after 10 to 12 trades, preferably spaced over several market environments, the bottom line is in the plus column, we can assume that there is promise with the strategy being deployed. On the other hand, if the bottom line is in the red, then, and only then, can we legitimately label the approach invalid? Our 25 years of combined experience has led us to the following realization. When the approach or strategy is sound, the money will take care of itself. We teach all of our students to focus on their technique. We tell them that if they do that, all that they are looking for will follow.

SEED OF WISDOM

It is imperative that a trader be able to separate those losses due to a faulty strategy from those that are due to the faulty implementation of a strategy. If the traders fail at this, they can find themselves forever chasing their tails. Progress eludes traders who jump from one approach to the next, without allowing it time to show its merits. Money or profits cannot be allowed to influence one's opinion of a certain strategy. In this regard, money isn't everything, simply because some of the most poorly constructed trading strategies can reward the trader with profits for a while. Conversely, some of the soundest can deliver losses for a while. But it will only be the sound ones that will ultimately stand the test of time and, for us, that time can be measured in blocks of 10. After 10 trades, if the strategy you are using has not rendered any fruit, then and only then, can it legitimately be questioned? As mentioned before, progress emerges in sets of 10. Do not forget this.

THE DANGER IN ASKING "WHY"

I am always amused whenever I hear market players make comments like, "The stock market is complex and very confusing." This is a notion to which we've never subscribed, and neither should you. The truth of the matter is that the mechanics of the stock market are very simple. While most people, at first glance, might disagree, a little thought will clearly show that this is undeniably true. Consider the following: A stock and/or the market can only do one of three things:

1. Go up
2. Go down
3. Go sideways.

That's it. That's literally all a stock can do. Up, down, or sideways. Simple. But "simple" doesn't mean "easy." Oh no. If trading were easy, everyone would be financially independent. While trading the market is far from easy, it is its mechanics that are rather simple. Consider another fundamental truism that is so simple that most have either missed its significance or chosen to ignore it:

Truth: A stock (or the market) can only go up if there is more buying than selling.

Of course this means that a stock can only go down if there is more selling than buying. "But Oliver and Greg, aren't you just stating the obvious," you ask? I'm not so sure this concept is as obvious as it sounds, especially given the countless questions we receive each day asking things like this:

Question: "I'm short Intel Corporation right here, but it's going up. Why is it rising?"
Pristine: Because more people are willing to buy the shares here than sell them.
Question: "Yeah! But why?"
Pristine: Our dearest sir. Intel Corporation came out with bad news this morning, yet despite this negative news, the stock is going up. This can only mean one thing: that the buy side (demand) is overwhelming the sell side (supply), and there is no regard for the negative news. To our way of thinking, there is only one course of action left for you. Why should the "reason" matter? A $3 loss is a $3 dollar loss, whatever the reason, is it not?"

This last statement brings up another point well worth mentioning. Whenever we find ourselves looking for the "why" versus the "what," we know with absolute certainty that we are in big trouble. *What* a stock is doing is far more important than *why* it's doing it. The "why" is always reflected in the price of the stock. In short, the chart tells it all! There are endless reasons *why* a stock can go up. Ask any fundamentalist. As technicians, we only care that the stock *is* going up and that we are in it for the ride. After all, isn't that what determines your profit?

SEED OF WISDOM

Asking the question "why" in the midst of a trade is a glaring sign that you are trapped in a state of confusion and perhaps paralyzed, and therefore unable to act. The word "why" in this regard is dangerous. Whenever we catch one of our traders asking "why," we have him or her immediately cut the position in half. If that does not briskly eschew the question "why," we have the trader kill the rest of the trade. Then we tell the trader, "*now* you can ask 'why' all you want." We do this because the battlefield is no place to be questioning your game plan. The moment you begin doubting your plan, that is your cue to exit. The quest for "why," the search for a reason, is proof that you are lost and have abandoned your command. The only correct time to ask "why" is before and after a trade. When you are in the throes of battle, action is the only option, not questions. Get your reasons ahead of time, or find them after you are back in the safety of your foxhole. There is a danger in doing this on the field of battle, unless you like collecting sniper bullets.

WHEN ACCURACY BECOMES A PROBLEM

As editors of one of the most popular trading advisory newsletters in the country, and with subscribers in 48 different countries, it was always our belief that we had literally seen and heard it all. And when we say all, we mean *all*. But not too long ago, that view was proven erroneous in a very big way. On one cold December morning in 1998, we received a call from a trial member who had been receiving the *Pristine Day Trader* for about a week. The performance of our picks had been quite stellar over the prior 5 trading days, and that impressive fact was not at all missed by our new friend. But strange as this may seem, our success was a very big problem for this gentleman, as he specifically conveyed the fact that he was in search of a newsletter that *lost* money, not made it. In no uncertain terms he said, and I quote "I have been monitoring your newsletter for 5 days, and I must admit that you are right far more often than you're wrong. But this does me absolutely no good, because I am looking for a newsletter that picks stocks that are going down. Your stocks don't go down. They go up." I was dumbfounded. "Well, how do you like that?" I asked Greg. "A man who *dislikes* our accuracy." At first, we laughed as hard as we could. But that was our first response. Shortly afterward, we stopped laughing as a deeper, more meaningful realization began to dawn on us. This gentleman was the prisoner of an ideology, one that purports the very popular idea that money is only made by buying stocks that are declining. It did not matter to him that our results proved otherwise. His loyalty was to the idea, *not* to any results. As soon as we realized this, it dawned on me that we have all been guilty of this crime in many other ways. I cannot begin to tell you how many times I've made the mistake of shorting a stock just because I thought the stock was rising too rapidly. Now isn't this the same idea I was so quick to laugh at? Sure it is. It's just in reverse. The point is that while ideas and trading concepts have their place, it is really the results that count in the end. At times the concepts we're following are so sexy that we tend to lose sight of the fact that our goal is not to be smart, not to be entertained, not even to be right, but simply to make money. Nothing more, nothing less. Now I am aware that we told you money isn't everything, and that is true. But if you find yourself liking your idea, while not making any money after 10 trades or so, it's time to either find another idea, or give up trading for bridge, dominoes, or philosophy where being ideological is much cheaper.

SEED OF WISDOM

As mentioned in a prior section, money isn't everything. But at a certain point, it really does become everything. When dealing with a concept, tactic, or technique, the first 10 attempts should not bring about any judgment. But after 10 or so trades, the concept we are using must be subjected to a microscopic review that has money as its basis. After all, we are trading to make money, not to make ideas. Those who fall too much in love with their approaches run the risk of ignoring signs that their sophisticated approaches need to be questioned, changed, or even discarded. As a professional trader, you cannot afford to render your loyalties to ideas or fancy trading concepts. In the end, your loyalty must be to the only thing that counts, and that is progress, advancement, and yes, *money!*

THE ENTRY IS 85 PERCENT OF THE TRADE

Being a successful trader is determined by a whole host of factors, all of which must be mastered, but my experience as a professional trader has thoroughly convinced me *that knowing how to enter a stock accounts for approximately 85 percent of a trader's success.* Now I am well aware of the fact that there are those who believe that selling properly is the key to good trading, but I'm compelled by my own experience to disagree. Most of the problems we encounter as traders can be directly linked to poorly timed and ill-placed entry points. By entering a stock inappropriately, a trader can actually turn a sound trade into a loser. Conversely, not so sound trades can actually turn out to be winners, if the entry happened to be at the right point and time. So it is the entry that serves as the foundation of short-term trading. Enter a stock properly and in a timely manner, and a trader is likely to be in profitable territory within minutes (hours in some cases). Enter sloppily and at a price that is too high, and the trade is likely to go against you almost immediately. Each experience is determined by one factor: when and where you make your entry, in other words, when you strike. What is amazing is how the professional investment community has managed to get away with ignoring this most critical of all points. How many times have you heard a major brokerage firm recommend a stock as a "Buy"? But what exactly does that mean? They've told you *what* to do, while leaving out the most important factor of *when* to do it. Your profitability will be determined by *when* you buy their recommendation, not *if* you buy their recommendation. Knowing the "what" (buy, sell, or hold) is good. But knowing "when" to do the "what" is what will make you a great trader. So master the art of the entry and you won't have to concern yourself as much about where to exit when you want to cash in those big bucks. In the second half of this book, we delve into the necessary components of the entry (see Chapter 14). By the time you finish, you will be well seasoned in the science of entering stocks.

SEED OF WISDOM

A commonly accepted axiom on Wall Street tells us that knowing when to sell is the key to mastering the trading game. While we cannot entirely discard this notion, we can say with a good deal of confidence that entering stocks properly greatly diminishes the problems associated with knowing when to sell. Every trader eventually realizes that the very best trades are those that become profitable instantaneously. They cause no pain from the moment they are initiated to the moment they are released. What is the difference between a stock that heads lower shortly after you bought it and one that zooms higher moments after you've initiated it? The difference lies solely with the entry. The properly entered trade is like a wonderfully behaved child who causes no problems. It does *what* it's supposed to do, *when* it's supposed to do it. It obeys your every command. Selling a properly entered trade becomes much easier because you are only concerned with the question, "when do I go to the bank?" This is very different from the question: "Will I ever go to the bank with this trade?" Or, "Will I have to kill this trade?" This first question is being asked by a winner. The latter two are the queries of a loser, a victim. A proper entry will frequently put you in the position of asking winning questions. Yes, knowing when to sell is important, but knowing how and when to enter is more important. We delve deeply into the art of entering stocks properly in Part 2.

YOUR PERCEPTION WILL BECOME YOUR REALITY

Most market players fail to realize that their trading reality, what they experience, is largely determined by their interpretation of the market. It is not necessarily determined by what the market does. In other words, it is not the market's reality that determines our results. It is our interpretation of, and our response to, that reality that determines them. While this statement may sound more philosophical than practical, we have found it to be enormously helpful in our trading. Let's consider the nature of the overall market for a moment. The market, by itself, is nothing but quantum soup. It offers absolutely no guidance, direction, or order. We as astute traders must bring order to *it*. Order is not the responsibility of the market, it is *ours*. Put yet another way, the market by itself cannot affect our lives or even determine our results. It is our response to the market that affects them, and our responses are determined by our very own interpretations. This view places full responsibility where it should be, with *us*. Think about how many times you've been greeted with the question, "How's the market treating you?" As if the market were capable of choosing its enemies and its friends! "How are *you* treating, or responding to, the market" is the real question. We are never victims. Yes, we may lose or experience pain because of an incorrect interpretation or a faulty reading of the market. But that interpretation is always ours, or at least one we've chosen to accept.

SEED OF WISDOM

The market is a near perfect mirror of life. This is why that which often makes for a successful life also makes for successful trading. Much of life and what it delivers depends on our perception. We need only take a quick glimpse at our great country to illustrate this view.

A Negative Perception

One person, living in this wonderful land of plenty since birth, experiences nothing but misfortune, disappointment, and failure. As a result of this, all that person sees is darkness, negativity, and a whole host of reasons that confirms the tragic conditions being experienced. Little does that person know that life, a perfect mirror of his or her perceptions, is casting the very reflection that was created and continues to be created. It is no wonder that each step this person makes leads to misfortune.

A Positive Perception

On the flip side of this we can find another individual who has just arrived to this opportunistic land. This individual's circumstances are nearly identical with that of the first individual, yet he or she sees and responds to conditions differently. Because this individual is in America, the great land of opportunity, this foreigner knows his or her plight won't be reality for long. Instead of asking the question, "why is life so angry with me," he or she asks, "how can I make my life better than it is right now?" Instead of seeing despair, this individual sees possibilities, chances, and opportunity. Instead of dealing with the current state as a victim, he or she takes the position of someone in control, a commander. Life for this person will almost have to start manifesting circumstances that match this view. Why, you ask? Because life is a perfect mirror of our thoughts, our responses, and our beliefs. We have found that the market as a whole acts in the same way.

The Market's Mirror Effect

Previously, we've referred to individuals dealing with the mirror effect of life in general, but the market has this same mirroring effect. Every consistently losing trader sees the market as this angry foe that must be overcome, tricked, or even conquered. In the loser's mind, the market is out to get him or her. It is perceived as an enemy of the highest order, and the market, being the perfect mirror that it is, casts that very negative perception back, in every detail. In other words, the losing trader's perception of the market becomes reality. The winner, on the other hand, sees the market in an entirely different manner. For the winner, the market is a friend. Its very purpose is to serve and reward him or her. The winner does not see the market as some bloodthirsty demon on a death hunt. Instead, the winner sees it as the place where dreams come true, a place through which his or her life is made better each and every day. To the winner, the market is a friend, a partner, and a sibling who is able and willing to open up the coffers of opportunity, fortune, and prosperity. To some, this may sound too philosophical, but we can't tell you how much our trading has been helped by making sure our perception of it is healthy and friendly. Just like life itself, trading is all about perception. Have the right one, and you win. Have the wrong one, and you will lose with great pain. You eventually get exactly what you perceive to be true. Why not decide to see the market as your friend and align yourself with it? Why not join forces with it?

As a final note I will say this. We have a student who after 2 years of training has risen to that grand level of development called trading mastery. It is not odd for that student to earn $60,000 to $100,000 in a week. That's right, 1 week. Do you think this immensely talented trader sees the market as an enemy or a friend? Case closed.

FACTS WILL NOT MAKE YOU MONEY

Have you ever wondered why one stock drops in the face of positive news, while another rises on the heels of what appears to be damaging news? How often have you scratched your head in absolute astonishment, trying desperately to understand why the market or a particular stock seems, at times, to totally defy the facts and/or logic? Well, the truth of the matter is that reality does not matter in the investment world. It is the *perception* of reality that is important. What's factual rarely, if ever, moves stocks. How investors as a whole *interpret* those facts is the reality, the true driving force behind stock movement. This is why and how stocks can—and do—part with logic. And this is the phenomenon that makes trading difficult. As market players, we simply don't place bets on stocks. And those who assume so will lose, often. We actually place bets on how others will *feel* about those stocks. Why? Because it's people and their feelings and emotions that ultimately move stocks, and, as you know, people are far more unpredictable than any other entity in existence. So the next time a company comes out with killer earnings that take the street by surprise, it would be wise not to blindly assume that the stock will rise. Of course, this goes for the reverse as well. We must never lose sight of the following fact. *We trade people, not stocks.*

SEED OF WISDOM

Traders who spend their trading lives delving into the facts that Wall Street and news services ceaselessly put out will not be as successful as those who learn to focus and capitalize on how the crowd reacts to those facts. The astute traders recognize that it's the reaction and/or the response that possesses the money-making potential, and the very best traders fully understand that the crowd's perception and/or reaction to the facts can be out of sync with the reality of those facts. There are times when the reaction can even be diametrically opposed to those facts, which is what really throws most novice market players. In essence, the master trader has come to terms with the knowledge that it is the understanding of people and what moves them that makes for truly profitable trading. Those who are the real captains of the game never ask, "What's the news?" Instead they ask, "How are people likely to respond to this news?" There is a big difference, and it usually makes a big difference in one's bank account.

THE TRUTH DOESN'T COUNT ON WALL STREET

If you, as a trader or investor, believe that the market responds to what is real and true, you are sadly mistaken. Worse, if you actually play the market based on this erroneous assumption, you have just about guaranteed yourself a losing market career. The truth of the matter is that stocks rise and fall based on belief, not facts. Did you get that? Please do, because it's enormously important. What we are trying to communicate here is that reality doesn't matter. It never has, and it never will. Rather, it is the perception of reality, the perception of the facts that drives the market. We are not playing stocks when we put our money at risk. It is not a company or even its fundamentals we are buying when we bring up our execution system to place an order. No. No. No. No. "Well, what exactly am I buying?" you ask. *We buy people and the beliefs they have about the underlying stock.* Think about it. When we, as traders, step up to the plate to put our money on the line, we are betting that we know how people, other investors, will perceive the stock we like in a day or so. It's *people* who are going to move the stock one way or the other, not facts. A fact has never moved a stock, and never will. And allow us to add a deeper dimension to our little discussion. Perception can be, and usually is, more dangerous than reality. Take the rekindled fears of an interest rate hike. How many times has the market sold off dramatically as a result of fears involving a *possible* rate hike by the Federal Reserve? Does it matter much that the Federal Reserve had not even hinted at raising rates? No. Not at all. What matters is that traders and investors *perceived* a rate hike as possible. That was and is enough to cause havoc. The point that must be fully realized by traders is that the market is anticipatory in nature. It tries to play on what *will* happen, not what *has* happened. Facts are remnants of the past. They tell us very little about tomorrow. This is why the real professionals tend to buy the rumors (perceptions) and sell the news (facts). So don't be fooled. It is not the truth that wins in the market. It is the perception of that truth.

SEED OF WISDOM

There will be times when the truth (facts) and the perception of the Wall Street crowd will be identical, perfectly in sync. There will be other times when the truth and the perception of it will be completely opposed or out of sync. It is the latter scenario that confuses and trips up the bulk of novice market players. In order to stay on guard so that these events can be utilized for profit, the trader must forever be mindful that the opportunity lies in the crowd's reaction to the facts, not in the facts themselves. In the short-term time frame, the truth does not always win out. This is why a perfectly sound company can get cut in half, when it deserves the very opposite, and a valueless company can be hyped up to a billion dollar market capitalization. One can certainly argue that the perception and the reality cannot stay out of sync forever, and that what is *real* will ultimately prevail. But who has forever? Someday does not exist for short-term traders. They do not have the luxury of a great deal of time. Their living, their livelihood, their very well being depend entirely on the Here and Now. And in this Here and Now, the truth does not always count.

YOU MUST BECOME INHUMAN TO TRADE SUCCESSFULLY

After very profitable winning streaks, there is a natural tendency for traders to become complacent, to get lulled to sleep by an accommodating market.

As individuals who do battle in the markets everyday, we have learned that *comfort* is the archenemy of the trader. Why? Because proper trading is one of the most *unnatural* activities an individual can undertake. If something is psychologically pleasing, in most cases *it is wrong!* On the other hand, if a particular strategy or approach is psychologically and emotionally difficult to pull off, the odds of it being right are very great. This is why the feeling of complacency or contentedness is usually a sign that you are doing something wrong. The right thing to do is not always the easy thing to do, and that which is wrong is often accompanied by an enticing sense of ease. Needless to say, it is this paradox that makes the art of trading so difficult to master. Unfortunately for us, it is the one great disadvantage of being human, of having human emotions. However, for the enduring trader, this condition, this war between what is right and what is easy, does not remain in place forever. Through vigilance and the constant effort to do what is right in the face of what is wrong and easy, traders will find themselves slowly becoming *in*human. Myriad experiences of pain and joy, triumph and failure, will begin to train their internal systems to feel as if they are *in reverse.* Through experience, new neurological paths will be established, which will set up new thought processes, new responses, and new feelings. After making decent progress, what is *right* will also start to *feel* right. Once this transformation has occurred, the wrong action, even the wrong thoughts, will send a message of pain and discomfort to the central nervous system, acting as an automatic internal alarm system. In other words, traders, through a process of continual growth, begin to change their entire network of psychological and emotional responses. Ever so slowly, they move from being pavlovian models who salivate at the tinkering of a bell to conscious thinking individuals who find that the easy thing to do is also the *right* thing to do. In short, traders who have reached a certain level of achievement reverse the natural process to become almost inhuman.

SEED OF WISDOM

Psychiatrists tell us that ever since the beginning of time, human beings have found the right course of action to be the most difficult course of action and the wrong action to the be the easy action. This is because we have been conditioned to seek the joys of pleasure and avoid the discomfort of pain. But the truth is that pain oftentimes accompanies what is right, while the wrong course of action often produces temporary comfort. Consider the following scenario as an illustration of this point. A trader, who has had a steep loss after buying a stock incorrectly, struggles with the question, "should I sell, hold, or buy more." The trader really knows that buying more is not the real answer, for that would be akin to someone adding more fuel to a fire that needs to be put out. The trader also knows that holding on is not the correct answer either, for that would be an exercise in the dangerous game of hope, and hope has no place in the world of sound trading. This leaves the trader with only one option, which is to sell. Intellectually, the trader fully realizes that selling is the only intelligent option and reasons that the trade was wrong from the start, and trying to correct it any other way besides killing it and moving on could result in exasperating the loss. But despite the prompting from the trader's intellect, his or her psychological self violently struggles against the notion of selling. Why? Because selling would make the loss seem more real by locking it in forever. It would send an acute message of failure throughout the entire mental and physical systems, causing psychological and physical pain in the process. So the trader opts for temporary comfort instead. Instead of acting, the trader decides to hold off, to sit tight, and do nothing. This holding off provides the trader with temporary relief. Despite the fact that holding on is not the correct action, doing so delivers a sense of hope, which in turns delivers a sense of comfort. The battle to do the *right* thing in the face of the *easy* thing has been lost. We can often judge our own progress as traders by judging how we feel about each action we know to be right. When the right thing starts to feel right, and the wrong thing is what brings with it pain and discomfort, we know that we are making that all-important transformation from the human to the *in*human.

OPPORTUNITY LIES WHERE THE MAJORITY IS AFRAID TO GO

Have you ever noticed that the most difficult trades to make are often the ones that go on to advance dramatically? Why is this? Why is our reluctance to act often rewarded or answered with missed profits? Well, the first thing that comes to my mind is the fact that opportunity often lies where most individuals dare not tread. Just imagine how many thousands of dollars are constantly left unclaimed by those who find it difficult to buy stocks with P/Es over 20 or 30? And hasn't the often repeated declaration, "I will not trade NASDAQ issues because of the volatility and the wide spreads," robbed many a trader of small fortunes? But the biggest culprit behind much of our reluctance is the yearning to be certain *before* we act, the need to be *sure*. We, as conditioned human beings, want to *know* if this will be a winning trade *before* we take the leap. We want to be sure this one will work out. But the hard, cold reality is that successful trading will always be difficult to accomplish because it requires that we act *before* we know. We must face the undeniable fact that each decision we make can never be a "sure" one. Why? Because the future is simply not known. It can never be known. All we can honestly do is develop a sound trading strategy based on carefully assessed odds. Our various newsletters, along with our Web-based Real-Time Trading Room, take care of assessing the odds. What we *cannot* do for our followers is act! That is their job.

SEED OF WISDOM

The need or desire for certainty is one of those natural human traits that every aspiring trader must learn to overcome. Why? Because, certainty is a myth. It does not exist in life in general, nor does it exist in the market. It is a phantom, a dream that has, and continues to be, chased by far too many market players. As traders, we must be capitalists of the unknown. We can never escape the fact that we are forced to act in the face of uncertainty. Those who must know all the facts before the trade will find opportunity forever leaving them behind. Fortune waits for its captor in the shadows of uncertainty. It lies hidden on the path least traveled. The active trader will find that the greatest opportunities will be found where no one else is willing to go. The trader can never be certain that the trade just taken will work. The trader can properly assess the odds and even devise an intelligent strategy in an attempt to exploit those odds. But each trade will still possess the ability to disappoint. Each attempt will carry with it the potential to fail. The aspiring trader must learn to deal with this and must learn to act before he or she knows. Because by the time the trader knows, the opportunity is long gone.

NOT A CLOUD IN THE SKY? WATCH OUT!

Not a cloud in the sky right now? Uh-oh! Watch out! We learned long ago that the time to increase one's watchfulness is when there isn't any sign of trouble, when things are rosy, peachy, and seemingly trouble-free. When making money has been too easy over a recent period, and when the "average" person on the street starts thinking he or she is hot stuff, that's when the astute traders start biting their nails. Why? Because the market rarely rewards the "average" for prolonged periods of time. Just when Mr./Ms. Mediocrity feels as though he or she has been given a break, the game starts to change. We can make sure that we are never in this person's company by always maintaining a contrary frame of mind at these critical points. We must protect ourselves from the herd mentality that so often is the undoing of many would-be successful traders. Remember that we can't predict the future, but we can be prepared for the possibilities. And one way to be prepared for possible danger is to run for the hills whenever things look too good.

SEED OF WISDOM

It has been said that the market climbs a wall of worry. Remove that wall of worry, and the market will start to lose its desire to climb. Astute traders recognize that the time to worry is when there is nothing on the horizon to worry about. It is almost as if the market does not care for periods of calm. Remember that the entire financial system in which we play was not designed to reward the majority. So when the majority is content and there is not a cloud in the sky, your best course of action is to run for cover, for history tells us we have just experienced the calm before the storm.

THE TRUE MEASURE OF A SUCCESSFUL TRADER

Tex Cobb, the only boxer ever to lose all 15 rounds of a championship fight, made a statement once that immediately grabbed my attention. He said, "Anyone can be a hero going uphill. The true measure of a man is what happens when nothing works and he still has the guts to go on." This statement adequately captures the essence of what truly makes for a successful trader. Those who have gone on to master the art of trading have undoubtedly learned how to proceed during times when everything seemed to go wrong. All developing traders go through periods when heaven and earth seem to be against them, when the very market itself appears to want nothing else but to thwart them at every step. But in order to succeed, in order to gain the necessary experience that ultimately leads to the state of mastery, traders have to muster up the courage to proceed in the face of these difficult times. They must learn to keep going, to keep pressing forward. It is not during the times when all is well that we make our biggest strides. Like fine gold, we make progress and rid ourselves of dross and imperfections while enduring the fire of hardships. Our character and trading acumen grow only when we are pressing forward in the face of mounting difficulties. During these hardships, if we manage to pick ourselves up from a fall and willingly face the next round, we do so as a more seasoned market player. It may not seem as though progress is being made when all is going wrong, and every choice you make shouts of your immaturity, but each time you manage to rise during these times, you will be making a giant leap forward. The very ability to rise itself stands as proof of that. During your developmental years, the true measure of your potential success can be gauged by your ability to face tomorrow when everything in your experience today begs you not to. What we must keep reminding ourselves is that in order to win, we must *last.* And while lasting alone will not guarantee that we win, we can rest in the assurance that we can't ever win without lasting.

SEED OF WISDOM

It is naturally very difficult to press forward in the face of frequent trading losses and failures. It is even tougher to see or accept the notion that in the midst of these losses, progress and growth as a trader are taking place underneath. But just like the flower that first grows below the surface before it shows its splendor to the world above, traders first develop from within. Their outer circumstances and P&L statements may seem in dire straits for a time, but all the while, hidden underneath, the wheels of progress are busily at work. But it must be known that this wonderful event only takes place for traders who properly handle this period. This law of hidden progress only works for traders who are determined to rise each time they fall, who face each successive challenge with ever-increasing resolve. Those who learn to do this will find, often times in retrospect, that the purpose of every lost round in their fight against failure is to help them prepare for the next. That every seeming knockout is only a knock *down*, if only to show them that the greatest act one can accomplishment is to rise after every fall.

WHEN NO ACTION IS THE BEST ACTION

When addressing the importance of thought as well as action during the 1960s war protests, Daniel Berrigan's frequent cry was, "Don't just do something, stand there." While short and obviously concise, this quote is power packed with a great deal of wisdom. It is very apparent that we, as human beings, are creatures of action, or at least we strive to be. The individual who strives, achieves, accomplishes, and does is idolized in our society. The "doer," the person of action, has always been treated kindly by history. And while action or doing holds great importance, we must never lose sight of the need for balance. If action is important, then a balanced existence calls for periods of inaction. In fact, I have found that the quality of my periods of action are often determined by the quality of the preceding periods of inaction. And so it is with my trading. Many active traders today, even those who are part of Pristine's in-house trading program, feel miserable and bored if they are not trading. When the market gets quiet and low-risk opportunities are scarce, these traders who feel they always need to be in something start forcing trades, as if they could force the market to cough up favorable conditions. These same traders don't realize that sometimes the very best action is *no* action. They fail to grasp the fact that standing still, at times, brings in a much-needed rush of calm and clarity. The moments during which the market enters into a lull offer us the chance to regroup and recollect ourselves. They help us regain our composure, grease our wheels, so to speak, so that we are prepared for the next period that calls for quick-rolling action. I've learned to respect the need for just standing still. I have learned how to use inaction as a means of preparing for the ultimate action. Ralph Waldo Emerson once said, "Do the thing, and you will have the power." This is so true. But he failed to tell us that standing still from time to time will help us *keep* the power. Be an active trader, please. But realize that, at times, just standing still helps.

SEED OF WISDOM

Standing still will, at times, be the most productive action we can take. Sometimes, it will be in the quiet periods of action that we find our balance. Mental clarity often returns when we have dropped all action to become an unbiased observer. We, as traders, need to recognize our need for these periods. Being involved in the struggle has its place, but we also need periods of nonstruggle, if only to rest our faculties and rejuvenate our senses. Each time we step back or bow out of the market to observe, we seem to come back more powerful. The next time the market is not cooperative, or something in the air seems wrong, *stand still*. Watch how *no* action will bring about a greater feel for what your *next* action should be.

STANDING STILL: THE HIGHEST ACTION OF ALL

Thirteen years of trading experience has taught me that there are times when *no action* is the very *best action*, that sitting is more appropriate than standing, and watching far superior than doing. In the western culture, too much emphasis is placed on the perpetual action individual, the doer, missing entirely the point that inaction can, at times, represent a higher, more intelligent action.

SEED OF WISDOM

Action is necessary, so much so that we could never get anything accomplished or make any money trading without it. But we have come to realize that many traders feel that they need to be perpetually in motion, always trading or always getting ready to trade. This idea is wrong and if put into practice too frequently, it can prove very damaging to those in the midst of their developmental stage. There are times when the highest action of all is simply to *stand still*, to do nothing but watch and observe how things are developing. The power to significantly manipulate the market's behavior has not been given to us. We cannot dictate which set of odds will be presented to us on any given day. We must face the reality that there will be times when all systems are go, and virtually everything we look at will scream of opportunity. And there will be other times— times when the market is so uncooperative that low-risk opportunities will be scarce and the number of booby traps and market-related land mines will grow abundantly. When we are dealing with the latter scenario, not only is no action the very best action, it is often the only money-saving action at our disposal. To illustrate how important this point is, let's look at the experience of a gung-ho market player who just started trading with us in our White Plains office. For purposes of this exercise, we will call this trader, Mr. Gung-ho.

A LESSON IN THE ART OF STANDING STILL

It was Mr. Gung-ho's first day as a Pristine in-house trader, and he was understandably very excited. Unfortunately, the market was not very welcoming on his first day with us. In fact, the market seemed outright angry as the S&P futures contract was down over 10 points before the opening bell, and concerns surrounding a key politician's resignation reverberated through the financial air. But this did not seem to matter to Mr. Gung-ho. With his squeaky-clean $50,000 account, he immediately began pressing his luck with several rapid-fire trades at the opening bell. That proved to be a rather big mistake. His total disrespect for the market's pre-opening message cost him over $850 inside of 30 minutes. Ouch! After taking a deep breath, it dawned on him that he was reverting back to his old ways of trading, and decided to settle down. He finally began to put to work some of the opportunity-finding techniques we taught him during his 2-week training course. But after 2 hours or so of this, he found himself coming up with very few trades that met the stringent criteria we purposely set in these techniques. This forced a "no action" stance on him that made him feel uneasy. This guy was used to action. It was obvious that "sitting still" was not his modus operandi, and I could almost see the frustration gaining control of his face. Had he still been trading at his old firm, he would have already completed 10 to 20 trades, if not more. Here it was close to twelve noon eastern time, and he was barely staying awake. Something *had* to change. Even though very few low-risk opportunities were meeting our predefined trading criteria, he was determined to *do something*. Within minutes, he took a number of trades that he would not have taken had he continued to abide by our plan. Not surprisingly, they delivered losses. Still feeling somewhat antsy, he tried his hand at a few more trades. As you might have guessed, they too delivered losses. On and on this continued, as we quietly watched from the sidelines (at times you have to allow traders to come face to face with their faults before they can appreciate the remedy). By the last hour of trading, the frustration that was gaining ground on Mr. Gung-ho's face relinquished its position to anger. At the close of trading, 1 hour later, Mr. Gung-ho was down over $2950.

Mr. Gung-ho got precisely what he wanted that day. Action. But he got it at the expense of sound trading. What he would have told you, of course, is that he wanted profits, but in reality his true desire was excitement. What this trader failed to realize is that inaction, prompted by our stringent trading criteria, was actually the element saving him from himself *and* the market's sloppy odds. Inaction, or no action in this case, should not have been something to combat but something to embrace, especially given the sloppy nature of the market. He also failed to see that the "no action" stance he was taking was not prompted by cowardice, which would have been just as problematic. Rather it was prompted by the implementation of sound trading techniques that simply had very high standards and conditions, conditions that the market was in no condition to meet. Little did Mr. Gung-ho know that this was an intelligent form of "no action." It was the money-saving form of no action. Had he continued to adhere to his *standing still* mode, he may not have been able to boast of a hugely profitable day at the day's end, but he certainly would have gone home more than $2000 richer. We think this clearly illustrates that, sometimes, no action is the very best action.

"HEY MAN, DON'T TEACH ME HOW TO THINK; TEACH ME HOW TO TRADE!"

"Hey man, don't teach me how to think, teach me how to trade!" This is a response similar to the ones we get whenever I address a topic that requires thought versus canned, thoughtless action. What the eager souls who demand this methodology fail to realize is that proper thinking *is* proper trading. We see it all too often. Traders think they can come to our White Plains, N.Y., location, take one of our detailed day-trading seminars, then go out and immediately win, win, win until they reap a fortune large enough to live out their days in the south of France, sipping warm cappuccino in the afternoons, and popping fine bottles of rare wine in the cool evenings. Surprise! As disappointing as it may seem, knowing *what* to do, which is the focus of our seminars, is no guarantee that you will do it. This is the hard, cold truth, and this is why the "thinking" part of trading is so important, so paramount. Consider this. We can give a trader every single tool, technique, and trading tactic that will ever be needed to be successful, all within the course of a short 3-day weekend. That's right. A weekend. Believe it or not, learning precisely what to do in the market and getting in your possession dynamic money-making trading tactics is *not* the hard part. It's following it, practicing it, doing it that's hard. How many times have you held on to a falling stock far beyond the point at which you *knew* it should have been sold? How many times have you, knowing that you should *not* be buying the stock, bought it anyway? The problem in most cases is *doing* what you know is right, not failing to *know* what is right. This potentially rewarding game we call trading is mostly mental. It's 85 percent psychological. Once you have all the trading tools and techniques under your belt, it will be the quality of your thought process that will determine your success or your demise. We don't always perish for *lack* of knowledge. In many cases, we perish for refusal to *heed* that knowledge.

SEED OF WISDOM

Eighty-five percent of the people who try to trade the market for a living fail within the first 6 months. The saddest part is that many of them fail because of one simple thing: lack of knowledge. There is no doubt that people in the market perish for lack of knowledge. It is the number one reason for failure. However, even those who manage to get the knowledge, through a seminar, a book, or years of trial and error, have a hard time advancing to a level that will pay them life-long profits. Why? Because knowledge is only the first hurdle that must be overcome in the long journey to trading mastery. Having the right tools will certainly place you head and shoulders above most market players. That is because most don't even get to the point of "knowing." But keep this in mind. Just because you've been given the carpenter's tool belt doesn't make you a master carpenter. It is the first step in mastering carpentry, no doubt, but one is not a master carpenter until proficiency and seasoning with each tool is achieved.

One of the greatest tools available to traders is their mind. Using it properly will almost ensure a successful trading career. Using it improperly and unproductively will surely lead to financial death. Another point that should never be forgotten is that traders can have all the right tools, like trading tactics and techniques, and have the wrong thinking process and they are still dead. Thousands of people can take a Pristine seminar, but thousands can't rise to the state of trading mastery, no matter how much they pay. And I, for one, say thank goodness. Thank goodness that most people don't ever get the right knowledge. I'll even say thank goodness that most of those who get the knowledge don't get the thinking right. Why? Because if it were any other way, the opportunities that exist for those who get the knowledge *and* the thinking would drastically diminish. Quite frankly, we are not ready for that to happen. Ignorance is an enemy to those who possess it. But ignorance in others is power to those who have knowledge, and it is a never-ending source of wealth to those who have the knowledge and know how to think.

WHAT ARE YOU DOING WITH WHAT YOU HAVE TODAY?

Wanting more than what we have has been arguably an American way of life for decades. Some careful watchers of history and social movements will argue that the intense desire for more has been part of the American culture from its beginning. Whatever the case, we feel that if we had *more* money, *more* time, *more* knowledge, then we'd really be able to take care of business, to move life itself. But what about the money we *do* have? What about the time and the knowledge, however limited, we have at our disposal right now? Are we taking full advantage of it? Are we exhausting it? In other words, are we being thoroughly responsible with our *limited* supply, before seeking a much larger supply? My personal observation, within my own daily life, has revealed an urgent need to watch this human tendency of reaching for more, without exhausting what is at my disposal right now. I am of the mind-set that we have no right to more time if we squander the bits of free time we have in our control right now. Excess money only seeks out those who intelligently use it, when it is in limited supply. And knowledge, one of the greatest riches of all, increases abundantly for anyone who is responsible with the amount they currently have. So how does this relate to trading, you ask? Well, all that pertains to our human tendencies will pertain to our trading. Because all our human tendencies, good and bad, will be acted out in our daily trading. The point is this. It is our duty to make sure that we are being responsible with what we have and know today, before seeking more. Today, every Pristine member knows the importance of stops. We not only use them in our services each day, we have written numerous educational pieces on their importance and explained in detail how they should be implemented. The question is, are we being responsible with that knowledge? Are we respecting it? Each of our subscribers knows how important waiting for the right entry point is, how important not chasing the stock is. But is that knowledge always adhered to? Some of our traders want more stock picks, especially on days when a good many don't meet our strict entry criteria. But are we being responsible with the stock picks that we do get? Let's master what we do have and know today, before we look for more.

SEED OF WISDOM

There is nothing wrong with the desire for more. The desire for more has been at the foundation of every great achievement known to humans. Therefore, we should never be ashamed of our urge to spread our wings. But whenever we grab for more without fully exhausting the portion we have today, we become guilty of the crime called greed. Aspiring traders very frequently fall into this trap. In their search for the holy grail, they move from one book to the next, looking for more. Seminar after seminar is taken in the endless quest for more of *this* and a lot more of *that*. More tactics, more plays, more tricks. More, more more. But many of these traders I see rarely, if ever, settle down to take a full inventory of what they have already accumulated. They rarely, if ever, watch or keep tabs on how well they are using the tactics they learned from here and the knowledge they picked up from there. We watch people all the time take our intense "One-Day Trading Boot Camp" seminar, and immediately want to move to our "Three-Day Trading" course, and then on to our "Two-Week Training" course. They have not even begun to digest, utilize, or maximize the knowledge that they've already gained. They have not allowed it to take root, to grow into anything substantial. Yet they want more. How do we know we will be responsible with *more* knowledge, *more* wisdom, *more* trading tactics, if we have not proven to ourselves that we can be responsible with the knowledge we already have? Maximize what you have today. Decide, right now, to take inventory of every trading technique you've learned. Then wear it out, my friends. Run it into the ground. Then, and only then, will you have earned the right to ask for more.

IS THE PAST IN YOUR WAY?

There is a very thought-provoking axiom, which states, 'If you do not know where you came from, you will not know where you are going." This rings true in my mind, and had I been aware of this wisdom when I was in junior high school, perhaps I would have paid more attention in history class. I'm sorry about that, Mrs. Nardiello. She was my sixth-grade history teacher. But is the past *always* valuable? Is it something that should religiously be respected, adored, cherished, and carried with you? I am not so sure about that. In fact, I'm willing to say that the answer is *no*. At least not always. And especially if it pertains to trading. Now this is a tricky point, I know, because even in trading one learns from past errors, mistakes, and blunders. There are even those rare times when we learn from our past wins. But carrying over too much of the past can cause serious trouble for the trader. In fact, it can be detrimental. The main reason behind this lies in the fact that 85 percent of the game we call trading is psychological. We can have all the tactics, techniques, tips, and tricks we can handle, but if our mind-set is not right, if we do not possess the right equanimity, the proper and much-needed mental clarity, we will undo ourselves every time. Take the trader who has lost four times in a row and is having a devil of a time finding balance in the market. This trader must be able to move into trade 5 as if none of the past four trades occurred. He or she cannot afford to allow "past" trading history to spill over into future trading. If the residue of trade 4 is carried over into trade 5, the trader is already working with a handicap. Trading successfully is hard enough without battling the trades from the past, in addition to the current ones. The present must be clean, pure, and innocent as a brand new baby. And in order for it to be so, prior losses must be like water under the bridge, like spilled milk. Signs that we are being contaminated by our prior losses are:

1. Chronic hesitation, which is really the hidden desire for certainty.
2. Fear of pulling the trigger, which is nothing more than the need to know more.
3. Grabbing at profits too quickly.
4. Failure to take a loss (stop).

So just remember, the past can be an enemy too.

SEED OF WISDOM

Successful trading is all about balance. We must delicately balance a great many things in order to move freely in the world of trading. We must balance good news with bad news that is often issued simultaneously. We have to balance opposing views from analysts, conflicting signals from technical indicators, and dueling emotions from the depths of our soul. It's all about balance, and when it comes to the past, it is no different. For a trader, there is no doubt that the past is important. In one sense, it serves as our greatest teacher and our "mirror, mirror on the wall" that will always tell us the truth about ourselves. But in another sense, it can serve as our archenemy, one that can ruin our future in a heartbeat. Simply put, carrying too much of the past with us can be damaging. This is where the balance comes in. We can't place so much emphasis on the past that we allow it to spill over and taint our tomorrows. The past should only serve as a window into what *was*, not necessarily as a window into what *will be*. It should only be utilized as a tool that helps us tighten our belts, so to speak. But once those belts have been tightened, the tool should be put down, as it has no more usefulness. Traders must learn to drop the past, each time they enter into a new play. It has no place when dealing with the myriad factors in the present. Leave the baggage at home. During the trading day, we have to travel light.

BREAKING THE CYCLE OF PAIN AND PLEASURE

Like all traders, in the delicate years of my trading youth, I perpetually vacillated between the extremes of pain and pleasure. Whenever I won, or experienced a string of profitable trades, a tremendous sense of accomplishment would well up in my chest, and the height of that sensation, called *pleasure*, would embrace my whole being. It was during these times that I, drunk with my success, would feel like a trading god. But whenever I experienced the pain of loss, my heart would sink. My body would ache, and a sense of profound despair would descend on my entire world. These were the treacherous times when all would go black, and the beauty of life that my prior wins delivered would instantly fade into the darkness. Then, suddenly, a few winning trades would bring back a glimmering of faith and, once again, the beacon of hope would shine bright. In other words, the cycle would begin anew. I spent years as a captive slave to these two masters, pain and pleasure. Sometimes I'd spend more time with one than the other, but I always found myself frequently visiting them both. But eventually, ever so slowly, these two extremes began to loosen their grip on me. At first, I found this strange, but each time I lost, I realized that the pain was not as acute anymore, no longer unbearably sharp. I curiously watched as my despair gave way to a feeling of ambivalence. So, too, did I begin to feel less pleasure from my trading wins. A careful observation revealed that the mental and psychological rise that at one time accompanied each success gradually turned quiet and serene. Shortly afterward, I found my personal trading catapulting to a brand new level, a much higher level. This experience taught me a very valuable lesson. You see, it is important that traders not be affected by their results. Many of us fail to realize that the outcome of any one trade shouldn't influence the way we feel or think. True traders, the ones who have been matured by countless market experiences, emerge out of each trade untouched, unperturbed, calm, and of course, serene. These fully developed traders know that the result is not nearly as important as the process. They recognize that winning or losing is simply a by-product of their choices. When we focus on the individual components of each trade, instead of applying our attention to what may happen at the *end* of each trade, we suddenly free ourselves from this vicious cycle of pain and pleasure. And only if that happens can we hope to rise to the level of trading mastery.

SEED OF WISDOM

It is a proven fact that most people spend their entire existence seeking pleasure and avoiding pain. This all too predictable pattern of human behavior also finds its way into the trader's world. As traders, we spend each and every market moment trying to escape loss, and doing everything in our power to experience only winning. While this is a very natural urge, the trader must find a way to rise above this dual struggle. Why? Because in reality, it's a trap. Let us try to explain. "The journey of a thousand miles begins with one step," right? Confucius said that. But in a sense, he didn't finish. What Confucius forgot to mention is that the journey will only lead to success if each and every step we make is correct and right. We all want to reach that distant destination we call winning, *but what about the steps?* Do you get the subtle difference? If we simply focused on making sure each choice, each decision was right, winning would take care of itself. We must not only want the win, we must crave to be a winner. And a winner is one who carefully takes each step in the journey, making sure it is right. The person who wants the win (successful journey), without working on what leads *to* the win (the individual steps) is really a thief. He or she wants the harvest, without the toil. That person seeks the fruit, without planting the tree, and if you don't watch that person carefully, he or she will sneak into your world, looking for freebies. "Hey, you got any good tips?" Our private students know that we believe in replacing the desire to win with the desire to *be* a winner, which really is the desire to get every individual part of the trade right. The analyzing, the thinking, the decision, the timing, the entry, the initial stop, the mental equilibrium, the waiting, the stop adjustment, the exit, etc. I tell them that the end result of their trade (the destination) does not matter, as long as the parts (the steps) are right. I tell them to ignore those who win by chance, those who win by playing tips, betting on rumors and gambling overnight on earnings reports. I tell them that if the individual parts of each trade are right, the winning will happen all by itself. This is the subtle but important difference between *being* a winner and just *seeking* a win. And this is the point we all must reach. There is a big gap between where a trade begins and where it ends. Instead of just focusing on where it may end, we need to make sure what happens in the middle is right.

SOUND TECHNIQUES LEAD TO SOUND INSTINCTS

A *New York Times* sports writer recently wrote, "Teaching a baseball player *instincts* is like trying to eat a bowl of soup with a fork. Impossible . . ." The same is true in trading. Instincts, as important as they are, can't be taught or transferred to traders. Instincts have to develop slowly, evolve gradually, through countless situations and over years of experience. What *can* be taught though is proper technique. Once traders have developed a technique, once they have put together an arsenal of profitable trading tools and tactics, instincts will gradually grow through their frequent use. In other words, instincts are the outgrowth of applying sound trading tactics over and over and over again. When we give our advanced 1- and 3-day trading boot camps, this is what we set out to do. We teach numerous *survival* trading techniques and a slew of guerrilla-like trading tactics that are not only designed to produce profits, but are engineered to gradually develop a growing level of professional instincts. Instincts, professional ones, are the hallmark of the true professional. The problem that many traders face is that they are applying the wrong techniques and, therefore, developing the wrong instincts. And I'm sure I don't have to mention that there is nothing more dangerous for a market player than having the wrong instincts. Trading is not an exact science, and because of that it requires an element of art, driven by properly developed instincts. Traders under our daily tutelage often ask us, "How is it that you knew to get out of this trade at that exact moment?" or "get into that trade just before it exploded?" More often than not, our timely actions will be the result of a subtle feel, a silent hint that gently tugs on the brain and the nervous system, producing the right action at precisely the right time. It frustrates us at times because we wish that these processes could be communicated adequately. But we rest in the assurance that our traders will eventually develop these instincts. Why? Because they are practicing the right techniques.

SEED OF WISDOM

Trading tactics and techniques are like the training wheels on a bike. They serve to keep us on balance and directed while we are learning to gain proficiency. Once that proficiency is achieved, we are no longer in need of the training wheels. At that point, we will have gained a trader's gut, or shall we say instincts, which, as we stated, can't be taught. These instincts will help us know when the rules of a certain strategy should be changed, ignored, or even violated. In reality, we will never be able to fit the market into a tight little box. Rules can't be rigidly applied to the market's behavior, and that is what tactics and techniques try to do. But that does not mean they have no value. Trading tactics and techniques, the training wheels, are immensely valuable, because they serve as guides for *our* actions. They systematize our responses and train our minds how to think. But after a prolonged period of use, the trader will begin to develop what we call the sixth sense. This sixth sense will, at times, diverge from the guided path of a rigid technique. It will urge a trader to change or even break the rules precisely when they should be changed or broken. When this sixth sense starts to take form, it is the sign that the trader has moved into a higher realm of mastery, a realm that needs the benefits of rigidity less. Before this realm is reached, it is necessary for the traders to rigidly abide by rules, tactics, and techniques, if only to protect themselves from the darker parts of their emotional and psychological selves. But when instincts, that sixth sense, emerge on the scene, the traders move into an almost techniqueless realm. And that is the realm in which instincts rule.

A LITTLE PARANOIA IS GOOD FOR THE SOUL

It is my belief that a certain amount of paranoia is an essential ingredient of success. I find this to be true in almost any endeavor. In the trader's formative years, I believe it is actually a *prerequisite* of success. Far too many novice traders looking for fast riches and an easy escape from their mundane 9 to 5 prisons fearlessly jump into the market without respecting its power to destroy. Being frightened, in the beginning at least, is a sign of intelligence. Being a wee-bit paranoid is how a trader honors the market's power. History clearly shows us that the bully and the brute, holding no respect for their opponents, eventually meet with annihilation. Underestimating what the market can do to you, especially in the formative years of your development, leads to financial ruin and perhaps destitution. Most former traders can only now fully appreciate that the market is a giant humbling mechanism.

> Fear is born of ignorance, but the beginner who fears not is too ignorant to know he is ignorant.
>
> —Oliver L. Velez

During the trader's developmental stages, it is all too easy to fall victim to the countless traps and snares that await those who lack the knowledge and the proper tools. This is why a certain amount of fear can be beneficial and a little bit of paranoia can save us. But when experience leads to more knowledge, and knowledge leads to more power, fear and paranoia give way to a profound sense of strength. And ever so gradually, quietly even, the market, once an ugly foe, becomes a loyal friend. And then, all is well. If you learn to respect the market, it will eventually respect you back.

SEED OF WISDOM

Fear is a primal instinct that has the ability to serve us very well. There are countless books on the market that are focused on the elimination of fear, which in my view is wrong. Fear is not something that should be annihilated. In its proper place, it is a friend, not an enemy. Like any other tool, it simply must be understood and used properly. When we face danger, fear helps us to run with greater speed or fight more ferociously. When it heightens our awareness and maximizes our capabilities, it is serving its legitimate purpose. Fear becomes particularly valuable to beginning market players trying to find their way. It will help them remain alert, careful, and forever on their toes. When it is time to take flight, it will quicken their speed and increase their awareness of the dangers. In short, it will help keep them out of trouble. But above all, it is fear that will prevent beginning traders from committing one of the gravest errors of all: *disrespecting the market's power to destroy.* If there is anyone who needs to fully recognize this power it is the novice trader. The number of traders who have been taken out of the market forever because they had no respect for this power is incalculable. We would much rather deal with a novice trader who has too much fear than have to deal with one who has no fear at all. The former has a chance for survival. The latter is a statistic waiting to happen.

WE TRADE PEOPLE, NOT STOCKS

The astute trader must never forget that we, as traders, really trade *people*, not stocks. So many novice market players fail to comprehend this critical point. As a result, they stay forever confused as to why stocks often contradict rationality and all sense of reason. Stocks can do nothing in and of themselves. Their prices are determined by the perceptions of people. And as you well know, people's perceptions are entirely controlled by their emotions. It is these emotions, primarily greed and fear, that often cause stocks to extend too far in both up and down directions. When the world seems peachy and very comfortable, greed dominates the landscape and stocks tend to move well *above* reasonable levels. This is when many traditional Wall Street analysts will become confused, frustrated, and sometimes irate. They don't understand why stocks are not behaving according to their neat little mathematical measurements of value. If they fully realized that stocks have no life of their own, they wouldn't be so perplexed. When the dominant attitude or emotion changes from greed to fear, stocks, driven by these same people, tend to drop well *below* reasonable levels. This is when the eternal market optimists become frustrated and confused, as they can't understand why stocks are not turning back up so quickly. This wide but frequent vacillation from overdepressed states to overextended ones has never stopped, and it never will. It is what creates trading opportunities in macro, as well as micro, time frames. It is what keeps the new people coming in, and the old beaten people leaving. *The astute trader, understanding this, builds his or her skill around knowing when one emotional state is about to give way to another.* That's it. *That* is trading in a nutshell. Not knowing when a stock's earnings will be better than expected or trying to guess when a company will announce a new product. It's all about people and their emotions, which is why chart reading is so important to us. Balance sheets and income statements present a picture of the past, a past to which people have already *emotionally* reacted. Charts, on the other hand, serve as a living map, built trade by trade, of the players' current emotional state. It is the ultimate tool for the active trader in our view, and those who play the market short term without them are at a huge disadvantage.

SEED OF WISDOM

It is an inescapable fact that we, as market players, trade people. We don't trade stocks. Of all the realizations we have ever made, this one stands as the most significant in our minds. The traders who see the market as people, as opposed to numbers or binary impulses on a computer screen, have a much better chance of reaching the state of trading mastery. They will better understand the reasons behind sudden price movements, which will put them in more viable positions to take advantage of those price movements. The true masters never forget that each time they place a trade, someone else is on the other side of it betting in the reverse direction. But because these master stock traders are really master people players, those poor souls taking the other side of their trades are usually the patsies. Recognize that you trade people and you have the potential to soar. Fail to recognize this, and you may be the next patsy.

A POSITIVE MENTAL ATTITUDE MAKES A DIFFERENCE

There are three major components to winning in the stock market: mind, method, and money. Dr. Alexander Elder, author of *Trading for a Living,* calls these "the three M's." While mastery of each of them is paramount, mind is, by far, the most important of the three M's. Because without a winning attitude, without the proper mind-set, and without the necessary mental equanimity, even the soundest of all methods will lead to lost money. In fact, *a winner is more defined by mental make-up than by method or money*. This is why the trader with a winning attitude and a faulty approach can still produce positive results, while the trader with a loser's mentality will stumble and fall, despite an excellent approach. Don't think so? What do you actually think causes one trader to play six winners in a row, and another to experience eight consecutive losses? How is it that one trader can use a daily newsletter and win, while another uses it and loses? What do you think differentiates the person who buys XYZ and wins from the person who buys the same XYZ and loses? The difference lies in the mind, plain and simple. One of the most revolutionary axioms I have ever come across is this: "As a man thinks in his heart, so is he," and this universal truth is just as applicable to traders as it is to anyone else. Monitor the attitude of a winner and you will find a level of confidence and certainty that is almost beyond belief. And while most people will make the mistake of assuming that winners are confident and certain *because* they win, the truth is that winners consistently win *because* they are confident and certain. No method, however sound, will work for traders who mentally picture themselves losing before each trade is placed. And no amount of money, however large, will save the individual who secretly harbors the belief that, "Whatever I touch, turns to mush." As choice-making individuals, we must choose a higher set of thoughts when approaching this sacred activity we call trading. You can never fail, or even feel like a failure, if you recognize the simple fact that *you are not your results*. You create them, which means that you possess the power to alter them if you happen not to care for them. There is room at the top for all dedicated traders, but the first step is to actually *believe* that. The second is to start *acting* like it. Think the part, then act the part, and the rest mysteriously takes care of itself. But don't take my word for it. Just try it.

SEED OF WISDOM

Mind or, shall we say, attitude can make all the difference in the world during a trader's developmental years. If you find this difficult to believe, all you need to do is find five losing traders (that should not be too hard) and take note of their attitudes. You may find that each trader loses in his or her own way, but the one thing they will all have in common is a bad attitude toward the market and/or a disturbed mind-set. As a result of bad thinking, their every action will lack power and be devoid of resolve. Their decisions will be weak and the eyes through which they meekly peer will reveal terror. If you were to find five winners, on the other hand, you would immediately sense an entirely different form of thinking at work. These traders would seem to be from another world. The position in their chairs would almost seem regal. Their eyes would be sharp, clear, and fierce as they await the next opportunity. The movements they make would be deliberate, their decisions quick and precise. While they would be all about the business at hand, they would also seem relaxed and comfortable. When they win, they would not have to shout it out to the rest of the world because it would be nothing strange. Many might make the common mistake of assuming that these traders can have mind-sets like that because they win. But that would be far from the truth. A more careful look would reveal they are winners because of their mind-set. The self-made successful trader does not have a positive attitude because he wins. He wins because he dared to have a positive attitude. Remember this.

TRADING WITH ATTITUDE

What is your mental view of the market? Do you see the market as a mass of chaotic hysteria that is rarely understood by market participants? Or, do you see the market as some big bad enemy that you must defeat each time you venture into a trade? In your mind's eye, is the market an enemy or a friend, good or bad, constructive or destructive? These are highly important questions because they help bring to light the attitudes with which we approach the art of trading. Aspiring market mavens spend a great deal of time honing their techniques, perfecting their trading strategies, and developing new tactics. But far too few understand the significance of the proper attitude. View the market as some giant monster who's out to demolish you, and guess what? Your every decision will be timid and lack resolve. Each of your actions will portray weakness and have no lasting effect, and the monster that you've created in your mind will haunt you all the way to the poorhouse. For lack of a better phrase, I prefer to view the market as "the field of all possibilities," my "playing ground," to use two popular phrases. It is the only place where I am truly on my own, and although that pure level of independence can be scary at times, I relish with deep pleasure the fact that my fate lies with me and no one else. If I fail, it is by my own hand. If I triumph, I am no less than a god. The market is no victimizer, my friends. On the contrary, it is a liberator and should be viewed as such. In it lies the potential fulfillment of our every desire, but this potential must be tapped, grabbed, taken, not begged for. So the next time someone asks you, "How's the market treating you?" You respond by saying, "No, you mean: "How am *I* treating the market?" As an astute trader, the market is *your* world. Trade it with *attitude.* That's what we do.

SEED OF WISDOM

The attitude with which we approach the market has a funny way of materializing in our experience. In a sense, it is like a mirror that will reflect both our strengths and our weaknesses and reveal our most hidden desires to the rest of the world. Fear that the market will not treat you like a friend, and you invite upon yourself the wrath of an enemy who won't quit. Look at the market as a place, or a field, from which you can extract obscene sums of money, and you have a better chance of making every one of your material desires become a reality. Each day I wake up, I remind myself that the market has opened up for one reason and one reason only: to allow *me* to make money. In my mind, the purpose of each participating trader is to take the other side of *my* trades, to give up their stock when *I* want it, and to take my stock when I want to rid myself of it. This may sound cocky, but I view the market as *my* world, and the results I often get from it would strongly suggest that it is.

DAILY FOOD FOR THOUGHT

We have provided a few of our thoughts on some commonly used words, actions, and emotions in an attempt to reveal how they may play a role in your daily trading decisions. Every so often, we encourage you to reread these points as they are specifically designed to keep you psychologically in shape and aware of some of the mental pitfalls that plague all active market players.

1. *Thinking.* Too much is not good. This may sound strange to most, but most master traders have moved beyond the need for thought. It is only if you ask them why they did a certain thing that they have to stop and "think." In my experience, the very best traders can't even seem to properly communicate what they do. Perhaps that's because they are "doers" who no longer have to think about "doing."

2. *Imagination.* If you have one, it could be a problem. Imagination is a quality or element that deals in the world of nonfacts. But successful traders stay rooted in what is real, actual, and factual. They are constantly processing what *is*, not

what may be or could be. They don't imagine, guess, or hope. They just process and react to the facts, second by second, minute by minute, with little to no imagination or opinion.

3. *Fear.* Fear is the bane of intelligent action. It not only cripples the mind, which in turn cripples the judgment process, but it erodes the intuitive faculties that become so important to seasoned traders. Fear is a poison, which destroys every virtue required to become great in anything. It is one of, if not the greatest, impediments to achievement.

4. *Greed.* This term is best summed up by the saying, "Bulls and Bears make money, but pigs make none." Home-run hitters should be left to baseball. Going for the big score does not work in trading, and, as surprising as it may seem, the desire to score big is the hallmark of a novice. Successful trading is largely a numbers game. Instead of going for the $10,000 score all at once, the master trader will go for the $1000 score 10 times. The $1000 gain will come more quickly, with less risk, and more certainly than will the larger $10,000 gain.

5. *Information.* The less the better. Too much information helps stimulate the imagination, which as you now know is not good. Opinions start to form and, before you know it, you have taken on the view of the information's distributor. It must never be forgotten that the importance of information does not lie in its message. Rather, its importance lies in how others will react to its message.

6. *Expectations.* Too many expectations or expectations that are too high are sure signs of an unseasoned novice. Reasonable expectations are always OK, but they must be safe ones. Overzealous expectations are always owned by those who don't know what they are doing. They are the hallmark signs of those who have not yet experienced the difficulties and hardships that go hand in hand with obtaining success. Show us traders with overblown expectations and we'll show you novices on their way to being taught how to respect the market, *the hard way.*

7. *Excessive Analysis.* Too much tinkering will prevent action and increase uncertainty. To analyze is to pick apart, to dissect. Consider the fact that a rose, once dissected, is no longer a rose. Every successful trader I know has a few basic, very simple, ways to determine if they should buy, sell, hold, or

ignore. They don't overcomplicate matters. And they are always willing to just "do it" and see what happens.

8. *Hope.* Hope is a dangerous thing, especially for traders. It is the archenemy of those who form the habit of holding losing positions. Hope, in this case, promotes inaction precisely when action is required. It fosters comfort and complacency, when the last thing one should do is sit still. Hope is like a dope that robs one of the very ability to reason intelligently. Those who hope become blind to the facts, and they will always be at the mercy of those who sell hope for a living. If I were presented with a choice, I'd always be a seller of hope, not a buyer of it. When trading, avoid hope like the plague.

3
C H A P T E R

LOSS

The Prerequisite to Trading Power and Success

THE POWER OF ADVERSITY

Thirteen years ago, at the very ripe age of 20, I experienced my very first stock market trade. It was a losing trade, but from that very moment, I knew that I had found my joy, my love, in short, my purpose in life. The excitement, the rush, and, yes, even the pain made me feel as though I'd discovered something that truly fit the description of being "the most fun you could have with your clothes on." Despite being a dismal failure at the game in the beginning, I was not deterred in the least. Why? Because I wouldn't allow myself to be deterred. I was determined to conquer the market, to learn its mysterious ways. But I will be the first to admit that the tuition I had to pay was very high. It took me a full 6 years before I started to see some consistent progress. Was I ever discouraged? Absolutely. Beaten? Heck no. There were points at which I was so close to rock bottom that the only other possible direction was up. Then it happened. At a certain point, I began to gain a rhythmic stride that lead me into a glorious twilight zone that I feel I've been in ever since. Two years later, I found myself consistently pulling big profits out of the market. I became a force to be reckoned with, and was no longer a victim. Today, I am asked almost daily, "To what do you attribute your remarkable market success?" And my answer is always the same. "I am a success today because I was a dismal failure yesterday." In the end, it was my losing trades that prompted me to discover every tactic, every technique, and every winning strategy I use to this very day. In retrospect, I see this very clearly now. My winners sent me to the local bar to brag to my friends, a very *unprofitable* activity, I might add. But it was my losers that sent me back to the drawing board, an exceptionally profitable activity. Now, I've told you all of this as a way to provide you with the most valuable tip I will ever be able to offer you. And it is this: *Adversity—losing—is the greatest gift the market can give you.* Losing is nothing more than an opportunity in disguise. Every mistake, every error, offers the trader an opportunity to kill a fault, to destroy a demon. From this day forward, I encourage you to start a "journal of losers." Write down every losing trade, starting with the symbol, the day, the entry point, the exit point, and the reasons for both. Once you've accumulated five or more losses, revisit them. Study them. Search for the common denominator in them all. Believe me, it will be there. Once you've found it, in no uncertain terms, *kill it!* Do this enough, and your problem will not be the loss of money, but the lack of losers from which to learn more.

SEED OF WISDOM

I have been trading for over 13 years, but it is only recently that I have grown to fully appreciate the enduring period of loss and frustration I had to suffer. At the time, I felt like I was battling for my life. Now I realize this period was helping me to gain my life. My losses kept me up at night, studying, correcting, and revising my thinking and my methods. They motivated me to rid myself of what was not working and accentuate what was. Today, with the benefit of hindsight, I can truly say that those years of frequent loss formed the foundation for the wonderful years of success I have managed to enjoy thus far. If I could have only one wish, I'd wish that every aspiring trader developed the mature understanding that losing is not the enemy. Failing to do something with your losses is the real foe.

MAKE YOUR LOSSES WORK FOR YOU

The path that leads to trading mastery is a journey often fraught with countless perils. The danger, the loss, the trials and tribulations that an aspiring trader must endure are enough to break the backs and crater the souls of most individuals who dare to trek its course. It is a shame that we are so quick to assume that individuals who have perfected their skills and command the markets with incredible dexterity have accidentally stumbled upon their gift by some innate tendency or natural endowment. This is far from true. Pain. Loss. Frustration. Confusion. Uncertainty. Inconsistency. These are the teachers that provide the education necessary to reach the desired heights of greatness. Each trader who enjoys a certain level of success today is guaranteed to have suffered through the pain and agony of being a loser yesterday. We, as human beings, simply do not learn very much from our successes. It is only our failures that seem to light the path and show us the way. We know that fire should not be touched because, at one time in our young lives, we got burned by it. So it is with trading. We learn how to win only after we learn *all* the ways to lose. This was the method used by Thomas Edison when trying to come up with the light bulb. So my question to you is this. What are you doing with your market failures? Are they wasted and for naught? Or are they serving as valuable examples of what not to do? Remember that we leap forward by great distances only after first stepping backward.

SEED OF WISDOM

Understandably, we spend a great deal of energy and effort trying to avoid the loss and the pain that goes with it. But have we ever stopped to contemplate the grand purpose that loss serves? Isn't it only through frequent loss that we can be sure our actions need correcting? In its purest state, the pain of loss serves as a personal messenger of change. Each time we violate a law, it tells us, in no uncertain terms, that our actions warrant dramatic change. This is why we grow through loss and excel by way of pain. The discomfort gets us to act, to get off our backsides and *do something*. Without the agony of defeat and the pain that rises from that, we doubt if our traders would ever grow. Learn to respect loss, because in a weird way, it is precisely what will lead the way to the future you want.

SMALL LOSSES: THE HALLMARK OF A MASTER TRADER

Losing money in the markets is never a pleasant ordeal, but as all intelligent traders know, it is—and always will be—a permanent part of the trading landscape. Far too many starry-eyed novices deplete their energies, not to mention their precious financial resources, searching for that perfect investment approach or trading system that promises to forever eradicate the losing side of the equation. Needless to say, these individuals are only deluding themselves, because the holy grail simply does not exist in the real world. In fact, a large part of traders' success is dependent on how well they manage their losses, not how well they *eliminate* them. What's even more significant is the fact that winners have an uncanny way of taking care of themselves, so astute traders who focus solely on managing their losers will always come out on top. In short, losing is an art, and it must be mastered if we are to ever reach a high level of proficiency. Why? Because our professionalism as traders is measured not by our winners, but by how adept we are at keeping our losses "controllable." Learn how to lose professionally, and the rest of the details seem to fall into place automatically. And what exactly is a professional loss, you ask? A small one, of course. Please keep this concept in mind. The underlying message is far more valuable than most would ever think.

SEED OF WISDOM

It has been said that the difference between a winning trader and a losing one can be measured in eighths and quarters. If this is true, and we believe it to be, the management of one's losses is what makes all the difference in the world between a winner and a loser. Let's face it. It is not uncommon for traders to luck into winning trades. In fact, during a bull market, one can luck into winning trades rather frequently, simply because a rising tide raises *all* boats. This leads us to the inescapable fact that winning trades are not always the truest indication that the trader is a winner. In reality, there is only one hallmark sign of a professional: *small losses.* No matter how lucky novices are, the truth about them can be found out by taking a look at the size of their losses. On the other hand, no matter how off professional traders are at the moment, you can be sure they are the real deal if their losses are consistently minuscule. The point is this. You can fake being a winner for a while, but you can't fake or luck into a record of consistently small losses. That hallmark sign belongs exclusively to the astute, the pro, the winner. Novices can't consistently lose small. It takes too much skill and discipline to pull that off. They may be able to luck into an occasional big win, but their losses will rat them out every time. The hallmark sign of winners is not how they win, but rather how well they lose. If you learn to manage your losses, you won't even have to look for wins. They will find you.

HOW THE MARKET SPEAKS TO US

The market, looked at properly, should be considered a friend, but a friend who is mute and incapable of common speech as we know it. This friend cannot pull up a chair and verbally anoint us with its plans to interrupt its steady course of action. It cannot speak of its intentions to take a wild and unexpected turn to the downside. What it can do is warn us via its actions. As a friend, it speaks to us in the form of *failures*—failing leadership in the mighty five [America Online (AOL), Citigroup, Inc. (C), General Electric (GE), General Motors (GM), and Microsoft (MSFT)], or failed attempts to rally beyond 2 or 3 days. Also, failure to respond to powerful, historical periods of strength, such as the late-year Santa Clause phenomenon, is part of its language. This is how the market communicates with us. This is how it warns us. This is how it speaks to us, through failure. Isn't that interesting? The market uses the language of failure to spread its gospel. And the players attentive and astute enough to receive the message early (easier said than done) will be the survivors, or at least the ones who fare the best. So the next time the market flat out refuses to do what it "should," consider it a friendly message of fatigue, and get the heck out of Dodge!

SEED OF WISDOM

Every master trader has learned how to decipher the market's hidden messages. If you watch them carefully, nothing seems to bypass their keen eyes, and no matter what the market delivers, these masters almost always seem to know how to interpret it. What is their secret? How are they able to do this? Their secret lies in their ability to understand *failure*. If a stock they bought should have acted one way, but suddenly acts another, handing them an unwanted loss in the process, they don't cry. On the contrary, they say "thank you." Why? Because they recognize that it is through failure that the market sends them warnings. If a reliable technical concept suddenly breaks down, they do not start doubting the efficacy of technical analysis. Instead, they see that as a friendly wink from the market, a forewarning of more ugliness to come. And let's say a proven trading strategy suddenly starts to lose its accuracy. Do you think they would scrap it? No. They would see that as the market quietly whispering the words, "Just wanted to let you know, my friend, that I'm changing my character again. Did you get the message?" Every aspiring trader who hopes to reach mastery must learn to do this. They must study and learn to understand the language of failure. It is one of the very few ways the market is able to communicate with us.

HOW TO LOSE YOUR WAY TO SUCCESS

In all my years of trading, one of the most valuable lessons I've learned is that problems can be a wonderful thing if only we allow them to cause a revolution within us—a change. This is because deep within every problem lies the answer we need. Consider the following example. Despite the fact that we are able to report on a daily basis that many of our stock picks have delivered attractive short-term gains, we frequently speak with a number of subscribers who never seem to find themselves in these $2, $3, and $4+ winners. If three out of four of our picks go on to be winners, they will almost invariably own the one loser. While the inability to buy every single one of our stock picks does create the necessity to pick and choose, one cannot ignore the fact that the simple law of mathematical averages still dictates that traders should experience a good share of the winners. So if consistent losses are the norm, a problem for these future market mavens does exist. The encouraging thing is that their problem actually contains their answer. A very close look will reveal that there is some characteristic common to the missed winners that is consciously, or unconsciously, being shunned or feared. For instance, traders may find that they are shying away from stocks over $50 in price. Or that stocks in the Internet sector won't be considered, or those with wide bid/ask spreads will be ignored. Whatever the case, something is preventing the selection of the winners and that something has to be found, because it is the answer. What we all must do is train ourselves to think out of the box, to be almost perverse. If we are shying away from stocks that gap up in the morning, but we're losing, then the answer is obvious. Buy stocks that are gapping up in the morning. If high-priced stocks are consistently where the quality setups are found, and you find that you repeatedly avoid them, then, once again, there is your answer. Buy higher-priced stocks. The winners are there, my friends. If you are not getting your fair share of them, just allow your losses to reveal what needs to be changed. If allowed, your losses will speak volumes, if only you listen.

SEED OF WISDOM

Every loss we experience tells us a little about ourselves. Put enough of these losses together, and they will reveal more about you than your loved ones will care to know. Since traders will never be able to totally eliminate the experience of loss (it is a permanent part of life's experience), they must learn to use it for their benefit by looking for the gem that lies deep within each loss. This gem, or lesson, will contain a valuable message that will reveal precisely what they have to do or change the next time. If you are perplexed, the answer will invariably be found in your losses. Decide today that you will not allow another loss to come into your life without extracting from it the gold it carries within. Make searching for the diamonds in all you losses your "magnificent obsession." Do this and that magnificent obsession will lead you to a magnificent trading career.

STARTING EACH DAY ANEW

Each day, I hear from market players who have been emotionally incapacitated by some recent loss or losses in general. And given the market's tendency to deliver frequent bouts of difficulty, I can only imagine that there are plenty of individuals reading this book today who need a bit of encouragement, in addition to a helping hand, which we're always willing to give. To these special souls I will say this: A trader's life should begin anew each and every day. If that supreme level of success, which is so difficult to obtain, is what you truly desire, you must develop the ability to forget about your past failures or, more precisely, to forget about the disappointment they caused, while retaining the valuable lessons they offer. It should be realized that every mistake you've made is really one less mistake you'll have to undergo in the future, as long as you've learned the lesson it was meant to teach. Taken this way, your losses actually become your power, your mistakes just another aspect of your future success. At times, I am quite surprised at how easily traders give up after a few losing trades. But after a little thought, the level of my surprise diminishes dramatically. Greatness, in any endeavor, lies within one's ability to persevere until all obstacles have been overcome. The "average" individual utterly lacks this determination, which is why superiority and greatness are such rarities. Today we outperform the markets year after year because yesterday we were failures, albeit smart failures who learned from our mistakes. Today we enjoy a level of market accuracy that others in our field can only dream of, because many years ago we realized that there's no shame in making mistakes, as long as you learn from them. In every loss, in every losing trade, lies a gem that needs to be discovered, a precious lesson that brings you one step closer to enrichment. Find them, and you will eventually reap big rewards.

SEED OF WISDOM

There is only a limited number of ways in which a trader can lose. This statement clearly points to the fact that there are only a handful of mistakes possible. The challenge we all face as aspiring traders is not to avoid loss. Rather it is to get on with it so that we can learn from each one. If we can somehow experience every possible way to lose, and completely absorb the lessons contained within them, our wisdom and trading skill would catapult to a level very few ever reach. But it must be remembered that each loss, after a brief examination, must be left on the operating table. It is the lesson that we must take with us. The loss itself, which is only the carcass that contains the lesson, must forever be dropped from our minds. This will ensure that we start each day fresh and new, only we will be more than new. Armed with a new lesson learned and another one of those limited ways to lose defeated, each day will be a step up to higher and higher states of mastery.

LEARN HOW TO ACCEPT WHAT CAN'T BE CHANGED

There is an incredibly powerful message for traders in the serenity prayer that says, "Lord, grant me the strength to change the things I can, the serenity to accept the things I cannot, and the wisdom to know the difference." Superb! Powerful! Deep! It is my firm belief that traders should forever be mindful of this prayer because within it lies an important key to profitable trading and a profitable life. It is fascinating how consistently the precepts that pertain to a successful life are those that also pertain to successful market play. I have the luxury of speaking to, teaching, and advising literally thousands of traders each year, and I have found that far too many of them are spending valuable time and effort trying to change, if not completely eliminate, the one thing that can never be changed: loss. In every business there are things we *must* deal with. And that which we must forever deal with as traders is loss. What exactly *can* we do, you ask? Well, astute traders can manage their losses. They can *curtail* them. *Cut* them short. *Keep* them small, controlled, and in check. But never will they be able to completely eliminate them. And focusing on doing so is futile and a complete waste of effort. Loss, my friends, is here to stay. It is something that we must learn to live with. Something permanent we must learn to manage. And the quicker one gains enough wisdom to realize that, the quicker one can get on with the business of what can be changed. *Wisdom has delivered the truism that a successful life is not so much determined by how much we win, but how well we manage our losses.* So it is with trading. Over the years, I have come to realize that winning, mysteriously, takes care of itself. We as traders will at times even accidentally stumble into winning plays and trades. Winning is not our problem. Losing isn't even our problem. Rather it is the failure to *manage* our losses that undoes us. *That* is what demands our attention. *That* is what we have the power to change. And *that* is what will, ultimately, catapult us into the stratosphere of success.

SEED OF WISDOM

It is ironic that every aspiring market player starts his or her trading career off by trying to do the one thing that can't be done: avoiding loss. We, as traders, will never be able to totally eliminate losing trades. They are with us forever. The only thing within our power is the ability to manage our losses, and if we do that correctly, these losses will lose their ability to hurt us. A careful look will reveal that the most talented traders of all lose, and sometimes quite frequently. Yet they still emerge each week as winners because they have stopped wasting energy on avoiding loss and spend the majority of their time managing it. Each trader we get to fully understand this point soon discovers something miraculous— that while focusing on the proper management of losses, the winning experiences that were once eluding them begin to happen automatically.

LOSING CAN BE WINNING

Winning consistently in the stock market is directly related to how successfully one loses. Did you hear that? Just to make this revolutionary truth stick, I'll say it another way: Knowing how to lose *correctly* is the cornerstone of any successful trading methodology. Finally, for those who only understand truths spoken bluntly, I'll say it like this: **If you do not know *how* to lose, you might as well pack you bags because your days as a stock market participant are numbered.** So enjoy the ride while it lasts. This may sound harsh, but this is reality. To think that you will not lose in this game is deluding yourself. Losing is a very real (and sometimes frequent) part of trading, and knowing how to do it *right* is the key to survival. Anyone can luck into the occasional big winner. The price of a stock goes up, the player makes money, and all is well. That is simple. But what about when a stock goes down? What then? Do you sell, and if so, where? When? How? Only the professional has these questions answered *before* he takes the trade. The novice, like an ostrich, sticks his head in the sand and ignores the downside. Why? Because he has no predefined plan to deal with it. If all traders adhered to our stop loss strategy, they would be forced into handling the downside like a professional. Today, we would never enter into a trade without having a predefined place at which we will cut our losses. Will some stocks rise as soon as our stops are acted on? Yes! At times will we kick ourselves for selling at the stop and not holding on? Absolutely! These distasteful occurrences are a permanent part of the game that we have chosen to play. But rest assured that we will never be down 5, 10, 15, or 20 points in *anything*. Never will we suffer losses of 15, 20, or 40 percent. In fact, as a result of our stop loss strategy, we tend to lose less than 3 percent on each trade. Yes, we may get stopped out frequently when the market gets sloppy, but when the good times start to roll again, we'll be the first on the bandwagon. Why? Simple! We'll have money! Those who don't have, or adhere to, stops won't.

SEED OF WISDOM

Each time a carefully chosen stock gets stopped out, you have not lost, you've won. This is what we teach and often preach over and over to our in-house trading students. We try to get them to change their paradigm, to regard every stop out as a win, not a loss. At first, many have a hard time believing us. They regard that statement as a mental trick that has no basis in reality. But this is not trickery. Being stopped out *does* mean that you've won. What have you won, you ask? First of all, traders who have been stopped out of their trades have won a good part of their money back. There are plenty of past traders who wish they could claim such a thing. Because they had no stops, they are now part of history, a forgotten history. Secondly, traders who have been stopped out have won another chance to get it right. Again, there are countless individuals, no longer with the market, who do not have any more chances. They can only wish they did. Lastly, traders who have been stopped out have won the greatest gift market players can receive: respect, self-respect. Each time traders adhere to their plan, their discipline grows stronger and the power of their resolve increases. When these traders do what they set out to do, their stock may not have risen, but the stock in themselves has. These are gifts that will pay great dividends in the future. Losing because you adhered to a well-placed stop is not losing at all. To our way of thinking, it is winning.

YOU MUST LEARN TO DESPISE BIG LOSSES

Whenever excessive volatility, due to an options expiration period or some other market-impacting event, makes the trading environment difficult, it is inevitable that the trader's number of stop outs will increase. That's the unfortunate part. What *is* fortunate, though, is that these losses will never be severe if one employs relatively tight stop-loss points. We at Pristine hate losses, but if we had to pick one thing that we abhor more than losses, it would be *big* losses. Losing trades are, unfortunately, an inevitable part of this up-and-down game we lovingly refer to as trading, but the market players' longevity is totally dependent on their ability to keep losses small. Let's face it. Anyone can luck into a winning trade. A stock is either going to go up or down, which makes the chances of a win close to a 50/50 chance. But only the professional trader is able to consistently keep the loss side of his P&L to a minimum. Show me the brokerage statement of a pro and I'd be willing to bet that each and every one of his or her losses will be small. On the other hand, show me the statement of a novice and I'll show you a string of losses large enough to fill several New York City potholes. While losing is never pleasant, it is an inevitable part of this game. If we *must* lose at times, why not lose small. Remember. You may not always have a choice, but when you do, you should choose small.

SEED OF WISDOM

Most of the things we seek in life are not small at all. In our most honest moments, many of us would admit to wanting a big bank account, huge profits, a long car, and an oversized house, complete with a massive jacuzzi on an extended deck overlooking a grand view of an endless ocean. But if we ever hope to become successful traders, we are going to have to get used to the notion that some good things do come in small packages. For the trader, there are two things that are best when they are small: losses and mistakes. Small losses are the hallmark of a professional trader. They speak to the trader's seasoning and skill in quickly getting out of harm's way. Small mistakes are even better because they often are the events that lead to small losses. If there were only one piece of advice I could give to aspiring traders, it would be to learn the *art of losing small*. Those who only focus on the *art of winning big* will not know what to do when the inevitable periods of loss make their presence felt and known. Those who have mastered the art of the small loss will ensure themselves plenty of time to get the winning part right. If you learn how to lose right, which is to say, if you learn how to lose *small,* you will last. And just as we've said many times before, you cannot even hope to win at trading unless you have first learned how to last. Losing small will ensure this.

THE TWO LIVES OF A MASTER TRADER

> If only one could have two lives: the first in which to make one's mistakes, which seem as if they have to be made; and the second in which to profit by them.

This wise statement, made by D. H. Lawrence, is surely food for thought, particularly for traders. But Mr. Lawrence seems to question if it is possible to live the two lives of which he speaks. Well, I will go so far as to say if you *don't* live these two lives, you will never be a success in anything, much less trading. You see, the very first phase of a trader's development always involves being a loser. Over the past 13 years, I have met and personally taught hundreds of traders, and I can honestly say, I've yet to meet a successful trader who has not first experienced being a loser. Of course, only those who profit from the first phase of their trading life earn the right to move into the second phase, which is the one that involves winning. No matter how you slice it or dice it, the truth of the matter is that we, as traders, must first learn how to deal with loss, before we can ever hope to be able to deal with success. In fact, success or winning is actually determined by how well we handle our losses. The sad part is that most aspiring traders never even get close to experiencing the joys of the second life of winning, mainly because they are not learning the lessons being offered by their first life of losing. What's even more unfortunate is that most are not even aware of the mistakes they are making *to* learn from them. We at Pristine have dedicated our professional lives to helping traders endure their first life as a trader, which involves walking, stumbling, and sometimes falling. Through dedication, discipline, and diligence, our traders are eventually reborn into their second life. And it is in that life that we will no longer be needed. But as long as we're needed, we'll be right here teaching traders how to survive the perils of the first life. Thanks for allowing us to guide you on your journey.

SEED OF WISDOM

Every individual, in a sense, lives two lives, one as a developing child or adolescent, the other as a developing adult. Every trader has a childhood as well, but very few end up enduring long enough to graduate to adulthood. Adulthood, as a trader, requires that all the lessons of childhood be learned, digested, and properly put into practice. If this maturing process does not occur, the trader stays trapped into the lower depths of childhood, struggling for maturity and seasoning. The very best way to ensure that you are maximizing the learning process during your childhood is to keep a trading journal. Not only should you track and make comments on each play you make, but your thoughts about trading should be written down, ideas should be maintained, and realizations kept. Each lesson learned should be immortalized by giving it a special place in your trading journal. This journal will act as a mirror that reflects who you are, and also serve as road map of where you should be going. By developing the habit of jotting down each experience, each emotion, each thought, you ensure the continual process of growth that will eventually lead to that much desired state of adulthood. It is in that second life of adulthood that all the hard work and struggle endured during the first will manifest itself in your trading experiences each day.

GROWTH IS A FLOWER THAT BLOOMS WITH TIME

I know it may seem strange, maybe even incredible. But it is imperative that developing traders refrain from judging their growth or success by the outcome of individual trades. Yes, the objective of each trade is to make money. And yes, we do call traders successful if they manage to win more often than lose. But winning traders are really the senior versions of traders who have become winners. In other words, traders are not successful because they win. Traders win because they are successful. Winning is the flower that blooms *after* the long, successful journey of growth has been made. Winning rarely, if ever, occurs during this journey, and it certainly cannot occur before the journey. Said another way, traders progressively making each step in their journey of growth are usually still losing. In fact, it is actually the losing that is planting the seeds of that very growth. You see, there is a period during which traders' outer successes, in other words their winning trades, will not reveal themselves, despite the fact that phenomenal growth is taking place underneath. This is because growth initially takes place below the surface. It gradually, almost secretly, builds mass within us, not unlike the conceived, yet unborn, child who develops for 9 months without any outside witnesses. Unfortunately, many traders never realize that growth is actually taking place amid their painful losses. They fail to recognize that each loss is actually propelling them closer to the ultimate goal of success. And it is this short-sightedness that causes many to drop out and quit, right in the middle of their progressive journey. Judging your internal level of growth by your outer wins and losses is a mistake. Judging how frequently you lose the same way is a better way to measure your growth. Let us repeat that. *Judging how frequently you lose the same way is a better way to measure your growth.* Just because your trading ledger is in the red does not mean you are not moving forward. If handled properly, the red will eventually give way to trickles of black, and before you know it, you will start to feel the first glimmerings of mastery. But it must never be forgotten that mastery is born. It is developed. It never comes into existence instantly. It requires an incubation period, during which it gains mass and strength. Those who realize this have much greater odds of lasting. And, once again, we feel compelled to remind you that in order to win, you must last.

SEED OF WISDOM

Whenever gardeners plant the seeds of new flowers, they understand that a portion of a seed's growth must take place underground. Those who walk by the garden looking for the outer signs of that growth too early will surely be disappointed, but not our gardeners. On their faces will be planted permanent smiles, produced by their full understanding of nature. Even though they will not be able to witness this process *without*, they rest securely in the knowledge that the miracle of growth is happening *within*. Soon this hidden growth will make itself known to the outer world. In time, they know it will emerge in the form of a glorious flower, and its splendor will delight all who come to see it.

We are the gardeners of many aspiring traders. The seeds we plant in the minds of our students will always take time to germinate. But once they do, a miraculous process of growth begins. Over the years, we have witnessed this miracle of growth countless times. It is almost always imperceptible to the naked eye, but just because it is not seen in the form of winning trades does not mean it is not taking place. There will be times when you, like many of our students, will get discouraged and lose sight of the fact that wonderful things are happening within. But try not to stay discouraged for long. If you can soothe your nerves, allay your fears, and last long enough for the process to be complete, a glorious trader will emerge, one that will stand as a living testament to the fact that those who last eventually win.

WHEN LOSING BECOMES UNBEARABLE

At one of our most recent trading camps, a student of mine expressed a life-long dream to me in enthusiastic tones and euphoric pitches. Her passionate desire was to become a professional trader, one who derives her entire livelihood from the market. "But," she said, somewhat saddened by a sudden realization that came over her like a dark cloud, "I'm losing, Oliver, and I'm scared," "Why?" I asked. "Because each time I lose," she continued, "it takes me one step further away from realizing my big goal. I have to stop losing, otherwise I will have to give up this grand dream of mine. Help me, Oliver. My boat is sinking and I need help." I sat there, silent for a few minutes, my mind racing, groping, and searching for just the right words to say. How could I tell my friend that what was happening to her was the best thing that she could ever experience? How could I explain, without sounding like some maniac, that in order to be a winner, one must first experience being a talented loser? Winning is always born out of losing. How many times have we all heard of the entrepreneur who struck it big only after failing time and time again? And doesn't the infant learn how to walk by first falling frequently for a time? As perverse and preposterous as it may sound, losing is the trader's ticket to the big time. It is the bridge that eventually gets him to that realm we call trading mastery. What many people fail to understand is that the desired state we call winning, the winner's circle, comes at a cost, a high cost. And truthfully, when it boils down to it, most are not willing to pay the price. Trading is not a game meant for everyone. That is why most have failed, and will always fail. It's only the ones who persevere, who last beyond the chronic period of losing, that have good odds of making it. Have you ever wondered why most of the best traders in the world were failures or messups in other parts of their lives? They are good at trading because they have learned to deal with failing. They have learned to cope with it, use it. I did not manage to come back with some profound thought for my friend, but what I should have said was "good!"

SEED OF WISDOM

George Bernard Shaw could not have been more right when he said, "You don't learn to hold your own in the world by standing on guard, but by being attacked and getting well hammered yourself." Life for the beginning trader is the continual story of getting well hammered. But like the mighty trees in the forest that grow strong by resisting the wind, the traders who manage to rise each time they fall will experience a day when they stand tall and command the awe and respect of those who appreciate the magnificence of a winner. We want you to know that each loss you endure only strengthens you for the next. Every time you rise, we want you to know that you do so as a more enlightened soul. We have over 20 years of trading experience between us, and all those years has led us to the same truth that Seneca the Younger discovered many centuries ago. "We become wiser by adversity; prosperity experienced too soon destroys our appreciation of what is right."

GET THE MOST FROM YOUR TUITION

George Bernard Shaw once said, "You don't hold your own in the world by standing on guard, but by attacking and getting well hammered yourself." I'm not certain if Mr. Shaw ever dabbled in the financial markets, but his insightful statement contains wisdom from which all traders can surely benefit. The market requires all traders who wish to learn its ways to pay a certain amount of tuition. And we, as traders, unfortunately pay that tuition in the form of lost money. But along with that lost money comes a rich education that will eventually lead to fewer losses and greater riches, if one uses them wisely. So, my question to you is, "What are you doing with your market experiences, particularly your losing experiences?" "Are they for naught, or are they used in such a way that they become welcome stepping stones to higher heights of market mastery? "Are you learning from your errors?" "Are you analyzing each and every one of your mistakes?" Are you finding the gem, the jewel that each trading error contains? I truly hope so, my friends. Because that is what it takes to gain market mastery, an enriching education gained through our losses.

SEED OF WISDOM

Our winners, although enjoyable, teach us nothing. It is our losses that lead the way to trading mastery.

4

EDUCATION OF THE MASTER TRADER

How to Save Yourself from Years of Lost Time and Money

FIND A WINNER TO FIRST EMULATE—THEN SURPASS THE WINNER

If you are truly serious about trading stocks for a living, one of the first things you should set out to do is find a winner to emulate. And when we say "winner," we mean a *real* winner, someone who trades daily or close to daily and makes money in the markets consistently. We are sure we don't have to alert you to the fact that there are countless winners in word, but very few in deed. Those who *talk* a winning game will always outnumber those who really *play* a winning game. So finding a winner will not be easy, much less one willing to take on the responsibilities of mentorship. However, despite how challenging this search may be, conduct it until you find one, and try not to give up. Why are we so bent on you doing this? Because there is simply no faster way to learning the ins and outs of this demanding endeavor we call *day trading*. And there is no substitute for the saved time and money a personal winning mentor can provide. We believe so much in the mentor approach to day trading success that we make sure each new Pristine in-house trader we take on is paired with a senior trader who is already making money. By paring up new traders with a winner who has already traveled the rocky roads that are still foreign to the novice, we are dramatically curtailing the money-losing period of trial and error that so many mentorless traders must suffer through. And the sad fact is that those without mentors rarely make it through that trial-and-error period alive. By having our new traders combine forces with an established trader who has already conquered demons not yet faced by the novice, we are speeding up that day when our younger trader can truly stand alone as an independent soul, free of worry and devoid of fear. Speeding up the educational process in this way helps to increase the odds of survival. It paves a much smoother path to that state we call trading mastery. But as we just mentioned, finding a winner on your own will be tough. Finding a winner willing to take you under his or her wing will be even tougher. But if you manage to find one, grip really tight and hold on for dear life. Whatever you have to do within reason to get him or her to guide you, do it. In other words, your goal is to become a leech so that you can drain the winner's brain. But you must make sure you become the most helpful leech on the planet. Bring lunch. Send gifts to his or her kids. Give up part of your trading profits if that works. Consider indentured servitude for 3 to 6 months if you must. There is no cost too great if the mentor you select is a *true* winner.

Once this winner has agreed to guide you through the first booby-trap–filled phase of your development, your mission will be to first emulate the winner, then surpass him or her. As a student of anything, you should never attempt to just match your teacher. This would make you nothing more than a mere follower. The goal is to *surpass* your teacher. And allow us to further develop this critical point by saying this. Every *true* teacher will impart his or her knowledge with the sole objective of raising a pupil above him or herself. This quality is rare, but we believe it is out there. It is too hard for us to believe that we are one of a kind in this regard. So search as hard as you can. There is no guarantee that you will find a true winner, but if you do, consider that day the beginning of a new life. Your new life as a Master Trader.

THE CHARACTER OF YOUR TEACHER MATTERS

An idea shared by many westerners is that the character of the teacher does not matter, as long as the teacher has the information. This is all wrong. It is actually the character and persona of the teacher that gives the information imparted vivid life. It brings the knowledge into true being. It is the teacher and his or her qualities that evoke true learning and that deep-seated passion and experience. As a person who trains and teaches traders all over the world, I have come to realize that teaching requires more than just spitting out knowledge. Facts, by themselves, don't give wings to the mind or lift the soul in any way. It requires special gifts to impart wisdom. It requires unique tools to raise the level of another's consciousness. These tools that make a teacher a great instructor can't be taught. Things like passion, enthusiasm, integrity, energy, conscientiousness, care, concern, and sensitivity are not items that can be purchased or picked up in some second-rate public-speaking class. They are priceless qualities that must evolve over many years. When they are present in a teacher, they stand as a dynamic testament that you have found a soul worthy of your time and attention. Those who seek out teachers who specialize in the art of trading should scout for those who possess the right information as well the right character traits. Easterners recognize, more so than westerners, how sacred the teacher/student relationship is. They have realized that the union between the two must be handled with extreme care. We suggest you handle your future in trading the same way. One can do this by making sure they speak with numerous people who have had learning experiences with the instructor they seek. This may seem like an insignificant point to some, but keep in mind that the teacher you choose will be the filter through which the knowledge you seek will flow. In many respects, you will be placing your future path and direction in the hands of this one individual, and it should not be taken lightly. Trust the wrong teacher, and you may be directed down a bumpy path that has no return. The quality of your teacher will determine the quality of the teacher's education. This must be remembered.

DON'T BE CHEAP WITH YOUR FUTURE

When it comes to your education as a trader, the very last thing you want to do is be cheap. It should never be forgotten that you get what you pay for, and nowhere does this ring home as soundly as it does in the trading field. Today, everyone and their grandparents are claiming to be masters of education in the trading field. But we are sure you realize that everyone and their grandparents are not real traders or real educators. One of the more blatant signs that you have stumbled onto a trading fake and/or an educational fraud is a cheap price. If you are being offered a supposedly first-rate trading education for a ridiculously low price, chances are there is no real education to be had. The business rule of thumb for many of the prevalent fly-by-night trading schools seems to be "whenever there is no value, compete strictly on price." We have found that when a real trading firm offers something of significant value, it will usually allow the merits of that value to stand on its own. It does not need the cheap antics of a used car salesperson to lure in takers. Think about it. Is a Ferrari ever offered for the lower price of a Ford? Of course it is not. And if it is, watch out. The same holds true for trading education. Now, we certainly don't mean to suggest that price is the only measurement of value. It is merely one of them, but one that far too few apply. The very best educators will not come cheap. You can bet big on that. The most talented teachers know their value and will not succumb to desecrating that value with an inexpensive price. If they have truly paid the price for their success, there is little to no chance that they will cheapen their achievement with a bargain basement offer. Why should a successful trader share the fruits of his hard labor for cheap? Why should the years he or she has invested in reaching adulthood as a professional market player be handed over for a few coins? If that is the case, perhaps there is no real fruit to share. Those who have much to offer know how valuable the knowledge they impart is. They know that what they have can positively alter the lives of practitioners forever. Because they are successful, they do not need to teach and would rather have no student than one who does not honor or respect the hardships overcome and the battles won. So when seeking out a teacher, make sure you have firm answers to the following questions:

1. *Does the instructor trade every day?* If the answer to this question is "no," walk out of the door or hang up the phone. There is no acceptable excuse for this. No "ifs, ands, or buts" will do. Would you pay for flying lessons from a flight instructor who does not fly? If a day trading firm can't provide you with a real instructor who trades and trades well, perhaps they don't have any. If the answer is "Yes," find out if the instructor is a *profitable* trader. You would be surprised how often you will run into firms selling classes being taught by tired, burnt-out traders who blew up their own accounts, and now want to show you how to do the same. Here is another question for you. Would you take flying lessons from a flight instructor who crashed on each attempt to fly? Need we say more?

2. *Is the price for the firm's education unusually cheap?* If the price for so-called one-of-a-kind day trading education is too good to be true, it probably is. Find out why they are offering

"priceless" knowledge on the cheap. If you get responses like, "We don't want to gouge the public" or "We are cheap because we make all our money trading," run away as fast as you can. Note that we did not say *walk* away. We want you to *run* away. For these are the lame disguises and excuses of charlatans. The fact of the matter is if you want a Harvard education, you're going to have to pay Harvard prices. Remember, a Ferrari won't ever sell for the price of a Ford, no matter how rich the car dealer is or how humane he or she claims to be. Philanthropic car dealers will give to the United Way or some other such charity, but don't ever expect them to offer you a Ferrari for the price of a Ford. If they do, watch out. For the Ferrari offered at a Ford price is sure not work.

3. *After the seminar or trading lessons, can you stick around for a day or two to watch the instructor(s) trade?* We feel if the instructor won't let you see him or her in action, perhaps the trading action and lessons are not worth seeing. Those who can, do. Those who can't may teach. But those who can do *and* teach should not mind you watching them in action. If they do mind or come back with a barrage of excuses, write them off.

4. *Does the class teach true trading techniques or is its purpose to teach you how to use a specific piece of trading software?* While learning to use trading software is important, it is our belief that trading firms should not be disguising this form of training with the form of education that delivers universal trading techniques and tactics. The truest form of trading education will be applicable no matter what trading system you use. This is the education that holds the greatest value. The type of instruction that is specific to a particular trading system, while useful if you plan to use that system, holds the smallest degree of value. What if you decide to use a different trading software system in the future? Will the education you paid for be obsolete? When we speak of trading education, we are not speaking of software training. This is something that we, as a trading firm, offer our clients free. When we speak of education, we speak of those timeless pieces of knowledge that can be used and profited from whether the trader uses a phone to place trades or the fastest NASDAQ level II trading system in existence. The vehicle from which you trade, while important, is not the real issue. A super fast trading system

put in the hands of uneducated traders will only provide a quicker route to their demise. Quick executions are only a plus if you know what you are doing. Otherwise they spell a painful, although quick death.

5. *Can you stay in touch with the instructor to make sure the fire of knowledge does not die?* This is very important. Why? Because the ever-widening gap between the current moment and the training course you've taken will often be accompanied by fading confidence in the beginning phases. A firm that offers follow-up courses for free or a nominal charge (remember, you already paid) is being responsible and has their students' progress genuinely at heart.

These are but a few questions that you should get answers to before you cough up your hard-earned funds. They are not exhaustive by any means but should help you start your process of inquiry on the right foot.

TODAY, THOSE WHO CAN DO *AND* TEACH

No longer is the saying true that those who can do, while those who can't teach. There was a time perhaps in the trading industry when it could be argued that this contained some truth. And perhaps, in a few cases, it still possesses some measure of reliability. But more than ever before, there are some talented traders in this industry who also happen to be taking up the grueling, yet rewarding, responsibilities of teaching. I am proud to say that many of the better instructors throughout the country are seasoned Pristine alumni. I have been teaching traders the art of making a living in the markets for nearly half a decade. One of the most frequently asked questions at our 1- and 3-day training camps is, "Why *do* you teach?" "If you guys are so good, why are you wasting your time with us," is another question often asked. Both are excellent queries that are difficult to answer without getting into some of my personal and philosophical beliefs. Over the past 5 years, I have discovered that the gentle coercion of seminar preparation has made the trading tactics and techniques I teach more mine. And whenever I've taken long sabbaticals without teaching, I've felt some of their intricate details leak from my bones. I can honestly say that I have never given a seminar without being changed in some way by it, for the better. Whenever I teach, I somehow leave the experience a grander, more elegant soul. Each experience leaves me more enriched, more knowledgeable, more powerful, and more astute. These realizations have led me to believe that somehow the sharing of your knowledge makes it more your own. In some mysterious way, I have discovered that whenever you offer your wisdom to another, you make room on your own plate for much more. Now that I look back on the past few years, I am extremely glad my passion for trading has turned into compassion for traders. As a result of 5 years of constant teaching, my growth as a trader has leapt forward at a rate that I could only have dreamed of matching without the aid of instructing. Today, teaching is what makes me complete. While I continue to grow as a trader, anyone who has taken my instruction can tell you that it is the teaching of it that really gets my juices running, my adrenaline flowing, and my body pumped. I don't know why this is, but it just is. So what is my point, you ask? What is the message I am trying to deliver to you? The message is simply to try it. Try helping another become a more intelligent trader. Try lifting someone to your level or even higher, and watch your progress as a trader soar. You will quickly come to realize that it is impossible to help a fellow trader without in some way helping yourself.

A very wise man once told me if I ever wanted something really bad, all I had to do was give away whatever it was I wanted. If I wanted love, I was to give away more love. If I wanted knowledge, I was to give knowledge away. Money, give that. He informed me that I may not have whatever it was I wanted in great supply, but if I gave what little I did have, my problem would not be the lack of it, but finding the accommodations for more of it. As a person who has dedicated his entire professional existence to teaching traders how to become Master Traders, I can attest that my friend was right. Whatever level of knowledge you have, teach it. Give it away. Shout it from the highest rooftop in your neighborhood. Then, watch what happens. I have only one question for you should you decide to take me up on this: "Are you ready to fly?"

5
CHAPTER

THE SEVEN DEADLY SINS OF TRADING

How to Combat Them and Defeat Them

DEADLY SIN #1: FAILING TO CUT LOSSES SHORT

As self-made professional traders who have taught hundreds of market players the art of earning a living from the markets, we are frequently asked the following question by our students: "What is the most frequently committed error by aspiring traders?" Our answer: *Failure to accept and take losses quickly*. We are of the school of thought that believes that traders' most precious commodity is their original capital, and that they are doomed to utter failure if they do not do everything in their power to prevent its erosion. Taking fast, but small, losses is the only approach, the only tool, if you will, that traders have to help ensure this. But not only must traders be willing to take quick but controllable losses, they must *accept* the fact that losses are, and will always be, a permanent part of their trading existence. This is perhaps the most singularly difficult fact to grasp. Most struggling traders spend their entire trading lives attempting to run away from losses. They perpetually move from broker to broker, service to service, newsletter to newsletter, trading system to trading system, hoping, praying, dying to find the "holy grail," that perfect pie-in-the-sky approach that will deliver juicy, unbelievable, mouth-watering profits without even a trace of a loss. In a word, that's *impossi-*

ble. Why? Because successful trading, like successful living, is determined by how well we *manage* our losses, not by how well we *avoid* them. If you truly desire to become an astute trader, learning how to lose professionally, by keeping losses small, is the master key. *That* is the skill we need, *that* is the way to big bucks, and *that* is what will deliver longevity in the trading business. Take care of your losses by keeping them small, and we assure you that the winners will take care of themselves.

SEED OF WISDOM

Every loss is like a cancer that has the potential to spread all over your account and destroy your entire financial life. Therefore, in order to ensure longevity in the trading business, traders must quickly rid themselves of this cancer whenever it rears its ugly head. Each loss usually starts off small. That's when controlling it, or completely cutting it out, causes little or no pain. The major problem for traders arises when they allow the loss or cancer to spread. Each time a stock is allowed to make deeper inroads into negative territory, the traders and their ability to act become weaker. Just like a cancer, the growing loss robs the traders of their intellect and eats away at their mental and physical abilities, until they are completely consumed and relegated to being a slave. If you want to become successful, any disease that has the potential to rob you of your future must be kept in check.

How to Eliminate the Sin of Failing to Cut Losses Short

The following action steps will help prevent you from falling prey to the deadliest enemy of all—failure to cut losses:

1. *Never place a trade without first determining where you will bail ship if things go wrong.* This is the same as saying, "never place a trade without a predefined stop loss." Taking a trade without determining the price at which you will run for cover is like racing down a steep hill at top speed without any brakes. You may wind up living, but only those who like to flirt with death would ever try such a thing.

2. *Always adhere to your predetermined stop loss.* This should go without being said, but so few aspiring traders are able to muster up enough discipline to do this that we feel compelled to mention it. Why is this so hard to do? Because selling your stock at the stop is clearly admitting that you are wrong. The

action does not bring about warm feelings of pride, nor does it boost one's confidence. But the true master traders have learned to overcome these difficulties. They have become experts at taking their stops with blinding speed. They have done this because they've developed an intolerance for stocks that are not working for them, and kill them at the first sign of trouble. We teach our traders to view each stock they buy as an employee who has been hired to perform only one job: to rise. If the stock even hints at failing to perform the task for which it was hired, we tell them to instantly fire it, just as they would fire an employee who utterly refused to do his or her tasks. We train our traders to be so intolerant of stocks that fail to live up to their expectations that, at times, they fire them *before* they hit their stops.

3. *If you are having a tough time adhering to your stops, start off by getting into the habit of selling half of your position.* Becoming disciplined enough to religiously cut losses takes time. Placing and adhering to stops deal with the art of taking a loss, which is why they are so often approached with reluctance and dealt with from a basis of pain. For those students of ours who can't seem to bring themselves to the point of taking their stops without a second thought, we encourage them to practice selling half their position. This alternative action is much easier to do, as it tends to please both dueling impulses: (a) the impulse to get rid of the failing stock and (b) the impulse to give it a chance to come back. By cutting the problem in half, the traders often gain a greater clarity and mental focus. Psychologically, traders find their plight to be less burdensome and therefore feel better about themselves. The problem of what to do with the second half still remains, but with half the problem gone, coming up with an alternative plan becomes much easier. *Note:* We deal with the art of placing stop losses in detail in Chapter 15.

DEADLY SIN #2: DOLLAR COUNTING

Oscar Wilde once said, "When I was young, I used to think that money was the most important thing. Now that I'm older, I know that it is." The goal and focus of every short-term trader is profits. Entertainment, action, the thrill of victory, even the agony of defeat can be attractive and very enticing lures. But it is the potential to dramatically increase one's wealth that wets the palate and lights the fire of most market players. In short, it is making money that is the driving force behind the desire to trade and invest. But while profitability is, and certainly should be, the primary objective, once a trade is taken, traders must work to forget their profits. Sound confusing? Let us explain. Constantly monitoring how much a trade is up or down is a destructive activity that has been robbing traders of big profits for years. This process, commonly referred to as *dollar counting,* not only increases fear, it promotes moment-to-moment uncertainty and prevents one from focusing on proper technique. And it is proper technique that ultimately determines how profitable we become. How many times has the fear of giving back a tiny profit knocked you out of a stock just before it went on to score big price gains? How many times has the paralyzing effect of a loss prevented you from cutting a stock loose precisely when you should have? The fact is, focusing too much on where you are, at the expense of what you're supposed to be doing, leads to knee-jerk reactions and quick responses that lack intelligence and reason. Instead, traders must make sure that their techniques are sound at every step; and if that is done properly, the profits will take care of themselves. "Am I entering the trade at the right place?" "Is my stop loss—mental or otherwise—properly set?" "What is my price objective and what course of action will I take once it's met?" These are just a few of the questions that traders should perpetually ask themselves. Your actions should be dictated by a well-thought out trading plan, which we will provide for you in this book, not by the minute-to-minute changes in your account. Good technique automatically leads to good profits.

SEED OF WISDOM

Dollar counting is a sin usually committed by traders who are not used to winning very often. As soon as these traders luck into a small gain, the fear of losing it causes their eyes to bulge, their hands to twitch, and their breath to quicken. In some cases, the money, not yet rightfully theirs, starts to burn a hole in their pockets, until the urge to cut the trade short completely consumes them. This dreadful habit of counting one's pennies in midstream like a Scrooge not only robs the trader of sizable gains, it fosters chronic uncertainty, fear of loss, and an emotional imbalance that can lead to destructive actions. Soldiers (traders) who start tallying the spoils (profits) of war before the battle (trade) is won are majoring in the most minor thing at hand. They fail or refuse to recognize that the spoils automatically come with a battle well fought and won. To focus too heavily on the spoils is to take one's attention away from the battle. And warriors, who take their attention off the battle, will often lose the spoils and their heads.

How to Eliminate the Sin of Dollar Counting

We teach our in-house traders to focus on their technique, not their profits or losses. We train them to let their well-executed strategies take them out of their trades. If you find yourself being robbed of bigger gains because of the deadly sin of dollar counting, consider the following steps:

1. *For each trade, establish two potential exit prices, at which you will sell your entire position.* The first of these sell points should be placed below the current price. This is what is called a *stop loss.* The second should be placed above the current price. This is where you expect the stock to go and serves as your price objective. Example: You buy XYZ at a price of $20. You immediately establish a stop loss at $19. This can be what is called a mental stop or an actual one. You also establish, in this case mentally, a price objective of $22. *Tip:* Each trade you take should always have one entry point and two exit points, namely, the stop loss and the objective. The stop loss is used for protection. The objective is used for profit taking. There will be more on this subject in a later chapter.

2. *Sell only if the stock you are in violates the stop loss point or hits your objective, whichever event occurs first.* By adhering to this rule, traders place the fate of each trade in the hands of their trading strategy, not in the hands of their greed or fear. To continue with the previous example, you would sell if XYZ declined to $19, resulting in a $400 loss. You would also sell if XYZ rose to $22, resulting in an $800 gain.

3. *If the urge to exit before either sell point is met becomes overbearing, satisfy the urge by selling only half and letting the remaining half sit until the strategy says exit.* For instance, let's say XYZ rises to $21, shortly after you buy it. You now have a paper profit of $400, but your strategy has not called for any action yet. However, the $400 gain you can lock in now is starting to look too delicious to ignore. While you recognize that $800 would be better, your dollar counting is preventing you from

thinking straight and the fear that the $400 gain may evaporate is creating a powerful urge to take the money and run. You can sell 200 shares at $21, locking in a gain of $200, while giving the remaining 200 shares a chance to go the entire distance. By doing this, you satisfy the urge to sell, while retaining the integrity of your trading strategy. These three steps will help you weaken, if not completely eliminate, the deadly sin called dollar counting.

DEADLY SIN #3: SWITCHING TIME FRAMES

There are four dominant time frames in which a market player can act: microterm, short term, intermediate term, and long term. In our world, the microterm engulfs minutes (sometimes seconds) to hours. The short term encompasses days to weeks. The intermediate term covers weeks to months, and the long term involves months to years. As the last three definitions clearly indicate, there is no precise point at which one time frame ends and another begins. Rather, they overlap at their meeting points. I am clarifying this to point out a very common trading error committed by scores of market players: *the error of buying in one time frame and selling in another.* It works like this. A trader buys a stock with the idea of capturing a nice short-term gain. But in this case the trade does not work out as planned, so instead of selling (within the confines of the short-term time frame), the trader decides that the stock will now be held as an intermediate or even long-term play. Sound familiar? Professional traders on all levels occasionally succumb to this deadly sin. The problem with this "switch" in time frames is that it is nothing more than a rationalization to ignore stops, which as you know is the only protection we have against disaster. *Switching* also protects the traders' egos by preventing them from admitting that they're wrong. As long as the trade is not sold, the loss doesn't seem real to the traders who indulge in this sin. This ostrichlike approach can actually work with the help of a very strong bull market. In fact, I have actually witnessed some traders get away with this sinful act for months, but far more often, it results in the trader getting wiped out. Sadly, this deadly sin has relegated countless traders throughout history to that dark, cold, musty dungeon that is so feared by those struggling for market survival today. In this purgatory I speak of, each zombielike prisoner bears a sign, which reads, "Beware of the switch. I was *once* a trader." Believe me. You don't want to go there. Avoid this sin.

SEED OF WISDOM

Switching time frames is really the act of a coward in disguise. It helps cowards temporarily escape their sad condition. By switching from one time frame to another, the traders postpone the ultimate feeling of being losers, camouflage their losses with a weak plan, and lull themselves into a deadly state of denial by fostering a false sense of hope. The traders guilty of this sin are really not fit for trading, and the market won't tolerate their presence very long. Eventually, the sin of switching time frames will eat away at the traders' resolve, rob them of their ability to think and act freely, and relegate them to the permanent position of pathetic victims.

How to Eliminate the Sin of Switching Time Frames

This deadly sin of switching time frames is not something that can be allowed to exist. It must be completely eliminated because it diminishes the trader each time it is committed. Once the habit is formed, it is very difficult to break, but we have outlined a few helpful guidelines designed to combat this sin:

1. *If you enter a trade in one time frame, make sure to construct your exit point(s) in the same time frame.* For instance, if you bought XYZ based on a daily price chart, make sure you use the daily price chart to construct your exit strategies. Remember that each trade should have one entry point and two exit points. Those who day trade using intraday charts particularly need to closely watch this error. Entering a stock based on a 5- or 15-minute chart must warrant an exit strategy based on the 5- or 15-minute chart. Switching in midstream to the hourly or daily chart would be an act of denial.

2. *Do not adjust your stop loss (exit point one) downward when long (upward when short).* This is the chief sign that you are committing the sin of switching time frames. Let's say you bought XYZ at $20, based on the daily chart (we will cover more about charts in Chapter 11). You also establish your stop loss and profit taking points based on the same daily chart. If XYZ declines and is close to stopping you out of the trade at $19, don't succumb to the urge to adjust your $19 stop to $18 or any lower price. Adjusting upward to protect profits is fine, when done correctly. But adjusting your stop loss downward

eliminates the benefit of a stop, and promotes cowardly
reluctance to do what you set out to do. Once you commit this
act, you will commit it again, and again, and again until stops
will have lost their power to save you from disaster. This pair
of guidelines will single handedly prevent you from
succumbing to the deadly sin of switching time frames.

DEADLY SIN #4: NEEDING TO KNOW MORE

In this exciting game we call *trading*, we, as active market participants,
are forced to deal with just about every conceivable deterrent to our success in existence. Each day, we must overcome the mass confusion created by the opposing views of myriad so-called experts. We must sort
through the endless stream of company reports and ceaseless news items
in an attempt to determine what has value and what is totally insignificant banter. And as if that were not enough, we are forced to forever be
the masters of ourselves because the psychological demons that plague
traders are far more dangerous than those we can see, feel, and touch.
One of the biggest of these psychological maladies is the fear of pulling
the trigger. How many times have you wanted to play a stock, but decided not to act until it rose an extra ⅛ of a point? How many times have
you missed a big winner because back-to-back losses made you hesitate,
second-guess, and/or pause, out of sheer fear of losing again? The main
culprit in these scenarios is the desire for certainty or the *need to know
more*. It is natural for us to want to be certain before we act, to be extra
sure. But the fact of the matter is that *the brass ring goes to those who can act
intelligently without the need to know more*. The market is anticipatory, and
big gains tend to occur ahead of the facts. He who needs to *know more* before the bet is placed will always be late and on the wrong side of the
curve. Traders who are not imprisoned by the need for more info are free
to act. When they truly understand the wisdom of uncertainty, they become chart makers, not just chart readers. So the point is this. You, as
traders, can't afford the comfort of certainty or the need to know more,
because by the time little old you knows all the facts, the opportunity is
already gone.

SEED OF WISDOM

"Buy on the rumor! Sell on the news" has been a well-recited Wall Street
axiom for decades. Yet, the need to know all the facts of a trade first has

forever compelled traders to do the exact opposite: buy on the news. During the rumor stage, or what technicians call the analytical stage, all the facts cannot be known. Yet, oddly enough, this is the stage where opportunity lies. If playing the market were as easy as collecting the facts and acting on them, or waiting for all the facts to be known, everyone would be a god on Wall Street. The needing to know more is a deadly sin, one that promotes inaction when action should be taken, and encourages action precisely when inaction is the better choice. This sin is like a thief that is out to rob traders of their opportunity. It also serves to perpetually keep traders on the wrong side of the game, giving up their merchandise (stock) when they should be holding on to it, and taking the merchandise of others when they should be steering clear of it. I wonder if Microsoft Inc. stock will report good earnings 2 weeks from now? Wait for the answer, and you will surely be acting late. Will that FDA approve the new drug? We can't know until it's too late to intelligently trade it. Will price support hold the third time? Who knows? All we can do is play, trusting our well-planned trading strategy to guide our steps. Can the 200-day moving average stop the stock from rising? Maybe. Maybe not. We are odds players, not fortune-tellers, and traders who can't act until all the facts are known will never be successful.

How to Eliminate the Need to Know More

If your need to know more is getting you into trades late and/or causing you to miss good trading opportunities all together, then you must take the following steps to rid yourself of this disease:

1. *Be very reluctant to buy immediately on the heels of good news.* This goes for the reverse when thinking about shorting bad news. Since professionals are in the habit of buying on the rumor and selling on the news, stocks reporting good news will tend to gap up, dangle for a period, and move back to the downside, sometimes sharply. This occurrence is commonly referred to as a *news reversal*, and it is one of the most prevalent traps for novice market players. It is very difficult for a company to release good news without the smart money having a good idea of what the news will be or entail. This is why the smart money is usually in the stock before significant news hits. The good news causes what we call the *wow effect* among the novice crowd. "Wow, XYZ just announced positive news. I think I'll buy some." The professional, already in with big size, uses the novice-driven rush to unload all or part of

the hefty load. *Tip:* Institutions need a large number of buyers in order to get out of a large number of shares. Anything that promotes a novice-driven run on the stock will be warmly welcomed by those who have big size to sell. "Come on in guys. The water is fine!" Yeah right.

2. *Use charts to form your buy decisions and sell decisions.* As you've already learned, charts don't lie. News can be, and often is, deceiving. Stocks can fall on good news (usually when the news is expected), and they can rise on bad news (usually when they have already moved down sharply in advance of the news). But either way, properly interpreted price charts will reveal what the big boys are doing and saying. We will go into some detailed charting techniques in a later chapter.

3. *If you find yourself hesitating because you'd like to know more, stop and ask yourself, "Is what I'm looking for necessary for the trade, or am I just looking for more comfort?"* This question will cut right to the chase. If you have a properly selected stop loss point for the stock you've bought, and find that you are looking for a reason why your stock has declined to the exit, you are most likely trying to feel more comfortable. There is no need to know more, or even why. The stock has dropped to your predetermined sell point. All that is necessary for the trade is known.

DEADLY SIN #5: BECOMING TOO COMPLACENT

When the market is being very kind to you, and all seems right with your trading, you cannot afford to fall into the destructive hands of carelessness. When a winning streak has fattened your purse, you must do everything in your power to keep your hard-earned gains and maintain the same intelligent mind-set that helped to produce those gains. It is unfortunate, but every trader eventually realizes that consistent winning often causes the lowering of one's guard, as the comatose state of complacency creeps in. But if you hope to remain a Pristine trader, you must not succumb to this all too common inclination. It is precisely when everything is right that you must increase the level of your caution. Why? Because you will learn that your greatest failures will come on the heels of your greatest successes. A lengthy and profitable run is a reason to step back and smell the sweet aroma of your wins. Even a professional poker player breaks from the table to count his chips from time to time. So too must the winning trader.

SEED OF WISDOM

In the same way that batting slumps follow hitting streaks in baseball, big losses often follow winning streaks in trading. It's almost as if the market saves up all the losses you were not suffering during your streak, in order to give them to you all in one or two trades. We teach our traders not to fight this mathematical tendency. After a few of our in-house traders have experienced an enduring profitable run, we encourage them to take a few cautionary steps, which are detailed here. We do this so that they don't fall victim to the sin of *becoming complacent.* Many novice traders won't understand this because they fail to realize that by the time they've won for a lengthy period of the time, the favorable market environment that they were so adeptly playing is close to taking on a different character. In fact, in many cases, it and the odds it is delivering have already changed. Think about this. A trader experiences 5 winning days in a row. During this time, the market has also strongly risen 5 days in a row. At this point, the market is clearly extended short term, and due for a 2- or 3-day breather. It is not the same market that the trader first started trading on day one. It has a different character, with a different set of odds. Yet, it is precisely when the market is about to change that the green trader feels cocky enough to step up his lot size and go for the gusto. Failing to realize that the environment that helped deliver his or her winning streak is no longer present, the green trader naively presses matters, and runs the risk of losing all his hard-earned gains. Whenever traders start to feel content, complacent, cocky, the market is close to a reversal, simply because it was probably a certain market environment that helped them feel cocky in the first place. And take our word for it. That environment won't last for long.

How to Eliminate the Sin of Becoming Too Complacent.

Learn to step back a bit after every enduring winning streak, by doing any one or both of the following:

1. *Reduce your lot size by half. If you typically trade in 1000-share lots, drop to 500 shares.* Most traders actually commit the

grave error of doing the reverse. Because they have experienced a string a wins, they feel more confident increasing their lot size. But they do so precisely when they are closer to breaking their winning streak with a loss. This is how so many traders manage to wipe out their entire string of gains in one or two trades. The very last thing you want to do is be guilty of winning with your small lots and losing with your sizable ones.

Tip: We have found that the best time to put action 1 into practice is after experiencing four to five winning trades in a row.

2. *Reduce the frequency of your trades.* If you were trading four times a day, drop the number of daily trades to two. We only suggest this option if the traders have already started to experience the turn of fortune. If the traders have not yet hit a pause in their winning streak, option 1 is by far the better choice. When you are hot, you are hot. There is no sense in retarding or stifling the streak by trading less. But as we mentioned earlier, trading *with* less is smart.

Tip: Action 2 is best put into practice after two consecutive losses have followed an enduring winning streak.

DEADLY SIN #6: WINNING THE WRONG WAY

We're all very much aware of the fact that money can be made honestly, and in an upright fashion. And on the other hand, we know it can be made criminally and dishonestly. The end result, which in this case is money, may very well be the same, but the means by which the money is made can be vastly different. This brings up the age-old question, "Does the end justify the means?" Needless to say, the answer is an emphatic no. That's very much like asking should a heart surgeon and a drug dealer, both of whom may make a great deal of money, be held in the same regard? Of course they should not. So too is this concept true in the world of trading. *Many novice traders do not realize that it's possible to make money in the market the wrong way.* Consider individuals who have failed to adhere to a protective stop on a certain position, and by doing so actually wind up making money on the play. While we at Pristine will have to report that we lost money on that play, these individuals feel pleased that they did *not* honor the stop because the "end result" turned out to be a profit. Little do these individuals know that they have committed a crime against the self, and retribution will surely have to follow. These individuals have gotten a taste of *false* success, and the market will ensure that they give back this unearned profit sooner or later. The very next time these individuals are in a play that triggers their protective stop, what do you think their action will be? To ignore the stop again, of course. Why shouldn't they? They were rewarded the last time they dishonored the stop, why should they not go for the same reward this time? But this time, the stock may not rebound as the last one did. This time they may have latched on to a stock that has just begun a multiweek free fall that won't end until it puts a large dent in their trading accounts. You must be aware that making money incorrectly reinforces bad habits and irresponsible actions. Once traders get the taste of success that comes the wrong way, they are almost compelled to repeat that wrong until it robs them and takes back what was incorrectly earned and more. The market is a very funny thing. It seems to dislike rendering profits to those who don't really deserve it. So try to win the right way. It's more lasting.

SEED OF WISDOM

Master traders are not interested in getting lucky in the market. They do not seek, hope for, or even enjoy the wins that come to them, in spite of their errors or faulty trading acts. In fact, each time a trade is rewarded by chance, instead of skill, many of these traders will feel as if they've lost. Why? Because the real winning traders fully understand that there are no gifts in the market. What appears to be a warm gift is really a cold debt in disguise, one that will have to be paid back with outrageous interest. It is only novices, lacking the necessary skills, who look for gains any which way they can get them. The undeveloped traders find themselves in winning situations so infrequently that they wish for and eagerly snatch at profits in any form they can get them. For the novice, each *unearned* win is followed by a childlike hoot and a naïve cheer. Because they should not have won, they feel as though they've been given a break. They feel they've gotten over, outsmarted the fox, and escaped the jaws of danger. But little do they know, they cannot lay rightful claim to any profit that is not the result of their skill. They fail to realize that profits achieved by way of faulty acts are not profits at all. They are loans that might as well have been accepted from a loan shark. For they will have to eventually be paid back, sometimes with blood. Right actions and right methods won't always produce profits for conscientious traders. But one thing is for sure. The wrong act, repeatedly committed, will eventually be a sloppy trader's demise. Stay debt free. Make sure you are winning the right way.

How to Eliminate the Sin of Winning the Wrong Way

Here are a few simple steps that will keep you on guard against this deadly sin:

1. *After every winning trade, review each component of the trade: the entry, the initial stop placement, the waiting, the money management, the exit, etc.* Check for errors or rule violations. If you find any, chalk the trade up as a *loss* and include it in your daily trading journal with comments describing what needs to be corrected next time. *Tip:* One of the key problems is associating the feelings of a winner to those trades that really are not wins. Whenever traders allow themselves to feel like winners on a trade, those are really not wins, they are sending a message to their entire being that what was done was correct and good. This will tend to reinforce the wrongful acts, and encourage one to repeat the mistakes. Needless to say, the errors eventually catch up to the trader.

2. *Recognize that the two evil Hs, hoping and holding, will be the major culprits that most frequently lead to winning the wrong way.* Playing the market like an ostrich might play it will often work when the market is in an impressive bull mode. Let's face it. A rising tide raises all boats. And if traders who mess up on a trade during a rapidly rising market can hold on long enough, the market will often erase their deficit. But when this redeeming event happens time and time again, these traders start to actually believe that the "stick-your-head-in-the-sand-and-wait" approach is correct behavior for traders whenever they're in a losing trade. This erroneous belief is really a poison, one that quietly spreads until it completely consumes the entire financial life of the trader. When the market is not so accommodating, it tallies all the unearned profits taken and submits a bill. This bill is often so big and painful that many traders go bankrupt and are never heard from again. Truly recognizing that the two evil Hs, hoping and holding, ultimately lead to a trader's demise is one way to keep it in check.

DEADLY SIN #7: RATIONALIZING

Let's see if you can tell what the trader in the following scenario did wrong. An excited trader sees a good play setting up on an intraday chart. All the pieces seem to be falling into place, an intraday pullback with good volume characteristics, at support, a tight intraday stop, etc. And all the market indicators are coming alive after an afternoon of sideways consolidation on an exceptionally positive market day. Then ... BAM! The entry price gets hit. The trader executes and gets filled. After a brief pop, the stock abruptly falls back, giving up its short-lived gain, and is now hovering around the entry price. "What's up?" The trader thinks. "This should be screaming!!!" With its late afternoon rise now totally evaporated, the market is clearly weakening, and with a vengeance. With his stop now just a tick away, the trader starts examining the stock, looking for clues as to why this perfect setup is going south. After checking for any news items (there is no news), the trader checks the daily chart. "Yes. The daily looks good. Really good," he observes. "I'll just move the stop down under the day's low. Yeah. It shouldn't break that!" Ten minutes later, the new stop is violated as the perfect setup heads down to Antarctica, taking his or her money with it. Frustrated, the trader cashes out and can't believe how much was just lost. Where did this trader go wrong? Was it that the trader ignored the developing market weakness? Not exactly. The trader made the three deadly mistakes of:

1. *Switching time frames.* Having picked and played the setup on a completely *intraday* basis with an intraday entry point and a tight intraday stop, switching to a *daily* chart and adjusting the stop based on the daily completely altered the original play, skewing the original risk/reward ratio against the trader.

2. *Planning the trade and failing to trade the plan.* Sticking to the original plan—whatever the timeframe—is absolutely *essential*. Failure to trade the plan puts you at the mercy of the market, and erodes the self-confidence necessary to trade effectively.

3. *Rationalizing.* The psychological root of the other two mistakes, rationalizing a change of time frames or plans is a form of denial—a denial of the reality of what's really happening. Honesty—*real* honesty—no matter how ugly the truth—will put you above most market players unable to summon such strength from within, preferring instead to be comfortable,

blaming their losses on something or someone other than themselves.

SEED OF WISDOM

If you ever hope to approach the market with intelligence, planning each one of your trades is an absolute must. Most losing traders are flying by the seat of their pants, without any knowledge of how to even construct a trade plan. However, planning your trade and then failing to trade your plan is a greater crime. Those who know what to do and then fail to do it are the least worthy of that knowledge, and the market typically sees to it that they get their reward: Losses. It should be clear that rationalizing is the culprit behind this and many of the other deadly sins. Because most people tend to be overly optimistic by nature, they have a hard time bringing closure to any event that will leave them with a loss and/or pain. When the time to act arrives, many can't summon the resolve and courage to leap, so to speak. So instead, they begin a process of rationalizing. This process of talking one's self out of correct action eventually winds up taking the trader completely out of the game.

How to Eliminate the Sin of Rationalizing

Eliminating or keeping the process of rationalizing in check can be done using the following two steps:

1. First the traders must realize they are rationalizing. Key signs that you are talking yourself out of an action are
   a. Asking "why" a stock is acting a certain way. The reason behind a stock's behavior should have no bearing on a trader's planned course of action. If the plan was to exit XYZ on a drop below $20, finding out why the stock has dropped has no value. The trader's correct course of action is to exit first, ask questions second.
   b. Checking for news. Staying abreast of news on a particular stock is not a bad thing, in and of itself; however, when the real purpose behind checking the news is to postpone an action that was planned, it is nothing more than an exercise in escapism.
   c Thinking in terms of "maybe." Whenever a trader starts using the word maybe when called into action by a stop or a target, uncertainty has been given the upper hand. It is

nearly always better to adhere to a trading plan that has been put in place in advance, than opting to change in midstream. This strict adherence to what you formerly set out to do may not always result in the very best outcome, but what it will do is foster discipline, which is a priceless quality to have as a trader. Once a trader has spotted the signs of rationalization, the only appropriate action appears below.

2. Exit the position. This may sound harsh but my many years of experience have convinced me that rationalization leads to harm more often than it leads to good. If you find exiting the entire position difficult to do, then at least lightening the load by selling half should be done. In short, if you are trying to find a reason to stay in a position, it is obvious no reason is apparent. Searching for a reason means you don't have one. And a trader who's in a stock without a firm reason will be a losing trader.

HOW TO FIND AND KILL YOUR *DEADLIEST* DEMON

Yogi Berra was fond of saying, "I just don't want to make sure I make the *wrong mistake*." This is a fascinating point made by a very fascinating man. I'm not sure if this legendary baseball manager ever played the stock market, but his statement certainly applies to the challenging game of trading. Traders must forever be mindful of the fact that there are two types of mistakes or losses: (1) those that are due to the law of averages and therefore unavoidable and (2) those that are the result of the seven deadly sins and/or the faulty execution of the trading plan. Not only must traders realize this fact, but it is very important for them to differentiate between the losses that occur due to the "sins" and those due to statistics. It must never be forgotten that loss is, and always will be, a permanent part of the trading game. No matter how knowledgable we become, losing trades will forever remain a part of our reality. Our challenge as traders is not to avoid loss entirely. Rather it is to manage our losses intelligently and make sure we are only experiencing the ones that occur simply based on the fact that we can't win them all. We also must set out to completely eradicate the wrong losses from our trading lives. In other words, we must forever maintain a "search and destroy mission" for the demons—the errors—that evolve from the "sins" and have the power to take us out of the game. We have detailed here a life-long activity that we teach and require all of our private in-house traders to follow. We are sure it will prove helpful to you as well.

The Setup

Before you begin differentiating the "good" losses from the "bad" ones, it is necessary to organize a section of your trading journal in a way that will make it easy to keep track of your progress. The following three steps will help you do just that:

1. Take a page in your Pristine trading journal and divide it into two columns.
2. Title the left column: "You Can't Win Them All."
3. Title the right column "Kill These or Be Killed." We're sure you get the point.

Now you are ready to start the all-important "separating" process. We call this activity, "separating the good losses from the bad losses."

Separating the Good Losses from the Bad Losses

1. Thoroughly review the individual components of each losing trade: the entry, the trade management, that is, the initial stop placement and the trailing stop method, the exit, etc.
2. If, after the review, you decide that no errors were committed, list it as one of those "you can't win them all" trades, and move on to the next trade. These "no-fault" trades can be largely ignored at this point.
3. If, after the review, you decide that an avoidable error was made, list it in the "kill these or be killed" column under a subcategory named for the error. This is done to help you differentiate one error from another. A few examples of such subcategories might be: "entered too late," "exited too soon," "ignored the stop," etc. As you will see, we have detailed a similar process in Chapter 6 of this book.

Finding and Killing the Head Demon in Charge of Your Demise

After a series of losing trades, you will find that one subcategory of errors begins to outpace the others. Once you have detected this, you have found the head demon in charge of your demise. And you must immediately set out to kill it, mercilessly. Your sole purpose in life at this point will be to entirely eradicate this frequently committed error from your existence. Whatever the cost, whatever the effort, you must vigilantly put an end to this error. If the error is "ignored the stop," then you must set out to adhere to your stops. If that means selling early, then do it. Sell early. But whatever you do, don't let another trade go beyond your predetermined stop, *ever*. Promise yourself that over the ensuing days, weeks, or months, the column titled "ignored the stop" will have the smallest number of entries.

Once this subsection of errors has become the least of your problems, start working on the next category that stands out as the biggest problem. Agree to continue this process for life, and eventually your biggest problem will not be deciding which demon to kill, but finding demons to kill, period!

6
CHAPTER

12 TRADING LAWS OF SUCCESS

Rules the Master Trader Lives By

LAW #1: KNOW THYSELF

It is crucial for traders to know *who* they are and *what* they are. Because only then will they be able to know *how* they should play the market. You see, traders' styles of play should be based entirely on their tendencies, likes, desires, fears, etc. If traders are trying to fit into a style that goes against their psychological grain, if you will, the results could be disastrous. For instance, take the trader we know who is incredibly impatient. This trader may find it torturous to hold a stock for more than 10 days. In fact, even 5 days would seem like an eternity. So with this dominant trait firmly in place, taking on a long-term trade for 2 months or more would be a big mistake. The trader would, in effect, be fighting him or herself via the market. But knowing this, the trader would want to limit plays to those that potentially offer a faster, more immediate move. And while the frequency of loss would be greater, those types of plays would gel, be in sync with his or her personality, a whole lot better. And as a result, better decisions would be made. Get the point? Here are a few questions you should ask in order to find who, what, and where you are as a market player. Once you know the answers, it will be a lot easier to determine whether you are a trader or investor by nature.

1. *Am I patient?* If the answer is yes, you are a natural intermediate to long-term market player. If you are not patient by nature, a short-term trading approach would better complement your emotional and psychological makeup.

2. *Do I feel safe in the hands of time?* Yes would mean you tend to think and trust that all things eventually work out with enough time. This would make you an intermediate to long-term investor by nature. If you feel prone to beat time at its work, to fix problems faster than time can heal them, you are inherently a trader by nature.

3. *Does the increase in time make me grow more nervous?* If the second after initiating a trade you begin to feel a light nervousness, you are definitely a trader. If you grow more and more nervous in a trade (win or lose) as time goes by, short-term trading is right for you. If you can buy a stock, and immediately walk away, call a friend, grab a sandwich, or read the paper, or run an errand, you are *not* a trader.

Knowing the answers to the following questions will determine if you should primarily focus on the micro, short-term or intermediate to long-term time frames.

1. *What is my comfort level for risk?* If being down $250 on a trade makes you feel like a failure, your correct style of play is short term. If you can be down $1000 in a stock play, and still feel good about its prospects, playing longer time frames is best for you.

2. *Am I one who is willing to take a bigger hit (loss) in exchange for potentially scoring bigger?* If so, playing over longer time frames is better for you.

3. *Do I tend to be more comfortable going after smaller, less significant price moves, while keeping my losses at a minimum?* If the answer to this question is yes, you are a short-term trader by nature and playing the micro time frames will work best.

These questions will help the trader determine which techniques and tactics to focus on.

1. Am I a gambler?
2. Do I like to put my stake on the line in a big way?
3. Am I the type who likes to score in tiny bits and pieces?
4. Am I cheap?

5. Does price or quality mean the most to me?

6. Do I hate even small losses?

7. Is the thrill just as important as winning?

We can go on and on. But we're sure you get the point.

LAW #2: KNOW THY ENEMY

While knowing yourself is the first order of the day for every trader, one must also be aware of who the enemy is. As we've mentioned on several occasions, trading is war. But with whom? As traders, our adversaries are mainly other traders and market players. Let's think about this for a minute. Each time you buy a stock, someone else is on the other side of the trade, selling it to you. In other words, someone else is getting rid of the very same stock you are buying, and using you to do it. And that someone, mind you, thinks he or she is smarter and more astute than you are. Do you know who that someone is? It's your enemy. Most market players miss this point. They somehow operate on the notion that they are buying from the market in general. They have a mental picture of some vague place or room where stockpiles of the issue they want are just sitting around for them to take. Wrong! Whenever you buy, you are buying the stock from *someone*. Conversely, whenever you sell a stock, someone else is buying it from you. The question is, do you know that person? Do you understand that person's thinking, motives, beliefs, feelings, and current emotions? Because if you don't, how do you know *he* or *she* is not the one who's right?

It is important to realize that when you are trading stocks on the NASDAQ, you are typically transacting with a *market maker*, the term used for members of the NASD who buy and sell stock for clients as well as their own accounts. Some of the major market makers are Goldman Sachs (GSCO), Merrill Lynch (MLCO), First Boston (FBCO), etc. Despite their respectable names, they're typically not your friends when transacting on the NASDAQ. These are the very players who are typically taking the other side of your trade. You're buying, while they're selling it to you. And vice-versa. Are they just being generous by giving you the stock you want? Heck no. They think that they're right, and you're wrong. They are betting against you, which makes them what? That's right, your enemy. But let us never forget that the biggest enemy of all is not some distant trader or market maker, it is us. We are our biggest enemy. We are the biggest impediment to our progress and success, and we are the only ones who possess the power to conquer ourselves. All the psychological and emotional demons that must be conquered are within us. They belong to us, and if we ever hope to become successful as a trader, this greatest of all enemies must be defeated, transformed, and re-born. But before we can conquer ourselves, we must first get to know ourselves. As Shakespeare told us several centuries ago, "the fault lies not in the stars but in ourselves." Here are a few ways to get to know thy enemy:

1. *Never place a trade without first asking, "who's on the other side of my trade?"* This question will keep you aware that the enemy always lies on the other side of your trade. Part of trading successfully is first getting to know the enemies on the other side of your trades, then learning how to outsmart them.

2. *Never look beyond yourself when laying blame.* If you are losing as a trader, you are the ultimate enemy behind those losses. While other traders and market makers serve as enemies they are really the minor ones. Traders who have conquered themselves (the emotional and psychological demons) have conquered all the rest. Trading mastering is the by product of self-mastery.

LAW #3: GET THEE SOME EDUCATION, FAST

When it comes to being an accountant, a lawyer, or even a plumber, most people seem to thoroughly understand the need for education. The national, if not worldwide, cry for higher education, is almost deafening. And as a result of this focus on learning, there are schools that teach everything from knitting to chemical and electrical engineering. But oddly enough, when it comes to trading, most people feel education is not needed. This is incredibly baffling to us, especially given the fact that trading is probably one of the most difficult endeavors in existence. But most market players, even the so-called serious ones, somehow lose the belief in education when it comes to their money. It does not matter that the market possesses the capability of causing financial ruin. Most are willing to either fly from the hip with no guidance, or even worse, en-trust someone else to fly from the hip. It does not even seem to matter that learning to trade successfully can reap rewards that far surpass most people's wildest dreams. Many feel the need to go it alone in the dark without any instruction. The truth of the matter is that while the average individual would never dream of going into a business like lawyering or doctoring without getting some education, that attitude is absent when it comes to trading. Somehow they have been sold the erroneous notion that they can naively come into the market, pit themselves against New York Stock Exchange (NYSE) specialists, NASDAQ market makers, and professionals like us, and win. Needless to say, this could not be further from the truth. We have been trading for more than 13 years. Reaching our current state of trading proficiency was not easy. The pain and hardships we experienced to get to where we are can still be remembered, and sometimes they are still felt. Do you think for one moment that we, and traders like us, are going to allow those with no knowledge at all, to come into our world and take food off our family's tables? It would be a cold day in the lower depths of purgatory before that happened.

We believe so strongly in the need for trading education that we have been training professional traders, market makers, and money managers for more than 5 years. There is no doubt in our minds that education is the first key that unlocks the door to trading mastery. We have been at this game we call trading long enough to know that everyone must pay for the right to be a winner. One does not get a Harvard education without paying a Harvard tuition. It should be recognized that your tuition must be paid. And as a trader, it will be paid one way or the other: Willingly or unwillingly. The market will certainly see to that. You will have to decide which route to take. We just think you should opt for paying it willingly. Here are a few steps you can take to get thee some education:

1. *Seek out a quality firm that offers a training program for traders.* It will shave years of trial and error and lost money off your developmental period. A few of the better training programs we are aware of, including ours, are listed here:

    a. *Pristine.Com (www.pristine.com)—the Rolls Royce of Trading Education.* We offer a variety of rigorous training programs ranging from 1- and 3-day training sessions to get your feet wet to full 6-month developmental courses. The more lengthy training we offer has come to be known as Pristine's Mentorship Program. Our focus is to train serious-minded traders how to earn a living in the markets. The attendees learn how to implement the same sophisticated trading tactics and techniques that we use to pull profits out of the market each day. Execution skills are taught, along with proper interpretation of NASDAQ level II, chart reading, and trading on news. Proper thinking, a crucial element of successful trading, is also a major focus. Various styles of trading are also taught such as microtrading for small but consistent day-to-day gains, swing-trading for more dynamic gains over a 2- to 5-day time frame, and intermediate-term trading for the purpose of building wealth via the markets. Many graduates of our training programs have gone to successful careers as professional traders. Some of these graduates offer training and individual mentorship as well, which is why Pristine.Com is regarded as the educational source for those who not only want to become successful traders, but for those who want to build on their success as well.

b. *Cornerstone Securities, Inc.—One of the First Companies to Specialize in Electronic Trading.* If you are looking for professionalism in the day trading industry, your search can stop at the doors of Cornerstone. This firm has over 20 offices countrywide, and offers the best overall program for those traders wanting to trade onsite. We particularly like the firm because it is home to several of the top traders in the United States. Cornerstone strongly believes in education, and most, if not all, of their trainers are graduates of Pristine's training program.

c. *Trader's Edge Net (www.daytrading.com)—the House of No-Frills, No-Nonsense Trading.* Traders Edge Net, run by Marc Freidfertig and George West, the authors of the best selling *The Electronic Day Trader,* offers a week-long seminar for those looking to learn how to trade like a professional. The course focuses mainly on basic NASDAQ level II interpretation, and grueling software training on the Watcher, a very sophisticated DOS-based trading platform that provides lightning-fast NASDAQ executions. While only one known instructor from Trader's Edge Net has received formal training from Pristine, we like the fact that Broadway Trading, LLC, their sister firm, is home to some very dynamic and profitable traders.

2. *Read the trading books that really count.* There is a preponderance of books on the market dealing with the subject of trading and market play. And the numbers are growing exponentially. Unfortunately, most of these books offer little more than basic facts and vague academic theories.

The very best books are those which help the trader think properly. Tactics and techniques are also important, and many books don't even cover that part of the game well. But the few that offer both the thinking and tactical elements are like fine gold. We have listed 10 books that will prove helpful to most developing traders. While not all of them possess the two important elements just spoken about, they are well worth delving into. The ones with stars have the dual elements and, as a result, they have had a dramatic effect on the way we think *and* trade.

Recommended Reading List

1. *How I Made $2 Million in the Stock Market*, by Nicholas Darvas (****)
2. *Trading for a Living*, by Dr. Alexander Elder, John Wiley (1993).
3. *Japanese Candlestick Charting Techniques*, by Steve Nison, Prentice Hall (May 1991).
4. *How to Make Money in Stocks*, by William J. O'Neill, McGraw-Hill (September 1994).
5. *The Disciplined Trader*, by Mark Douglas, Prentice Hall (June 1990).
6. *Winner Take All*, by William Gallacher, Irwin (March 1997).
7. *Reminiscences of a Stock Operator*, by Edwin Lefever, Market Place Books.
8. *The Electronic Day Trader*, by Marc Freidfertig and George West, McGraw-Hill (1998).
9. *How to Get Started in Electronic Day Trading*, by David Nassar, McGraw-Hill (November 1998).
10. *Strategies for the On-line Day Trader*, by Fernando Gonzalez and William Rhee, McGraw-Hill (July 1999).

LAW #4: PROTECT THY MOST VALUABLE COMMODITY

As an active trader, you will be forced to deal with those occasions on which numerous brokerage downgrades, negative earnings reports, or negative economic news items will wreak havoc with the overall market as well as your open stock positions. While losses are a permanent, inevitable reality for every market participant, they are never pleasant for us, especially when they come as a result of things outside of our control. Because the element of uncertainty can never be totally eliminated from the financial markets, it is always necessary to have a protective sell strategy. We call this sell strategy the Pristine Insurance Policy. As many of our subscribers know, this is a theme which we perpetually emphasize, almost to a fault. But prudence dictates that we must do everything in our power to protect the most precious commodity we have: our initial capital. Once that goes, my friends, you can stick a fork in us, because we're done, cooked, finished. Get the drift? It is essential that you do. We believe that every professional trade should have one precise buy point and two sell points. One of those sell points addresses the upside and gives a profit-taking reference point. However, because we live in the real world, we must also have a sell point which deals with the possibility of the trade going sour. Because human beings are naturally optimistic and too often naïve, the "protective sell" typically gets the smallest degree of the trader's attention. Needless to say, this is why most trading gains are much smaller than trading losses. As Pristine traders, we can't afford to be human, at least in this regard. The pocket book simply can't take it. So make sure that you have three prices in mind each time you make a trade. The entry price, the profit-taking price, and the protective stop price, better known as your Pristine Insurance Policy. Always recognize that the protective price, your stop, is by far the most important price of all, at least during the initial stages of your trade. This price represents the line in the sand that you have intelligently drawn for the market. It provides you with an advanced notice as to what your maximum cost will be for being wrong, and most importantly it is your protection from the only thing that can take you out of this wonderful game we call trading: a runaway collapsing stock. You may step up the frequency of your losing trades by instituting a stop loss strategy, but the losses will be so negligible on balance, it won't matter in the long run. Take our word for it. We've lost big, and we've lost small. Losing small is *much* better. Protect your precious capital, at all costs.

We have outlined here basic instructions on how we set our Pristine Insurance Policy for both swing trades, which cover the 2- to 10-day holding period, and the intraday trade, which covers minutes to hours:

The Swing Trade

1. First, we enter each swing trade based on one of three entry methods. The specific entry price is typically based on the daily price chart. We cover these three entry methods very thoroughly in Chapter 14.

2. Once we have bought the stock, we establish a protective sell at $\frac{1}{16}$ to $\frac{1}{8}$ below the current day's low, or the previous day's low, *whichever is lower.* Here's an example: We buy WXYZ at $20. The current day's low (the entry day's low) is $19.25. The previous day's low is $18.50. Because the previous day's low is lower than the current day's low, our protective stop would be placed at $18\frac{7}{16}$ or $18\frac{3}{8}$.

3. This initial protective sell price would stay in place for two complete days, with the entry day counting as day one. After 2 days, we often make adjustments upward to protect some of our profits. More detailed instructions on stop adjustments will be given in Chapter 16.

The Intraday Trade

1. First we enter each intraday trade using one of the intraday entry methods. This entry price is usually based on the 5- or 15-minute price chart. We cover intraday entry methods very thoroughly in Chapter 17.

2. Once we have bought the stock, we place a stop $\frac{1}{16}$ below the low of the current 5- or 15-minute bar that was bought. If our buy was based on the 5-minute chart, our stop would be placed directly under the current 5-minute bar, which would be the entry bar. If our buy was based on the 15-minute chart, our stop would be placed directly under the current 15-minute bar, which would be the entry bar. Again, detailed explanations on how we enter stocks using 5- and 15-minute charts are discussed in Chapter 17, and money management techniques designed to protect capital are discussed in Chapter 15.

LAW #5: KEEP IT SIMPLE

For the most part, it is our firm belief that traders, in a desperate search for the "holy grail," will unnecessarily grasp at anything that suggests, "super complexity." Logarithms, neurological mechanisms, and confusing mathematical trading equations are but a few of the examples of how far we have transgressed away from the basics. Basics such as major trend lines, price support and resistance, volume increases and decreases, major moving averages, core chart patterns, and the like. The western frame of mind, in particular, assumes that if it isn't complex, it isn't workable. Our view is closer to the exact reverse of this misconception. The clarity of mind and the certainty of action that are born from a simple approach are almost indescribable. And all of our students get a healthy grounding in the basics, and learn the value of ceaselessly revisiting them. Decide today that you will become a master of the basics, and you'll quickly understand that simplicity is the mother of clarity.

If you answer yes to any of the following questions, your trading approach may be too complex:

1. Will your trading tactics and techniques thoroughly confuse an intelligent 12-year old?
2. Does your approach call for mathematical calculations?
3. Do you need a calculator to trade?
4. Are more than three pieces of software required to come up with your trades?
5. Will it take more than 5 minutes to write out your trading strategy on paper?

These are only a few questions that point to overcomplexity. Make sure you keep it simple.

LAW #6: LEARN FROM THY LOSSES

The path that leads to market mastery is a journey fraught with countless perils. The danger, the loss, the trials and tribulations that an aspiring trader must endure, are enough to break the backs and crater the souls of most individuals who dare to trek its course. It is a shame that so many are quick to assume that an individual, who has mastered his craft and commands the markets with incredible acumen, has accidentally stumbled upon his gift by some innate tendency or natural endowment. This is far from the truth. Pain. Loss. Frustration. Confusion. Uncertainty. Inconsistency. These are but a few of the states and circumstances that provide the education necessary to reach the desired heights of greatness. Each trader who enjoys a certain level of success today is guaranteed to have suffered through the pain and agony of being a loser yesterday. We, as human beings, simply do not learn from our successes, but rather from our failures and shortcomings. We, as adults, know that fire should not be touched because, at one time in our childhoods, we got burned. So it is with trading. *We learn how to win only after we learn all the ways to lose.* So my question to you is this. What are you doing with your market failures? Are they wasted, ignored, left to fester and grow more potent as time goes on? Or are they serving as valuable examples of what *not* to do in the future? Within our losses lies the secret to the success that we are looking for. We must lose first, then use those losses as a springboard to winning. Remember, we leap forward by great distances only after first stepping backward. In other words, we step back, *then* leap forward. That is the law of nature. That is the blueprint of success. And that, my friends, is the way to trading mastery. Without stepping back first, our attempt to leap forward will be feeble and weak. So do not moan and whine when you experience a losing trade. On the contrary, you should rejoice. For that loss, dealt with properly, is a wonderful angelic guide that has the potential to lead you to a winning future.

SEED OF WISDOM

One of the most valuable tools available to a trader is not some fancy market indicator or some sexy trading technique, but a simple, yet effective diary of losing trades. I have found that keeping a log of all my losses makes it easier for me to spot trends and recurring mistakes and errors. For instance, after reviewing a string of five losses, one might discover that a late entry was made on four of them. That valuable discovery, if dealt with properly, holds the key to dramatically improving one's winning percentage. At that point the trader would focus his or her attention on entering sooner or refraining from chasing the desired stock too far. I recall making an interesting discovery years ago, after using my log to review all my losses made the prior year. After a careful review, I found that 78 percent of my losing trades were in stocks that cost between $8 and $15 per share. I remember that day like it was yesterday. It was an amazing discovery that I'm sure I would have missed without the use of my log. Clearly, that review revealed the simple fact that if I had stayed away from stocks in the lower-price ranges, my performance would have at least doubled. So many incredible things can be derived from a careful review of one's failures. A daily diary of these failures tells a lot about who, what, and where we are. Used with dates, it can also tell us where we are going, and if we are going anywhere at all. I wouldn't leave home without it. Heck, I wouldn't even *be* at home without it. My 5-year-old daughter learned how to walk by falling. Now she's running. This 33-year-old trader and author learned how to trade by first losing. Now I'm teaching traders all over the world how to win in the markets just like I do. Winning takes care of itself. Just learn the art of losing properly, and your dreams may just become your reality.

LAW #7: KEEP THEE A TRADING JOURNAL

One of the most valuable actions a trader can perform is to keep a personalized journal of trading errors. As most of our students and subscribers know, we are firm believers that our failures (in life as well as in the market), used properly, serve as stepping stones to higher heights of market mastery. And keeping a detailed history of your market mistakes will help you know *who* you are, *what* you are, and *where* you are going. Over 7 years ago, this simple task helped raise my trading accuracy to a level I thought could never be achieved. There is no reason for me to believe that it won't do the same for you. Here's how I carried out this simple, but effective task. First, I took all of our pitiful brokerage statements, and wrote down the gritty details—date of trade, stock symbol, entry price, exit price, total commission, reason for trade, etc.—of every single losing trade. With the aid of a chart book (today I use the *www.executioner.com's* charting feature), I reviewed and dissected each losing decision and found that many of the same mistakes were being repeated time and time again. So I began grouping these errors into separate classes such as "entered too late," "sold too soon," "held too long," "got too greedy," "got too nervous," "ignored stop," etc. Once this was complete, I was left with an unmistakable picture of who I was as a trader (a failing novice), and what I needed to immediately work on to become someone different (a successful pro). I then took the group that had the greatest number of entries and, ignoring the rest, went to work on eradicating it from my life. I did not rest until that specific error was dead. Then I started on the next most frequently committed error, and killed that one. Then I killed the next one, and the next one. Ten months later, while working on my last group of errors, it dawned on me that I had been trading profitably for several months, *without fully realizing it.* I was so focused on eliminating my errors that the collective effect of my winning trades virtually went undetected. This was living proof to me that winning takes care of itself. A successful trader is more defined by the way he loses than by the way he wins. The trader who wins right, but loses wrong will eventually be a statistic. The trader who wins wrong but loses right will be around long enough to eventually get it right. The trader who wins right *and* loses right will have to find creative ways to spend and give away the money earned. Through this thorough process of tracking my errors, I learned what not to do, and my trading account grew. Journal your way to success, my friends, and watch your level of trading mastery soar. You will be amazed at how this one simple task of keeping a trading journal will help eliminate some of your biggest trading demons, and therefore enhance your ability to win.

Here is an example of how my students and I set up our personal trading journals:

Trade 1

Date of Trade: 6/15/99

Market Rating: Positive (more about how to rate the market in a later chapter)

Symbol: PSFT

Share Size: 100

Type of Trade: Long

Style of Trade: Swing-trade (2 to 5 days)

Entry Price: $18.50

Reason for Entry: 30-minute buy rule (see further details in a later section)

Initial Stop Price: $17.50 (below prior day's low)

Objective: $20.50 to $21 (expecting a move to the 200-day moving average)

Sell Date: 6/16/99

Sell: Price: $16.75

Reason for Sell: Violated initial stop

Result: $1.75, or a $175 loss (omitting commissions)

Error 1: Fear of pulling the trigger. Hesitated at the entry, which resulted in buying ¼ point higher than I should have bought. This error alone cost me $25.

Error 2: Ignored stop. At my stop price of $17.50, I succumbed to the enemy called hope, stuck my head in the sand so to speak, and tricked myself into believing the odds of a rebound were great. This error cost me an extra ¾ point or $75.

Error 3: N/A

This journalized trade reveals a world of information about the trader. The two most common errors, fear of pulling the trigger and ignoring the stop, suggest that the trader is experiencing skepticism instead of experiencing optimism, and is feeling naively optimistic instead of being the most skeptical. This is an all too common condition that usually goes undetected. However, journalizing our losses, in this way, will uncover such hidden things and show us clearly who, what, and where we are as traders. If this pattern persisted, this trader's sole goal in life would be to reverse these two feelings, to make sure the next 10 trades, for instance, did not repeat either of the two errors. The trader could either take one error at a time or attempt to tackle them both. Either way, the trader's focus would not be to make money, but to make sure not one single trade dropped below the predefined stop. Even if that meant fanatically selling *before* the stop, the trader would not want one trade to violate or get by the defined sell point. In fact, the trader should almost hope every trade made declines so that he or she can break the back of this dangerous habit (demon). The trader would also have to practice executing initial buys with heightened expediency. Once the buy signal comes, the trader's job would be to eliminate all thinking, and become one minded in terms of getting the trade done. Again, even if this meant being a bit fanatical, it should be done on every trade, at all costs. The idea is not necessarily to make money, although this may very well be the final effect. Rather, it is to "kill" the two demons that have the potential to take the trader out of the game forever.

Journalizing each losing trade in this manner will do wonders for you. We know this all too well because after practicing it for a while, our own trading rose to a brand new level. Journalizing losses is also a required practice for our private in-house trading students. Try it. We are sure it will help your trading immensely.

LAW #8: DON'T MAKE LOW-PRICED STOCKS THY MAIN FOCUS

If there is one mistake, one cardinal sin I've run into a zillion times, it's deciding on a stock play based on price. I have seen this one novice mistake cause more casualties of war than anything else, besides not adhering to stops of course. I understand where it comes from and why the urge exists, but it's faulty and should be recognized as such by all traders. Limited capital is the main motivator for this urge. Because of limited funds, many traders opt for taking the trades in the lower-priced areas. Wrong! What you must realize is that the odds of winning often increase as you climb the price ladder. Consider this. In order for a $10 stock to move $2, it must rise a whopping 20 percent. That is the type of gain some investors would be delighted to get on the entire year. In fact, over 60 percent of professional fund managers don't even produce annual gains near that, and there are traders who want it in a day or two. "Can it happen?" You bet. "Then what is the problem, Oliver?" Well, the problem is that the trader with limited funds is precisely the one who desperately needs a higher winning success ratio. Yet if he exclusively concentrates on the lower-price range, the trader is swinging for the fences in the land of lower probability. I would much rather see the trader buy fewer shares in the higher-price ranges, simply because the odds are much better. Let's consider the other side now. How much easier is it for a stock, priced at $60, to rise $2 in a day or two? The answer: Much easier. A $2 move, even in one day, is closer to a normal occurrence for a $60 stock. A $2 move in a $10 stock often gets it mentioned in the next day's paper, it's so rare. This game we call trading is based almost entirely on odds. In a sense, it's a simple, although difficult to execute, numbers game. And the trader, who fails to recognize where the best odds of success lay, will have a very brief market career. But one thing is for sure. It'll be exciting. However, I suspect if you are reading this book, you want more than excitement. If that is the case, play a little more frequently in the higher-priced stocks. They will work a lot harder for you. Besides, didn't mom ever tell you, "You get what you pay for?"

SEED OF WISDOM

This commandment is not to suggest that stocks in the lower-price range should not be played at all. In fact, we initially train our new in-house traders exclusively on the lower-priced stocks because the risk associated with them is less. But once these trainees get a thorough understanding of how market makers work, and how our applied trading strategies take full advantage of their sly activities, we begin inching them up the price ladder. We also utilize the lower-price stocks when we are implementing our "accumulation approach." *Note:* Our accumulation approach involves building a rather large position in a stock over the 1- or 2-day period preceding an expected move. This is an advanced strategy in which our senior in-house traders get schooled. Just remember that sometimes good things come in small packages, but in most cases, the higher-priced stocks will come more frequently bearing the gifts you really want.

LAW #9: DON'T DIVERSIFY

One of the most frequently used terms among investment professionals is "diversification." Today, you cannot open a brokerage account, read a financial book, meet with an investment advisor, or even have a beer with a financial planner without hearing the command "you must diversify" at least half a dozen times. Almost before we learned the difference between preferred stock and livestock, the concept of not keeping all our eggs in one basket was thoroughly drilled into us. But as time moved on, we began to question the validity of this dogma and, in the process, discovered some very interesting things. *Tip:* As an astute trader, you should question everything and put to the test of reality even the most fundamentally accepted axioms. You'll be quite surprised at what you discover. Curiously, we found that being well diversified actually curtailed one's progress and cut short the potential profitability when a trader was right. However, when the trader was wrong, diversification effectively served as a protective buffer against big losses. Isn't that interesting. Diversification did not actually prevent losses, nor did it increase the odds of being profitable. It simply provided a thicker cushion whenever the trader was wrong. Now we don't know about you, but we're far more interested in concepts that increase the odds (and therefore the frequency) of being right than those that merely help us to be more comfortable losers. Now don't get us wrong. Diversification does have its place. And as we've preached many times, losing right is a big part of the game. It's just clear to us that diversification has less of a place when a trader has talent. In short, heavy diversification is nothing more than a substitute for lack of talent. It is a concept that was created to make one's losses more satisfying. While there are appropriate times to diversify, we would prefer you to throw your energies into becoming an overall winning trader. Think about it. What traders need diversification when they can produce eight winning trades to every two losses? Traders who have reached that level of mastery are looking to leverage their high winning percentage as much as possible. Diversification would only dilute that winning average.

SEED OF WISDOM

We do not want to minimize the fact that diversification does have its place. But we have found that it is largely an overrated practice when it comes to the somewhat different challenges of short-term trading. Not only do master traders want to use concentrated positions to maximize their accuracy, the novice trader is better off building proficiency trade by trade as well. The very last thing developing traders want to do is multiply their frequently committed errors by increasing the number of their decisions. In the beginning, the fewer decisions that have to made, the better. But even on the other side of progress this is true. The more accuracy and proficiency is attained, the less one needs the safety of diversification. In the world of trading, an increase in talent should correspond to a decrease in diversification.

LAW #10: REALIZE THAT NO ACTION IS, AT TIMES, THE BEST ACTION

After many years of speaking, counseling, teaching, and lecturing to thousands of market players all over the world, we have come to realize that many of the problems that plague developing traders fall into two main categories: (1) lack of patience and (2) failure to know when doing "nothing" is the right action. How many times have you decided to sell a stock, only to watch it skyrocket a day or two after you sold it? Now ask yourself how many of those sell decisions were based on a predetermined sell strategy and how many were initiated because you just got nervous, bored, or distracted by some other issue or event. Having a sell strategy established *before you enter a trade* is one of the hallmarks of a seasoned trader. But even seasoned traders make the mistake of violating their preset sell strategies by prematurely selling their stocks despite them having done nothing wrong. If you are guilty of this tendency, it needs attention, because if allowed to continue, it will likely deprive you of some of the greatest moments of your trading career. The second problem is, by far, the most damaging, and is what is responsible for the endless vacillations we experience between "profit and loss." This nonprogressive profit and loss cycle deserves a well-written book in and of itself, but knowing when *not* to trade is the magic elixir that will virtually put an end to it. Most traders fail to see the benefit of knowing when to sit on their hands. They erroneously assume that if you're good, you'll always be able to find something to do or some stock to trade. This is not only naïve, it is potentially ruinous. As professional traders, we are little more than odds players, very much like the professional poker player. And he who correctly assesses the odds will consistently win a healthy share of the kitty. The truth of the matter is that *no action is, at times, the best action,* and knowing when and how to deftly shift between the polar states of activity and inactivity will place you in a rare class of traders. Please keep these two points in mind, as they are worth a great deal more than the price of this book.

SEED OF WISDOM

One of the most valuable possessions of master traders is their ability to properly time "inaction." Inaction is a very potent tool that only the most successful traders have learned to use, a tool that not only saves them tens of thousands of dollars, but one that helps make them tens of thousands of dollars too. I sit and watch developing traders each day make decent money in the initial phases of the day, only to spend the rest of the day giving it all back. They easily cough up their hard-earned gains because they fail to appreciate the benefits of properly timed "inaction." Each winning trade makes them want to press harder, to grab more. Inaction during a winning spell is often the furthest thing from their minds. But it is an inescapable fact that there are times when the wind is just not blowing right, and you should stay home. There are times, when going up to bat is not what should be done, even if its your turn. And there are times when you should stop trading for a moment, a day, or maybe even a week. Trading is a very enriching profession if mastered. But the would-be trader who does not quickly learn that *not* trading can at times be the better choice will have a hard time reaching that state we call trading mastery.

LAW #11: KNOW WHEN TO BOW OUT GRACEFULLY

The ability to sidestep or reduce one's activity in a timely manner during periods of erratic market behavior is the hallmark of a professional trader. Too many uninformed market players assume that a supertrader is one who combats and successfully overcomes even the most treacherous market environments. This couldn't be further from the truth. The astute trader understands that above-average performance is more a result of keeping losses small than making profits big. Therefore, being skilled at bowing out of the market at the right time is an integral part of successful trading. Consider the following fact. If a long-term investor happened to be out of the market during the 20 most positive days of the past 14 years, about 30 percent of the total 14-year gain would have been missed. Amazing, isn't it? A very powerful argument for the buy-and-hold approach, right? Wrong! What is missed in that statement is the flip side. If that same investor stayed fully invested, but instead managed to sidestep the worst 20 days of the 14-year period, profits would have more than doubled. Avoiding the bad periods is more profitable than capitalizing on the best periods. But let me say this. Being able to do both, side step the worst, and play the best, is what makes a *supertrader*. So stay on the sidelines when the odds are not in your favor, and rest in the fact that "missed money is better than lost money."

If any one or more of the following occurrences take place, perhaps it is time to bow out gracefully:

1. You've lost two times in a row after an enduring winning streak.

   Tip: Traders often undo themselves by self-destructing immediately after a winning streak. In other words, our biggest failures often follow our biggest successes.

2. The market, as measured by the S&P futures contract, violently turns negative.

   Tip: The S&P futures contract is a key market-leading indicator. It often gives watchful traders advanced notice of market turns.

3. You feel offbase, uncertain, confused, disoriented, and you don't know why.

   Tip: Over time traders tend to develop what is called a trader's "gut." This gut, developed over years of seasoning and experience, speaks via our emotive and intuitive faculties. The master trader with a well-developed gut learns to respect these "hints."

4. Your predetermined trade plan is shattered by some sudden market event.

   Tip: It is always best to step aside whenever a monkey wrench gets thrown into your trade plan. Many novice traders try to fight the inevitable need to bow out, when something like an unexpected negative news item is released, but this often results in the trader gambling, which in turn leads to bigger losses.

5. You feel ill.

   Tip: Traders are like professional athletes. They must keep themselves in good physical and mental health. If you feel ill, you will not perform up to par.

6 Your frame of mind is frazzled.
     Tip: The trader's most potent weapon is a serene mind-set.
     If mental equanimity is absent, sound-trading decisions will
     be absent.

7. You are dealing with a personal problem.
     Tip: Personal problems affect the mental equanimity,
     which in turn affects trading decisions. The market acts as a
     near-perfect mirror image of who and what we are. Our
     personal problems have a funny way of manifesting
     themselves through our trading.

LAW #12: DON'T EVER MAKE EXCUSES—THEY NEVER MADE ANYONE A DIME

"You can make excuses, you can make money, but you can't do both."
We find this wise statement so incredibly true, on virtually all fronts. But
it particularly rings true for traders. As active stock market players, we
deal with complexity and the shadows of uncertainty each day. In our
search for consistent profitability, we take real risks (albeit intelligent
ones) with our hard-earned capital with every passing trade. The word
"difficult" does not even come close to describing the trader's plight. Yet,
the real trader acts. When you think about it, it's quite amazing. The path
that leads to trading success is no easy one. We all know that. Yet thousands of us survive and choose to press on each day. The arduous journey to the high lands of consistent profitability is one we all hope to
complete. And while many do fall by the wayside, there are those who
continue the good race. Consistently, beginning traders flirt with financial doom. Daily they battle the psychological demons that stand in their
way. And despite the enormous difficulty, the extreme hardship involved in being successful as a trader, we are thoroughly impressed with
the fact that there remain some who refuse to make excuses. And it is
those who ultimately wind up making the money, that "sweet dollar," to
use another term. Whenever I am down and out, beaten up by a soul-
bending losing streak—and we all have them—I remind myself that no
one ever promised me that a successful life, or successful trading, would
be easy. Yes, excuses can be easily made. But they never put a dime in the
pockets of their promoters. I love and respect traders—the real ones that
is—because they recognize that courage is best described as being afraid
and "doing it anyway." Excuses are for losers. The real money, that

"sweet dollar," will always go to those who recognize that. So when going after the Mighty Moby Dick, don't bring excuses, bring tartar sauce.

SEED OF WISDOM

Trading is the last bastion of total freedom. The partners in law and accounting firms really work for their clients. Doctors really serve their patients. Traders work for and serve only themselves. No one can rightfully lay claim to the traders' successes, because it can only come from within. And failure cannot be co-owned or passed off to others. In short, traders live in a world that is all their own. Every peak and every valley belong to them. But because there is nowhere to hide or escape the personal responsibility of each act, losing traders often find it easier to create excuses. Blaming others makes it psychologically easier to cope with shortcomings. Accusing a newsletter, blaming an analyst, and faulting the Wall Street system are just a few of the ways losers evade the fact that they alone are responsible for their decisions. Don't become one of these excuse makers. The path they are on is clear. The final destination, which can only be failure, is already known. Take full responsibility for your every action in the market. Recognize with deep honesty that no one has the power to make you act. Know in your heart that the final endorsement of any act belongs only to you. The very best traders live their lives in a world built on self-reliance and total independence. In that world, the fault for all losses lie with themselves, but also, they know that they have a right to lay claim to all the wonderful gains. And the traders who make no excuses will eventually have many more gains than losses.

7
C H A P T E R

SECRETS OF THE MASTER TRADER

15 Things Every Trader Should Know, But Doesn't

SECRET #1: THERE ARE NO GIFTS ON WALL STREET

There are not many certainties in the larger game of life. Death and taxes are two that immediately come to mind. It can be said that another certainty is change. But when it comes to the smaller game of trading or the market, the only certainty we can bet on is the simple fact that *there are no gifts on Wall Street*. If you think you have gotten lucky with a trade, time will usually reveal that what you initially felt was luck is actually misfortune. Take the trader who waits to enter a running NASDAQ stock after most of the market makers have disappeared from the inside offer price. If the trader gets filled when there is only one or two market makers left on the offer, it is almost certain that the trader really doesn't want it, or shall I say *shouldn't* want it. Whenever you think you've been *given* something, chances are you *have* been given something, something you don't want. This is akin to receiving a gift. And the simple truth is that no one on Wall Street is going to give up anything for free. Yes, there will always be mistakes made by even the most astute. And yes, there will always be the ignorant who perpetually buy and sell merchandise at the wrong time. But capitalizing on these events is what artful trading is all about.

This is very different from being given what you think to be a gift. I am referring to being lucky, to getting something you know you did not deserve. This is what the trader must be watchful of. In other words, profits and/or opportunities are *taken* in the market, not *given*. When someone gives you something, chances are it's a hot potato that you should immediately dish off to someone else, if you do not wish to get burned. This may not make you feel very good about yourself, but the Darwinian-like law on Wall Street is survival of the wisest and shrewdest, *not* survival of the luckiest. Take what you will, but accept no gifts. They don't exist, not on Wall Street anyway.

MASTER TRADING TIP

If you get something you know you did not deserve, chances are it's a trap. Always be a skeptic when something seems too good to be true. Here are a few examples of potential negative warnings being passed off as "gifts":

1. *Your bid gets hit (you buy) below the current market price.* This means someone wanted out of the stock so bad they were willing to sell it to *under* the current bid price. While most novices would be delighted, the master trader immediately becomes skeptical. The fact is, this person may know something that you don't. Whenever this happens, be on guard and ready to get rid of the stock at the first sign of trouble.

2. *Your offer gets hit (you sell) above the current market price.* This is the exact reverse of the previous scenario. It means someone was so anxious to get the stock they were willing to pay up for it. This could very well be a novice who does not know what he or she is doing or an excited trader who's been bitten by the greed bug. But there are times when those willing to pay above the current offer (ask) price are true professionals. When they want all the stock that's available in the current area, they will be willing to buy above the market. This means the stock is likely on the verge of exploding on the upside. We teach our traders to get ready to aggressively buy back into the stock when this happens as a result of professional positioning.

3. *One market maker is on the offer (ask price) displaying small size and you still get filled with blinding speed.* This often means that the picture of strength being advertised is not really strength

at all. Let's look at an example. Four market makers are bidding for (wanting to buy) a stock at $40 and only one market maker is offering 1000 shares of the stock at $40.25. At first glance, the stock looks strong because four people are willing to buy at $40, while only one market maker is willing to sell. However, numerous transactions go off at $40.25, yet the market maker posted at $40.25 still remains. *Note:* This means the market maker is "refreshing" his or her offer. In the midst of the flurry of trades going off at $40.25, you place a buy order for 1000 shares at the $40.25 offer price. You instantly get filled. While a novice trader might feel lucky about getting the stock at $40.25, the master trader would instantly become skeptical. Sometimes the master trader's skepticism would result in an immediate offer of these shares for sale at $40.25 or even $40\%_{16}$.

There are, of course, many more scenarios, but we are sure you get the point.

SECRET #2: SOMEONE'S ON THE OTHER SIDE OF YOUR TRADE, AND IT'S *NOT* YOUR FRIEND

I have always believed it necessary for our students to understand that each time they place a trade, there is someone on the other side of that transaction betting in the opposite direction. For instance, each time you buy a stock, there is someone on the other side of the trade selling it to you. The $64,000 question is "Who's smarter?" Who is right, you, or the person on the other side? Far too many traders and investors operate in the market as if they buy and sell stock from some large warehouse in the sky in which piles of the securities they want have been stacked and stored. This vague and erroneous concept ignores the most crucial element of trading and fosters an incorrect state of mind. Trading must always be viewed as a battle, a battle first and foremost with the self, but also a battle against other market players. As a trader, you must always be aware that with each trade, you are pitting yourself against the opinions and beliefs of other traders and investors, and they could very well be the ones who are right. As a trader, it is imperative to understand that you are only able to buy a stock because someone else is anxious to sell it. Conversely, you are only able to sell your stock at a certain price because someone is anxious to buy it at that price. In order to be the party who's right more often than not, you will first have to fully understand what successful trading is. This may sound simple enough, but you will be surprised to find that many traders do not know it. We have asked the question, "What is successful trading" to thousands of people across the country at our 1- and 3-day trading seminars. And each time we have, we've gotten the typical answers like, "successful trading is buying low and selling high," and "successful trading is winning more than losing." While both of these statements contain some truth, they fall far short of the real answer, mainly because they are vague and eliminate the personal element we've spoken of earlier. In order to approach the game of trading in the proper mind-set, you must know the answer to this simple question. So, let us reveal the right answer here and now, before we delve deeper into the subject matter. **Successful trading is buying merchandise (stock) from someone who is selling it too cheaply, and selling that merchandise back to him or someone else when you know it to be too expensive.** Reread this statement several times, before moving on, for it contains one of the most important keys to trading mastery. If you understand it properly, you will realize that, essentially, successful trading is the art of finding and taking advantage of a fool, someone totally unaware of the current value of the merchandise in or at hand. This is the truest definition of successful trading, and those who approach each trade with it in mind will be playing the game with a deeper and keener insight. The problem with other definitions of successful trading is that they miss the most valuable point. In every winning trade, someone must be the patsy, the idiot, the fool who gives up the merchandise to someone else too cheaply, and buys it back too expensively. Our job is to make sure you and our students are not the fools.

MASTER TRADER TIP

Master traders in many ways play the role of the Good Samaritan. They relieve the downtrodden by buying stock from them when they are in pain, and satisfy those who are anxious by selling their stock to them when they get greedy. In a sense, master traders are relievers of pain and satisfiers of greed.

SECRET #3: PROFESSIONALS SELL HOPE; NOVICES BUY HOPE

Many traders new to the market—and some not so new—think that given enough time and money trolling the aisles of the nearest mega bookstore, thumbing through the pages of one trading tome or another, they will find it: the holy grail of indicators, sure to make them a fortune by its ease of use and inherent logic. Others hold a similar hope that perhaps it will just be the next trade that will deliver the mother lode, the out-of-the-park grand slam, or maybe just bring them back to breakeven in one glorious round trip. But every master trader knows that hope is a dangerous thing when it comes to the market. While it is often that which initially brings people of all persuasions to the market, hope itself rarely helps one achieve success in the market. It is rather the ability to see what *is* that leads to consistent profits. By this, we mean the ability to read what is displayed in the price chart without projecting one's hopes, desires, and fears upon it. As with most things worthwhile, this is much easier said than done. The level of clarity required is one of mature, healthy detachment. In other words, rather than the focus being on oneself and the fortune to be had just around the corner, it demands complete focus on the facts of the potential trade. It demands that one adopt the attitude of the scientist, diligently gathering all the facts before reaching a conclusion. Facts such as the nearest support and resistance areas, the direction and age of the current trend, the relationship between the last price and the aforementioned facts in order to determine the entry price, the stop and the price objective. It also demands that one ask uncomfortable, yet realistic questions like "What if it doesn't work out?" "Am I prepared to lose that amount of my precious capital, or should I go lighter, or simply sit tight?" And "Am I disciplined enough to get out according to my plan?" It is this process of seeing what is—a process that eventually becomes speedier and ultimately second nature—that allows one to make informed trading decisions, stay in the game, and, most importantly, be a winner in the end.

MASTER TRADING TIP

Hope is a state of mind that the professional traders do not often partake of. Whenever they feel themselves hoping for something that does not exist, they know they are in trouble and immediately take the necessary steps to get out of the trade. Hope is something reserved for novices, those individuals devoid of knowledge and a concise trading plan. The master trader fully knows that selling hope is far more profitable than buying it. The options game, for instance, is largely a game of hope, so much so that we refer to it as the poor man's racetrack. It is not a coincidence that the biggest winners in the options game are those who *sell* options (hope), not those who buy the options (hope). When given the choice, the master trader will always be a seller of hope, rather than a buyer of it. It's more profitable.

SECRET #4: HOME RUNS ARE FOR LOSERS

The master trader knows that Mark McGwire and Sammy Sosa, the two baseball superstars who battled for Major League baseball's home-run record in 1998, would *not* make good day traders. Why? Because it is in their nature and their blood to go for the *big* one, the *long* ball, the all-mighty home run. And while that approach may work in baseball, it does *not* work in day trading. Professional traders, I mean the ones who have mastered the game, are consistent "singles" hitters. They only occasionally experience doubles. And when they get very lucky, which does happen every now and then, they may score a triple. But the master trader never goes for the gusto, or what some call the "big one." They are never looking to make a huge score. The push to score big, to hit the jackpot, is usually the occupation of a loser who, lacking skill, tries to stay or get back in the game via one big giant win. Going for home runs in day trading is typically an act of desperation, and just in case you did not know, it is characteristic of wisdom *not* to do desperate things. We see it all too often. A struggling day trader is down 3 days in a row, or 3 weeks in a row, maybe even 3 months in a row, and the pain is so unbearable that he or she starts to get desperate. The stocks hit their stops, and they're ignored because the trader is convinced that he or she can't take another loss. Or, the trader gets handed a $1 or $2 gain, but can't seem to make the decision to sell because it's not nearly enough to get back to breakeven. So the trader holds on (as if the stock knows he or she needs more) until the stock finally moves down to deliver another devastating loss. We've seen some traders so imprisoned by this vicious cycle that they don't realize they are speeding on a self-destructive kamikaze course that can only end in psychological and financial bankruptcy. We, as master traders, need the heart of a McGwire, accentuated by the smarts of a Pete Rose. We need the power of a Sosa, directed by the mind of a Rod Carew. In short, we need to become masters of the single, the base hit, the small but consistent gain. And if we do that right, every now and then that approach will reward us with an unexpected gift. A gift called the home run.

MASTER TRADING TIP

A big win is usually the hallmark sign of a novice. This is not to say that a large point gain in a stock is something that should be pooh-poohed. But every master trader knows that successful trading is all about consistency, and consistency is more attainable as a singles hitter than it is as a home run hitter. This is why they leave the homeruns to novices, as enticing lures to stay in the game, while they take the smaller but more consistent gains right from under them. Think about it. The ultimate masters of the game are specialists and market makers. Firms like Spear, Leads & Kellogg (SLKC), Goldman Sachs (GSCO), and Merrill Lynch (MLCO) represent the blue bloods of Wall Street, the titans of the game, and they are by far the most profitable groups in existence. Do you think for one moment that they are looking for a $27 gain in Amazon.com or a $14 score in AOL? The answer is no. Only novice traders seek such things. These masters' sole mission on each trade is to simply gain the spread, the difference between the bid price and ask price. These masters of Wall Street and their representatives preach the buy-and-hold approach, but any NASDAQ level II quote system will reveal that they do not practice the buy-and-hold approach. They are perpetually vying for ⅛ths and ¼s, and they have more money than the gods. In fact, they are the gods, the gods of Wall Street. If you believe the recent hype that short-term trading does not pay, perhaps you should take a few notes from the real masters.

SECRET #5: *MAKE* THE CHART AND THE CROWD WILL FOLLOW

It is estimated that the typical person experiences over 60,000 thoughts per day. Unfortunately, 95 percent of us have the very same thoughts today that we had yesterday, making us nothing more than bundles of conditioned responses. However, if one truly desires to excel as a trader, one must learn to think independently of others, to think completely "out of the box," if you will. As traders, there exists a dire need at times to be *proactive* versus *reactive*. The master traders create market reaction at times, they don't merely respond to it. In other words, they single handedly move markets when they can, not merely react to them. Those players who are using a trading approach that hinges largely on the constant movement and actions of others are really followers, not master traders. Acting confidently, independently, and with great certainty is a must in the high-stakes game of trading, but this only becomes possible if one is acting on one's own knowledge and conviction. Now don't get us wrong. To a certain extent, we do follow the lead of what we term "smart money." That's what charting is all about. But I experience far too many instances when a trader of mine has decided to do one thing and never does because he or she has received no confirmation from others. But once independent traders decide what their action will be, they should need no confirmation from others before leaping into action. Let's say a trader decides to buy XYZ above $40. The breakout comes. And instead of acting instantly as planned, the trader now thinks things like, "Well, XYX is now at $40⅛. Maybe I'll wait to see if the volume picks up." "Let's see if it can move up one more ⅛ before I commit." "Let's see if the market makers start to lift, or the size on the offer gets smaller." "I'll wait until Goldman Sachs (GSCO) leaves the offer." These are nothing but excuses not to act based on the need for others to confirm a decision. True master traders *become* the volume others are looking for. They help *create* that extra ⅛ with their own buy orders and they are not willing to let GSCO or the size of the offer weaken their resolve. They know what they want to do, and believe in it enough to leap into action whenever their sound approach gives them the OK. This is being independent. This is being a master, and it is key to not only being happy, but being profitable.

MASTER TRADING TIP

We teach our traders to be the *creators* of those market events that others are waiting for. "If the crowd is waiting for a stock to trade above $40 before they buy," we say, "then get the stock up to $40⅛." In other words, "make the chart!" This is true mastery and often requires many years of experience before it can be done, but we thought it would be beneficial for you to know how the professionals are playing the crowd. The idea is to ignite the action of your desire by getting to the crowd to take your lead. It can't always be done, but our master traders pull it off more often than some might think.

SECRET #6: ALL MAJOR STOCK MARKET AVERAGES LIE

Every serious market player should be aware of the fact that major stock market indices, such as the Dow Jones Industrial Average (DJIA), the S&P 500 Index (SPX), and the NASDAQ Composite Index (NASDQ), are very often inaccurate gauges of what is really happening behind the scenes. This fact is true, despite the enormous day-to-day focus they receive by the media. We certainly don't mean to suggest that these popular indices have no value at all. But the master trader, particularly the short-term one, knows he needs a sharper, more accurate picture than these broad averages are capable of delivering. We have witnessed market periods during which the SPX was off by only 12 percent, while the average stock trading on the NYSE was down some 36 percent. We have experienced pockets of time during which the NASDAQ 100 Index (NDX) was in negative territory by some 18 percent, while the average NASDAQ traded stock was off by a whopping 46 percent. The technical rule of thumb is that any decline greater than 20 percent signals a bear market crash. The numbers just stated show clearly that it is possible for the market to actually be in the tight grip of a vicious bear market while externally painting a much rosier picture to the world. This is living proof that major stock market averages do not always tell the truth about the overall market's condition. More often than one might expect, they flat out lie to the general public, and the master trader is forever bent on exposing their lies. How are they allowed to lie, you ask? These broad-based gauges can lie because stalwarts like Proctor & Gamble (PG), Merck (MRK), Microsoft (MSFT), Dell Computer (DELL), and the like dominate them. These large stocks are so heavily weighted in most averages that they often skew the numbers to one side in a very big way. The astute trader of today must be able to go "inside" of the market for a true read, to take an x-ray, if you will. Looking on the surface no longer cuts it. Relying exclusively on the most touted averages cannot be done, if today's traders want an accurate picture of the market's health. Today, the trader must know how to look deeper.

How the Master Trader Looks Deep Within

As short-term day traders who hold positions for minutes at a time on the short end to days on the long end, we've found it incredibly important to have a crystal-clear view of the current state of the broader market. As we've mentioned before, the major stock market averages do not and cannot provide that accurate view. So we rely on other technical items that zero in on the internal goings-on that give us our edge. One such technical indicator is the New York Stock Exchange TICK indicator ($TICK). This excellent intraday market gauge measures the number of NYSE stocks trading on an up tick versus the number currently trading on a down tick. If, for instance, the TICK reading is a +400, we know that the stocks currently trading on an up tick (being bought) outnumber those trading on a down tick (being sold) by 400. In other words, there is a lot more buying then selling taking place. If the TICK reading is –400, the reverse is true. Now, here's where this can be important. Let's say the DJIA is down some 120 points (negative), but the NYSE TICK is steadily rising and has crossed the +600 area. Would you be biased to the "sell side" or the "buy side?" If you were one of our in-house trading students, you'd be eagerly looking to position yourself in long (buy side) plays. While high-paid news anchors would be talking about the blood bath stocks are taking, your internal read would have you looking on the rosier side of things. This is just one indicator that helps the master day trader take accurate reads on the market, which in turn leads to accurate trading decisions. Other internal gauges used by our trading students are the NYSE TRIN indicator ($TRIN), better known as the ARMS Index, the S&P futures contract, the Utility Index, and U.S. bonds. All of these gauges help our master traders maintain an edge that most players only dream they could have. Looking deep within is an art that many fail to master, but only the trader capable of deciphering what is real (the truth) and what is not (a lie) will move to the high lands of trading accuracy. We accomplish a lot of this for the subscribers to our services, but it is a priceless ability all should work diligently to have for themselves.

SECRET #7: BUYING *AFTER* THE OPEN IS USUALLY BETTER

Despite the growing capability of buying and selling stock in the pre-open market, the master trader knows that it is usually best to initiate stock positions (buy) after the stock market opens. Allowing the market to open first gives the trader a chance to know more accurately where the stock will open, which in many cases allows for a more intelligent decision. This becomes more critical when the environment becomes treacherous because gaps in share prices (up and down) at the open can be an unwanted nemesis for traders. Placing your order before the open not only contributes to these gaps, it increases the odds that you will pay at or close to the highest price of the morning. By simply waiting a few moments to see where the stock will open, and what side the novice crowd is leaning on, a trader can measurably improve the accuracy of his or her entries. Also, *it should be remembered that stocks gapping open by more than 50 cents should be purchased based on our 30-minute gap rule.* See details in Chapter 14. Gaps always change the approach and this change can't be made if you don't wait a minute or so to allow the market to open.

MASTER TRADING TIP

Greater access to Instinet (INCA), and other ECNs (Electronic Communication Networks), has brought pre- and postmarket play to the ordinary individual. Not too long ago, this was a privilege enjoyed only by the powerful, the wealthy, and the wise. But despite the fact that professional trading systems offered by companies like Executioner.Com have made trading before the open commonplace, we encourage our traders to largely stay away from the practice. While there are times when buying before the opening bell can be lucrative, more often than not the picture being presented is a false one. A great many games are played during these "outside" times. Because the volume is so scarce, manipulation and legal forms of price fixing often serve as death traps to the novice. On balance, the very best action is to wait to see what is real, and that will not be revealed until the game has truly commenced. Remember, there are no gifts on Wall Street. If you're getting something you feel you don't deserve, you will not want it when you finally get the real scoop.

SECRET #8: IT USUALLY DOESN'T PAY TO TAKE PROFITS *BEFORE* THE OPEN

As mentioned in Secret #7, in today's age of electronic access, traders have the same ability to sell in pre- and postmarket hours as the professionals do. Through the use of the Executioner.Com's trading system, our in-house and remote traders can access the market several hours before the market opens and several hours after it closes. Soon, 24-hour trading will commence on all the exchanges, and conducting trades during any time period will be considered normal; however, until this occurs, we actually teach our traders to refrain from trading heavily in these extraneous time frames. We teach our traders to especially refrain from selling a stock before the open, if it is trading up in premarket activity. Why? Because we have found that stocks trading up in premarket activity generally trade a bit higher right after the open. This is because market makers on the NASDAQ will rarely reveal the true picture of the stock before the opening bell. And why should they? Wouldn't this be akin to them showing the world what their hand is before the game commences? Of course it would. My experience has taught me that if I am able to sell my merchandise (stock) before the rest of the crowd at a price perceived to be attractive, the price is really not that attractive. We must always remember that there are no gifts on Wall Street. Let's look at a quick example to further illustrate this point. Let's assume you own 1000 shares of WXYZ, which closed at a price of $20 the day before. About 30 minutes before the opening bell, you turn on CNBC and your level II execution system. You are pleased to find that WXYZ is being bid up $1.25 by several market makers. On your level II screen you see that you can hit Merrill Lynch's bid of $21.25, locking in a $1.25 gain or $1250. You think to yourself, "not bad for two clicks of a mouse button. Life is grand." Yes, life in this scenario is grand, but in most cases, life would become grander if you simply waited for the market to open. Staying in the trade until a few minutes after the opening bell will statistically result in a higher sell price. Of course this is not always the case, but it certainly is the case more often than not.

MASTER TRADING TIP

The master trader knows that most stocks being bid up in premarket activity trade a bit higher after the opening bell. They recognize that novice traders tend to place market buy orders before the opening bell, and these accumulated buy orders often add more fuel to the stock's upward rise. If the market, as measured by the S&P futures contract, is strong during premarket hours, we might yell out something like the following to our traders: "Hey guys! The market is strong and the WXYZ we bought yesterday is up very nicely in premarket trading! This means there are a lot of greedy novices who want what we have, and they are willing to pay up for it! This is why the market makers are adjusting the price upward. They want to make these novices pay, and so should we! Don't even think about selling your WXYZ until the market opens! That would be giving up your merchandise too cheaply. We will have plenty of novice-driven market orders to get us even better pricing!"

Note: Whenever we have a trader, who is holding a rather large but profitable position that is trading up in premarket activity, we instruct him to sell half before the bell, with the idea of letting the rest ride into the open. This is an excellent alternative if the premarket gain you have starts to burn a hole in your pocket. *Tip:* When in doubt about which one of two possible actions should be taken, try to do both. The truth is usually in the middle.

SECRET #9: 11:15 TO 2:15 EST IS THE WORST POSSIBLE TIME TO TRADE

Many day traders, those active market players who trade numerous times per day, do not realize that there are specific times of the day during which the odds of success drop precipitously. And some of these pockets of time are quite lengthy. Once such period is 11:15 to 2:15 EST or so. We often refer to this 3-hour time frame as the *midday doldrums*, because stocks tend to settle into a very distinct nondirectional mode during this time period. It is during this pocket that many day traders get whipped around. False starts and short-lived breakouts proliferate, while fake-outs are a frequent occurrence. In all actuality, it is the first part of the day and the latter part of the day that have always offered day traders the very best trading odds. This is why we tell our traders to play the middle of the day lightly, with the idea of only scalping stocks for small change. While this only applies to active day traders, those who want to instantly eliminate 50 percent or more of their intraday losses can do so by simply sidestepping this unpredictable period. Try it. We dare you.

MASTER TRADING TIP

Master traders recognize that the most lucrative trading opportunities often occur in the first part of the day and the latter part of the day. While they will often still dabble here and there, they are fully aware that the midday doldrums period requires a change in their approach. Why is 11:15 to 2:15 typically dull and uneventful? Because that's when a good part of Wall Street goes to lunch and hands the controls over to their flunkies. Their flunkies have less authority to make big bets or run with things, and it is not until the big guys get back that stocks start to regain some life and direction. Whenever I reveal this fact at my seminars, I invariably get someone who says, "But Oliver, 11:15 to 2:15 EST is a very long lunch. Are you sure its because they are at lunch?" My answer is always the same. "If you've ever seen a group of market makers, I don't think you'd be asking that question. When we say, "at 2:15 the big guys come back," we mean that literally. Their lunches are big and *they* are big. *Note:* This is a generalization that is becoming less true today, but the power traders on Wall Street are notorious for being overweight. Now you know why.

SECRET #10: IT'S ALWAYS DARKEST BEFORE THE DAWN

We've got a dark secret to reveal to you. Something many of our followers would never expect. In a sense, it's an admission. One that communicates a very important message to all active traders. Every time we've decided to list all short plays in our daily newsletter, the market actually quickly reversed back to the upside. That's right. Reversed. And rather sharply at that. Now, many may not find our little secret comforting at all. In fact, there was a time when this revelation would have made us feel somewhat embarrassed. Today, we've either grown too callous to feel the sting of embarrassment, or we've simply grown up. At any rate, the question I know you're asking is "Why?" Why is it that with all our knowledge, skill, and talent, our timing on the market is usually wrong whenever we see only short plays? Well, in reality it's quite simple. A long list of short plays testifies to how negative things have become. Note here that "become" is the operative word. The market is not *becoming* ugly when we recommend only shorts. It has already *become* ugly. In other words, *it's usually the darkest just before dawn.* If the market has gone through an extended period of selling, at some point things will look so bad that not a single leading stock will look even close to a long play. And that is when the astute short-term trader will recognize that the crack of dawn—a relief rally—is close at hand. We've decided to reveal this because the "darkest before dawn" concept is an important one to know. It is something that every master trader we know is fully aware of, and it will forever keep you watchful. It will prevent you from committing too much to one train of thought, which, as you know, can be harmful when dealing with the market. *Tip:* The master trader reserves a small portion of uncertainty at all times, even when things appear very certain.

MASTER TRADING TIP

Whenever things seem the most certain, the master trader knows they are extremely uncertain. Whenever things seem too one-sided, the master trader knows to consider the opposite side. It does not even matter that he or she is the one doing the seeing. The trader has learned that the market is nothing more than a reflection of what the crowd is experiencing. And when the crowd has already experienced a great degree of pain and anguish, nothing, nothing at all, will look appealing. But oddly enough, that will be just when things are about to improve. Ugliness and sloppiness in the market can only be caused by those who have already sold. Get it? *Already sold.* Once the selling is over, once the darkness is complete, the buying part of the cycle is right around the corner. It is *always* darkest before dawn. Whenever things look their worst, you are likely to be in the final hour of darkness. Never forget this simple fact.

SECRET #11: WALL STREET GURUS WILL ALWAYS BE WRONG

There have been times when some of Wall Street's top market strategists called for the end of financial civilization, as we know it. During these times, gloom and doom were being touted by such a large chorus of professionals that even the most jaded market supporters started to grow grizzly hair. In each case, the market seemed to laugh in the face of these gloom and doom calls. By now, you'd think these gurus would have figured out why their timing is typically so poor. Perhaps if they realized "it's always darkest before dawn," the fact revealed in Secret #10, they'd have a clue. But let me reveal why the market almost *has* to reverse if a large number of these professionals start yelling "fire in the theatre" at the same time. Wall Street market strategists have a responsibility to inform their firm's major clients of their views ahead of time. In fact, responsible market strategists would not dare go public with a bearish market call until most of their clients have either sold out or at least repositioned for the expected event. In other words, these gurus only go public with their bearish calls *after* they feel their clients have prepared for the doom. No wonder the market always seems at odds with these guys. All the selling from their big clients (mutual and hedge funds, etc.) has already taken place. Who do they think is left to sell, my grandpa Bill? Maybe it's the warm-hearted custodian in my office building who owns two mutual funds that they fear. They just don't get it. My grandpa and the hard-working custodian I know don't listen to them. They don't even know they exist. They simply stay put in the market. And even if they didn't, don't these "experts" realize it's *their* clients they need to fear? I guess they don't. That's why the market is always laughing at them. Can you hear it? It's still laughing?

MASTER TRADING TIP

The master trader knows that whenever a large group of Wall Street's most-watched analysts start looking for trouble, the reverse will likely take place. We know some traders who profit enormously by betting in this contrary way using S&P futures contracts and Equity Index options. The nature of fear and greed works the same for the gurus as it does for the novices. It's just that the gurus will be less willing to admit it. This is why the market laughs especially when it proves them wrong. Learn to always look for the reverse when Wall Street, as a whole, is thinking in one direction, because if and when the professional crowd is proven wrong, the move in the opposite direction will be violent. When the big boys are forced to scramble, the market really moves.

SECRET #12: PLAYING EARNINGS IS A GAME FOR NOVICES

If I have said it once, I've said it a thousand times. Earnings reports don't move stocks. It's the expectation of earnings that moves stocks. Too many novice market players miss this point. And because of it, they find themselves frequently perplexed as to why some stocks actually rise on bad earnings and some fall on good earnings. The key point every master trader knows is that the market is a discounting mechanism. It will attempt to anticipate what each report will say. The *anticipation* of positive results will help bid stocks up in advance of their reports and the *anticipation* of negative results will cause many stocks to drop before their reports. The master traders also know that those stocks, which have risen very sharply in advance of their reports, are the most susceptible to a decline when the report is out, even if it is positive. Why? Because the positive nature of the report was expected and lacked the element of surprise. Of course, if the report comes in negative right after the stock has been bid up, the stock will plummet. The reverse of this scenario is also true.

MASTER TRADING TIP

The master trader is always looking to sell positive facts. Why? Because facts, such as a company's earnings results for a prior quarter, are events staged and packaged for the public. These eagerly awaited facts almost always cause large crowds to act in one direction. This is why the master trader, who tries never to act *with* the crowd, will often sell positive facts against the crowd, especially when they are positive facts that were expected to be positive. Buying during the anticipation period in order to sell to those who buy during the factual period is the modus operandi of a true master trader. This approach does not always capture the biggest gains, but as we've said before, home runs are for losers.

SECRET #13: PAYING UP FOR STOCKS BETTERS THE ODDS

One of the most frequently asked questions regarding our stock market approach is, "Why do most of your trading strategies call for buying a stock *above* the current price?" "Why not buy the stock exactly where it is, which would result in a cheaper price?" Despite covering this topic in much greater detail in a later chapter, I will attempt to answer these questions in two parts. First, it should be clear that we specialize in two forms of trading. We are professional *swing traders* who focus the bulk of our efforts on discovering stocks that are on the verge of a near-term multiday move (1 to 5 days). We are also professional *intraday* traders, who focus on discovering stocks on the verge of a micromove over the next few moments. Obviously, with such short-term time horizons, we can't afford to tie up huge chunks of our capital in stocks, which may linger on the launch pad for days, weeks, or even months. As a result, we demand a stock to demonstrate its ability to move in the desired direction *before* we jump on for the ride. If it fails to show the strength, power, and tenacity required to take out the many sellers *above* it, it gets eliminated from our consideration. *Tip:* Remember that all stocks are bad unless they go up. Secondly, and just as important, our approach of buying a stock on strength has saved us more money than any other trading tactic (besides the stop loss) in our arsenal. I cannot even count the times a stock in which we were interested failed to rise above our buy point, only to close down $2, $3, or sometimes even $4 on the day. I can say with great confidence that if we were in the habit of buying stocks at the market, right at the open, as many novices do, we'd be a little bit poorer today. Now, some people may say that we are wrong when a stock fails to meet our buy criteria and subsequently moves to the downside. However, we regard ourselves as being absolutely right when this occurs. Keep in mind that each one of our buy recommendations is really saying, "We like XYZ, but *only* if it can show strength enough to trade above this price." In short, our specific "buy-above-the-current-price" strategy saves us from a lot of unnecessarily hefty losses. Isn't knowing exactly "how" to buy just as important as knowing "what" to buy? You bet it is.

MASTER TRADING TIP

The master swing trader, one who looks for 1- to 5- or 10-day moves, typically looks to buy a desired stock once it trades above the prior day's high. The master microtrader or day trader looks to buy once the desired stock takes out the high of a 2-, 5- or 15-minute bar on the price chart. The master microtrader knows that picking the exact bottom would be more profitable, but has learned, often the hard way, that the only traders able to consistently pick off the bottom are liars. So, the master trader lets those who think there are supermen or superwomen waste their money away in a futile attempt to catch the bottom. The master microtrader simply waits for the stock to signal that the coast is clear. That signal is the stock's ability to trade above the last period's high as described earlier. Only when it has gained the strength to do that does the master trader consider risking his family's financial future. *Note:* We thoroughly cover the art of properly entering stocks in a later chapter.

SECRET #14: THE BUY-LOW SELL-HIGH METHOD IS WRONG FOR DAY TRADERS

It has always fascinated me that when it comes to playing the market, whatever we find psychologically easy to do is almost guaranteed to be the wrong thing to do. I have found that in no other endeavor is this more so, which is precisely why trading the markets successfully is such a difficult undertaking. Let's take the universally accepted concept of buying low and selling high. This approach to the market has been touted as the basis of correct market play for many decades. "Buy low, sell high." It's simple. It's basic. It's succinct. It's apparently true. But it's also terribly wrong, at least most of the time. Why? Because buying low typically entails purchasing a stock that is going in the exact opposite direction (down) from the most desired direction (up). When we take time to apply even a cursory level of intelligence to this concept, we quickly discover how silly it sounds. In order to buy low, one must focus on buying stocks that are going down, while our true desire is for them to go up. Does that make sense? Would we entertain, even for a brief moment, the idea of taking, let's say, a train that is going in the exact opposite direction from our desired location? Wouldn't every 6-year-old be able to tell us that going west, first, in order to go east is a tremendous waste of time, especially when one can simply start the journey going east? Why then don't most people apply the same simple wisdom to trading or investing? Why not simply buy stocks that are already doing what we want them to do, going up? Why? Because buying low is appealing to our nature. It's comfortable. It sounds right and feels good. Hey, after all, isn't paying less the American way? Yes, but when it comes to the market, it leads to wasted time, money, and potential profits. Now granted, I may have oversimplified this matter a bit, but not much. Concentrating on stocks that have already demonstrated their ability to rise is intelligent trading and investing. Focusing on stocks that are doing what we *don't* want them to do, in hopes that they will soon do what we *want* them to do, is nothing more than guessing and gambling.

MASTER TRADING TIP

All master traders, particularly those who day trade, know that a stock is not good unless it's going up. Short-term traders, however astute, do not have the luxury of time. When they enter a trade, they must be reasonably sure of attaining their profit goal with a very minimal amount of time. Time for the investor is a friend, but for the master short-term trader it is an archenemy. While buying a stock that is headed down may turn profitable, master traders learn to wait for the stock to head in the desired direction before jumping on with all their might. This is not to say that master traders buy late, as much as it is to say they buy smart. They are not interested in guessing or gambling. They simply know that jumping on board a train that has just begun its move toward the destination of profitability is far smarter than trying to luck out on those train that they think will eventually move in the desired direction.

SECRET #15: KNOWING WHAT'S NEXT CAN MAKE YOU RICH

Many short-term traders erroneously assume that the macroview of the market (intermediate to long term) has little relevance to, or impact on, the short-term trader's world. While the macroview is certainly not as important to the trader as it is to the investor, to think it has no importance is a mistake. We must not forget that a top-down approach to the market (macro to micro) can help us devise our short-term strategies with a greater degree of intelligence. For instance, let's say our view is that the market, once cooled off a bit, is likely to regain a big portion of its lost luster. Let's further assume that we used this view to come up with specific sectors that will likely respond very favorably if we happen to be right. The short-term trader would then want to apply a great deal of focus to the leading stocks in those groups, with the idea of building a list of potential plays to take when the environment does turn. You see, a big part of winning at the game of trading lies in the ability to capitalize on what is happening *now*. But the greatest rewards will always go to the players who can build a strategy based on what lies *beyond* the now. Knowing how to profit from current occurrences is a must, no doubt. But traders who can use their macroviews to prepare for what will come *next* will never have a problem making big money in the market. The very best traders are constantly asking two questions:

1. How do I profit from what is happening in the present?
2. How do I prepare myself for the opportunities that will likely happen in the near future?

The first question (the micro part) provides for decent day-to-day gains in the market. But the big money is always made with the second question (the macro part). Why? Because the correct answer to question 2 is what provides for being early. And as you all know, it's the early bird who catches the worm. Of course, our challenge is to be the bird and *not* the worm.

MASTER TRADING TIP

We have always taught a dual approach to trading, one that looks to earn a healthy living, the other that looks to build wealth. Position trades and swing trades are designed to build wealth, while day trades and scalp help a trader earn a day-to-day living. The trader who becomes a master at both styles of market play will never have many financial worries.

8
CHAPTER

10 LESSONS FOR THE MASTER TRADER

LESSON #1: CASH IS KING WHEN THE STREET GETS BLOODY

It is said that a timid person is frightened *before* the danger, a coward *during* the danger, and a courageous person *after* the danger. If this is true, I suppose we as traders fit into the latter category. We are rarely frightened before or during the danger. More often, we find ourselves feeling the pain of a sloppy market *after* the danger has already struck. But this is not the case for the professional community. For instance, we have found that most young mutual fund managers get frightened *during* the danger, which would make them cowards if we take this statement to heart. As advisors to many money managers and mutual fund companies, we speak to those in charge of vast sums of money each day. And we can tell you for sure that whenever the market goes through a rough period of uncertainty, a great deal of panic and bewilderment sets in for these young guys (the average age of a U.S. mutual fund manager is under 30). During one sharp market downdraft, a young fund manager who seeks out our daily take on the market couldn't have summed up the sheer fright of these professionals any better when he said, "Oliver, I am really, really very nervous *this* time. I don't know what it is, but I suddenly feel like a pizza on the way to a starving person." When we hear things like that from professionals, we can't help but get nervous for the public, because these young guys actually hold in their hands the financial futures of many Americans. But the scariest thing of all is the fact that these fund managers, who have billions of dollars in their control, only know how to do one thing. In other words, they have only one market tool. One methodology. One single approach. They only know how *to buy more.* Why is that? Because it has worked like a charm during most of the 1990s. For almost an entire decade, if not longer, buying more stock on the way down was the thing to do; the thing that delivered; the tactic that helped create fortunes and the method that built comfortable lifestyles. And most importantly, it was easy. But the hard part will come when the market truly starts to sour, because we're not so sure at that time that the "buy more" approach will still be a viable approach. But in all fairness to these young professionals, what else is there to do? What action do you take when you own 2 million shares of a collapsing stock? Do you sell, *adding* to the panic and chaos? Or do you boldly look chaos in the eye and buy more? Do you just sit idle, hoping and praying that all will soon be well, as your assets erode hour by hour, day by day? Or do you get up and go for broke? It's a dilemma, my friends. One that you and I should feel fortunate not to be involved with. All I can say is "thank heavens I'm a trader." As traders, you and I don't have to grapple with such concerns. When we see a stock which we feel has good odds of moving higher over the next 2 to 5 days, we buy it. But realizing that we don't live in a perfect world, we bring along an exit plan, a bailout point that we call a stop. This is not being a coward, this is being smart, and it's being realistic. You see, many novice traders get upset when the protective stops that they have placed on their trades get triggered. While triggered stops can be frustrating, they should be viewed as welcome friends, not as enemies. Think about it. The purpose of the stop loss is to protect. To save. To safeguard against disaster. What's even more important is what they force the trader to do. Stops, triggered ones that is, force the trader to "raise" cash that will be very necessary to have when a falling market finally does bottom out, and opportunities begin to proliferate. You see, the person who has the most cash at the bottom wins. *In other words, cash is king when the streets get bloody, and being stopped out of certain plays on the way down helps to prepare us for the next round of opportunities.* This is not something to be sad about. On the contrary, it is something that we should be glad about. Just guess how many fund managers wish they had the luxury of a protective stop. Guess how many wish they were not locked into the buy-more-and-pray approach. Stops are a benefit. A privilege. Perfect they are not. That is for sure. But they are the best form of protection we have. So appreciate them, and most of all, use them. They are one of the few things that are only available to individual traders.

LESSON #2: TIME DIVERSIFICATION MINIMIZES MARKET RISK

One of the questions we're asked very often is, "Should I buy every stock on your daily pick list?" The answer is almost always a resounding *no!* Here's why. First of all, buying every recommendation would likely take financial resources greater than most individuals possess. Secondly, and far more importantly, buying all your picks today, for instance, will increase your odds of becoming what we refer to as "a victim of the times." What this means is that individuals who deplete all their capital on one day's picks become totally dependent on how that *one* specific day performs. What if an unbelievably dynamic opportunity presents itself 1 or 2 days later? Where would the money come from, which is now all tied up in say, Monday? Even worse, what if our picks "stink up the joint" on the very day you decide to buy *everything?* We encourage our swing traders to spread their picks over a 1- or 2-week period. For example, a $30,000 account owned by a developing swing trader might be put to work by investing a quarter, or $7500, twice a week. At the end of a 2-week period, the entire $30,000 will have been put to work. Now here's the beauty of a plan such as this. By the time the trader is investing the final lot of $7500, he or she will more than likely be selling out of the first lot, and maybe even the second, if swing trading. This methodology guarantees that you will always have funds available for those occasional "major" opportunities. And don't you dare think that two plays a week are not enough action during your developmental phase. It should be remembered that every play is comprised of two major actions—the entry *and* the exit—not to mention the other items involving the management of the trade. In reality, the person who plays four times a week has to make a total of eight decisions. And we're willing to bet that eight decisions will be of a higher quality than say, fifteen. Try it! I think you'll like it.

LESSON #3: BUYING VERSUS ACCUMULATING

Stocks making bottoms must be handled differently than stocks that are well into their established trends. It is our belief that traders should buy stocks that are trading in up trends, while investors should accumulate those that are in the process of bottoming. There is a major difference. *Buying* implies a one-time purchase at one specific price, while *accumulating* involves multiple purchases spread out over multiple time frames and prices. The latter approach provides for two forms of diversification: time diversification and price diversification. The only other form of diversification that exists is stock diversification, which calls for spreading your bets over multiple issues. While we are not very big promoters of stock diversification, applying all three forms can prove beneficial at times, particularly when finding an intermediate to long-term play in which to invest.

LESSON #4: THE ULTIMATE DECISION-MAKING TOOL

It is our belief that far too many traders overemphasize the importance of the overall market and its potential direction. This tendency is largely due to the media, which has to report a more macro view of the financial climate. While market climate and direction have their place, direction should not be entertained at the expense of proper trading technique and proper money management. This is why we focus primarily on providing our subscribers and private students with helpful trading tips, which in our opinion is far more valuable than giving them our view of what the market "might" do. This is certainly not to say that market direction is unimportant. In fact, there are times when having an accurate assessment of the general market will mean the difference between winning consistently and winning only sporadically. However, the shorter one's time frame, the less important macro or overall market analysis becomes. Why is this so? Because short-term price moves (up or down) can be found in virtually any market environment. But far more important than this point is the fact that market direction should never be a trader's ultimate decision maker. One should almost never decide to liquidate an existing position on the basis of what a specific index is doing or not doing. The ultimate decision maker must be your stop loss order or your predefined sell point, not the market. Let's look at it this way. If the Dow is down 200 points and your stock hits its stop loss, the master trader *sells!* If the Dow is up 200 points and the stock hits its stop loss, the master trader still *sells!* Where does market analysis come into the picture? Nowhere. Not if the ultimate decision maker is your stop loss. So while market direction does have its place when considering entering a new position, if you are already in a stock, it should be secondary to your initial sell strategy. This rigid approach does require very strict discipline, but if adhered to, the trader will be richly rewarded with very small losses.

LESSON #5: SELLING THE DOGS AND BUYING THE DOLLS

Many people run their business affairs with a very high degree of professionalism but fail miserably when it comes to handling their trading/investing program in a financially sound manner. I know a very prominent retail magnate who rids his stores of poor selling items faster than you and I can say "Pristine" on a profitable trading day. These "dogs," as he calls them, get dramatically reduced in price; and once they're sold (usually at a fraction of the original cost), he quickly puts the money to better use by buying more of his best-selling merchandise. This simple, but powerful concept of quickly selling his losers (dogs) to buy more of his winners (dolls) has made him a millionaire many times over. But ask this shrewd entrepreneur to get rid of one of his nonperforming stock market dogs, and you'll get a heated argument invariably sprinkled with phrases (or sayings) such as "but now it's really a bargain" and "I have to buy more." In his successful retail concern, he quickly does away with the "dogs" that fail to produce positive results. However, in his investment concern, he reverts to buying more of his "dogs," while grabbing at every little profit that his winners produce. Does this make sense? To him it does. But I'm working on him. Our concern at the moment is you. If you're finding yourself unable to take advantage of new opportunities because your money is tied up in old, nonperforming stocks, consider having a garage sale. Be determined to keep your money working for you in the best merchandise available. Let's leave the dogs to my friend.

LESSON #6: BRAINS OR A BULL MARKET?

Being able to profitably capitalize on negative market environments places the trader head and shoulders above the rest of the pack. Why? Because most market players can only experience gains in the most bullish of markets, but totally lack the ability to adequately handle themselves when the environment turns sour. I call this "confusing brains for a bull market." Please be aware that it requires no talent whatsoever to make money when 90 percent of all stocks are rising, but a trader's true talent will certainly be revealed when the market turns ugly, and agility, pinpoint accuracy, and above-average stock picking become necessary requirements. To find out the true colors of your broker, financial advisor, mutual fund manager, and/or newsletter writer, you must monitor how they fare when nearly everyone else on planet Earth is losing money. We have demonstrated our ability to shine in these environments. We suggest that you demand the same from all your "paid" advisors, unless of course they're willing to forego the "paid" part.

LESSON #7: RATING NEWSLETTERS AND OTHER ADVISORS

There are times when the stock picks in our daily newsletter, the *Pristine Day Trader*, will put in a phenomenal weekly performance. During these times, our weekly performance review might state something similar to the following: "Fifteen of the twenty plays rose $2 or more, offering short-term traders more than enough opportunities to make money." While actual performance will always vary from trader to trader, there is no doubt that any week warranting the preceding statement will bring tons of e-mail and numerous congratulatory notes from our subscribers. But is this the proper way to judge the overall success of our (or anyone else's) advisory letter? The answer, my friends, is "no." Absolutely not. Far too many market participants fall for this type of hype. Yes, these statements are true, but the proper way to determine the effectiveness of any service is to look at the "losers." The important questions to ask are "How do these so-called experts *lose*? How do their losing trades compare to their winning trades?" "And are their losses consistently smaller than their winners, or will I suffer devastating blows to my capital following their advice?" This is how you gauge the effectiveness of newsletters, advisors, mutual funds, systems, etc. It's how they *lose* that counts, not how they win. In the best of all environments, almost everyone will be able to show you winners. But only the true professionals will be able to show you consistently small losses during the rough times. Want to become an outstanding trader? Then learn to lose professionally. Winning will take care of itself. Remember, the professional loss is always a small one.

LESSON #8: TIME EQUALS MONEY

A recent study revealed that we, as parents, spend less than 60 seconds a day with each child when they are the most receptive to valuable input, right before they go to sleep. This is not only unfortunate, it's a high crime as far as I'm concerned, the victim of which is not only the child but the parent(s) too. While it is very easy to recognize the tremendous importance of time well spent with our children, life and its myriad details do, at times, make it difficult to do. But difficulty is not, and cannot ever be, an acceptable excuse. Not regarding our children. They're just too important. Any caring parent would agree with that. But let's turn our thoughts to trading. My question to you today is, "How much time are you spending each day developing yourself to be a better trader?" If the child's mind is most receptive after the activities of each day, then the trader's mind is the most receptive after the market's close. Are you spending quality time after the closing bell, collecting your thoughts, reviewing your actions, analyzing your trades, preparing for tomorrow, and/or taking notes in your personal journal? Or are you one of those traders who dash out of your office, your home, or your chair at 4:01 p.m. (EST) like a wild bat out of hell, looking for relief? Most would-be traders don't readily recognize that becoming a successful trader requires hard work. It's a long evolutionary process that takes place ever so gradually over time. Most do not recognize that spending quality time reviewing their actions at the end of each day helps season the mind and fatten the purse. Frequently committed mistakes are left alone to rob the trader of his or her future, because less than 60 seconds a day is spent developing into a better trader for tomorrow. If you want to be a winner, you must spend time planting the seeds of improvement each and every day. Time, in this case, really does equal money. Spend a little on your future.

LESSON #9: WINNERS MAKE IT HAPPEN; LOSERS LET IT HAPPEN

It has always been my belief that a successful life is made, created not found. So too do I believe that those who enjoy success in their trading life have, through their own work, struggle, and relentless effort, *made* it happen. The problem for many is that they think success is simply going to occur without really earning it. Somehow, they miss the point that winning is the end result of a long process of trying to make it happen. In short, "Winners *make* it happen; Losers *let* it happen." Take aspiring day traders who spend their whole day with the market between the hours of 9:30 a.m. and 4:00 p.m. EST. Perhaps they trade with others in a trading office like ours, or they spend the trading day at home. During this time, they concentrate, focus, look continuously for plays, enter some trades, exit others, etc., and minutes, if not seconds, after 4:00 p.m. EST, they're gone. Poof! These want-to-be traders unfortunately think success in trading is just going to happen between 9:30 a.m. and 4:00 p.m. EST. They do nothing in between to make it happen. Yet they expect the wins to pour in just because they sit down at 9:29 a.m. EST (1 minute before the open) to trade. Life, particularly a successful one, does not work that way. In order to make success happen, traders must work, study, review, practice, analyze, dissect, ponder, think, write, memorize, categorize, and organize hours after the close or hours before the open. If success is truly what they want, traders must prepare for it in the cool of the evening and in the early hours of the morning when the world and the market are not yet watching. Then the wheels of progress will have already been set in motion, by the time 9:30 a.m. EST has rolled around. But many traders delude themselves. They think because they are *with* the market during trading hours that the market is *with* them. Wrong! The market is funny. It yields only to those who study and spend quality time with it outside of trading hours. *That's* how you make it happen. *That's* how you win.

LESSON #10: USING THE POWER OF PROMISES

Recently, I took the mandatory tour of my daughter's new elementary school. She starts kindergarten this upcoming September. What an experience it was. I was amazed at how much things have changed since I was in kindergarten. No hard wooden rulers used to make little knuckles into *big* knuckles. The rulers I saw at my daughter's school were made of a much softer material. No teachers were trained in the art of jujitsu to apply on mischievous students. They seemed kind, wise, and very nurturing. The books were all new, and every instructor, including the teaching assistants, spoke two or more languages, fluently. I must admit all of this dazzled me to no end. Shoot! I was sold as soon as I saw sponge rulers. But what struck me the most was how simple, yet wonderfully effective some of the new teaching methods are today. In passing through one class, I happened to glance up at the wall. It was plastered with personal promises made by each child in the class. Jimmy said, "I promise to use my hands for only good things." Mary said, "I promise to use kind words." Betsy said, "I promise to ask permission before taking things." And my personal favorite came from Joey who said, "I promise to keep my mouth to myself." Oh, there were many, many more. But this simple method of teaching correct behavior struck me, not only as a father, but as a trader. Why? Because trading successfully ultimately comes down to proper behavior. And as an instructor and teacher of traders, it is necessary for me to find ways to promote the *right* behavior in my students.

How many of us have made promises to ourselves, real ones, about our trading conduct? How many have actually written down things like, "I promise to never chase a stock more than ⅜." "I promise to always adhere to my predetermined stops." And, "I promise to never place a market order before the open." What about this one. "I promise to always consider the risk before going after the reward." And let's not forget these. "I promise to accept responsibility for each one of my trades." "I promise to write down the lesson learned from each losing play." "I promise to keep tabs on my two biggest shortcomings as a trader." As strange as it may seem, there is a power that accompanies personal promises, especially if they are written down. Somehow, the soul seems to recognize that a crime against the self has been committed when a promise is violated. They work. Why not make some today? Write them down. Look at them each day. Why? Because knowing what's right is not always enough. Sometimes it takes making a "blood" promise to yourself that you will do what you know is right. Knowing and doing are often two entirely different things.

9

FINAL WORDS OF WISDOM FROM A TRUE MASTER

EIGHT ELEMENTARY LESSONS FOR LIFE AND TRADING—BY MOTHER

As an intent observer with an insatiable thirst for knowledge, I consider myself to be a very astute student of life. As a result, I've managed to learn some very valuable lessons in my life. But after recently contemplating this subject, I realized that everything I needed to know about trading I learned from my mother before I was 10. Here are just a few things she taught me as a small child.

Lesson 1: It is OK to fall, as long as you learn from the process of getting up. To this very day, I preach and practice the art of learning from my trading errors. Each of my trading losses serves as a springboard to a higher level of trading mastery.

Lesson 2: Always recognize what others are feeling. This is precisely why my partner, Greg Capra, is such a successful trader. He always seeks to understand what the other traders in a particular stock are feeling. Pain for other traders can mean opportunity for you. Why? *Because successful trading is nothing more then buying stock cheaply from those in pain, and selling it expensively to those who are greedy.* To be really astute at the game of trading, you must know what other traders in the market are feeling (pain or greed). Gaining that ability can make you rich. Thanks Mom.

Lesson 3: No matter how bad things are today, tomorrow will present another opportunity to get it right. As a trader, you cannot bring the baggage of yesterday into the possibilities of today. The residue left from a prior losing trade must be wiped clean before you take the next. Otherwise, you are doomed.

Lesson 4: Know why you are making every action you make. Never make an action (buy or sell) from the emotional state of fear or greed. It is imperative that we, particularly as traders, understand that intelligence lies between these two emotions. In other words, there is a gap between fear and greed, and that is where all our actions must spring from. To this very day, I will never sell a stock if I'm feeling fear. At times I lose more money as a result of this, but more often than not, I fare better by making sure I wait for a moment of intelligence to emerge.

Lesson 5: Never take yourself too seriously. Whenever I am on a big winning streak, I hear those words ring in my ear. Despite the fact that I win in the market nearly every day of my life, all of my in-house traders will attest to the fact that I am never too serious when I trade. In fact I'm silly, but this is because of Mom.

Lesson 6: Only fight battles you can win. From this wisdom, I learned to pick my stocks, my entries, and my exits very carefully. Whenever I enter a stock, for instance, I feel comfortable that it is on my side, ready to work for me. I try never to fight the market, because that is a battle I know I can't win. When I realize I have made a choice that conflicts with the market, I exit and immediately align myself with the power. In the Bible, David may have won his battle against Goliath. But let me tell you this. In the market, Goliath *always* wins.

Lesson 7: Life is not something to conquer but to befriend. This lesson from my Mom taught me to work *with* the market, not against it, to view it as an ally that can enrich, not as an adversary that can take away. The market is not Frankenstein. It is a friend. It is not a killer of dreams. It is a liberator of them. In short, the market is the field of all possibilities.

Lesson 8: A loss does not always make you less. Sometimes, losing is winning. Far too many day traders miss this valuable point. If I get stopped out of a stock for a $1 loss, and the stock drops another $2, I have not lost. I've won. The art of winning is determined by how intelligently you lose.

Take these lessons from my Mom. She would be delighted if you used them in your daily living. I would be content if you just used them in your daily trading. But I will say that they are lessons that have served me well in every corner of my life. I hope they serve you well too.

TOOLS AND TACTICS FOR THE MASTER TRADER

Developing the Arsenal of a Master Trader

DEVELOPING THE ARSENAL OF A MASTER TRADER

In the following chapters, we will reveal a few simple tools and tactics that will greatly aid the master trader in understanding how the market works. The following techniques form the cornerstone of Pristine's approach to professionally trading the market. These are some of the same tactics and techniques we have taught to professional traders all over the world. After gaining a clear understanding of these building blocks, the trader will never again be confused and not know what to do. In fact, once the following tools and tactics are mastered, the trader will rarely find him or herself on the wrong side of the market. And we are sure you realize, 65 percent of all trading losses can be attributed to being on the wrong side of the market. Let's move to the next step, which is building a repertoire of trading tools and tactics that will help hasten your trek to trading mastery.

10

MARKET TIMING TOOLS AND TACTICS

There is an old Wall Street adage, which says, "The market is always right." And while most so-called words of wisdom regarding the stock market are useless at best, this is one that rings very true, particularly for the short-term trader. Being caught on the wrong side of a major market move can be very distressing, but failing to admit the error (arguing with the market, in other words) can result in a trader being taken out of this wonderful game, forever. This is why every would-be successful stock trader must learn how to correctly "read" the market, "feel" its mood, and "anticipate" its very next whim. Despite comments and views to the contrary, part of our survival as traders will always depend on our ability to properly align ourselves with the market's power. It must be realized that knowing what the "will" of the market is, and how to give one's self over to it, promotes long-term trading success.

Now, we will be the first to admit that short-term market timing is a skill that is very difficult to attain, but there are several market-timing tools that can help you be right, much more often than wrong. In the following pages, we'll be revealing several of the highly reliable tools and tactics we use to accurately assess the market's short-term direction. As most of our followers know, we at Pristine are human, and do make our share of mistakes. But thanks to the following market-timing tools, we aren't human very often. We will now attempt to pass on these simple, but very effective, timing tools to you.

MARKET TOOL #1: S&P FUTURES (S&P)

S&P FUTURES DESCRIPTION

The Chicago Mercantile Exchange is home to one of the largest and most liquid financial instruments in the world, the Standard & Poor's 500-stock Index Future. This instrument is quite different from its cash equivalent, which is the S&P 500 Index. The S&P futures contract, distinct from its cash equivalent, allows large traders and investors (usually institutional in size) to bet on the future direction of the overall market. For this reason alone, it is carefully watched by every sophisticated economic and market professional in existence. The master trader, particularly the master intraday trader, would not even dream of trading without it as a guide. Here are some interesting facts of which each trader should be aware.

HOW THE MASTER TRADER INTERPRETS THE S&P FUTURES

- The S&P is a key barometer of the overall market.
- The S&P often leads the direction of the entire market.
- The S&P is a leading indicator for many individual stocks like America Online (AOL), Cisco Systems (CSCO), Dell Computer (DELL), Microsoft Corporation (MSFT), etc. In other words, intraday moves in the S&P futures contract often precede similar moves in the preceding stocks. This fact frequently offers the alert intraday trader some interesting scalping opportunities.
- We monitor the S&P futures contract using 2-, 5- and 15-minute charts (Figure 10.1).

HOW THE MASTER TRADER PLAYS THE S&P FUTURES

- The master trader prefers to take intraday long positions when the S&P is above its opening price and rising.
- The master trader prefers to take intraday short positions when the S&P is below its opening price and dropping.
- The master trader uses support and resistance analysis with the S&P to time intraday buys and sells.
- The master trader combines reversal periods with the S&P to anticipate potential market turns.
- The master trader looks at 5- and 15-minute charts of the S&P with 200 simple moving averages (SMAs) superimposed on

F I G U R E   **10.1**

Five-minute line chart of the /SPU9. Note how meaningful the 10:00 a.m. and 10:00 p.m. reversal times were. A mild decline at the 10:00 a.m. period took place, and the 12:00 p.m. period stopped the /SPU9's advance dead in its tracks.

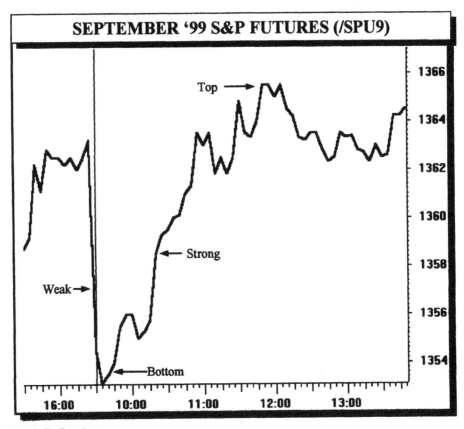

Chart by The Executioner.com

them. The 200 SMA often serves as significant intraday support and resistance for the S&P (Figure 10.2).

MARKET TOOL #2: NYSE TICK INDICATOR ($TICK)

NYSE $TICK DESCRIPTION

The $TICK has proven to be one of the most reliable market gauges available to the intraday trader, and we believe it deserves a special place in every master trader's arsenal. This simple, yet powerful indicator measures the number of NYSE stocks currently trading on an uptick (rising)

Five-minute chart of the S&P Futures contract. The master trader tries to time intraday longs and shorts with the predominate trend of the 5-minute S&P Futures contract.

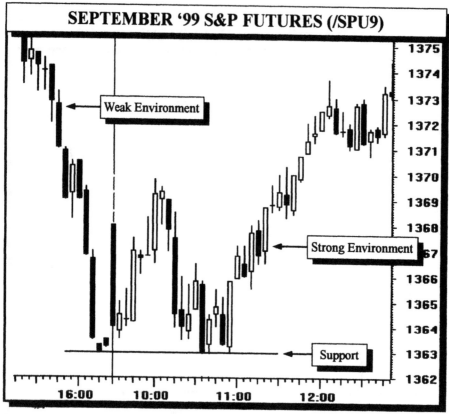

Chart by The Executioner.com

versus the number of NYSE stocks trading on a downtick (declining). An uptick is a transaction executed at a price higher than the preceding transaction, while a downtick is the sale of a security at a price below the preceding sale. For instance, a $TICK reading of +500 would mean that the number of stocks currently trading on an uptick outnumber those trading on a downtick by 500. A reading of –500 would mean the reverse, 500 more down ticking than up ticking. In a nutshell, the $TICK helps the trader monitor the level of broad buying and selling in the market, moment by moment. It also provides an instant snapshot of who's dominating the action, the bulls or bears. Here's how we use the $TICK in our daily trading.

HOW THE MASTER TRADER INTERPRETS THE $TICK

- $TICK readings between –300 and +300 indicate a generally neutral market environment.
- $TICK reading near the +1000 level indicates excessive bullishness, which is usually followed by a reversal to the downside.
- $TICK reading near the –1000 level indicates a excessive bearishness which is usually followed by a reversal to the upside. Note that in bear markets TICK readings well below –1000 are common.

  As an example, let's assume that the market has been declining for four consecutive days. On the fifth day, the market breaks to the downside again, producing a negative $TICK reading of –1100 (remember, this means that the stocks currently trading on a down tick outnumber those trading on an up tick by 1100). The astute trader would start preparing for the market to reverse back to the upside on an intraday basis. *Tip:* A highly negative $TICK reading indicates that someone has yelled, "fire," and those with the "herd" mentality are all trying to simultaneously make an exit (sell). This climatic down ticking activity causes the market to use up all of its "selling bullets" in one day, leaving very little selling potential left over for the ensuing days.

  The same thing applies to the upside. A high $TICK reading of say +1000 after a robust number of up days would be warning of a market that has spent all of its "buying bullets" in one climatic day, very much like a little boy who spends all his allowance in one place. Figures 10.3 and 10.4 are examples.

- A $TICK spread reading of +1000, after an enduring market correction typically puts in a significant bottom which often kicks off a multimonth rally. The $TICK spread measures the difference between the high $TICK reading of the day and the low $TICK reading of the day. For instance, a high $TICK reading of +1200 and a low $TICK reading of –200 on the same day would qualify as a $TICK spread of +1000.

HOW THE MASTER TRADER PLAYS THE $TICK

- The master trader prefers to take intraday long positions when the $TICK is rising.

F I G U R E   10.3

Five-minute line chart of the $TICK showing the neutral zone.

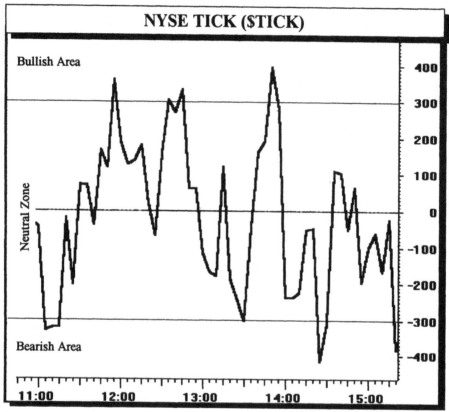

Chart by The Executioner.com

- The master trader prefers to take intraday short positions when the $TICK is dropping.
- The master trader looks for potential intraday longs when the $TICK reading reaches an extreme −1000 or better.
- The master trader looks for potential intraday shorts when the $TICK reading reaches an extreme +1000 or better.
- The master trader uses support and resistance analysis with the $TICK to time intraday buys and sells (Figures 10.5, 10.6, and 10.7).

F I G U R E   10.4

This 15-minute line chart of the $TICK shows how reliable the extreme 1000 levels are. After reaching the +1000, the $TICK quickly reversed back to the downside. An extreme reading below −1000 kicked off a sharp reversal back to the upside in the same manner.

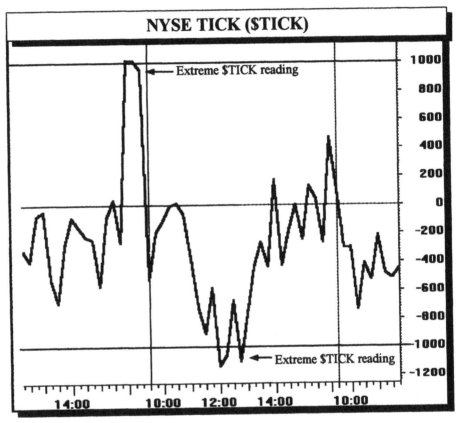

Chart by The Executioner.com

MARKET TOOL #3: NYSE TRADER'S INDEX (TRIN)

NYSE TRIN DESCRIPTION

The formula for TRIN is as follows:

$$\frac{\text{Advancing issues / advancing volume}}{\text{Declining issues / declining volume}} = \text{TRIN}$$

The NYSE Trader's Index (TRIN), known also as the Arm's Index, is one of the most valuable intraday market-timing tools we and our in-

F I G U R E   10.5

This 5-minute chart of the $TICK shows a very severe drop well below the −1000 mark. This extreme move suggested that most of the selling had already occurred. It should be noted that the $TICK bottomed near the 1:30 p.m. reversal time, and proceeded to rally strongly into the close.

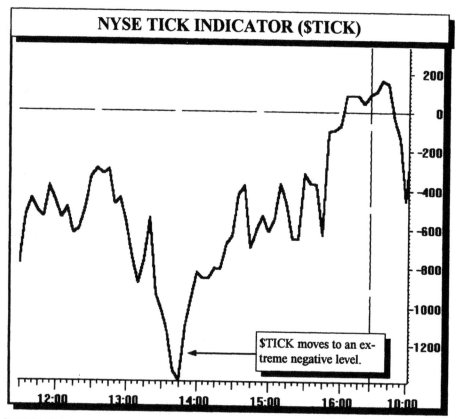

Chart by The Executioner.com

house day traders use. It is a marvelous tool that helps us monitor the level of intraday "trading" risk in the market. As a loyal companion to the intraday scalper or microtrader, it is unrivaled. Using a 5-minute line chart of the TRIN, we use it to interpret the market in the following manner.

HOW THE MASTER TRADER INTERPRETS THE TRIN

- A rising intraday TRIN is short-term bearish, indicating that risk for the intraday trader is increasing. In other words, a rising

F I G U R E   10.6

This 5-minute chart shows how the bottom in the /SPU9 corresponded perfectly with the extreme $TICK reading. The subsequent rally into the close was also in lock-step with the $TICK.

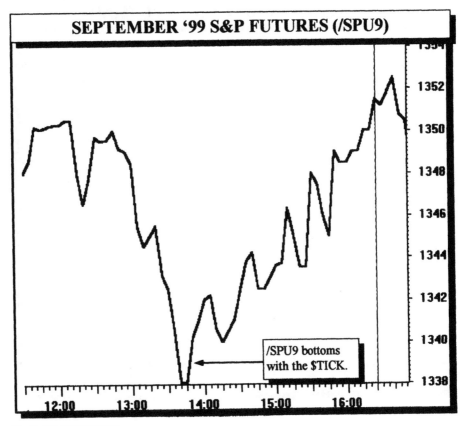

SEPTEMBER '99 S&P FUTURES (/SPU9)

/SPU9 bottoms with the $TICK.

Chart by The Executioner.com

TRIN equals rising risk. This assumes a buy-side bias. Keep in mind that the short seller would consider a rising TRIN bullish.

- A declining intraday TRIN is short-term bullish, indicating that risk for the intraday trader is decreasing. In other words, a declining TRIN equals declining risk. This assumes a buy-side bias.

Aside from directional analysis, the TRIN, as an intraday indicator, also helps the master trader determine the general health of the market. Here's how we use the TRIN to determine the market's current condition:

F I G U R E   10.7

This 5-minute line chart shows the $INDU simultaneously bottoming with the extreme $TICK reading as well. The INDU's subsequent rally into the close was also in lock-step with the $TICK and the /SPU9.

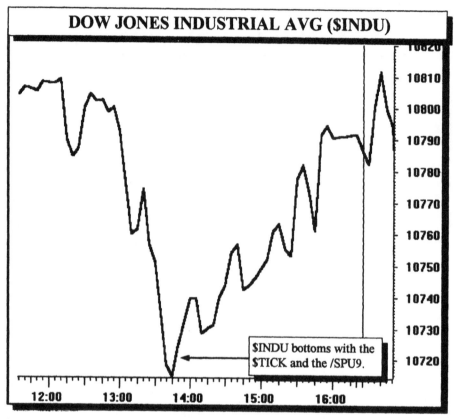

DOW JONES INDUSTRIAL AVG ($INDU)

$INDU bottoms with the $TICK and the /SPU9.

Chart by The Executioner.com

- An intraday TRIN reading below 1.00 generally means we are dealing with a healthy market environment. Remember that this assumes one is taking an intraday snapshot of the market environment. Its relevance from a longer-term perspective is insignificant.
- An intraday TRIN value above 1.00 generally means we are dealing with a riskier market environment, which is one more susceptible to an intraday decline or sell-off.

Aside from directional analysis, the TRIN also lends itself to over-bought and oversold analysis, or what we sometimes refer to as *threshold analysis.* Here's how we use the TRIN to determine when the market is excessively overbought or oversold:

- If and when the intraday TRIN drops below .35, the market environment has become too euphoric. In other words, a bullish intraday TRIN that drops below .35 tells us that the majority, the crowd, the masses have already committed to the market, and the market is in store for a strong intraday pullback.
- An intraday TRIN reading above 1.50 would suggest too much bearishness, and a market that is poised to surprise the bears with a strong intraday rally.
- A closing TRIN at 1.50 or above shows a great degree of pessimism and late-day bearishness. This suggests that panic selling has taken place right into the close, setting the market up for a reversal or snap back to the upside in the morning. *Tip:* A closing TRIN of 1.50 or greater, combined with a closing $TICK of –500 or more, increases the odds of a positive open the following day. While we can't cover all the nuances of each tool in this book, those interested in further education can access additional reports on our web site at *www.pristine.com.*

A few examples which demonstrate these points are presented in Figures 10.8 and 10.9.

HOW THE MASTER TRADER PLAYS THE TRIN

- When the intraday TRIN is rising, the master trader becomes more defensive by curtailing intraday plays on the long side.
- When the intraday TRIN is declining, the master trader becomes more aggressive by stepping up intraday plays on the long side.
- When the TRIN is below 1.00, the master trader generally maintains a buy-side bias.
- When the TRIN is above 1.00, the master trader generally maintains a sell-side bias.
- When the TRIN drops to or below .35, the master trader looks to sell out of all longs, and begins a search for potential opportunities on the short side.

Five-minute line chart of the $TRIN showing the 1.00 threshold and the extreme 1.50 threshold.

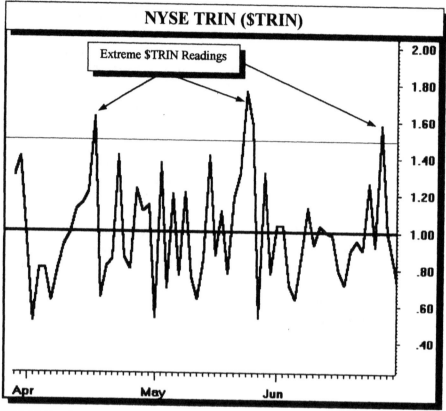

Chart by The Executioner.com

- When the TRIN rallies above 1.50, the master trader looks to cover all shorts, and begins a search for potential opportunities on the long side (Figures 10.10 and 10.11).

MARKET TOOL #4: NEW LOWS (NLS)

The NYSE daily new lows (NLs) indicator reports the number of Big Board stocks that have hit a new 52-week low. This single (daily) statistic offers one of the quickest and most accurate ways to measure the market's health. So let's take a closer look. A basic fact that is often overlooked by traders is this: "Selling" is the only thing that can cause a market to weaken or a stock to reach a new 52-week low. It is selling,

F I G U R E   10.9

Five-minute line chart of the $TRIN. *Tip:* A rising $TRIN indicates rising intraday risk. A declining $TRIN indicates a decline in intraday risk. Note that the $TRIN's bottom and top occurred at key reversal times.

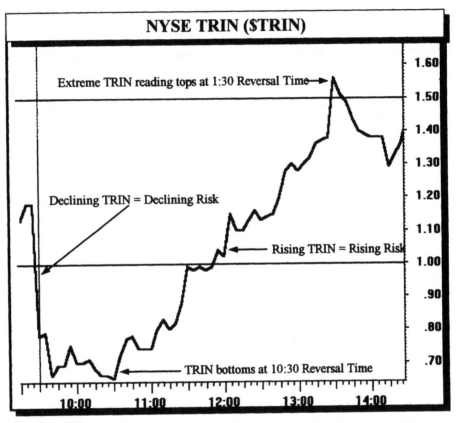

NYSE TRIN ($TRIN)

or the lack thereof, that really reveals how well the market is. Therefore, it is crucial to keep close tabs on any abrupt changes in the degree of selling. And the NLs very accurately monitor the market's degree of selling pressure. Here is how we use the NLs to interpret the market's condition.

HOW THE MASTER TRADER INTERPRETS THE NLS

- Rising NLs indicate that the market's selling pressure is accelerating, and the environment will likely become increasingly difficult.

F I G U R E   10.10

This 5-minute line chart shows a closing $TRIN greater than 1.50. This extreme reading suggests a
market bottom is close at hand. After the extreme spike into the close, the $TRIN begins a multihour
decline the following morning. *Tip:* A closing $TRIN greater than 1.50 typically leads to a rally the
following morning.

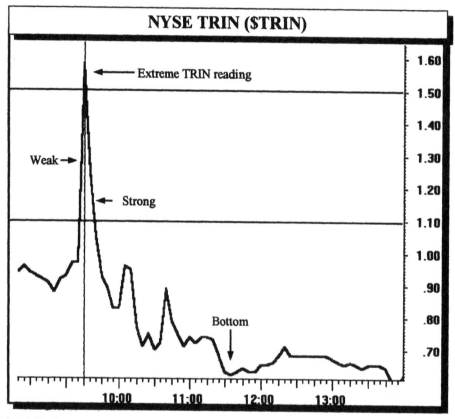

Chart by The Executioner.com

- Declining NLs tell us that buying interest is increasing, as
  selling is becoming more sparse, and an improving market
  condition will emerge.

We have found several levels of NLs to be quite significant in terms
of the story they tell about the market's condition:

- Daily NLs less than 20 represent the most bullish
  environment imaginable. This euphoric state does not

F I G U R E   10.11

This 5-minute line chart of the /SPU9 shows how much in sync the S&P futures and the $TRIN can be. Note how the /SPU9 bottoms and tops in perfect accordance with the $TRIN.

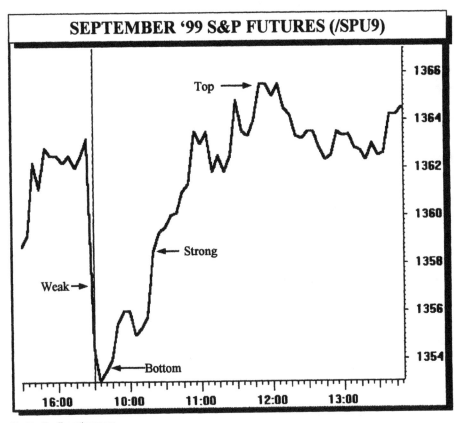

Chart by The Executioner.com

normally last long. In fact, it tends to quickly lead to an easing of the market.

- Daily NLs between 20 and 40 represent a positive market environment.
- Daily NLs greater than 40 represent a neutral or cooling-off period for the market.
- NLs greater than 60 signal a sickening or somewhat troubled market.

- NLs greater than 80 represent a bearish environment. Shorting opportunities will typically abound. This is the environment that typically crushes the dedicated buy and hold players, as moves to the upside are quickly and emphatically neutralized by abrupt turns to the downside.

Tip: It should be noted that the NLs reading can register much higher than 80, but these occurrences are not very frequent. As an aside, we have witnessed the NLs exceed 1000 in August 1998.

Monitoring this simple statistic will help you maintain your sanity in the midst of some very questionable times. We suggest you use this guide week to week. It will go a long way toward helping you keep your finger on the five dominant states of the market listed here:

1. The state of greed and extreme euphoria (NLs below 20)
2. The state of health (NLs below 40 but above 20)
3. The state of rest (NLs below 60 but above 40)
4. The state of turmoil and confusion (NLs below 80 but above 60)
5. The state of fear and pessimism (NLs above 80)

HOW THE MASTER TRADER PLAYS THE NLS

- NLs under 20 represent an extremely bullish market environment. During this bullish phase, the master trader will look to play the long side exclusively. The master trader will also want to be more aggressive in terms of size and profit objectives.

- NLs over 40 represent a cooling-off phase. This reading typically provides an early warning sign that the market is a bit fatigued. The market will likely offer short-term trading opportunities in both directions. But the master trader, in this environment, will want to trade in and out quickly, as moves will be very short lived (see Figure 10.12).

- NLs over 80 signal a sloppy market environment. The master trader focuses exclusively on finding shorting opportunities, as rallies will be sparse at best, and the path of least resistance will most definitely be to the downside.

The daily charts of the S&P 500 Index and the NYSE NLs clearly show how bearish the overall market is when the NLs remain above 40. *Tip:* The 40 NLs threshold is the dividing line between the bulls and the bears..

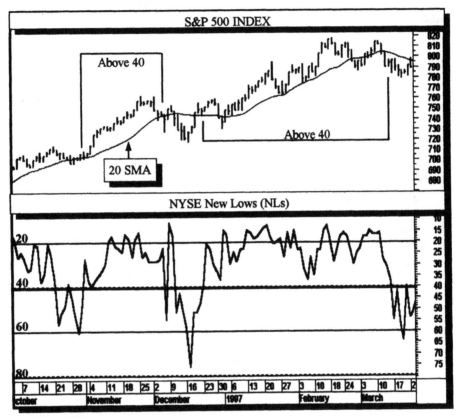

Chart by The Executioner.com

MARKET TOOL #5: MIGHTY 5 INDEX

The Mighty Five Index developed by Pristine is a mini five-stock index that we created to help our in-house traders keep close tabs on the overall health and condition of the market. Over the years we have come to discover that certain key stocks not only mimic the actions of the general market, they often lead it. This tendency to lead can provide invaluable clues and profitable opportunities to the watchful trader. By simply monitoring these key stocks on a day-to-day basis, the master trader can maintain a "feel" for the market that would rival that of the so-called Wall Street pros. We have detailed the five individual stocks that make up the Mighty 5 Index. We are sure you will find the story each tells quite interesting.

THE MIGHTY 5 INDEX

General Electric (GE). GE *is* the market. If we had to pick one stock to use as a general proxy for the health of the entire market, GE would be it. Whatever the market does, GE will eventually do. Whatever GE does, the market will eventually do. This is one of the biggest companies in the world, and it sells just about everything on planet Earth. GE is so encompassing that no long-term portfolio should be without it.

CitiGroup, Inc.(C). This stock single handedly encapsulates the entire financial industry. Through its divisions, it represents the big three financial sectors: banks, brokers, and insurance. C's Citibank division represents the banking sector. The Solomon Smith Barney division represents the brokerage sector. And C's Travelers division represents the insurance sector. It should be noted that there can be no enduring market rally without cooperation and thorough participation from the financial sector. In C, you have the whole financial picture.

Microsoft, Inc. (MSFT). There is no one today who can doubt the tremendous impact technology has made in our lives, in our markets, and in our world. Over the past decade, the technology sector as a whole has been the heart of the stock market, the lifeblood, if you will. And it is our view that this will be the case for several more decades. This is why keeping close tabs on this large section of the market has become paramount today, and astute traders can easily do this by monitoring the day-to-day action of MSFT. With this one megastock, the ebbs and flows of the entire technology sector can be seen and felt. If the technology sector is the heart of today's market, MSFT is the heart of today's technology sector. Don't step into the technology sector without carefully considering what MSFT is doing.

America Online (AOL). Internet mania has captured our imaginations, taken hold of our lives, and altered our market like no other frenzy in history. The future prospects of the Internet are no less than mind-boggling, and no matter what the skeptics say, the Internet, like the phone, will be affecting the way we communicate and do business with the rest of the world for a very long time. Because this emerging industry has become so critical to the overall psyche of the market, keeping tabs on it day by day is a must for astute traders. Those who follow this sector would never be able to doubt AOL's dominance in this field. In a very real sense, AOL is the granddaddy of all Internet stocks, and it can single handedly serve as a barometer of the entire Internet sector.

General Motors (GM). Cyclical stocks are extremely important to astute traders because they serve as a near-perfect barometer of the economy. And as we are sure you know, a healthy economy equates to a healthy stock market. GM is a key cyclical stock, and therefore a key barometer in and of itself of the entire economy. If people are willing to buy cars, they are willing to assume debt, which means they have confidence in their jobs and the economy. Confident consumers, willing to take on additional debt, make financial stocks thrive. Intermarket analysis is a topic that deserves a book in and of itself. But the master trader can be almost as astute as a professional economist by simply monitoring GM. It comes very close to telling it all.

HOW THE MASTER TRADER INTERPRETS AND PLAYS THE MIGHTY 5 INDEX

- When all five stocks in the Mighty 5 Index are up, the master trader focuses exclusively on the long side.
- When all five stocks in the Mighty 5 Index are down, the master trader focuses exclusively on the short (sell) side.
- When Microsoft Corp (MSFT) and America Online (AOL) are simultaneously performing well, the master trader looks for most, if not all, trading opportunities in the key technology stocks.
- When MSFT and AOL are both down, no intraday long plays in technology stocks are taken. Short plays, however, are an option under this scenario.
- When CitiGroup, Inc. (C) is performing well (up decently on the day), the financial sector is supporting the overall market. This

will often mean that intraday pullbacks in the market are buying opportunities as opposed to reasons to get worried. Trading opportunities in the bank, brokerage, and insurance sectors can also be looked for. The same applies in reverse.

- When MSFT is down big, many technology stocks will experience selling. Intraday rallies in the techs will tend to peter out quickly when MSFT is down big. This offers prime shorting possibilities. The same applies in reverse.
- When AOL is up big, trading opportunities on the long side will proliferate in the Internet sector. Under this scenario, the master trader assumes pullbacks in Internet stocks are potential buying opportunities. The same applies in reverse. *Tip:* Internet stock traders who try to fight the direction of AOL will be playing with fire.
- If General Electric (GE) is up decently, and the market is down decently, the master trader assumes the market will eventually follow. Therefore, the master trader looks for early buy opportunities using support and resistance analysis and other trading strategies and techniques. The same works in reverse.

Needless to say, we could go on and on with possible scenarios, but it is of paramount importance to note that these scenarios are only guidelines. They serve to provide general direction and/or a rough intraday game plan, which most novice traders fail to form (Figure 10.13).

A STOCK MARKET QUIZ

Question 1: What is historically the most *bearish* month of the year? Knowing this ahead of time can help investors as well as traders position their portfolios and their trading plans accordingly.

Answer: September. In the past 15 years, September has only been up five times.

Question 2: What is historically the most *bullish* month of the year? Knowing this answer can also give astute traders an edge.

Answer: May. In the last 12 years, May was the best month 11 times.

Question 3: Which 3-month period is the *best* time to be fully invested and/or margined? Knowing this can reap the astute trader huge gains that outperform most market averages.

F I G U R E   10.13

This list shows how we use the Executioner.com's market minder feature to stay on top of the overall market as a whole. This watch list is monitored throughout the day, and provides an easy way to determine which sectors are being bought and which are being sold. ① TICK and and TRIN ② S&P and NASDAQ 100 Futures contracts, ③ DJIA, Transportation Index, S&P 500 Index (cash), NASDAQ Composite. ④ The Mighty 5. ⑤ Semiconductor, Financial, Internet, Broker Dealer, Drug, and Oil Indices. Note that the day shown was a very negative one.

Symbol	Last		High	Low	Change
$TICK ①	513	S	609	-793	+513
$TRIN	1.84	S	1.84	.65	+.64
/SPU9 ②	1331.80	S	1358.00	1330.00	-18.00
/NDU9	2276.50	S	2327.00	2276.00	-10.75
$INDU	10655.15	S	10825.80	10647.86	-136.14
$TRAN ③	3333.24	S	3366.48	3327.62	-15.71
$INX	1328.72	S	1350.92	1328.49	-12.31
$COMPX	2638.49	S	2676.45	2631.87	-1.52
GE	109	S	112 5/16	108 11/16	-3
GM	61 1/8	S	64 1/8	60 3/8	-2 13/11
C ④	44 9/16	S	46 1/4	44 1/2	-1 3/16
MSFT	85 13/16	S	88 5/8	85 1/2	-1 1/8
AOL	95 1/4	S	100 1/2	94 1/4	-1 5/8
$SOX.X	493.97	S	501.93	490.99	+1.33
$NF.X	532.39	S	541.95	532.11	-9.40
$IIX.X ⑤	278.33	S	285.51	276.77	-3.69
$XBD.X	389.71	S	398.22	389.56	-8.41
$DRG.X	349.02	S	352.77	348.84	-.54
$XOI.X	514.68	S	519.73	508.70	+5.88

Chart by The Executioner.com

Answer: November, December, and January. Thanks to late-year tax planning and last-minute attempts by mutual, corporate, and private pension funds to work on performance bonuses, these 3 months represent the best period to be stock market friendly.

Question 4: Which month historically *ends* bear markets? Knowing this answer can help the astute trader call turning points and bottom fish at precisely the right time.

Answer: October. The former bear markets of 1946, 1957, 1960, 1966, 1974, 1987, 1990, and, of course, 1998 all ended in October.

Question 5: What 5-day span of the month is the very best to be fully invested in the market? Knowing this can help investors and traders time their level of aggressiveness and size.

Answer: The last, first, second, third, and fourth day of the month. This 5-day period historically outperforms the rest of the days of the month, thanks to the fact that funds get their biggest cash inflows around the end or beginning of each month.

Question 6: Which single day of the month is historically the best day to be in the market?

Answer: The second day of the month. The market rises more often on the second day of the month (62.3 percent) than any other trading day.

Statistical facts were obtained from *Yale Hirsch's Stock Trader's Almanac,* an indispensable guide to market tendencies.

A FINAL WORD ON THE MARKET

As we forever leave behind the twentieth century, it is almost impossible for us not to ponder the question, "What are traders and investors in store for in the new millennium?" Over the last decade of the 1900s, the robust advance in stock prices has brought out countless doomsday prognosticators, all with the same repetitive message of overvaluation. As computer-related shares soared beyond anyone's expectations and Internet stocks rocketed to far-away galaxies, the word that has been repeated over and over by many professionals is "overdone." To a certain extent, this "overbought" cry is understandable. The NASDAQ-100 Index was up an incredible 82 percent in 1998 alone, its best performance ever. Up until that year, a 65 percent gain in 1991 was its crowning glory. Stocks that helped the index soar to incredible heights were Microsoft Corporation (MSFT), Cisco Systems (CSCO), MCI Worldcom (WCOM), Dell Computer (DELL), and Sun Microsystems (SUNW), all of which more than quintupled over the past 5 years alone. Needless to say, leading Internet stocks performed even better in recent years, with Amazon.com (AMZN) up more than 10-fold and Yahoo! (YHOO) up more than eight-fold in a single year. Can this continue? Is the frenzy that has driven Internet stocks up faster than any other group in history the sign of a euphoric top? Many professional Wall Street market watchers feel so, but then again these same experts felt a DJIA crossing 3000 was too rich. Our view is that instead of a market that is *overdone*, we have and will continue to enjoy a robust market that is *overdue*. While we, more than most, know the danger in saying "things are different this time around," the undeniable fact remains that they really are. We live in a different world today, driven by different dynamics and different mediums. A technological explosion, which is only in its infancy, has lit fire to the hearts and given wings to the minds of people, companies, and countries around the globe. The complete cycle of communication—from source to public—is fast approaching the instantaneous mark, and the powerful barriers, once solidified by space and time, have given way to an industrial oneness and a universality that is staggering to even the broadest of minds. If the new technological miracles of the world have given flight to our minds, why should this not translate into a market that has also taken flight? If today's advancements help our achievements soar to higher and higher levels, why should not the market, which reflects these things, soar as well. *The market is only a mirror of what we, as a human race, experience and become. If we advance, so must the market that reflects our human experience.* What the Wall Street pros, locked away in their plush offices, seem to forget is that the market ultimately serves as a reflection of the people. Not the reverse. If our lives are being made better with each passing year, no P/E ratio is going to stop the market from responding favorably, no matter how astronomical. The rapid pace of technology is moving us higher and higher. And as long as this is the case, the market must also move higher and higher. Sure, we will have abrupt ups and downs and an occasional case of severe hiccups. But as my mother used to say, "hiccups mean you're growing, be glad!"

11

C H A P T E R

CHARTING TOOLS
AND TACTICS

INTRODUCTION TO CHARTING

It should be no surprise by now that our style of trading is short term in nature. This is to say, all of our entry and exit points are based on technical events, not fundamental or economic ones. Each specific action we take is based on a number of very reliable chart patterns that represent key short-term shifts in market psychology. Now this is where the Pristine approach to the market gets very interesting. Consider the following fact: *Each specified period (that is, day, hour, 15 minutes, 5 minutes, 1 minute) is nothing more than a battle or mini skirmish between the only two groups of players in existence: the buyers and the sellers, better known as the Bulls and the Bears.*

When you are looking at a daily chart, for instance, each bar you see represents an individual battle that was conducted in the context of an ongoing war. If you are looking at a 2-minute chart, each bar you see represents a 2-minute skirmish in the context of a never-ending war. If this is true, and believe us, it is, the master traders' success lies entirely in their ability to accurately determine which group is currently dominating the war. While one group can be winning the current battle (period), the other group can be dominating the war (the trend). It is the master traders who consistently align themselves with the group dominating the war who will always be able to use the market as an avenue of income. However, master traders who can consistently spot the moment just before one group takes control of the other will be able to use the market to produce income *and* accumulate wealth.

We have discovered a number of very reliable chart patterns that pinpoint exactly when a change in the balance of power between the buyers and sellers has occurred. After reading and thoroughly studying the following sections, you will not only know how to identify these chart patterns, you'll know how to build tactics and strategies that are designed to profitably exploit them.

As we've pointed out earlier, charts are the footprints of money, and they don't lie. They are like a doctor's x-ray, which provides deeper insight into all the patients. In our case, the market, and the individual stocks that make it up, are our patients. This chapter will provide you with the tools that will make you a market doctor of the highest order. But before we delve into the individual tools, we will have to touch on a few basic charting concepts that are essential to the more advanced ones we cover later in the chapter. Let's do that now.

A CHARTING PRIMER

CANDLES WILL LIGHT THE WAY

The master trader has a vast variety of chart types to choose from. There are western bar charts, which are by far the most commonly used, point and figure charts, which are the least used, line charts, seen sometimes in daily newspapers and stock market reports, Japanese candlestick charts, which are rapidly gaining in popularity, thanks to us, and a relatively new form called equivolume charts. And that's just to name a few. While the spiciness of "variety" has its benefits, it is our belief that the Japanese candlestick chart is by far the best and only form needed by the master trader. In fact, we regard the Japanese style of charting so superior that we would not look at a chart today if it were not in candlestick form. That is how vital to our success candlesticks have become.

Now this is not to say that candlesticks possess some magical power not shared by the others, or that they contain more information than regular bar charts do, because they don't. We are immensely in love with candlesticks for only one simple reason: They make it easy to visually see which group, bulls or bears, is controlling the market. They also make it easy to see which group is about to lose or regain that control. That's it. They provide no additional facts. They do not have any capabilities that the others lack. Candlesticks simply allow the trader to visually determine, with greater ease, who's winning the battle. Put another way, they provide the ability to more quickly determine which side Goliath is on:

the buyers' side or the seller's side. As we've mentioned before, it is the trader who bets with Goliath, not against him, who consistently emerges as victor. Let's look at two examples to demonstrate this point. The first example will show Goliath siding with the buyers. The other will show Goliath siding with the sellers.

DETERMINING WHEN THE BULLS ARE IN CONTROL

Each time a stock closes *above* the opening price, the bulls (buyers) have won the specific period being viewed.

Close > open = bulls rule

Figure 11.1 is an example of bulls/buyers winning the battle using the western bar chart form of charting. Figure 11.2 shows the same example of bulls/buyers winning the battle. Only this time, we are using the Japanese candlestick form of charting. Note that in both examples, the stock closes above the open, which signifies that buyers were strong enough to drive or push the sellers back to higher ground. We teach our traders to think of the open as the starting point of a battle. If the battle ends at a level higher than where it began, the buyers won that battle. If the buyers are winning most of the individual battles, it is clear that they are currently dominating the war. Counting or tracking who won each battle is what many chartists call *trend analysis*. An up trend is nothing more than a war, comprised of many battles won by buyers.

F I G U R E   11.1

Bulls/buyers winning the battle using the western bar chart.

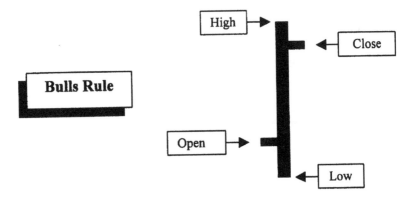

F I G U R E   11.2

Bulls/buyers winning the battle using the Japanese candlestick chart.

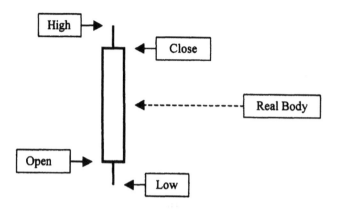

But let's take a closer look at the second example to see how much better the candlestick charting form displays the outcome of this battle. Because the Japanese fully understand the importance of determining who wins each individual battle, they visually accentuate the relationship between the opening price and the closing price with a cylinderlike body, or *real body* as it is more commonly referred to. In the candlestick example in Figure 11.2, the bottom of the body represents the open, while the top of the body represents the close. The tails on each end, or the "wicks," represent the extreme high and low prices of the period. While the high and low are important as well, it is always the range between the open price and the closing price that holds the greatest importance because it determines who has won the battle. When the bulls win the battle, the real body will always be white. We teach our traders to think of white as being light in weight. When the bulls win, the price floats upward from the open price, because it is light in weight. So, in essence, a white or light-colored candlestick bar immediately tells us that the bulls/buyers have won the battle. Let's look at the reverse scenario.

DETERMINING WHEN THE BEARS ARE IN CONTROL

Each time a stock closes *below* the opening price, the bears (sellers) won the period being viewed.

Close < open = bears rule

Figures 11.3 and 11.4 show an example of bears/sellers winning the battle, which we've displayed in western bar chart form (Figure 11.3) and candlestick form (Figure 11.4). Note that in these examples, the stock closes *below* the open, which signifies that sellers were strong enough to drive or push the buyers back to lower ground. Note also how much easier it is to determine the ominous outcome of this battle. The Japanese candlestick, with its dark, heavy real body, shows with greater clarity that the bears are in control. When the bears win the battle, the real body

F I G U R E   11.3

Bears/sellers winning the battle using the western bar chart.

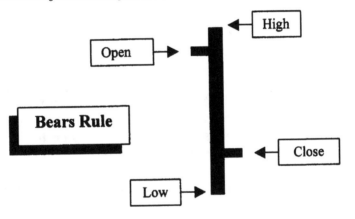

F I G U R E   11.4

Bears/sellers winning the battle using the Japanese candlestick chart.

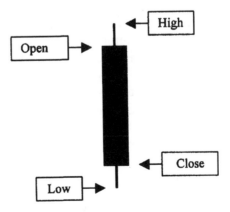

A stalemate condition is seen in candlestick form as a bar with no real body.

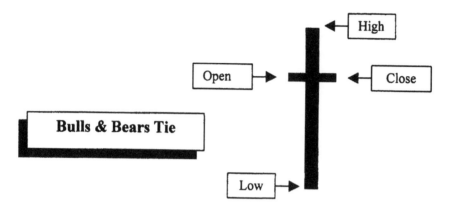

will always be black or dark in color. So, in essence, a dark candlestick bar immediately tells us that the bears/sellers have won the battle. Again, keep in mind that you must think of the open as the starting point of each battle. If the battle ends at a price or level lower than where it began, the bears/sellers won that battle. If the bears are winning most of the individual battles, it is clear that they are currently dominating the war. A downtrend is nothing more than a war being dominated by the bears/sellers.

WHEN THE BULLS AND BEARS TIE

It is worth noting here that there will be times when neither the bulls nor the bears will win. If the bulls win by closing the stock above its open, and bears win by closing the stock below its open, a tie or draw is formed when the open and close are the same. This stalemate condition, or state of neutrality, will be seen in candlestick form as a bar with no real body. An example is shown in Figure 11.5.

While this example appears to be, and is, in western bar chart form, it is also in candlestick form. Because the open and close is the same price, there is no real body or range between prices to depict. These ties, so to speak, can be very informative, depending on when and where they occur.

In the following section we will reveal some of our most powerful charting tactics and techniques. In our view, the following section is by far the most valuable one in the entire book, and we encourage you to study and reread it many times. Those who truly become intimate with the tools and techniques that follow will be well on their way to becoming a master trader of the highest order. We want you to know that what you are about to read has fared us very well. Once you learn how to identify, use, and combine the following tools, we are sure they will reward you for many years to come. Let's now move to our first charting tool.

CHARTING TOOL #1: NARROW-RANGE BAR (NRB)

NARROW-RANGE BAR DESCRIPTION

A *narrow range bar* (NRB), as we call it, is defined as a bar with a smaller than normal range between the high and low. The appearance of an NRB indicates that a dramatic decrease in volatility has occurred, and strong moves tend to emerge from these periods of low volatility. Let's take a look at an example of an NRB.

If XYZ traded on Monday as high as $22 and as low as $20, the day's range would total $2 ($22 – $20 = $2). If on the following day, XYZ traded between $21 and $21.50, it would qualify as an NRB. See the example in Figures 11.6 and 11.7.

FIGURE   11.6

A narrow-range bar using a western bar chart.

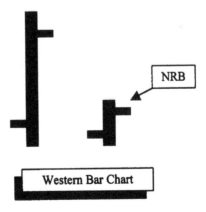

Western Bar Chart

A narrow-range bar using a candlestick chart.

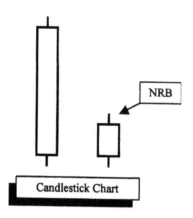

Candlestick Chart

HOW THE MASTER TRADER INTERPRETS NARROW-RANGE BARS (NRBS)

- The presence of an NRB signifies that buyers and sellers are near equal in power (Figure 11.8).
- An NRB is only significant when it occurs *after* several normal-to-wide range bars.
- An NRB offers the master trader one of the clearest possible signs that a strong turn is close at hand.
- A turn (rebound or decline) after an NRB will tend to be more potent and reliable than a turn from a more normal size bar.
- When an NRB occurs after a several bar decline, the master trader looks for the stock to turn to the upside.
- When an NRB occurs after a several bar advance, the master trader looks for the stock to turn to the downside.

HOW THE MASTER TRADER PLAYS NRBS

- The master trader looks to buy above the high of an NRB after a several bar drop (Figure 11.9).
- The master trader looks to sell below the low of an NRB after a several bar advance.
- The aggressive master trader often buys on an NRB following a several bar decline, if it is closing *above* the open.

F I G U R E   11.8

Narrow-range bars (NRBs) mark significant tops and bottoms in CNCX.

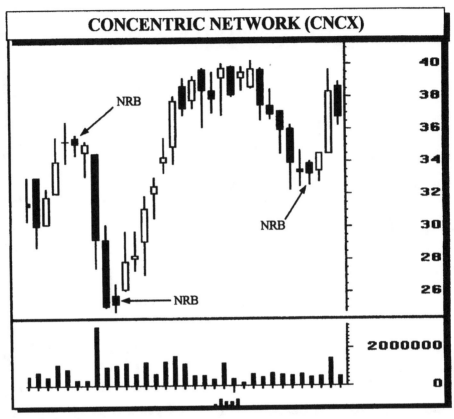

Chart by The Executioner.com

- The aggressive master trader often sells short on an NRB following a several bar advance, if it is closing *below* the open.

CHARTING TOOL #2: REVERSAL BARS (RB)

REVERSAL BAR DESCRIPTION

A *reversal bar* (RB), as we call it, is marked by an initial, and often sharp, move in one direction, followed by an abrupt turn, which ends the period in the opposite direction, below the starting point. For instance, after ini-

F I G U R E   11.9

After a several bar decline, AAPL experienced an NRB, which kicked off a very robust advance. The master trader buys above the NRB.

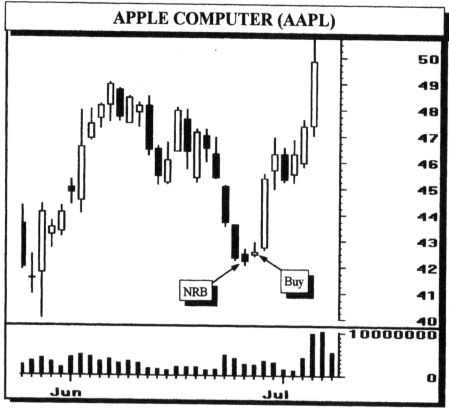

Chart by The Executioner.com

tially dropping sharply to the downside, a *bullish* reversal bar will turn and close at or near the period's high, above its opening price. After rallying to the upside, a *bearish* reversal bar will turn and close at or near the period's low, below the opening price. Let's take a look at two examples.

Bullish reversal bar. XYZ opens on Monday at $20, trades as low as $18 throughout the day, then reverses back to the upside to close at $20.50 (see Figures 11.10 and 11.11).

Bearish reversal bar. XYZ opens on Wednesday at $20, trades as high as $22 through out the day, then reverses back to the downside to close at $19.50 (see Figures 11.12 and 11.13).

A bullish reversal bar using a western bar chart.

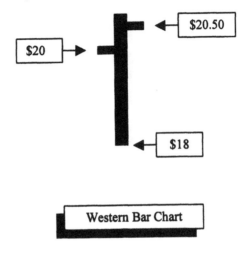

Western Bar Chart

A bullish reversal bar using a candlestick chart.

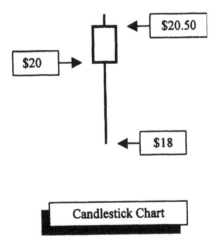

Candlestick Chart

HOW THE MASTER TRADER INTERPRETS REVERSAL BARS (RBS)

- The presence of an RB signifies that a sharp turn or change of trend is close at hand.
- A turn (rebound or decline) after an RB will tend to be more potent and reliable than a turn from a more normal bar.

F I G U R E   11.12

A bearish reversal bar using a western bar chart.

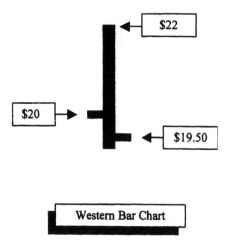

F I G U R E   11.13

A bearish reversal bar using a candlestick chart.

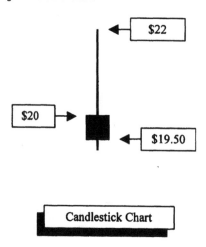

- RBs show where shakeouts have occurred.
- The bullish RB indicates that control of the market has shifted from the sellers back to the buyers.
- The bearish RB indicates that control of the market has shifted from the buyers back to the sellers.

- A bullish RB is most significant when it occurs *after* a several bar decline.
- When a bullish RB occurs after a several-bar decline, the master trader looks for the stock to turn to the upside.
- A bearish RB is the most significant when it occurs *after* a several-bar advance.
- When a bearish RB occurs after a several-bar advance, the master trader looks for the stock to turn to the downside (Figure 11.14).

HOW THE MASTER TRADER PLAYS RBS

- The master trader looks to buy above the high of a bullish RB after a several-bar drop.
- The master trader looks to sell below the low of a bearish RB after a several-bar advance.
- The aggressive master trader often buys on the bullish RB just prior to the close.
- The aggressive master trader often sells short on the bearish RB just prior to the close.

CHARTING TOOL #3: TAILS

TAIL DESCRIPTION

Tails mark where shifts in the balance of power between buyers and sellers have occurred. A *topping tail*, which points toward the high, is formed by an initial move to the upside, which suddenly gives way to a sudden drop to the downside. A *bottoming tail*, which points toward the low, is created by a stock dropping, and then suddenly reversing back to the upside. Let's quickly look at two examples.

Bottoming tail. XYZ opens at $30, trades as low as $27 throughout the day, and then reverses back to the upside to close at $29. In this case, the tail is $2 in length, which is equal to the range between the low of the bar ($27) and the bar's closing price ($29) (see Figures 11.15 and 11.16).

Topping tail. XYZ opens at $31.50, trades as high as $34 throughout the day, and then reverses back to the downside to close at $31.75. In this case, the tail is $2.25 in length, which is equal to the range

F I G U R E   11.14

DCLK declined sharply after forming bearish reversal bars (RBs). A bullish reversal bar (RB) also kicked off a major rally.

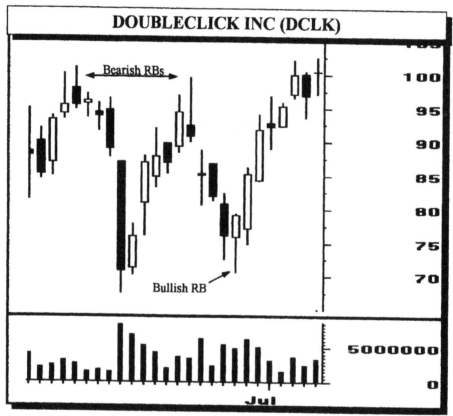

DOUBLECLICK INC (DCLK)

Chart by The Executioner.com

between the high of the bar ($34) and the closing price ($31.75) (See Figures 11.17 and 11.18).

HOW THE MASTER TRADER INTERPRETS TAILS

- A turn (rebound or decline) after a tail will tend to be more pronounced.
- Tails show where shakeouts have occurred.
- A topping tail reveals where professional sellers are hanging out, dumping stock on the general public.

F I G U R E   11.15

Bottoming tail using a western bar chart.

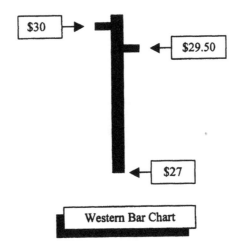

F I G U R E   11.16

Bottoming tail using a candlestick chart.

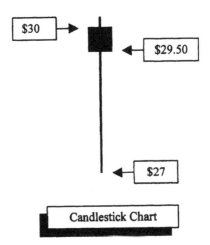

- A bottoming tail reveals where professional buyers are hanging out, accumulating stock inexpensively.
- The bottoming tail indicates that control of the market has shifted from the sellers back to the buyers.
- The topping tail indicates that control of the market has shifted from the buyers back to the sellers.

F I G U R E   11.17

Topping tail using a western bar chart.

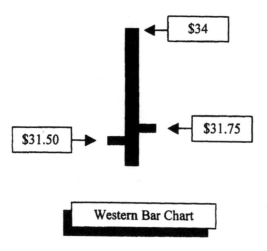

Western Bar Chart

F I G U R E   11.18

Topping tail using a candlestick chart.

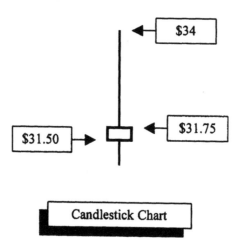

Candlestick Chart

- A bottoming tail is the most significant when it occurs *after* a several bar decline.
- When a bottoming tail occurs after a several bar decline, the master trader looks for the stock to turn to the downside.
- A topping tail is the most significant when it occurs *after* a several bar decline.

This chart of Novellus Systems (NVLS) shows how informative bottoming tails can be. The bottoming tails revealed that buyers were very busy at work accumulating stock in the $46 area.

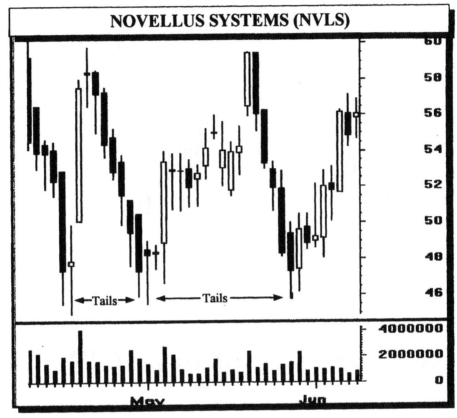

Chart by The Executioner.com

- When a topping tail occurs after a several bar advance, the master trader looks for the stock to turn to the downside.

HOW THE MASTER TRADER PLAYS TAILS

- The master trader looks to buy above the high of a bottoming bar after a several bar drop (see Figure 11.19).
- The master trader looks to sell below the low of a topping bar after a several bar advance (see Figure 11.20).

F I G U R E   11.20

NSOL declined sharply after forming two topping tails. Note that these topping tails also help make two bearish reversal bars.

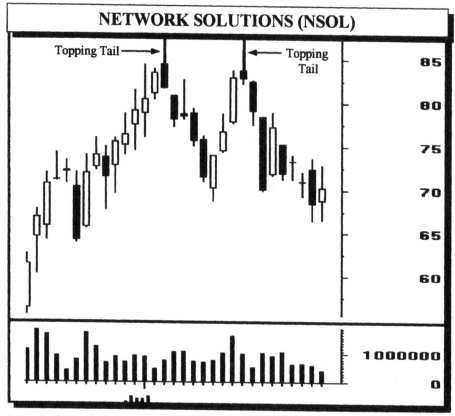

Chart by The Executioner.com

CHARTING TOOL #4: GAPS

GAP DESCRIPTION

Gaps are one of the most watched for charting events among the master trading group, as they form the basis for numerous trading techniques. Strictly speaking, gaps fall into two groups, upside gaps and downside gaps.

An *upside gap* occurs when the opening price of the current bar is above the close and or the high of the previous bar. A *downside gap* occurs when the opening price of the current bar is below the close and or the low of the previous bar. The gap, or window, as some traders call it, forms a void in which no trades have taken place. Let's look at two examples.

Upside gap. XYZ trades on Wednesday between $30 (low of the day) and $32 (high of the day) and has a closing price of $31.75. If the stock opened for trading on Thursday at $33, it would create a space between $31.75 (close of the previous day) and $33 (open of the current day) that would represent an upside gap of $1.25. If XYZ opened for trading on Thursday at $28, the space between $30 (low of the previous day) and $28 (open of the current day) would represent a downside gap of $2 (see Figure 11.21).

Downside gap. XYZ trades on Wednesday between $32 (high of the day) and $30 (low of the day) and has a closing price of $30.25. If the stock opened for trading on Thursday at $29, it would create a space between $30.25 (close of the previous day) and $29 (open of the current day) that would represent a downside gap of $1.25 (see Figure 11.22).

Depending on where the upside and downside gaps occur, they are events that can alert the trader to major turning points.

F I G U R E   11.21

Example of an upside gap.

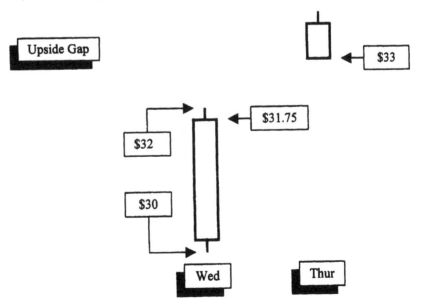

F I G U R E   11.22

Example of a downside gap.

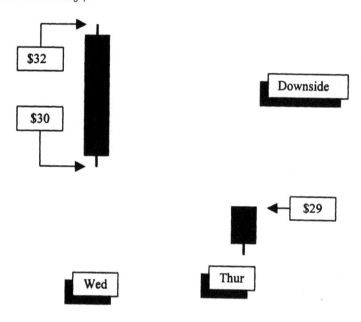

HOW THE MASTER TRADER INTERPRETS GAPS

- The market does not like gaps. As a result, gaps are normally filled shortly after they are formed, particularly intraday.
- Gaps often serve as price support and resistance, meaning they can halt and/or reverse rallies and declines that move into them.
- Upside gaps that occur *after* several down bars are professional in nature. In other words, upside gaps from oversold conditions are typically signs of early professional buying.
- Upside gaps that occur *after* several up bars are typically amateur driven. In other words, upside gaps from overbought conditions are typically signs of late novice buying.
- Downside gaps that occur *after* several up bars are usually professional in nature. In other words, downside gaps from overbought conditions are typically signs of early professional selling.
- Downside gaps that occur *after* several down bars are typically amateur driven. In other words, downside gaps from oversold

F I G U R E   11.23

The downside gap after TXN's major rise led to a very sharp collapse. After the decline, an upside gap kicked off a major rally.

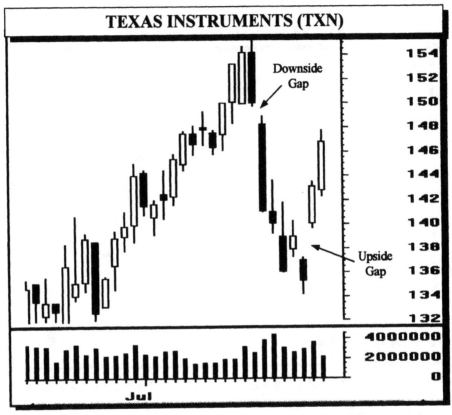

Chart by The Executioner.com

conditions are typically signs of late novice selling (Figures 11.23 and 11.24).

HOW THE MASTER TRADER PLAYS GAPS*

- The master trader looks to buy above the high of an upside gap from an oversold condition.

*See the 30-minute gap rule developed by Pristine for another sophisticated way to play gaps. Visit *www.pristine.com* to gain access to an informative report detailing a unique trading strategy using the 30-minute gap rule.

F I G U R E   11.24

This daily chart of Sep 99 S&P Futures shows how deadly a downside gap from the area of new high can be. These downside gaps are so bearish when they occur that we often say the underlying stock or index is suffering from "gap disease."

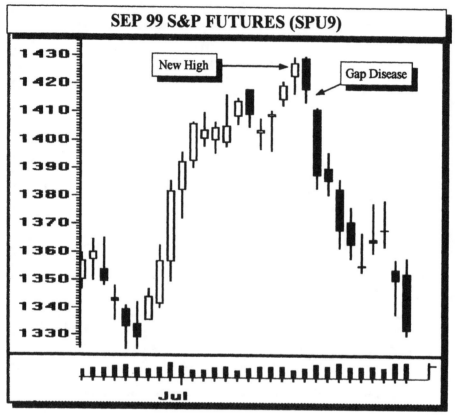

Chart by The Executioner.com

- The master trader looks to sell below the low of a downside gap from an overbought condition.
- The master intraday trader looks to buy the first pullback after an upside gap from an oversold condition.
- The master intraday trader looks to sell the first rally immediately following a downside gap from an overbought condition.

CHARTING TOOL #5: SUPPORT AND RESISTANCE

SUPPORT AND RESISTANCE DESCRIPTION

The concept of support and resistance forms the foundation for a whole host of day trading tactics. Many master traders earn a living in the market by using the concept of support and resistance exclusively. *Support* a price level or area at which the demand for a stock will likely overwhelm the existing supply and halt the current decline. Conversely, *resistance* is a price level or area at which the supply for the stock will likely overwhelm the existing demand and halt the current advance. Unknown to most traders, there are major and minor forms of support and resistance. For instance, *major support* comes into play when a stock is declining to retest a prior low. *Minor support* comes into play when a stock is declining to retest a prior high. The reverse is true for major and minor resistance. Here are two examples.

> *Major support and resistance.* After declining to $20 (Figure 11.25a), let's say XYZ rebounds to $24 and stalls (Figure 11.25b). From the $24 area, XYZ falls back toward $20 (Figure 11.25c). The $20 area would likely serve as an area of major support. This is where the master trader would look for XYZ to rebound again (Figure 11.25c). If XYZ were to rebound from $20 once again, the $24 area would likely serve as major resistance (Figure 11.25d). This is where the master trader would look for XYZ to start another potential decline.

F I G U R E   11.25

An example of major support and resistance.

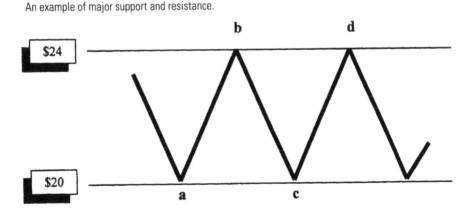

An example of how major resistance becomes minor support.

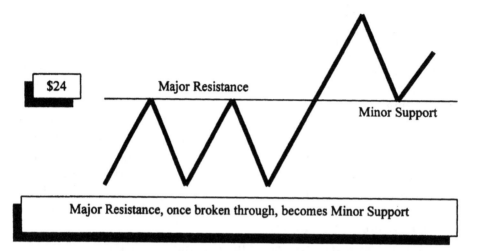

$24 | Major Resistance | Minor Support

Major Resistance, once broken through, becomes Minor Support

Minor support and resistance. Let's continue with the previous example to demonstrate the minor form of support and resistance. If XYZ were to significantly break through $24 (major resistance) and trade as high as say $26, the area of $24 would become minor support. *Tip:* In other words, major resistance, once broken through, becomes minor support. If XYZ were to decline and break through $20 (major support) and trade as low as say $18, the area of $20 would become minor resistance (see Figure 11.26). *Tip:* In other words, major support, once broken through, becomes minor resistance (see Figure 11.27).

HOW THE MASTER TRADER INTERPRETS SUPPORT AND RESISTANCE

- Major and minor support and resistance are areas, not specific price points. They should be viewed as fences that the bulls and bears can lean on, not as glass floors and ceilings that break at the first point of contact.
- A prior low that has kicked off a sharp rally will typically serve as major support if and when it is retested (Figure 11.28).
- A prior high that has ignited a sharp decline will typically serve as major resistance, if and when it is retested (Figure 11.29).

An example of how major support becomes minor resistance.

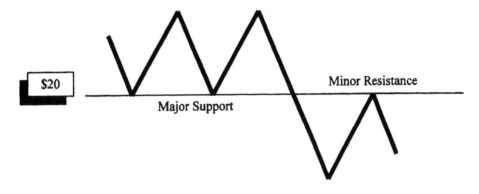

- Low-risk buying opportunities often present themselves in the area of major support.
- Low-risk shorting opportunities often present themselves in the area of major resistance.
- In up trends, areas of minor support become key potential buy points (Figure 11.30).
- In down trends, areas of minor resistance become key potential sell (short) points (Figure 11.31).
- Major and minor support and resistance used in conjunction with any one or more of the other Pristine charting tools makes for powerful buy and sell opportunities.

HOW THE MASTER TRADER PLAYS SUPPORT AND RESISTANCE

- The master trader looks for any one of the key buy setups* in the areas of major and minor support. A key buy setup at or near support will trigger a buy (Figure 11.32).
- The master trader looks for any one of the key sell setups* in the areas of major and minor resistance. A key sell setup at or near resistance will trigger a sell (Figure 11.33).

*The key buy and sell setups will be discussed in a later chapter.

This 15-minute chart of Lattice Semi (LSCC) shows how significant major support can be.

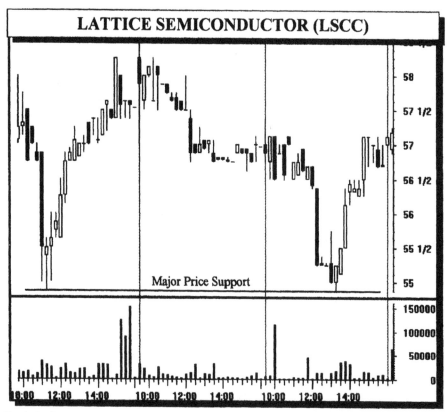

Chart by The Executioner.com

CHARTING TOOL #6: RETRACEMENTS

RETRACEMENT DESCRIPTION

The concept of retracements is one of the main keys that unlock the door to predicting price movements and picking low-risk entry points. They give the master trader a reference point for predicting where price turns might occur, and they also serve as a way to measure just how strong the preceding move was. Most importantly, retracements keep the trader's expectations in check. They prevent the trader from projecting his or her hopes and fears into expectations of the next move. In other words, retracements help keep the trader objective.

F I G U R E   11.29

This daily chart of Lucent Tech (LU) powerfully demonstrates the powerful concept of major resistance.

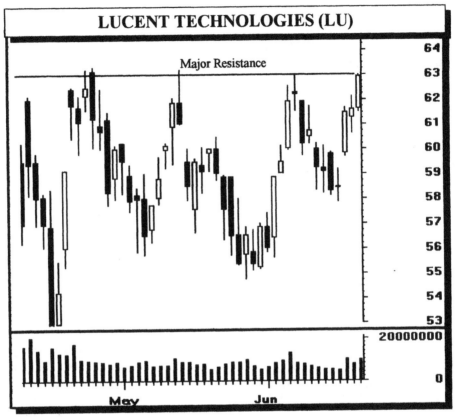

LUCENT TECHNOLOGIES (LU)

Major Resistance

Chart by The Executioner.com

   In its most basic form, a *retracement* is a price move in the exact opposite direction of the most recent price move. For example, if a stock advances $4, then pulls back by $2, it has experienced a 50 percent
retracement. If the stock were to pullback the entire $4, it is said to have
experienced a 100 percent retracement, which potentially sets up what
chartists call a double bottom. The same is true for the reverse. If a stock
declines $4, then rallies back by $2, it is said to have experienced a 50 percent retracement. It should be noted that the most important retracement
levels for master traders are 40, 50, 60, and of course 100 percent, also
known as a double bottom (see Figure 11.34). Let's take a look at the following examples.

F I G U R E   11.30

Prior highs, once broken through, often serve as minor price support. This daily chart of Motorola Inc.
(MOT) clearly demonstrates that.

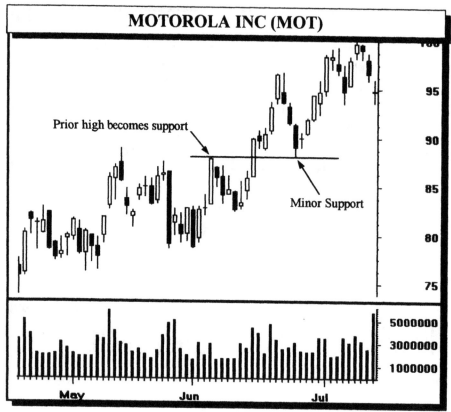

Chart by The Executioner.com

HOW THE MASTER TRADER INTERPRETS RETRACEMENTS

- Key retracement levels are general guidelines or areas, not exact points.
- If a stock experiences a shallow retracement (40 percent or less), the prior move is considered to be strong, and as a result the counter move should be strong.
- If a stock experiences a deep retracement (60 percent or greater), the prior move is considered weak, and as a result the countermove should be weak.

F I G U R E   **11.31**

Prior lows, once broken through, often serve as minor resistance. This daily chart of APOL clearly demonstrates that.

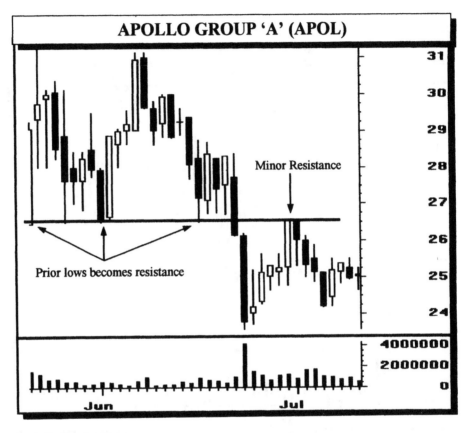

Chart by The Executioner.com

- The first retracement after a strong up move is buyable nearly 100 percent of the time.
- The first retracement after a strong down move is sellable nearly 100 percent of the time.
- A 40 percent retracement after a strong advance is typically followed by a move to a new high.
- A 40 percent retracement after a strong decline is typically followed by a move to a new low.

F I G U R E   11.32

This daily chart of Oracle Corporation (ORCL) displays perfect examples of major support and major resistance. Keep in mind that support and resistance must be looked at as areas, not as specific price points. The areas marked by S are potential sells (shorts), while the areas marked by B are potential buys.

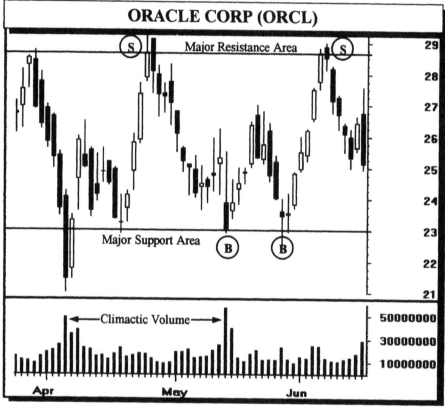

Chart by The Executioner.com

- A 50 percent retracement after a strong advance often leads to a move with a 50/50 chance of exceeding the prior high. The same applies in reverse.
- A 60 percent retracement after a strong advance often leads to a move with a 1 in 3 chance of exceeding the prior high. The same also applies in reverse.
- 100 percent downside retracement, which sets up a potential double bottom, is typically followed by a 50 to 60 percent rebound.

FIGURE   11.33

This 5-minute chart of DoubleClick (DCLK) shows major support in the $96 area and major resistance in the $98 area. The area marked by B indicates a buy, the area marked by S indicates a potential sell (short).

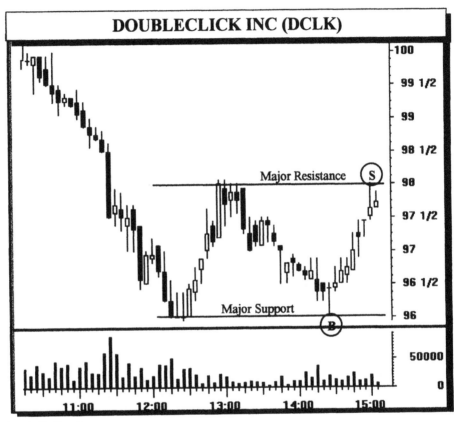

Chart by The Executioner.com

- A 100 percent upside retracement is typically followed by a 50 to 60 percent decline.
- Excellent entry points present themselves at or near all key reversal points: 40, 50, 60, and 100 percent. However, the objectives on each are quite different (Figures 11.35 and 11.36).

HOW THE MASTER TRADER PLAYS RETRACEMENTS

- The master trader looks for buying and selling opportunities at all key retracement levels: 40, 50, 60, and 100 percent.

Example of a 50 and 100 percent retracement.

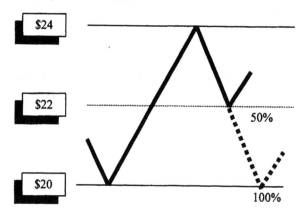

- The master trader looks to take profits decently above the prior high on shallow retracements (40 percent or less). The same applies in reverse.
- The master trader looks to take profits at or slightly above the prior high on 50 percent retracements. The same applies in reverse.
- The master trader looks to take profits slightly below the prior high on 60 percent retracements. The same applies in reverse (Figure 11.37).
- After a 100 percent retracement, the master trader looks to take profits on the counter move between 40 and 50 percent levels (Figure 11.38).

CHARTING TOOL #7: REVERSAL TIMES

REVERSAL TIME DESCRIPTION

A decade of trading stocks and other financial instrument has led us to the amazing discovery that there are specific points or pockets of time around which stocks and the general market as a whole consistently experience price reversals. These *reversal times,* as we call them, are generally so accurate that many of our students and subscribers familiar with the concept stay perpetually amazed. It should be noted that these reversal times are intraday in nature. They serve as a valuable tool for

F I G U R E   11.35

This daily chart of AMAT demonstrates a near-perfect 40 percent retracement. Note that AMAT's move from bottom to top was quite robust. This alerts the master trader to the likelihood of a shallow, but playable decline. Note that the formation of a bullish reversal bar (RB) also signaled a potential turn at the 40 percent retracement level.

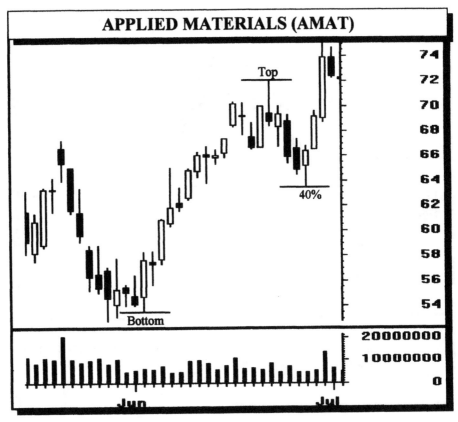

Chart by The Executioner.com

microtraders who constantly look to exploit small price moves through-out the day. The key reversal times are as follows: (1) 9:50–10:10 a.m., (2) 10:25–10:35 a.m., (3) 11:15–11:30 a.m., (4) 12:00–12:15 p.m., (5) 1:15–1:30 p.m., (6) 2:15–2:30 p.m., (7) 3:00 p.m., and (8) 3:30 p.m.

HOW THE MASTER TRADER INTERPRETS REVERSAL TIMES

- *9:50 – 10:10 a.m. EST.* Often times, a stock that is moving up into this reversal time zone will either stall or reverse and head lower. The same is true for the reverse. A stock that is moving

F I G U R E   11.36

This daily chart of CNCX demonstrates a near perfect 50 percent retracement. Note that CNCX's move from bottom to top was quite robust. this alerts the master trader to the likelihood of a playable decline. Note that the formation of a narrow-range bar (NRB) also signaled a potential turn at the 50 percent retracement level.

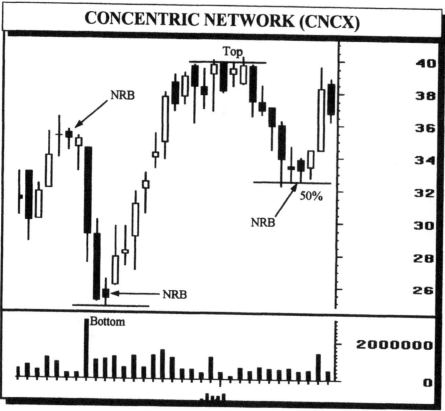

Chart by The Executioner.com

down into this reversal time zone will tend to stall or reverse and head higher. The 9:50 to 10:10 a.m. reversal time is by far one of the most reliable reversal times in existence.

- *10:25 – 10:35 a.m. EST.* A stock that is moving down into this reversal time zone will also tend to either stall or reverse back to the upside. If a stock is moving up into this time zone, it will often halt its advance or reverse and head lower. This is also one of the more reliable reversal times (Figure 11.39).

F I G U R E   11.37

This daily chart of CEFT demonstrates a near perfect 60% retracement. The move from bottom to top was quite robust, alerting the master trader to the likelihood of a shallow, but playable decline. Note that the bottoming tails and the formation of an NRB also signaled a potential turn at the 60 percent retracement level.

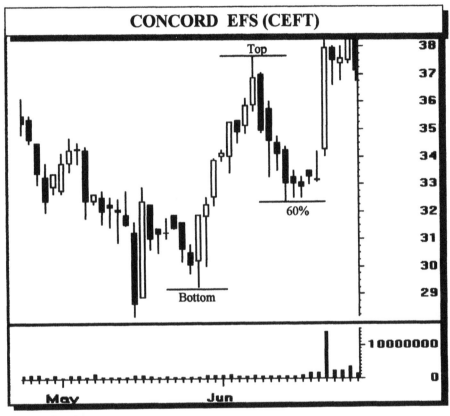

Chart by The Executioner.com

- *11:15 – 11:30 a.m. EST.* This reversal time tends to accomplish two things. First, it tends to halt the prevailing trend preceding it. For instance, if a stock is rallying strongly into this time zone, chances are its advance will be abruptly halted in the 11:15 – 11:30 a.m. time period. We have further found that the stall that this time zone puts in will tend to be an enduring one. Needless to say, the same goes for the reverse. Second, the 11:15 – 11:30 a.m. reversal time kicks of the period we call the *midday doldrums.* The midday doldrums is an elongated period that

F I G U R E   11.38

This daily chart of IBM shows a near perfect 100 percent retracement. Note that the 100 percent retracement ties in with the concept of major support.

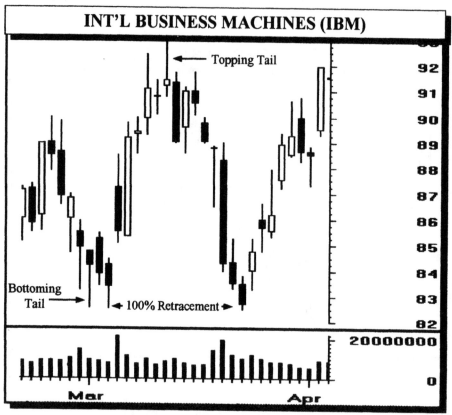

spans from 11:15 a.m. – 2:15 p.m. During this extended time zone, many stocks, as well as the market as a whole, often go into a major lull.

- *12:00 – 12:15 p.m. EST.* We have found this time period to be most important on days in which the morning has been quiet or directionless. Despite the fact that it is in the midday doldrums period, we have seen the 12:00 – 12:30 p.m. time zone kick off some major moves in both directions, but only when the preceding period was very quiet. Keep in mind that these 12:00 – 12:30 p.m. reversals are far less common than the preceding three reversal periods.

- *1:15 – 1:30 p.m. EST.* This is one of the more minor reversal periods. We have found it to be most significant when it coincides with the retest of a prior high or low. For example, lets say XYZ tops out around 11:15 a.m. After a pullback, it rallies back to retest the 11:15 a.m. high in the 1:30 p.m. time period. The odds of a double top dramatically increase, because the retest of the prior high is coinciding with the 1:15 – 1:30 p.m. time period. These retests that occur in line with the 1:15 – 1:30 p.m. reversal time can present some interesting trading opportunities.

- *2:15 – 2:30 p.m. EST.* As mentioned previously, this time period puts an end to the *midday doldrums* period. It also serves as a very reliable reversal period for stocks and the general market as a whole. The most important thing to remember about the 2:15 – 2:30 p.m. time period is that it often marks the precise period when things start heating up again. The 2:15 – 2:30 p.m. time reversal is so pronounced at times that many master traders regard the period as the market's second open (Figures 11.40 and 11.41).

- *3:00 p.m. EST.* This reversal time often brings change because it coincides with the close of the bond market. Bonds often have a pronounced effect on the equity market. Once they have closed, traders feel as though there is one less thing to worry about. In other words, once bonds are out of the way, they can't help or harm the market. This often results in stocks or the market taking on a different, more accelerated character. We have found the 3:00 p.m. reversal time to be most valuable as a guide for S&P futures.

- *3:30 p.m. EST.* We have found that this time often reverses any move that was kicked off at the previous 3:00 p.m. reversal time, particularly when the market is in a sideways trading range. For instance, if the market started dropping from 3:00 p.m. and continued to do so right into the 3:30 p.m. reversal time, the next move would most likely be up. The same situation occurs in reverse. Keep in mind that the last half hour is one of the most active for many day traders, as it often represents the last flurry of activity.

- *4:00 p.m. EST.* We have found that shortly after the 4:00 p.m. time, almost everything stops. Could this have anything to do with the fact that the market closes at 4:00 p.m.? Of course. Just

FIGURE   11.39

After opening down on the morning of July 25, AMAT rallied into the 9:50 – 10:10 a.m. reversal time, filling its gap in the process. The subsequent decline bottomed in the 10:25 – 10:35 a.m. reversal time.

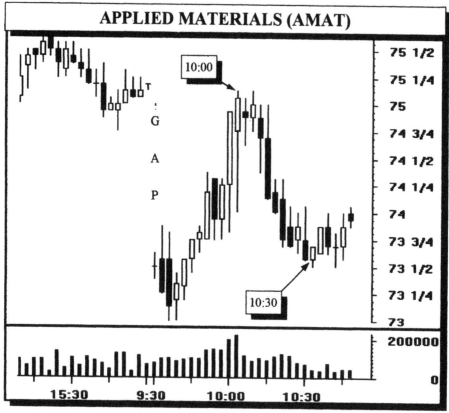

Chart by The Executioner.com

making light of the obvious. But keep in mind that 24-hour trading is close at hand. Once this extended trading takes place, look for the 4:00 p.m. time to be an important reversal time.

HOW THE MASTER TRADER PLAYS REVERSAL TIMES

- The master trader looks for buy setups and other low-risk entry points at or near the key reversal times.
- The master trader combines the other trading tools, like narrow-range bars, tails, climactic volume, and support and resistance, with the reversal times to predict the probability, direction, and potency of the potential turns.

FIGURE 11.40

On July 16, Concord EFS (CEFT) gaps up to the 200 SMA on the 15-minute chart. The stock then drops into the 10:30 a.m. reversal time and reverses. CEFT rebounds back toward the 200 SMA, and tops out at the 2:30 p.m. reversal time. The rest is history.

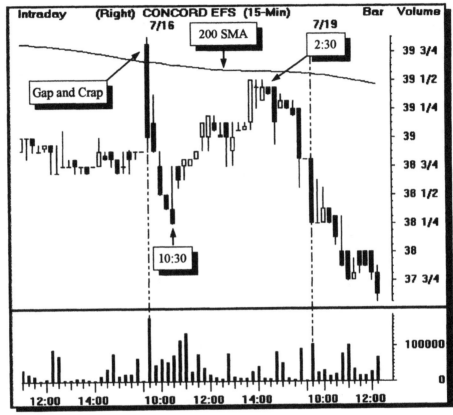

Chart by The Executioner.com

- The master trader also uses reversal times as profit taking guides.
- Numerous buy and sell (shorting) opportunities will present themselves at the key reversal times.

CHARTING TOOL #8: CLIMACTIC VOLUME

CLIMACTIC VOLUME DESCRIPTION

Volume is to the stock market what fuel is to a car. Not only does it represent the level of interest among buyers and sellers, it can serve as a ba-

F I G U R E   11.41

ANDW's early morning decline bottoms at the 10:25 – 10:35 a.m. reversal time. The subsequent rally stalls in the 11:15 – 11:30 a.m. reversal time. Around the 1:30 p.m. reversal time, ANDW begins another microdecline, which bottoms in the 2:15 – 2:30 p.m. reversal time.

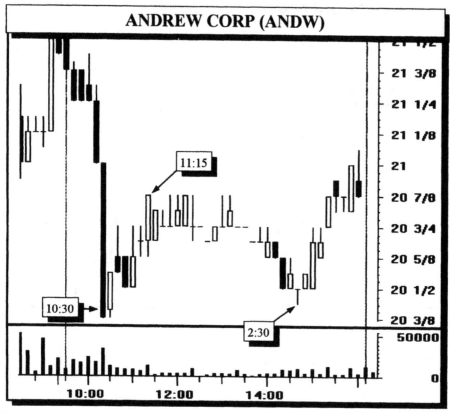

Chart by The Executioner.com

rometer of greed and fear. There is no doubt in our minds that volume, in particular climactic volume, is one of the most valuable keys to predicting price turns. The trader who masters the art of reading price/volume relationships will be able to pick reversal points in stocks with an amazing accuracy.

Over the years, we have found that far too many traders believe that a rising stock, accompanied by an explosive increase in volume, is positive, and a falling stock accompanied by an explosive increase in volume is negative. While at times those general assumptions can be true, in most cases they are not. Volume, in its most useful form, tells us when a stock is running out of buying fuel or selling fuel. This brings us to what we believe is the most important volume rule in existence. **Climactic volume,** *after* **a strong advance or decline, indicates that a near-term price reversal is at hand.** The operative phrase in the above rule is "*after* a strong advance or decline." While there are several more useful volume rules, the one just revealed is by far the most valuable for traders. Let's look at the two examples in Figures 11.42 and 11.43.

HOW THE MASTER TRADER INTERPRETS CLIMACTIC VOLUME

- Volume is considered climactic when it exceeds two times the average daily volume over the past 10 days.
- Climactic volume typically brings an end to the preceding up or down move.
- Climactic volume, after a strong, multibar move to the upside, indicates a top. In this case, buyers have used up all their fuel.
- Climactic volume, after a strong, multibar move to the downside, indicates a bottom. In this case sellers have used up all their fuel.
- Climactic volume is more powerful as a concept when it occurs in conjunction with other charting tools.

HOW THE MASTER TRADER PLAYS CLIMACTIC VOLUME

- When climactic volume occurs after a strong move to the upside, the master trader gets into buy mode.
- When climactic volume occurs after a strong move to the downside, the master trader gets into sell mode.
- When long, the master trader looks to take profits when climactic volume follows a multibar move to the upside.
- When short, the master trader looks to take profits when climactic volume follows a multibar move to the downside.

CHARTING TOOL # 9: MOVING AVERAGES

MOVING AVERAGE DESCRIPTION

Moving averages (MA) are mathematical items that smooth out the rough data of a price chart, effectively eliminating the bar to bar "noise."

F I G U R E   11.42

This daily chart of Compaq Computer (CPQ) shows how climactic volume can abruptly put in a major bottom. Note that the bullish reversal bar (RB) with a bottoming tail also helped put in the low. These events are the footprints left by big buyers.

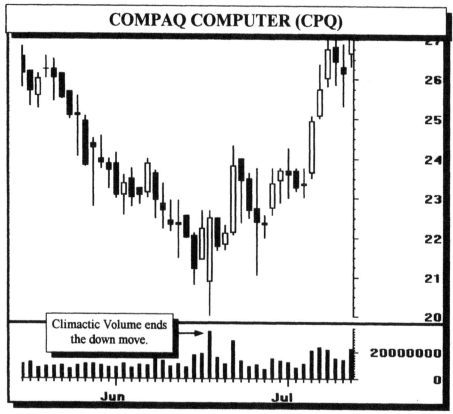

Chart by The Executioner.com

Moving averages are, by far, the most superior trend-following tools in existence, so much so that we don't consider a price chart worthy of our attention unless it is accompanied by one or more of the following five dominant moving averages. It should be noted that there are different types or versions of moving averages. We use the "simple" version of moving averages. Despite the arguments, we have yet to find any hard evidence that suggests that the sexier versions, such as exponential, triangular and weighted, enjoy greater reliability when it comes to equities. Futures, however, do call for a greater use of the exponential form of

FIGURE 11.43

This daily chart of VRIO demonstrates how climactic volume can abruptly put in a major top.

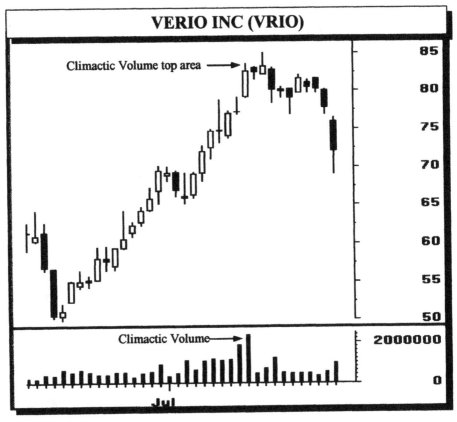

VERIO INC (VRIO)

Climactic Volume top area →

Climactic Volume →

Chart by The Executioner.com

moving averages, simply because the majority of futures traders now predominantly use exponential moving averages.

$$\text{Formula for simple MA} = \frac{P1 + P2 + \ldots + PN}{N}$$

where P = the price of the stocks being averaged and N = the number of bars the trader wants to include in the moving average. For example, if a stock's last five closing prices were $20, $20.75, $22, $21.25, and $21, the 5-bar simple moving average of closing prices would be plotted at $21 ($20 + $20.75 + $22 + $21.25 + $21), divided by 5.

THE FIVE DOMINANT SIMPLE MOVING AVERAGES (SMA)

1. *10 SMA.* A short-term MA used on stocks in the most powerful up and down trends.

2. *20 SMA.* A short- to intermediate-term MA. This is our most dominant MA. We train our traders to regard the 20 MA as a permanent part of every chart, irrespective of time frame.

3. *50 SMA.* An intermediate-term MA. This is one of the most popular MAs, especially among institutions. As a result of this professional attention, it should be referred to frequently. *Note:* We have found that the 40 MA can be interchanged with the 50 MA.

4. *100 SMA.* An intermediate- to long-term MA. This is not a frequently used MA for day traders, but can prove valuable when a stock or the market nears it.

5. *200 SMA.* A long-term MA. This is one of the most reliable MAs in existence. We use it on daily charts and 15-minute intraday charts where its accuracy is unrivaled.

While the mathematical computation to construct a simple moving average is basic and easy to implement, computers and today's prevalent charting software do it all automatically. Most master traders today use direct access electronic trading (DAET) systems, which offer everything a trader needs, including charts. For instance, the Executioner.com's DAET system, which is the one we use, offers real-time quotes, real-time charts, real-time news, NASDAQ level II access, ECN access, live portfolio tracking, and the complete capability to customize the design and format. Its charting package is particularly robust and makes placing or plotting moving averages on charts effortless. Let's take a look at how the master trader looks at MAs.

HOW THE MASTER TRADER INTERPRETS MOVING AVERAGES (MAS)

- There is no tool more reliable than MAs when dealing with stocks in up or down trends.
- There is no tool worse than MAs when dealing with stocks in sloppy sideways trends.
- *Rising* MAs, particularly the 10, 20, and 50 SMAs, mean the stock is positive. As a result, declines will tend to be short-lived and present very decent buying opportunities.
- *Declining* MAs, particularly the 10, 20, and 50 SMAs, mean the stock is negative. As a result, rallies will tend to be short-lived and present very decent shorting opportunities.

- The sharper the slope of the MA(s), the more powerful the trend.
- Strong stocks tend to halt their declines at or near rising MAs.
- Weak stocks tend to halt their rallies at or near declining MAs.
- The 10 SMA is best used on stocks in the daily time frame that are in very powerful up and down trends.
- The 20 SMA is the trader's most dominant MA, and should be used on virtually every chart, irrespective of time frame (Figures 11.44 and 11.45).
- The 50 SMA should be referred to on the daily chart.
- The 100 SMA should become a focus when a stock in an up or down trend has significantly violated the 50 SMA.
- The 200 MA is best used on the daily chart and the 15-minute intraday chart (Figure 11.46).
- All stocks can be divided into three broad groups: (1) stocks with rising 20 MAs, which represent a good starting point for buy candidates; (2) stocks with declining 20 MAs, which represent a good starting point for short candidates; and (3) stocks with relatively flat 20 MAs, which represent stocks in directionless trading ranges and/or sideways consolidations.
- Other events, like NRBs, RBs, and climactic volume, that set up at or near rising or declining MAs will offer amazing buy and sell opportunities.

HOW THE MASTER TRADER PLAYS MOVING AVERAGES

- When a stock in a strong up trend pulls back to retest a *rising* MA, the master trader goes into buy mode.
- When a stock in a strong down trend rallies back to retest a *declining* MA, the master trader goes into sell mode (Figures 11.47, 11.48, and 11.49).

CHARTING TOOL #10: 3 TO 5 BAR DROP

3 TO 5 BAR DROP DESCRIPTION

The 3 to 5 bar drop is a very simple event that forms the basis for numerous profitable trading opportunities. As far as we are concerned, it is one of the master keys to finding low-risk entry points, and, as a result, we have heavily used it in our day-to-day analysis for nearly a decade. *If there were only one trading concept we could teach, the 3 to 5 bar drop would be it.*

F I G U R E   11.44

Applied Materials (AMAT) finds support on its rising 20 SM.

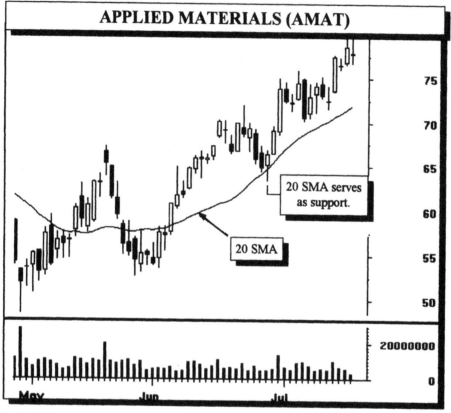

Chart by The Executioner.com

In its simplest form, the 3 to 5 bar drop is just that, a decline comprised of 3 to 5 consecutive down bars, the operative word being *consecutive*. But before we delve deeper into this indispensable charting event, we must define what we mean by a down bar. For purposes of the 3 to 5 bar drop, a *down bar* is defined by the following criteria:

1. Current bar's closing price is lower than the prior bar's closing price.
2. Current bar's closing price is below the current bar's opening price.
3. Current bar's open is at or near the high of the current bar's range.

F I G U R E   11.45

This daily chart of Electronic Arts (ERTS) shows how supportive the rising 20 SMA can be. Note that the 20 SMA serves as an "area" of support, not as a glass floor that shatters at the first point of contact. MAs are flexible items that have a certain degree of "give."

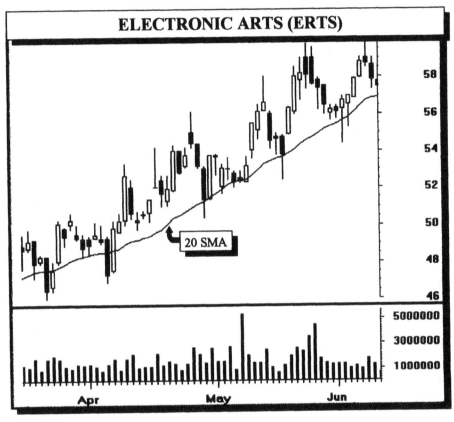

Chart by The Executioner.com

4. Current bar's close is at or near the low of the current bar's range (see Figure 11.50).

We have found that strong stocks (those in up trends) tend to rebound sharply after experiencing 3 to 5 consecutive down days. The strongest stocks will tend to rebound after 3 down days, while those, which are moderately strong, will do so after 4 or 5 down days. *Tip:* Any decline that exceeds 5 consecutive down bars is signaling weakness. The 3 to 5 down bars rid the stock of its weak hands (those who exit at the first sign of trouble), creates a moderately oversold condition, which attracts new

F I G U R E   11.46

3COM Corp (COMS) rallies to its 200 SMA and collapses.

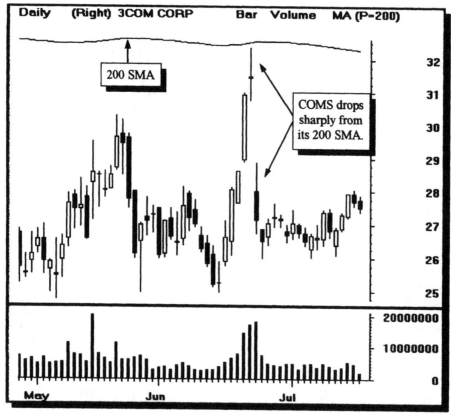

Chart by The Executioner.com

buyers, and effectively dries up the supply. It is after this simple but powerful event that the master trader steps into the arena to look for the right moment to strike (enter). When is the right moment, you ask? *After a 3 to 5 bar drop, the master trader buys the very next time the stock trades above a prior bar's high.* Let's look at an example in Figure 11.51.

HOW THE MASTER TRADER INTERPRETS THE 3 – 5 BAR DROP

- Stocks in strong up trends will tend to halt their declines after 3 to 5 consecutive down bars.
- Excellent, low-risk buy opportunities tend to set up after 3 to 5 bar drops.

F I G U R E   11.47

This 5-minute chart of ALTR clearly shows how powerful the 200 SMA can be. *Tip:* An overhead 200 SMA on the daily, 5- and/or 15-minute charts can serve as excellent profit-taking areas.

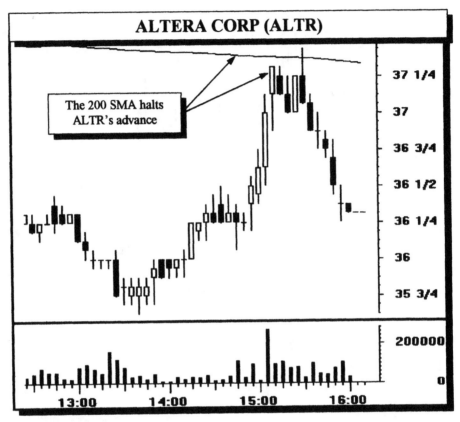

Chart by The Executioner.com

- The best 3 to 5 bar drops are those in which each down bar's opening price is near the prior bar's closing price. In other words, 3 to 5 bar drops that involve gaps to the upside or downside generally weaken, if not violate, the pattern.
- A 3 to 5 bar advance, in the context of a downtrend, sets up good shorting (selling) opportunities. The 3 to 5 bar advance is obviously the reverse setup.
- The 3 to 5 bar drop, combined with other tools and events, such as NRBs, tails, climactic volume, support and resistance, and moving averages, set up near-perfect buy opportunities. *Note:*

F I G U R E   11.48

The 200 SMA on the 15-minute is the "law," and this 15-minute chart of MSFT clearly shows that. Note how the sharp drop halted right on its 200 SMA. *Tip:* The master trader will not even consider looking at a 15-minute chart without 200 SMA superimposed on it.

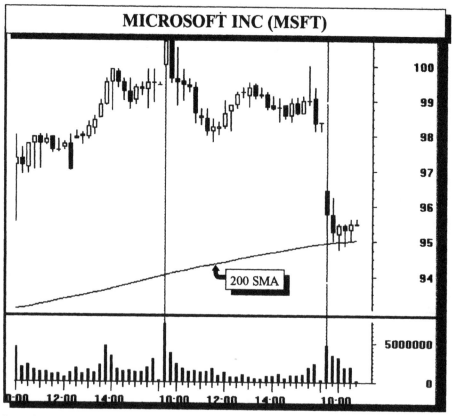

Chart by The Executioner.com

These combinations form the basis for nearly all our trading tactics and techniques.

HOW THE MASTER TRADER PLAYS 3 TO 5 BAR DROPS

- When a strong stock experiences a 3 to 5 bar drop, the master trader generally looks to buy above the prior bar's high (Figures 11.52 and 11.53.

This 5-minute chart of CTXS demonstrates how powerful the 200 MA is as support. Note how strong the rally of the 200 MA was.

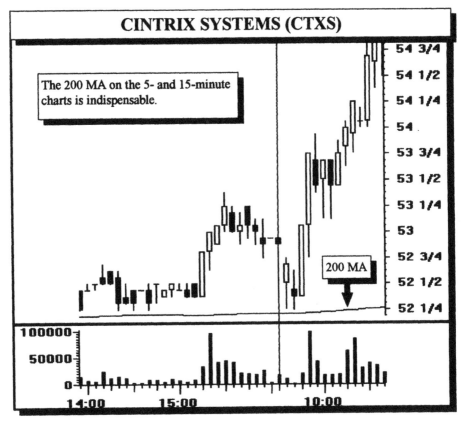

Chart by The Executioner.com

- When a weak stock experiences a 3 to 5 bar advance, the master trader generally looks to sell short below prior bar's low (Figure 11.54).

F I G U R E   11.50

A 3 to 5 bar drop that meets the four criteria. It is important to note that these criteria only form a general guide. Being too strict or precise may result in missing viable setups that lead to trading profits.

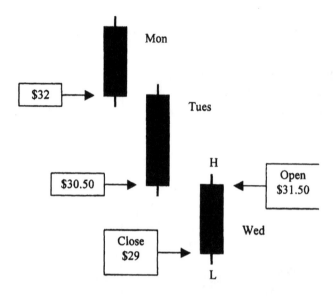

F I G U R E   11.51

After a 3 to 5 bar drop, the master trader buys the next time the stock trades above a prior bar's high. In this case, the master trader buys on Thursday above $31.

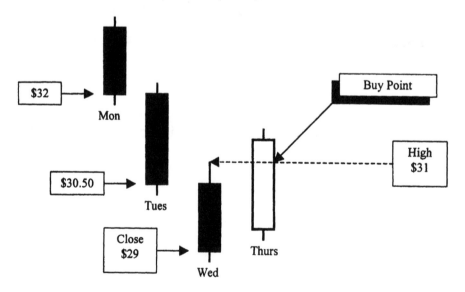

This daily chart of BGEN shows a near perfect 3 to 5 bar drop setup. After a 3 to 5 bar drop, the master trader buys the very next time the stock trades above a prior bar's high. *Tip:* Aggressive master traders would buy on any bullish RB following a 3 to 5 bar drop.

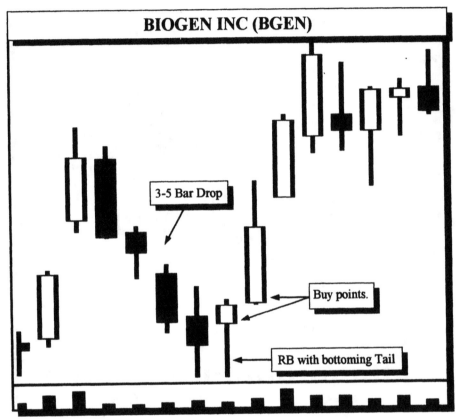

BIOGEN INC (BGEN)

3-5 Bar Drop

Buy points.

RB with bottoming Tail

Chart by The Executioner.com

F I G U R E   11.53

This daily chart of LXK shows two 3 to 5 bar drops, which in turn set up two buy points. *Tip:* After a 3 to 5 bar drop, the master trader buys the very next time the underlying stock trades above a prior bar's high..

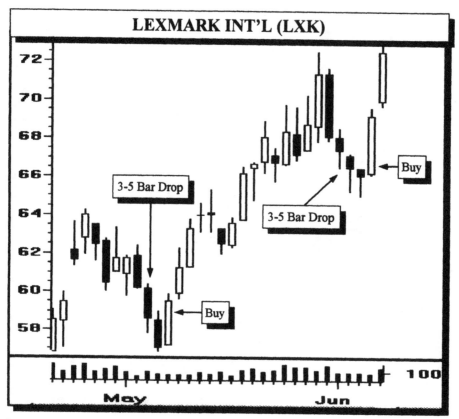

Chart by The Executioner.com

F I G U R E   11.54

This 15-minute chart of AOL shows a 3 to 5 bar advance which sets up a perfect sell (short) setup. After a 3 to 5 bar drop, in context a downtrend, the master trader sells the very next time the stock trades below a prior bar's low.

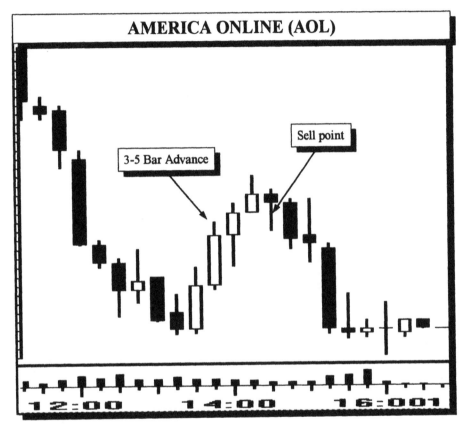

Chart by The Executioner.com

12
CHAPTER

EXECUTION TOOLS AND TACTICS

Once traders have defined their trading strategy and identified a trade opportunity, they must determine how best to capitalize on the opportunity. Master traders recognize that their trading success is heavily influenced by their order-placement methods. An otherwise successful trading strategy can result in net losses through improper order-placement techniques. In fact, one of the most difficult parts of trading is determining the best way to get your orders executed.

Most investors understand the difference between the most elementary kinds of orders such as market orders and limit orders. A *market order* is a request to buy/sell stock immediately at the best available price, with no restriction placed on the ultimate price paid for the stock. A *limit order* is a request to buy/sell a stock, restricted to a specified price or better. For example, a trader may place a limit order to buy Intel Corporation (INTC) stock at a price of $82 per share or lower.

Master Traders recognize that these elementary order types are only the foundation for developing their order-placement strategy and maximizing the benefit of direct access to the marketplace. Different trading methods will require different order-placement techniques. Traders looking to win the spread and "play market maker" will have a totally different order-placement strategy than momentum traders trying to catch a fast-moving stock. Fortunately, master traders have a wide variety of order-execution options available at their disposal. For NASDAQ stocks, these options include utilizing one of the Electronic Communication Networks (ECN's), the Small-Order Execution System

F I G U R E   12.1

The Executioner.com's order-execution module shows the various ways by which a master trader can execute trades. Executioner.com users have direct access to two ECNs: Archipelago (ARCA) and Island (ISLD)*, the Small-Order Executioner System (SOES), Selectnet (SNET), and SuperDot (ISI). These execution vehicles are crucial tools for the master trader, and a thorough understanding of how each one works and when each one should be used is essential.

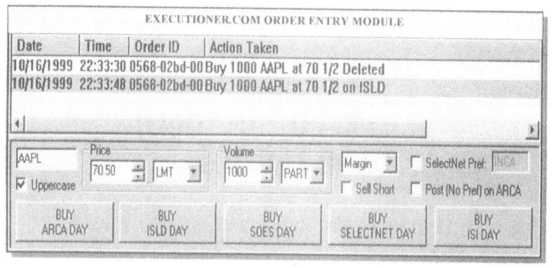

Chart by The Executioner.com

(SOES), the SelectNet system (SNET), and the more sophisticated automated order-routing options such as the Archipelago system (ARCA). For NYSE orders, master traders will predominately be using the SuperDOT (Designated Order Turnaround) system to route their orders to the exchange floor. All of these order-execution options are available to traders using powerful order-entry software offered by firms such as The Executioner (*www.executioner.com*). It should be noted that The Executioner was one of the original firms providing individuals with this powerful trading software and it's the system used by all Pristine in-house traders (Figure 12.1).

Finally, some traders may be executing their orders through discount brokers, such as Datek, E-trade, Ameritrade, Fidelity, and others, and their orders will be sold to market makers for execution. Let's explore each of these available order-execution options and discuss when each might be most appropriate to use.

EXECUTION TOOL #1: ELECTRONIC COMMUNICATION NETWORKS (ECNS)

ELECTRONIC COMMUNICATION NETWORKS (ECNS) DESCRIPTION

ECNs were created by NASDAQ in 1997 for the display and execution of limit orders. As of this writing, nine ECNs have been formed with many more to come. The current nine are: Island (ISLD), Archipelago (ARCA), Instinet (INCA), Bloomberg Tradebook (BTRD), Spear, Leeds and Kellogg (REDI), Attain (ATTN), Strike (STRK), BRUT, and Next-Trade (NTRD). Any other quotes seen on the Level II display are from market makers. On some Level II displays, ECNs will be shown with a "#" after their symbol, such as ISLD# or INCA#. This is to facilitate quick identification of those quotes that are from ECNs. ECNs should not be confused with market makers; there are hundreds of market making firms, some of whom are Goldman Sachs (GSCO), Merrill Lynch (MLCO), and Solomon Smith Barney (SBSH), just to name a few (Figure 12.2).

An ECN is merely a computerized limit order book, comprised of hundreds or thousands of individual orders to buy or sell stock at a certain price. The function of an ECN is to electronically match buyers with sellers, eliminating the need for human traders or market makers. As you will soon see, ECNs are very much like ministock exchanges. The best bid and ask limit orders for each stock are communicated to NASDAQ for display as the bid/ask quote for the ECN. For example, assume the following limit orders are on the ISLD book for stock INTC:

Buy 100 shares at $70\frac{7}{8}$*   Sell 400 shares at $71\frac{1}{16}$*
Buy 200 shares at $70\frac{7}{8}$*   Sell 1000 shares at $71\frac{1}{4}$
Buy 200 shares at $70\frac{5}{8}$ Sell 100 shares at 72
Buy 300 shares at $70\frac{1}{4}$

At this time, the best (*) bid price on the book is at $70\frac{7}{8}$, with a collective size of 300 shares. The best (*) ask price is $71\frac{1}{16}$ with 400 shares offered. Therefore, the NASDAQ Level II display for ISLD would show these best bid/ask prices and sizes (Figure 12.3).

Master traders will be able to execute against existing limit orders on any of the ECNs using the SelectNet (SNET) system. However, only with direct access will the trader be able to actually *post* a limit order on the ECN limit order book for display on NASDAQ Level II. Traders will typically have *direct* access to no more than a few ECNs, with the most common being ISLD, ARCA, and REDI.

F I G U R E   12.2

This figure shows a NASDAQ Level II quote screen for MCHP. It is the NASDAQ Level II screen that provides the master trader with the ability to see a stock's depth, meaning the bid and offers of ECNs and market makers. The circles highlight, INCA and ISLD, two ECNs. All the other bids and offers (asking prices) shown are from market makers. We cover NASDAQ Level II quotes and market maker characteristics more thoroughly in Chapter 13.

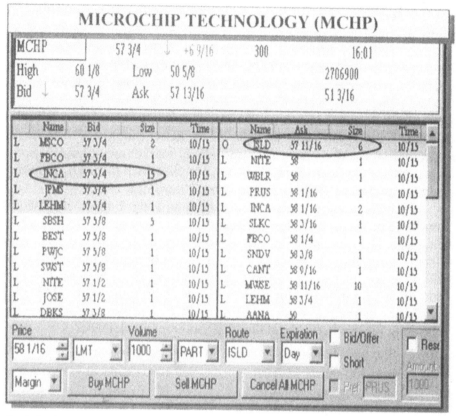

Chart by The Executioner.com

ADVANTAGES OF ECNS

- Enables extremely fast fills (as little as 0.2 seconds) when placing a matching order to execute against an existing order on the ECN limit order book.
- ECN quotes are real. If you see a quote on an ECN, it is a real quote at that price and at that size. If you are the first person to send a matching order to execute against an ECN quote, you *will* get filled.

FIGURE   12.3

The two orders on ISLD bidding for INTC stock show up on the NASDAQ Level II quote screen as one single ISLD post for 300 shares. See the left-hand side, which is the bid side. The one order to sell 400 shares of INTC on ISLD shows up on the right-hand side, which is the offer or asking side.

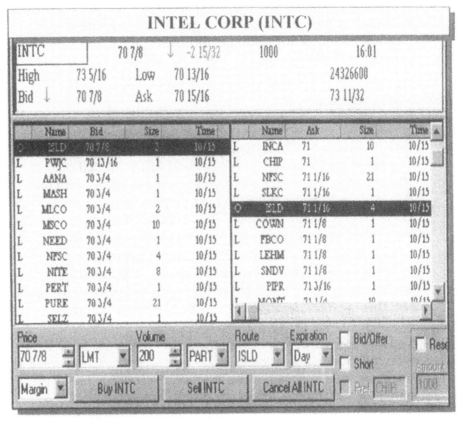

Chart by The Executioner.com

- ECNs will show their entire size (unless originators have specifically requested that their order not be displayed). If an ECN has collective orders of 14,200 shares to buy at its best price of 81, you will see all 14,200 shares displayed on your Level II display.
- ECNs allow the traders to post their limit order for display on NASDAQ Level II. This gives you broad advertising for all market participants to see your order.
- ECNs can quote prices in much finer increments than is possible on NASDAQ. ISLD, for example, allows for orders priced as

finely as $\frac{1}{128}$ for stocks above $10 and $\frac{1}{256}$ for stocks priced below $10. These orders will be rounded to the nearest $\frac{1}{16}$ or $\frac{1}{32}$ (stocks less than $10) for display on NASDAQ Level II. However, they will be displayed on the ECN book and executed based on actual price priority.

- ECNs avoid the many disadvantages associated with direct interaction with market makers through the SOES and SNET systems.

DISADVANTAGES OF ECNS

- Some ECNs are not very liquid, making execution by way of a match infrequent. The most liquid and therefore the best ECNs to post on are INCA, ISLD, ARCA, and REDI. We tell our students not to consider any direct access trading system that does not provide the ability to directly post on ISLD and ARCA. These two ECNs are indispensable, as far as we are concerned. We will delve deeper into the features of ARCA shortly.

- In a quickly rising stock, it will be difficult to buy using an ECN at or below the inside ask price. In other words, it will be unlikely to get your bid filled at the inside bid price of the stock and there will not typically be any ECN limit order offers available to execute against the inside ask.

- You may frequently get filled with partial executions. ISLD is the worst offender with this problem, as they accept orders as small as one share of stock. Imagine the frustration of getting filled with only 14 shares out of a 1000 share order. *Note:* All other ECNs require that orders be placed in increments of 100 shares.

HOW A MASTER TRADER USES THE ECNS

Master traders recognize the many advantages of ECNs and uses them often. Specific examples of when ECNs should be used include:

- When master traders are bidding for a stock below the current offer (ask) price. Best results are achieved by placing the bid on the most liquid available ECN, which is typically ISLD.

- When master traders are offering a stock out for sale above the current bid price. Best results are achieved by placing the offer on the most liquid available ECN, which is typically ISLD.

- Whenever master traders are willing to buy a NASDAQ stock at the ask price or sell at the bid price. If an ECN is available with acceptable size, the master traders will always execute their orders against the ECN first, rather than deal with the less reliable market makers. *Note:* Because of the additional cost to trade against INCA, many traders will opt to route their order to a market maker if no other ECN is posted at the desired price.

- When a stock is fast rising the master traders may seek to fill their buy orders by preferencing a liquid ECN several levels *above* the ask price. By paying a premium price in a rapidly rising stock, the master traders are often able to establish a position and profit from the subsequent rise in the stock. The reverse is true for selling a long position in a rapidly falling stock.

EXECUTION TOOL #2: SMALL-ORDER EXECUTION SYSTEM (SOES)

SMALL-ORDER EXECUTION SYSTEM (SOES) DESCRIPTION

The SOES system was created in 1984 to give the small investor better access to the NASDAQ market. The SOES system, up until recently, could be used to get near instant executions of up to 1000 shares at the inside ask price (for a buy order) or the inside bid price (for a sell order). This system only became widely used, however, after the stock market crash of 1987, when market makers simply refused to answer their phones and therefore could not be traded with. It's interesting that the public still barely knows about SOES. But ask active traders today, and you'll find that SOES is a permanent part of their vocabulary, if not their lives.

The first basic thing that should be understood about SOES is that it is the only obligatory execution mechanism for the market makers. In other words, if a market maker is posted or displayed at a certain price, an SOES order obligates that market maker to fill it for the amount displayed. The only caveat is that market makers have 17 seconds to update their displayed quote, so at times a trader may SOES a market marker not realizing that he is no longer posted at that price. There also may be many SOES orders ahead of yours, reducing the odds of getting filled. But, if the market maker quote(s) are real, and there is no large number of SOES orders ahead of yours, the market maker(s) is obligated to fill yours. Now it must be understood that SOES is far from a guaranteed way to get filled on the NASDAQ market. In fact, at the time of this writing, the fill rate on SOES orders was only approximately 38 percent. In other words, only 38 percent of all SOES orders resultèd in a fill. So let's not confuse the obligatory nature of SOES with the concept of guaranteed fills. But even with this declining fill rate, SOES, used properly, still offers the master traders some creative and advanced ways to quietly and quickly enter a NASDAQ stock.

The hours of operation for the SOES system are from 9:30 a.m. until 4:00 p.m. Eastern time. Note that SOES market orders can be placed as early as 7:15 a.m., for subsequent execution at the 9:30 a.m. market open.

The SOES system can be used to place both market orders and marketable limit orders to buy or sell NASDAQ stocks. For example, let's assume that INTC is trading at $70\frac{7}{8}$ bid, $70\frac{15}{16}$ offered, and a trader wants to *buy* the stock. There are several ways that a trader can use the SOES system to purchase the stock. The trader can

- Place an SOES buy limit order at $70\frac{15}{16}$. The trader would expect to be filled on this order if a market maker is available at this price and the trader's order is the first to arrive to the market maker at this price. *Note:* ECN quotes are non-SOESable; therefore if the lone quote at $70\frac{15}{16}$ is ISLD, INCA, or another ECN, then your order will be immediately rejected and returned.

- Place an SOES buy limit order at a price above the inside ask, $71\frac{1}{8}$, for example. If the stock is quickly moving higher, traders may be willing to pay a higher price, if necessary, to get their orders filled. In this case, traders may have their orders filled as low as $70\frac{5}{16}$, or as high as their limit price of $71\frac{1}{8}$. If the stock is moving higher extremely rapidly, there may be so many other SOES orders in front that the stock price exceeds the order price of $71\frac{1}{8}$ and the traders will not get filled at all. In this case, the order will be returned "rejected" or "deleted," depending on the system being used, after the ask price of the stock exceeds $71\frac{1}{8}$.

- Place an SOES market buy order. In this case, traders are so eager to get their orders filled that they will accept whatever best price is available. The order may be filled immediately at $70\frac{15}{16}$, or it could get filled a minute or more later at a substantially higher price. This kind of order should be used with caution, as it is impossible to limit or control the actual execution price of the order. Typically, this order will only be used by traders eager to exit a position that is going against them quickly (Figure 12.4).

F I G U R E   12.4

The master trader routes an order for 1000 shares of INTC via SOES. Note that ISLD is not posted at $70$¹⁵⁄₁₆, the inside offer price. ISLD's closest offer is at $71$¹⁄₁₆. Had ISLD been posted at 70¹⁵⁄₁₆, the master trader's best bet would be to route the order via ISLD. With only market makers on the offer, SOES is a better choice here.

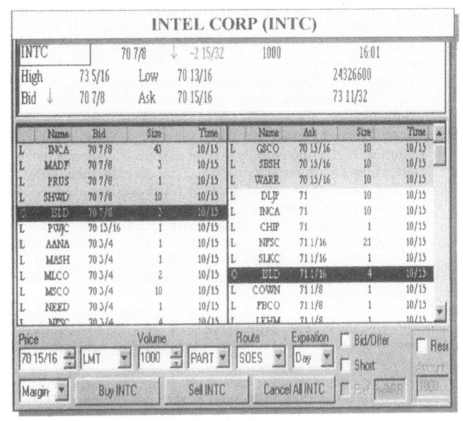

Chart by The Executioner.com

ADVANTAGES OF SOES

- It is possible to get extremely fast executions (that is, 1 second or less)
- It is very easy and uncomplicated to place this kind of order, since there is no need to select to whom the order is to be sent.
- The SOES system is controlled by NASDAQ. All SOES executions are electronically determined by the SOES system

and reported back to each side of the trade. Therefore, any potential for market maker abuse is avoided.

DISADVANTAGES OF SOES

- In active stocks, the SOES queue will be frequently loaded with many orders from other traders, leading to a very low probability of getting *your* order filled before the price moves away from you.

- Recent rule changes allow market makers to quote sizes as small as 100 shares in all stocks. As a result, it can be very difficult to get larger orders (up to 1000 shares) filled at the current posted prices.

- Another SOES rule permits market makers a 17-second delay after filling an order at their posted price, before they must either change their posted quote or fill an additional order. As a result, you will often see "stale" market maker quotes at the inside bid or ask from market makers who have already filled an order and are waiting their full 17 seconds before adjusting their quote to a less favorable price. There is no way to tell whether the posted market makers quotes are real or whether they are stale quotes subject to being adjusted in the near future. *Note:* The 17-second delay is reduced to 5 seconds anytime the bid/ask price in the stock is locked (that is, the same) or crossed (that is, the inside bid is higher than the inside ask price).

- ECNs are not SOESable. As a result, your SOES order will never fill an existing ECN order at your desired price. This flaw is overcome with the usage of more sophisticated order-routing systems such as the ARCA system to send your order by the most appropriate means for execution. More on this shortly.

- As its name implies, SOES is designed for only small orders. Order size is limited to a maximum of 1000 shares in most active stocks, and either 500 or 200 shares maximum in less active stocks.

- Since you can only buy at the inside ask price, or sell at the inside bid price, you will *always lose the bid/ask spread* on this kind of order.

HOW A MASTER TRADER USES THE SOES SYSTEM

The master trader recognizes the flaws of the SOES system and therefore uses it sparingly. However, there are several times when SOES may be appropriate:

- The master trader, willing to give up the spread, uses an SOES order when buying/selling a slow moving stock, provided the collective size of the market makers at the inside bid/ask are sufficient to fill your order. When a stock is not moving actively, it is unlikely any SOES orders are in the queue in front. As a result, the master trader can expect to get executions instantly on orders such as these.
- The master trader often uses SOES orders as an effective way to enter a stock just as it begins to reverse directions. The key for being executed is being able to detect the directional change *before* other traders notice it. With an early decision and quick order placement, these SOES orders will often be filled. However, you can't wait until the reversal is obvious to everyone or your order will find itself way down in the SOES queue and will be left unexecuted as the stock moves in the expected direction.

EXECUTION TOOL #3: SELECTNET (SNET)

SELECTNET (SNET) DESCRIPTION

SelectNet (SNET) is a computerized system instituted by NASDAQ to forward buy and sell orders to other parties. Its hours of operation are from 9:30 a.m. – 4:00 p.m. eastern time. In addition, "pre- and after hours" SelectNet trading is available from 9:00 – 9:30 a.m. and from 4:00 – 5:15 p.m.

The SNET system can be used in three "flavors":

1. SNET preference to a market maker
2. SNET preference to an ECN
3. SNET broadcast

Let's review each of these alternatives:

SNET Preference to a Market Maker

Let's assume you send a *preferenced* SNET order to buy 1000 DELL at 36½ to the market maker Goldman Sachs (GSCO). Your order will immediately show up on the Level III display of the GSCO market maker for DELL. *Note:* Level III systems are what market makers use to place their orders. They have numerous options on how to handle your order:

- They can immediately execute your order, assuming they want to sell you the shares.
- They can give you a partial fill of only 100 to 900 shares, if they don't want to sell you the full 1000 shares.
- They can refuse your order, and send it back rejected/cancelled.
- They can ignore your order and simply not reply.
- They can negotiate your order by sending back a message that, for example, they will sell you the full 1000 shares at a price of $36\%_{16}$. *Note:* This typically only occurs with larger orders placed between market makers. Traders will typically never see this.
- They can fill all or part of your order at an improved price. Traders will likely never see this happen. As we've mentioned before, there are no gifts on Wall Street.

Now let's review what the market maker is *required* to do with your order. If you are *preferencing* GSCO at their currently posted ask price, and they have not filled any other orders within the past 17 seconds, then they are *required* to fill your order up to the size of their posted quote. However, if they have filled another order within the past 17 seconds, then they can withdraw their posted price anytime within 17 seconds and are not required to fill any additional orders at that price. Also, they have no obligation whatsoever to fill your order if it is at a less favorable price than their quote (that is, stock is at $36\%_{8}$ bid and $36\%_{16}$ offered, GSCO is at the offer price of $36\%_{16}$, and you preference them to buy at $36\%_{2}$, trying to split the spread).

SelectNet Preference to an ECN

Let's assume you send a *preferenced* SNET order to buy 1000 DELL at $36\%_{2}$ to the RediBook (REDI) ECN. Since ECN is simply a computerized limit order book, it will handle your order in one of the following ways:

- The ECN will *immediately* execute your order, assuming their order book has sufficient shares in a matching order and your order was the first to reach them for these shares. Immediately after filling your order, the ECN will update their quote to reflect their adjusted order book, minus the order(s) you filled against.

- If the ECN has matching orders for some, but not all, of the shares you request, then you will *immediately* get a partial fill of 100 to 900 shares. Instantly after filling your order, the ECN will update their quote to reflect their adjusted order book, minus the order(s) you filled against.
- If someone else sent their order to the ECN before you, and there are no remaining matching orders on the ECN limit order book, your order will immediately be returned to you rejected. You should instantly notice the ECN update its quote and it should no longer be displayed on your Level II screen at the original price. The limit order at the original price has been filled and is no longer displayed. No games, no 17 seconds, etc.

Note that the *preferenced* ECN order is really just the same as the *preferenced* market maker order. I only separate them because you avoid all of the market maker games when you deal with ECN's. The playing field is truly level when dealing with the first come, first serve nature of ECNs. As you now know, this is not the case when dealing with market makers and the rather unfair advantages they have.

A Few General Points to Mention

Market makers have no requirement to display their true size. When they want to sell 100,000+ shares, they may only post an offer of 100 shares. By comparison, ECNs typically display their full size (90+ percent of the time), unless the order originator specifies otherwise. You will notice at times, especially with INCA, that an order may be shown for 1000 shares. Then 400 shares will be executed, leaving 600 left. Finally, the 600 remaining shares will be filled, and the order will immediately be refreshed at 1000 shares again. This typically happens with institutional orders, which are sent with "Max display size" selected, at 1000 shares in this example. Many ECNs have this feature, but it is rarely used except by institutions, and you'll primarily only see this with the ECNs: INCA, REDI, and BRUT, which are heavily used by institutions.

SelectNet Broadcast Order

Let's assume you send an SNET broadcast order (that is, unpreferenced) to buy 1000 DELL at 36½. This order will immediately show up on the Level III display of *all* market makers in the stock. Any of these market makers now have the opportunity to fill against your order. However, none of them has any requirement or obligation to fill any part of your order. In addition, note that your order will not show up on the Level II display for the stock and will not affect the inside bid or ask price in the stock. Sometimes a SelectNet broadcast order can be a successful way to exit a rapidly deteriorating position, if you are willing to give up an additional $\frac{1}{4}$+ points, for example, below the inside bid for a sell order or above the ask for a buy order.

ADVANTAGES OF SELECTNET SYSTEM

- Enables the traders to control where their orders are routed.
- Ability to get very fast and reliable fills when preferencing any of the ECNs.
- Ability to place all-or-none (AON) orders to eliminate the chance of getting a partial fill. For example, a trader can preference a market maker to buy 1000 shares of a stock with an AON order, even if the market maker is only quoting a size of 100 shares. This prevents the market makers from giving a partial execution of only 100 shares, requiring them to either fill the entire order, or refuse to fill the entire order for 1000 shares. This can be an effective way to reduce commissions caused by numerous 100-share executions.
- Ability to trade before and after hours (that is, 9:00 – 9:30 a.m. and 4:00 – 5:15 p.m. EST), particularly when preferencing ECNs.

DISADVANTAGES OF SELECTNET SYSTEM

- Executions via market makers can be unreliable, due to stale market maker quotes caused by the 17-second rule.
- The desired number of shares will not always be available, since market makers are only *required* to execute their posted size, which can be as low as 100 shares.
- SelectNet orders cannot be canceled by the initiating party until they have been active for a minimum of 10 seconds to give the recipient sufficient time to decide whether to accept or reject the trade.
- Preferenced orders can be a more tedious and difficult order to place in a fast market, since you must select to whom the order is routed.

HOW A MASTER TRADER USES THE SNET SYSTEM

The master trader appreciates the flexibility that the SNET system offers and is able to use this system in a variety of ways:

- The master trader uses SNET as a fact-finding tool, by placing preferenced orders to market makers for more shares than the market maker is displaying. For example, although market makers are only displaying 100 shares at their inside bid or ask, they will often fill a preferenced SNET order for 1000 shares or more, revealing their true intent as buyer or seller.

- In a fast-moving market, the master trader is often willing to give up several price levels in order to get an order filled. For instance, to get filled on the long side, the master trader can either preference a specific market maker several levels higher or place an SNET broadcast order (that is, unpreferenced) several levels higher, in an attempt to get filled. To sell a rapidly declining stock, the master trader can either preference a specific market maker several levels lower or place a SNET broadcast order (that is, unpreferenced) several levels lower, in an attempt to get filled.

- Because most trading firms do not offer direct access to all of the ECNs, the master traders use SNET to route orders to any other ECN to which they do not have direct access. Remember that interacting with posted ECN orders is *always* preferable to routing SOES or SNET orders to market makers.

- The master trader uses SNET orders for pre- and after-hours trading to interact with ECN orders. Typically, market makers are unresponsive during pre- and after-hours trading, therefore, ECNs should be used more often during these times of day.

EXECUTION TOOL #4: ARCHIPELAGO (ARCA)

AUTOMATED ORDER-ROUTING SYSTEMS (ARCA) DESCRIPTION

Sophisticated order-routing systems were designed to help traders more quickly and efficiently access the SelectNet and ECN systems. These systems are not widely available, but can be very useful for traders that have access to this technology. For example, The Executioner (*www.executioner.com*) offers the sophisticated ARCA order-routing system to automatically route your order in a manner to maximize the likelihood of getting shares executed. This is a very fast and complex system designed to relieve the trader from the very urgent task of proper order routing and is especially valuable for larger orders that need to be broken down into smaller pieces for execution. *Note:* ARCA has a dual function of serving as an ECN and a sophisticated order-routing system. Some trading firms offer just the ECN capabilities of ARCA, while failing to offer the sophisticated order-routing capabilities of this indispensable system. Executioner.com is one of only a few firms which provide both functions to the public. When shopping for a direct access trading system, make sure you are dealing with one that offers the posting capabilities (ECN) as well as the order-routing functions of ARCA. Only then will you truly have access to the same tool used by many large institutions.

Let's review how this complex routing system works, then I'll further clarify this process with an example. The ARCA order-routing system uses the following priority for processing and executing your order:

- First, it checks for internal matches on the book of the ARCA ECN.
- Second, it checks for any matching orders found on the other ECNs.
- Next, it checks the availability of market makers and prioritizes them based on their price and size.
- Finally, any remaining shares on your order will be evenly distributed among the market makers already identified.

This complex process is more easily understood with an example. Let's assume that a trader wants to buy 5000 shares of INTC at the inside ask price of 80. Let's further assume that the posted offers on the Level II display are as follows:

Size	MM*	Price
1	GSCO	80
10	MLCO	80
14	SLD#	80
4	ARCA#	80
3	MSCO	80
4	REDI#	$80\frac{1}{16}$
1	HRZG	$80\frac{1}{8}$
10	NITE	$80\frac{1}{8}$

As you can see, there are only 3200 shares posted at the inside ask price of 80, versus the order size of 5000 shares. Going through the preceding prioritizing process yields the following:

1. A 400-share order will go to ARCA .
2. A 1400-share order will go out to ISLD.
3. The market makers GSCO (100 shares), MLCO (1000 shares), and MSCO (300 shares) will each receive a preferred SNET order.
4. Since an additional 1800 shares need to be allocated from the 5000-share order, these remaining shares will be evenly distributed among the three available market makers at that price (600 additional shares each).

As a result, the following orders will be instantaneously generated by the ARCA order-routing system and routed for immediate execution:

Buy 400 shares from ARCA at 80 directly off the ARCA book.

Buy 1400 shares from ISLD at 80 using direct ISLD connection.

Buy 700 shares (that is, 100 + 600) from GSCO at 80 using SNET.

Buy 1600 shares (that is, 1000 + 600) from MLCO at 80 using SNET.

Buy 900 shares (that is, 300 + 600) from MSCO at 80 using SNET.

In this way, the order-routing system very quickly and efficiently processes and routes your order for ultimate execution. If any of these orders are rejected or not fully filled, the system will automatically reroute the remaining unfilled shares to other available market makers or ECNs that are still available at that price. Finally, when there are no market makers or ECNs left at the desired price willing to fill an order, the remaining unfilled shares will be posted on the ARCA ECN limit order book and displayed on NASDAQ Level II as an ARCA# bid at a price of $80 per share.

ADVANTAGES Of ARCA

- Allows the trader to quickly place orders to the best possible ECNs and market makers at that time.
- Allows the trader to fill a large order quickly with multiple partial fills from several different ECNs and market makers, *while only being charged a single commission. Note:* This point alone makes ARCA an indispensable trading vehicle that no trader should be without.

- Can be an effective way to get an order filled in a quickly rising market.

DISADVANTAGES OF ARCA

- If a market maker chooses to ignore an SNET preferred order generated by the ARCA system, the order will remain active for 30 seconds before it is automatically canceled and rerouted. This can be an eternity in a very active market

HOW A MASTER TRADER USES ARCA

The master trader understands this order-routing technology and realizes that it is capable of making excellent decisions. The master trader also recognizes that ARCA places orders far more quickly than is manually possible. As a result, the master trader finds many uses for this technology. Let's look at a few:

- The master trader uses the ARCA order-routing system when placing larger orders that need to be broken down into smaller pieces for execution.
- In very fast-moving markets, the master trader gets filled using ARCA by placing buy (sell) orders several levels higher (lower) than the inside ask (bid). *Note:* The ARCA system is able to quickly reroute orders to second and third options subsequent to being rejected on any of the initial fill attempts.
- The developing master trader, who may need help in quickly and efficiently placing the most appropriate order among the wide variety of options, uses ARCA exclusively.

EXECUTION TOOL #5: SUPERDOT

SUPERDOT (DESIGNATED ORDER TURNAROUND) SYSTEM DESCRIPTION

Master traders seeking to trade stocks listed on the New York Stock Exchange (NYSE) will typically place their orders using the SuperDOT system. While the NYSE is not an electronic exchange such as NASDAQ, the SuperDOT system electronically routes customer orders directly to the NYSE specialist who manages that particular stock. The specialist can then manually fill the order or post the order on his or her limit order book.

ADVANTAGES OF THE SUPERDOT SYSTEM

- Typically able to get much better liquidity for your orders. Traders are often able to fill orders of 5000 shares or more, without difficulty.
- SuperDOT limit orders are managed by the specialist on his or her limit order book. All customer limit orders have priority and must be executed by the specialist before executing any orders for his or her own account at the same price. This establishes a fundamental fairness in the system, since the NYSE specialists are not working against you, as is the case with the market makers on the NASDAQ market.

DISADVANTAGES OF THE SUPERDOT SYSTEM

- The SuperDOT system is much slower than the fully electronic NASDAQ system. Marketable orders could be filled in as little as 5 to 10 seconds, or as long as several minutes, which is an eternity to an active day trader.

HOW A MASTER TRADER USES THE SUPERDOT SYSTEM

- While recognizing its limitations, the master trader uses the SuperDOT system for all NYSE and AMEX listed stocks. It is the only viable option for trading NYSE stocks using a direct access broker such as the Executioner.com.

EXECUTION TOOL #6: ONLINE BROKER

ONLINE BROKERAGE FIRMS' DESCRIPTION

Some traders are able to find success trading through traditional discount brokers such as E-trade, Ameritrade, Fidelity, E-Schwab, etc. These brokers are known in the industry as "payment for order flow" brokers since they typically sell customer orders to market making firms for execution. Often, the discount broker can receive a larger payment from the market maker than they can receive from the customer commission on the order. This brings about a possible conflict of interest for discount brokers, who must decide whether to route their customer orders to the market makers that offer the best execution prices or route the orders to the market makers willing to pay the most for the order flow. It is our view that this practice will soon become a thing of the past. The lines between direct access brokers and online brokers will begin to blur in ways that will only benefit the trader. Until then, some of the disadvantages of dealing with online brokers just have to be suffered. But let us not ignore or discount the power that these massive new behemoths wield. They are a force to be reckoned with, and because of that, we feel every astute trader should have an online brokerage account, as well as a direct access account. As far as online brokers go, E-trade is by far the most progressive, offers the best free services, and has the best overall business model. As for direct access brokers, the Executioner.com offers the slickest system, the best education, and most importantly the best support staff in the industry. It is for these reasons that we trade through both of these entities. Some of the most popular online brokers are listed here:

Charles Schwab *(www.eschwab.com)*

E-Trade *(www.etrade.com)*

Ameritrade *(www.ameritrade.com)*

Muriel Siebert *(www.siebertnet.com)*

Datek Online *(www.datek.com)*

Brown and Company *(www.brownco.com)*

SureTrade *(www.suretrade.com)*

Waterhouse WebBroker *(www.waterhouse.com)*

Web Street Securities *(www.webstreetsecurities.com)*

Scottrade *(www.scottrade.com)*

ADVANTAGES OF ONLINE BROKERAGE FIRMS

- They typically charge lower commission rates than direct access brokers, which they can afford due to the payments received by the market makers executing their orders.
- They typically offer the ability to place stop orders on NASDAQ stocks, in addition to the more common market and limit orders.
- Their limited order execution options make them much more simple to use.

DISADVANTAGES OF ONLINE BROKERAGE FIRMS

- They can be very slow to execute market orders. In rapidly moving markets, this can translate into drastically inferior execution on market orders. For example, on the day after Thanksgiving 1998, many investors placed sell orders for ONSL when the stock was faltering at a price of $90 to 95 per share. Their orders were filled 15 to 30 *minutes* later at a price below $60 per share. OUCH!

- They can be very slow to display your limit orders on NASDAQ. The NASDAQ Limit Order Display Rule requires that market makers either execute or display your limit order within 30 seconds of receipt. However, in practice, market makers don't seem to be very good at complying with this rule.

- Discount brokers offer very limited choices for order routing and execution. This prevents the master traders from being able to route their orders in the most effective manner and can make successful trading more difficult.

HOW THE MASTER TRADER USES DISCOUNT BROKERAGE FIRMS

Typically, the master trader does not use discount brokerage firms for short-term trades, although these brokers may be somewhat acceptable for swing trades of several days or longer. The slower order executions and inferior prices create too many disadvantages for the part- and full-time master trader to accept. However, discount brokers may be a viable option for new traders who are just beginning to learn the trading business and need the simplicity of a web-based broker, along with the ability to easily place orders 24 hours per day. Also, the ability to place stop orders is certainly a useful feature for these traders. As the traders develop their skills and confidence, they would be well advised to investigate opening an account with a firm specializing in servicing the needs of active traders, such as The Executioner.

13 CHAPTER

NASDAQ LEVEL II TOOLS AND TACTICS

A NASDAQ LEVEL II PRIMER

LEVEL 1 QUOTES: WHAT THEY ARE, WHY THEY ARE INCOMPLETE

Level I quotes primarily display the inside (best) bid and offer prices of NASDAQ stocks. Some Level I displays will even show the number of market makers willing to buy and sell at the inside (best) bid and offer prices. In addition to the best bid and ask price, the typical Level I display will also include technical items such as accumulated volume, high of the day, low of the day, last trade price, last trade size, and the net change on the day. All of this information included in Level I is referred to as *first-tier* quotes (Figure 13.1).

It should be understood that Level I, by itself, is inadequate for gauging real market making interest in a stock. It fails in a number of ways. First, it does not tell the trader *who* is bidding or offering the stock. Second, it gives the trader no information regarding how much stock each individual market maker/ECN is advertising to buy or sell. For instance, in the example in Figure 13.1, there is a bid to buy Exodus Communications (EXDS) at $74⅝, and an offer (ask) to sell it at $74¹¹⁄₁₆. The trader has no idea who's doing the bidding or offering, or how many players actually make up the current bid or offer. What's more, Level I quotes fail to tell the trader who's bidding and offering beyond the current bid/ask spread, and how much is

F I G U R E 13.1

EXODUS COMMUNICATIONS <32T.0969.VELE.82015425>					
EXDS		74 11/16	↑ +1	500	9:40
High	76	Low	74 1/2		332600
Bid ↓	74 5/8	Ask	74 11/16		73 11/16

Chart by The Executioner.com

being bid and offered. In other words, first-tier quotes do not provide the trader with an in-depth view of the stock's current condition. As a result, they are incomplete and grossly inadequate as a tool for trading. A trader armed only with Level I will never be able to determine the true picture of strength or weakness in the stock.

Unfortunately, Level I quotes are the only form of quote information offered to clients of conventional Wall Street brokers. Even in today's more advanced world, over 95 percent of all retail brokers don't even have access to Level I quotes. In our opinion, this forces most conventional retail brokers to provide incomplete information to their clients, which in our view is a major disservice. Thanks to technological advancements, growing sophistication on the part of investors, and the willingness of firms like Executioner.com, greater transparency and easy access to more in-depth quote information is available to the individual. The vehicle that provides this deeper level of information is appropriately called the Level II Quote Display.

WHAT IS LEVEL II?

Level II is what really gives the behind the scenes look for active traders. This color-coded box displays all the individual market making firms, specialists, and ECNs that are making a market (buying and selling) in the underlying stock. Each buyer (bid) and seller (offer) is identified by a four-letter designation for NASDAQ stocks and a three-letter designation for firms trading NYSE or ASE equities. It shows us not only the first-tier Level I bid/ask prices, but also the secondary and tertiary prices that are underneath. This secondary level of quotes is where the real value of Level II quotes is.

Level II windows are referred to as *marker maker windows*. There are two parts to this window. The top part typically shows what was described earlier in the Level I section. The bottom portion of this window

F I G U R E   13.2

The upper portion of the screen displays Level I quotes, while the lower portion shows all the individual market participants buying and selling Adaptec Inc (ADPT). Note how each price level is separated by a different color or shade for easy reference.

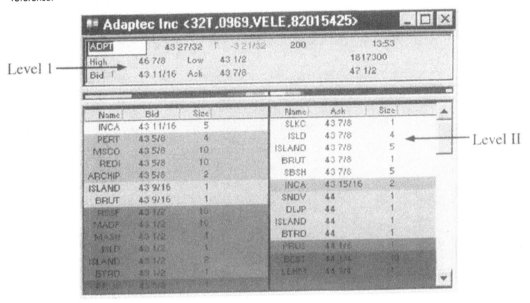

Chart by The Executioner.com

displays all participating market makers and ECNs at each price level, along with the number of shares each is offering. Prices are segregated by colors. Other than the inside bid and offer, which is typically in yellow on most systems, the other colors are there only to separate the different price levels (Figure 13.2).

UPWARD MOMENTUM

On a Level II screen, upward momentum, or a steady rise in price, is shown by an increase in the number of market makers joining the bid, willing to buy, and a decrease in the number of market makers on the ask, willing to sell. A stair-stepping action occurs in a counterclockwise fashion, as competing market makers continue to improve price by raising the prices at which they are willing to buy and sell the stock. When prices are moving higher, the trader looking at a Level II screen will actually see market makers literally step in front of each other to compete and jockey for the best position to buy. Traders using ECNs are also compet-

During upward momentum, the bid side (left) of the screen will tend to move downward and grow deeper, while the offer side (right) will rise as each level thins out.

Chart by The Executioner.com

ing to buy, and will step in front of the market makers, narrowing the spread as the demand increases for the stock. As this jockeying and competing is going on, a barrage of trades will be going off at the offer price. The top-most bid and ask prices will be increasing or rising steadily. The screen's movement will occur in a counterclockwise motion. The bid side of the Level II screen will be pressed down with higher bid prices appearing on top of them, while new ask prices on the right side will be rising to the top. In other words, the price levels, segregated by color, will grow wider on the bid side and shrink in comparison on the ask side, indicating greater buying demand than selling supply (Figure 13.3).

DOWNWARD MOMENTUM

On a Level II screen, downward momentum, or steady decline in price, is shown by a decrease in the number of market makers bidding and an increase in the number of market makers offering. The motion or movement on the Level II screen will take place in a clockwise fashion, as the top-most price on each side will steadily decrease in price. During a pe-

During downward momentum, the offer side (right) of the screen will tend to move downward and grow deeper, while the bid side (left) will rise as each level thins out.

Chart by The Executioner.com

riod of downward momentum, the majority of prints (trades) seen will be occurring at the bid price in red. The offer price levels on the right side will tend to grow larger and wider than the bid side, meaning diminishing demand and increasing supply or selling pressure. The market makers, as well as the general public, will be competing with each other to exit the stock by jumping in front of each other on the offer/ask side. This in turn narrows the spread and drives the bid price lower (Figure 13.4).

NO MOMENTUM OR EQUILIBRIUM

Once equilibrium between the buyers and sellers has been reached, better known as a *saturation point*, the trader will notice that the color bands separating each price level will move toward being evenly matched. In other words, the number of buyers and sellers on each side will start to equalize. The master trader will then know that momentum

F I G U R E   13.5

When there is a lack of momentum, the frequency of individual trades or prints will slow, while the bid (left) and offer (right) side will often appear neutral.

Cyberonics Inc <32T,0969,VELE,82015425>					
CYBX	27	↑ <7/16	200		14:17
High	27 1/8	Low	26 9/16		104900
Bid ↑	26 7/8	Ask	27		26 9/16

Name	Bid	Size	Name	Ask	Size
INCA	26 7/8	4	SMMI	27	1
REDI	26 7/8	1	PIPR	27	1
BTRD	26 7/8	20	FLTT	27	2
MONT	26 13/16	1	ISLAND	27 1/8	25
PIPR	26 13/16	1	ISLD	27 1/8	25
ARCA	26 13/16	5	MASH	27 1/8	1
ARCHIP	26 13/16	5	MONT	27 3/16	1
SHWD	26 3/4	1	ISLAND	27 1/4	50
HRZG	26 9/16	1	CANT	27 3/8	1
CANT	26 3/8	1	NITE	27 1/2	1
ISLAND	26	1	SLKC	27 5/8	1

Chart by The Executioner.com

is slowing and either look to reduce risk in an open position, or consider entering a new position depending on the directional bias (Figure 13.5).

USING ISLD TO GAUGE MOMENTUM

An excellent way to gauge momentum is to keep a close eye on the ISLD bid or offer. Let's assume you, a master trader, are long on a stock that has been moving up. You start to notice that the inside color level (the inside bid/ask) is starting to even off on both sides. The ISLD offer, representing the general public, is just hanging. In other words, no one is willing to buy from the ISLD offer. Seeing this, you, the master trader, decide to exit your position by hitting the bid. You've decided to lock in whatever profit you have simply because if the public, represented by ISLD, isn't willing to buy, then the stock has obviously lost its euphoria, at least in the short term. It should not be forgotten that the professional is more prone to *sell* stock as it rises. Buying, during upward momentum, is typically done by the public. ISLD is one of the mirrors through which the master trader can view the fear and greed of the public. Level II quotes, which provide for watching the movements of both profession-als and the public, become indispensable in this regard.

WHERE'S THE BEEF?

When it comes to trading NASDAQ stocks, it is important to make sure you are dealing with stocks that have what we call "beef." The beef refers to lots of market maker participation and interest. In other words, the stocks we like to deal with have depth. When deciding to put on a trade in a NASDAQ stock, the master trader should always look to the Level II screen to see how deep the market maker participation is at each price level. This allows the trader to determine a few things up front. Stocks that have few market makers posted at each price level tend to have less volume and wider spreads. We teach our traders to shy away from these types of plays, because the spreads tend to be wider and fewer hands usually control the stock. This makes for greater risk as wider spreads translate into greater price slippage, and fewer hands controlling the stock allow for more price manipulation by the pros in control. In these "thin" stocks with no beef, there will be little to no representation by ISLD, which usually means the stock is completely dominated by profes-sionals. If the general public is not participating in the stock, the job of making money will be a lot tougher. Why? Because it is the mistakes of the public and the public's lack of knowledge that offers the master trader the greatest chance to profit. So, shallow price levels and no ISLD participation are tell-tale signs that we should be looking for more fertile pastures to graze.

On the other hand, stocks with decent market maker participation at each price level are the kinds of stocks we like to trade. Whenever we decide to enter a long trade in a NASDAQ stock, we just want to make sure that if one or two participants on the bid are lost, the next price level is not half a dollar away. The risks involved in that kind of play far out-weigh the reward for the beginning trader. While the payoffs in these thin stocks can be substantial, the master trader understands that the risks are much greater (Figure 13.6).

Keep in mind that, as a general rule, the number of market makers lined up on either side gives us a general indication of the strength or weakness in a stock. If a stock has 10 market makers lined up on the in-side bid and only two on the inside offer, this initially tells the trader that there are more participants willing to buy the stock than sell. In strong market environments, we would look for this stock to move higher. But

F I G U R E   13.6

(*a*) Thin levels with no ISLD participation make for added risk. The inside spread for Farmer Bros (FARM) is $10. It should also be noted that FARM trades primarily in whole numbers, with few fractional points shown. There is no beef here. (*b*) Beefy price levels indicate a great deal of interest among the public and professionals, and offer added safety for the master day trader.

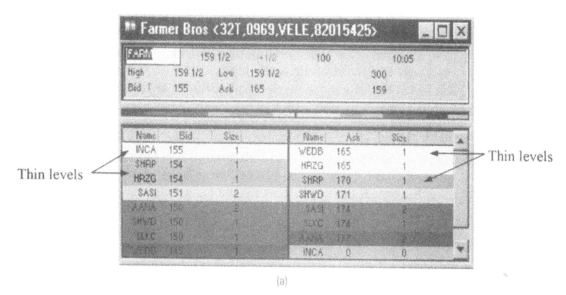

(a)

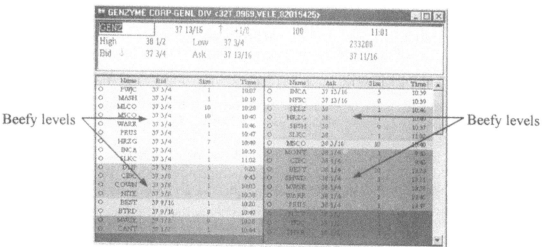

(b)

(*a*) A big bid in an overall strong market environment indicates more buying interest than selling interest. Caveat: If the market environment as a whole is weak, this is not necessarily the case. (*b*) A big offer in an overall weak market environment indicates more selling interest than buying interest. Caveat: If the market environment as a whole is strong, this is not necessarily the case.

Big bid ———

——— Smaller Offers

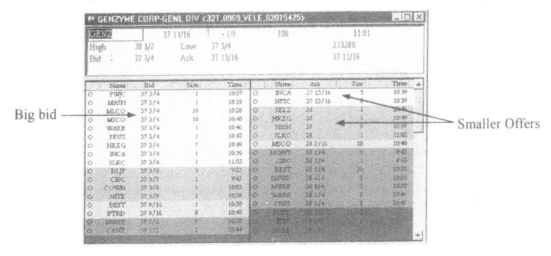

(a)

Small bids———

——— Big Offer

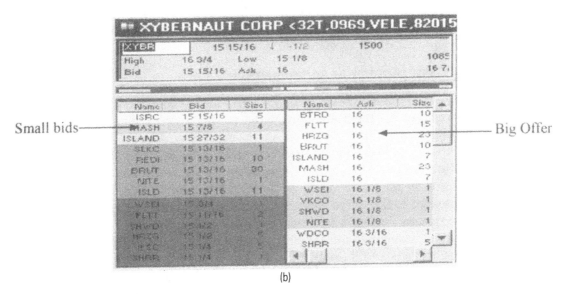

(b)

Charts by The Executioner.com

in weak environments, it could actually indicate lower prices. We will discuss this concept in the Pancake Stack Play section later in this chapter. The reverse is true as well (Figure 13.7). An additional factor of "Where's the Beef" is who the players are. The depth of participation is important, but just as important is the quality of "who's coming to dinner." The master trader always wants to be involved with the Goliaths and the 800 pound gorillas, not opposing them. Young David may have beaten Goliath in the *Bible*, but when it comes to the market, Goliath *always* wins. The master traders fully understand that they lack the capital of the Goliaths, and do not have access to their unlimited order flow. This makes it impossible to match up with the big players. Taking things personally and trying to go head to head with them will only help the traders quickly dispose of their capital income.

If the master traders are bidding for WXYZ stock, for instance, and GSCO joins the bid, they know they're on the right side of things. If MSCO won't lift off the offer in ABCD stock, and continues to refresh (reload) its size, the master traders will not put the trade on until MSCO either lifts to a higher price, or flips to the inside bid, in which case they'd be announcing their intent to buy. It is important that you size up your opponents first. Verify if they are real. Then verify how potent they are. *Then* put your plan into action. The master traders are always reassessing the conditions while trading. Information and trading environments are not static and must constantly be monitored for any changes. We, as traders, cannot control the markets we trade in. But we can certainly control ourselves.

TIME AND SALES: THE INDIVIDUAL FOOTPRINTS

The truth will always be in the print. It is not what the market makers show me. It is what they do, the trades they make, that gives me the best insight into their true intentions. The *time and sales window*, known as T&S, is what helps us view the individual footprints of the big players and the public. You can choose to either set up a separate time and sales ticker, or your software may provide a function that has a built-in ticker that scrolls alongside your market maker window. Many day trading firms teach their traders that if trades are going off in red at the bid, the stock will go down. Conversely they teach that if trades are going off in green at the offer, the stock will go up. While those basic statement are true sometimes, it is by far not always the case. The time and sales ticker paired with your Level II display and charts can be a powerful combination. Market makers are aware that most traders have been taught to monitor key player movements and so use this to their advantage. They head-fake, jiggle, wiggle, and who knows what else to shake all the weak hands and loose fruit from the tree. It is our responsibility, as master traders, to realize this and be ready to counter. The fake-outs can come in a variety of ways: how they display their markets to us as buyers or sellers, how they display their lot size, the size of their prints, and when and where they occur (Figure 13.8).

Let's take a look at a scenario that shows how the time and sales window can prove insightful for the master trader. We pull up a Level II quote on a stock and see market makers stacked at the bid, advertising that they are buyers. We notice that this stock is near the lows of the day, in a strong market. There are only a few market makers on the offer. We are already feeling queasy. Something is not right. We look for the print in our time and sales window to confirm our feelings. We see trades popping off on the offer. Our screen lights up in green. Positive, right? No. We take a closer look and notice that those prints at the offer are for small 100-share lots or nominal compared to the size of the prints that have been occasionally occurring on the bid side. We see 1000 shares on the bid go off, then a flurry of smaller trades at the offer price. Probability dictates that this stock will head lower during the day. What's the moral of this story? Watch where the size is being traded. Are the sizable prints occurring on the bid or the ask? This sounds basic but somewhere it gets lost as people sit in front of their computers. They somehow get lost in the huge information flow that is being thrown at them.

The master trader will always watch the size displayed by market makers and ECNs and the tape (time and sales) to determine the major players' real intentions. Instinet is famous for showing, say 1000 shares, alone at the bid or offer, while trades are going off for well in excess of the displayed size. We realize that trades do go off on other mechanisms, such as Selectnet, but as that price action continues, we then have to believe that a size buyer or seller is reloading and masking his or her real intentions. We may choose to pass on this or look for this buyer or seller to be cleaned up before making a commitment.

The tape helps us when a market maker tries to either bull up a stock or press it down by displaying a huge bid or offer and then immediately pulling it. If we see no print when this order disappears, we know that the major player was simply trying to press the stock higher to get a better price. If a trade actually occurs on my time and sales, we then have to believe that someone out there is a size buyer or seller and we may want to think about joining in.

F I G U R E   13.8

(a) The basic Time and Sales window shows each individual (foot) print in the stock, and the time it was posted. The share size of the print is also displayed in the basic Time and Sales window. *(b)* The Executioner *(www.executioner.com)* and other select direct access trading systems offer an expanded Time and Sales. With this expanded view trades, individual market maker movements, and the direction of each market maker move can be monitored and scrutinized.

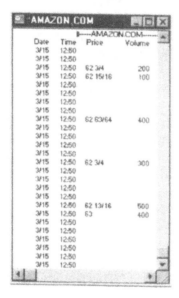

(a)

Date	Time	Price	Volume	Exch	Type	Bid	BSize	BEx	Ask	ASize	AEx	Cond
3/15	12:47				Best Bid	62 5/8	1000	NAS	62 11/16	900	NAS	
3/15	12:47				Best Ask	62 5/8	1000	NAS	62 11/16	900	NAS	up
3/15	12:47	62 5/8	500		Trade							
3/15	12:47				Best Bid	62 5/8	1000	NAS	62 11/16	900	NAS	
3/15	12:47				Best Ask	62 5/8	1000	NAS	62 3/4	3000	NAS	up
3/15	12:47	62 11/16	200		Trade							
3/15	12:47	62 11/16	500		Trade							
3/15	12:47	62 3/4	400		Trade							
3/15	12:47	62 3/4	190		Trade							
3/15	12:47	62 3/4	200		Trade							
3/15	12:47	62 5/8	100		Trade							
3/15	12:47	62 3/4	400		Trade							
3/15	12:47				Best Bid	62 5/8	1000	NAS	62 3/4	3000	NAS	
3/15	12:47				Best Ask	62 5/8	1000	NAS	62 3/4	2900	NAS	up
3/15	12:47	62 3/4	100		Trade							
3/15	12:47				Best Bid	62 5/8	1000	NAS	62 3/4	2900	NAS	
3/15	12:47				Best Ask	62 5/8	1000	NAS	62 3/4	2700	NAS	up
3/15	12:47	62 3/4	100		Trade							
3/15	12:47	62 3/4	200		Trade							
3/15	12:47	62 3/4	200		Trade							
3/15	12:47				Best Bid	62 5/8	1200	NAS	62 3/4	2700	NAS	
3/15	12:47				Best Ask	62 5/8	1200	NAS	62 3/4	2700	NAS	up
3/15	12:47				Best Bid	62 11/16	100	NAS	62 3/4	2700	NAS	
3/15	12:47				Best Ask	62 11/16	100	NAS	62 3/4	2700	NAS	up
3/15	12:47	62 3/4	500		Trade							
3/15	12:47				Best Bid	62 11/16	1000	NAS	62 3/4	2700	NAS	
3/15	12:47				Best Ask	62 11/16	1000	NAS	62 3/4	2700	NAS	up

(b)

Charts by the Executioner.com

MARKET MAKER CHARACTERISTICS

Each major market player has a distinct set of characteristics that, if known, can provide the master trader with some insightful clues. Getting to know how your competition thinks and acts will only help to improve your game.

- *GSCO.* Goldman Sachs, often referred to as Goldy, is the most formidable firm on Wall Street. It garners the highest respect of all market makers on and off the street, particularly among day traders. Why? Because it is not only considered to be the most powerful market maker in existence, it is also considered to be the most honest, meaning its bids and offers are real. This brings us to another important point. GSCO's heavyweight clients, most of whom are wealthy individuals, large institutions, municipalities, and governments, allow for GSCO to be more than a one- or two-lot player. *Note:* A lot is equivalent to 1000 shares. In other words, GSCO will typically transact or be good for 3000 shares or more at each price (bid or offer) posted. When trading a stock that GSCO makes a market in, you will be right more often than not assuming GSCO is the key market maker in the group. Some traders will refer to the key or controlling market maker as the AX. Watching the buying and selling activity of GSCO will provide valuable clues to the master trader. We often use the Executioner's Level II screen to highlight GSCO in black, which makes watching its every move easier.

- *SBSH.* Solomon Smith Barney is one of the largest firms on the street with a very hefty list of large institutional clients. SBSH is so significant as a market maker at times that we often refer to it as the "stock stopper." We also refer to it as "son-of-a-B" which reflects the dogged tenacity that this market maker can display. What is most interesting is that we have found that SBSH's weight is far greater on the sell (offer) side than it is on the buy (bid) side. For the most part, this is the case with all key market makers, and it reflects that institutions typically exit stocks more aggressively than they enter them. If SBSH is consistently conducting business on the inside bid and offer of a particular stock, know that it is a key player and deserves to be watched carefully.

- *MLCO.* Merrill Lynch is the largest brokerage company in the United States, and, as a result, it deserves a degree of respect whenever it is seen on your Level II screen. MLCO's large institutional base, coupled with its large retail base, warrants watching the moves of this market maker carefully. While it is not as formidable as GSCO, MLCO is often the key market maker or AX in some of the most popular Nasdaq stocks. Before it decreased the number of stocks it made a market in, MLCO was one of the most omnipresent market makers in existence. Its presence in the market has declined a bit, but not enough for the master trader to lose any respect for it.

- *NITE.* Knight/Trimark came out of nowhere to become the world's largest market maker, all within a few short years. It represents a new breed of market makers, and the key role it has played in dominating a big part of the online brokerage business has made it the most visible market maker today. While it still does not hold the same weight as a GSCO or a MLCO, it should get special notice whenever it is consistently doing business on the inside bid and offer of a stock. It is important to note that NITE's volume is primarily retail in nature. In other words, much of its volume comes from its relationships with online brokers. This makes NITE a near-perfect mirror into the actions of the public, or individual market players. They will be formidable in the highly coveted Internet stocks that online traders have come to love.

- *SLKC.* Speer, Leeds & Kellogg is the largest NYSE specialist firm in existence, which should give the master trader some insight into the power behind this market maker. It does not play a dominant role in every stock it makes a market in, but when it does, its power and tenacity can be mind-boggling. In other words, SLKC can at times single handedly hold up a stock's momentum, taking in unbelievable amounts of stock. It can also be insignificant as a market maker, so its role has to be determined on a stock-by-stock basis.

- *MASH.* Meyer Schweitzer is a subsidiary of Charles Schwab, the largest online brokerage company in the United States. While a good deal of its volume and activity represent the retail market, it tends to show some size from time to time.

- *HMQT.* Hembrecht & Quist is a very respected boutique firm that specializes in small- to medium-sized technology companies. Its research is considered to be top notch, which is what attracts large clients to its firm. The strength of HMQT as a market maker must be determined on a stock-by-stock basis. When it's a key market maker in a stock, its power and weight can be felt big time. The master trader will find that HMQT will be seen most often in stocks in the mid- to lower-price range.

- *HRZG.* Herzog is another respected boutique firm that focuses on the smaller, but rapidly growing, technology stocks. Its characteristics are similar to that of HMQT. It will most often be seen and felt in the mid- to lower-priced technology stocks.

- *PRUS.* Prudential Securities, despite its size, does not hold a great deal of weight each and every time it is seen. But like many other second-tier market makers, it can be formidable from time to time. One thing is for sure, when PRUS is a big player in a stock, its tenacity will be felt in an unbelievable way. The master trader determines how significant PRUS is on a stock-by-stock basis.

MARKET MAKER EVALUATION

Over the years, we have developed and used with great success a market maker evaluation, which has served as a general "Who's Who" list of the key players. We are certain this ranking of the most influential market players will guide you in your daily dealings with them. They are ranked in order from 1 to 10, with 10 being the most influential:

GSCO	10
MLCO	9.5
MSCO	9
FBCO	9
SBSH	8.5
NITE	8
PWJC	8
HRZG	7
HMQT	7
MASH	7
MONT	7
PRUS	7

It is important to note the following: GSCO, MLCO, MSCO, and FBCO are all considered institutional market makers. In other words, they have the beef. The beef is the considerable real order flow they possess and they should always be taken seriously as players. The *real* order flow I am referring to is a way of describing the probability that they will stay at the quoted price and trade with you rather than fill an order once and immediately leave. They are there to "work it." So be ready when facing them to put your chinstrap on, because they don't play. If you feel you want to take one on and tow the line, rest assured you will be looking for a new hobby. They have the power to take your lunch if you don't know what you are doing.

It is just as important to know that there are market making firms who rarely hold on to long-term positions, nor are they willing to commit firm capital. They are typically looking to get a piece of the action on the large volume of retail orders. This practice is known as *getting in between orders*. Arrangements are made with retail firms for the order flow and they quickly flip the shares to anyone for small fractional profits. Market making firms, such as Mayer & Schweitzer (MASH) and Herzog (HRZG), are known as "trade houses" and are often real only if they have an order in hand. They seldom commit firm capital to a position, and they are rarely real factors in pricing (without an order in hand). In other words, they trade for the spread.

DETERMINING WHO'S THE BIG CHEESE

Each NASDAQ stock will typically have at least one dominant market maker who controls most, if not all, of the action. We call this market maker the "big cheese." One of the master trader's first tasks is to determine exactly who the big cheese is. The second task is to determine what the big cheese is doing, buying or selling. Of course this is easier said than done because no market maker will intentionally show his or her hand. But we have made note of a few tips that will help the master trader determine, with a good degree of accuracy, who the big cheese is and what the big cheese is doing. Armed with this knowledge, the master trader will be able to improve on the timeliness of entries and exits.

- The market maker who is consistently the last one to leave the inside bid or offer is the big cheese. Highlight that person, and watch him or her.

- The market maker who consistently transacts 3K or more at each level is typically the big cheese. The big cheese often moves in nominal price increments. In other words, key players tend to transact at price levels that are close to each other. For instance, GSCO is bidding for stock at $40⅜. After taking in a few thousand shares at $40⅜, GSCO drops to $40¼. The big cheese will typically not drop to $39¾. While this does at times occur, the key players in a stock will tend to be active at level.
- The market maker who consistently transacts more shares than displayed is typically one of the key players. For instance, PWJC, while showing an offer for only 1000 shares, sells 8000 shares. Or, HRZG shows a bid for only 100 shares, yet takes in (buys) 2000 shares, refreshing the 100-share quote continuously.
- The market maker who continually steps up to bid for a declining stock at a price higher than any other market maker is the big cheese. This is called *supporting the stock* and usually occurs as general market conditions are slipping and weakening. Here's an example. WYYZ is declining steadily. The current price of WXYZ is $40 bid, $40¼ offered. SBSH, MLCO, HRZG, and SHWD are bidding for stock at $40, while PWJC is offering stock for sale at $40¼. SBSH steps up the bid price to $40⅛, and becomes the lone quote at $40⅛. SBSH gets filled for 1000 shares, and lowers the bid back to $40. Several minutes later, SBSH raises the bid to $40⅛ once again, takes in several thousand shares, then drops back to $40 once more. SBSH may raise the bid once again in a weakening market and others start to recognize this and you will see an ECN join the bid, most likely INCA or ISLD and then get ready because the game has just begun. This action signals to the master trader that the market maker is a key accumulator of the stock, and its future moves should be watched carefully and be stalked as to when general market conditions improve to see if indeed it will continue to act accordingly.

THE JAMMIN' SESSION PLAY

There are times when it is in the best interest for a key market maker to help ignite a sharp and/or steady price advance in a stock. Let's say a market maker has received an order from one of its large institutional clients to buy 100,000 shares of ABCD, Inc. The market maker has already accumulated (bought) 78,000 shares of the 100,000-share order primarily using Instinet, leaving 22,000 shares that still remain unfilled or bought. In this case, the market maker decides to use the 22,000-share buying power still left to drive the stock higher. If the market maker can accomplish this, his or her client will make money on the 78,000 shares bought, and the market maker will be able to satisfy some of the remaining 22,000 shares from his or her own personal inventory at much higher prices, making a hefty gain in the process. In other words, the market maker will use the power of his or her client's money to drive the price higher, then satisfy the last bit of the client's buy request by selling to the client directly, but not before working to get the stocks to a more favorable (profitable) price. Jammin' the bid is one method used by key market makers to ignite such an advance. Here's how it works:

- ABCD is trading at $40 bid to $40¼ offered. GSCO has already accumulated 78,000 shares and has 22,000 shares to go before the entire 100,000-share buy order is filled.

- Using Instinet (INCA), GSCO "pegs the bid" by ¹⁄₁₆. What this means is, GSCO will use INCA as its buying vehicle, and it will instruct INCA to maintain a bid price ¹⁄₁₆ *below* the best offer, whatever the current price. In this case, the best offer (asking price) is $40¼.

- Suddenly INCA, manipulated by GSCO, pops up on the Level II screen on the bid side at $40³⁄₁₆, ¹⁄₁₆ below $40¼, the best offer. Publicly, GSCO will be sitting on the offer displaying that it is a seller of the stock. The master trader looks past the obvious and uses the tape as a friend. The public believes that GSCO is a seller and dumps their shares, when in fact after its offer is taken, GSCO "fades" and raises its offer price.

- This aggressive move by INCA sends a message to the world that there is a major buyer who wants stock so badly he or she is willing to sharply raise the price to pay for it.

- Seeing this move, other traders, investors, and market makers join the bid. Others decide to take (buy from) the offers at $40¼. This continues to send the message that the buyer using INCA wants the stock bad enough to chase the rising stock.

- The offer price quickly moves to $40⅜, and INCA, which GSCO has "pegged" by ¹⁄₁₆, lifts to a new bid price of $40⁵⁄₁₆.

- Once again, other market makers join INCA's bid, *while others take the offer*. Remember, GSCO has to fill an additional 22,000 shares, which can be done in two ways: (1) buying at the bid on INCA, provided some sellers hit GSCO's INCA bid or (2) the most likely scenario to really get this rocking and moving upward is to start aggressively taking out the offer. Using that remaining balance GSCO starts pounding that offer and then flips to the bid simultaneously, publicly displaying itself on the Level II as a buyer. Traders notice that Goldy has flipped and see the subsequent prints at the offer begin now to pile in. All across the nation trader's tickers start humming and buzzing with a flurry of green prints. The ham and eggers get excited as well and jump on, creating further momentum to the upside. "Hello Houston we have blast-off !"

- INCA continues to jam the bid as this orchestrated tango continues. The offer lifts. INCA jams the bid by $\frac{1}{16}$, stair-stepping this up. On and on this goes until next thing you realize ABCD is $40\frac{7}{8}$ offered.

- GSCO, using INCA to jam the bid, has effectively ignited the dry kindling and fanned the flames a bit, effectively moving the stock higher and has made the client's position that much more profitable. Most likely at those higher levels, after creating the last burst of momentum, it will be selling some of that stock it picked up on the cheap at lower prices to the public now through an ECN making a hefty $\frac{5}{8}$ of a point plus gain. Nice deal. Remember, our key was INCA. Once we realize that INCA will no longer raise its bid and the stock starts to experience a stalling-out effect, we'll then call this jammin' session a wrap and ring our cash registers.

The master trader who catches the start of what we call a "jammin' session" and can properly interpret these actions can get involved and play along. Once you have sized up the situation, bid the stock, join INCA out there by using ISLD or even stealthily bid for it using a Selectnet broadcast order. Once you have built yourself a position, look for the telltale signs mentioned earlier and then gladly assist anyone who would like to get involved by selling them your position at a higher price! Keep in mind that the moves are not typically large. However, in some cases, they can be very strong, steady, and certain to produce a decent day trading gain.

We teach our traders to buy only twice, and to sell two to three times, after spotting a jammin session. This will increase the odds that the trader is not buying size at or near the top, but is already in sell mode when the top of the micromove sets in. *Tip:* When microtrading, master traders sell on the way up, while novice traders wait for trouble first, and then sell on the way down. The Pristine mantra is: *Sell when you can, not when you must.* This process is precisely the reverse of when shorting a stock that is being jammed to the downside.

THE PANCAKE STACK PLAY

The "pancake" was coined by our in-house trainer, Mike Campion, whose affinity for fine cuisine and trading has resulted in a transfer of sorts as the art of trading has taken on a new "flavor" for all of us.

Most novice traders with access to NASDAQ Level II quotes automatically assume that when a lot of market makers are stacked up on the bid (buy) side, there is great demand for the stock, which in turn suggests strength. They also assume that when a lot of market makers are stacked up on the offer (sell) side, the stock is weak. While it is understandable why these are basic assumptions on the part of ill-informed traders, they are far from being correct in many cases. What's unfortunate is that there are still many day trading firms with so-called advanced training programs teaching these erroneous concepts. The master traders not only know that "all that glitters is not gold," they know that if it glitters, it probably isn't gold. Beware of the obvious! Let's look at an example to demonstrate the pancake play.

EGGS is trading at the high of the day. The current bid is 10% and the current offer, which is also the high price of the day, is $11. A quick look at the 5-minute chart shows us that after making its early morning run from 9% to the day's high, EGGS has hardly pulled back. Second, on the Level II screen, we immediately notice that while there is only one ECN making a bid at 10%, there are a slew of market makers sitting, like a high stack of IHOP pancakes, on the $11 offer. At this point we say, "Hmmm." The current picture being presented to us is one of weakness. In other words, the major market makers are blatantly advertising to the world that they are sellers. The Level II picture also insinuates that there is really no one willing to step up to the plate and bid for it/buy it. The natural inclination is to view the stock as weak, saturated with supply, devoid of demand, and therefore poised to decline. While this is the picture, we recognize that something does not quite add up. Could this be a *false* picture presented by the key players to just throw us off, to deflect our scent? Why would real sellers be so eager to show themselves to the world as, well, big sellers? You see, the master traders, under this scenario, will ask themselves this, "If everyone really wants to sell this stock, why is it trading at the high? Better yet, why isn't the stock backing off, or taking out the sole bidder at $10¾ if it's so saturated with supply at $14." If the stock were truly under huge selling pressure, as the stacked-up offer suggests, the stock would immediately start drifting lower. Something is obviously wrong with the picture!

A closer look reveals that the sizeable prints are occurring at the offer, and those going off at the bid are nominal in comparison. The point to understand is that they, "the MM's," know that the "sheep" are watching and that the ill-informed Level II watchers will likely fall for this "false" display of weakness. They are trying to divert your attention, to force you into giving up your shares too cheaply, right before another potential upward move ensues. It has not escaped us that this "pancake phenomena" is occurring at a flat number like 13, 19, 22, etc. versus a fractional number like 12⅛, 15³⁄₁₆, 25¹¹⁄₁₆. Noting all of this, we check our 5- and 15-minute charts for any signs of overhead resistance that could cause a break above $14 to fail. There is no resistance such as a prior high or a 200 simple period moving average near by to deter us. Lastly, we note the time of day, just to make sure we are not planning an entry in EGGS in the mid-day doldrums period (11:15 a.m. to 2:15 p.m. EST), as most breakouts to new daily highs generally fail during this time period. By now, we are already ordering ourselves a healthy plate of pancakes with our EGGS. We know through much experience that this scenario is a market maker fake-out and this "stacked offer" will soon be eaten through, sending EGGS to a new high.

There are two things that have to occur before we pile into the stock. Let's go over those two things now. The first prerequisite is that we need the time and sales window to reveal a couple of good size 1000-share lots being printed at $14. Once we have witnessed a small flurry of trades at $14, the second and final requirement is that two to three market makers at the offer have to either lift to a higher price or flip to the bid. It does not matter how many market makers are presently posted at the offer. We only need to see two to three lift. That is our sign that the stock is about to rip. Once we get that, we drill (buy) the offer at $14. Then we put our seatbelt on because if the thousands of pancake plays we've done over the years are any guide, we're in for a cool ride. That seemingly weak set-up displayed to fool the novice is pure pay-dirt for us and hopefully it will now be pay dirt for you as well.

It must not be missed that the stacked pancake play works just as well in reverse, although getting a short off during downward momentum is a lot tougher than getting a long off during upward momentum. We also must point out that the stacked pancake play is a pure scalping or microtrading strategy. It is not intended for those who are looking for large gains which involve holding stocks overnight. The stacked pancake play is the quintessential buy 'em and flip 'em trading strategy.

14

ENTRY TOOLS AND TACTICS

A Step-by-Step Guide to Entering Stocks Like a Pro

A PROPER ENTRY IS 85 PERCENT OF A WINNING TRADE

Make no mistake about it my friends. The most critical part of every trade is the entry. Traders who enter stocks properly and in a timely manner will enjoy a much higher winning percentage than those who enter stocks poorly. We will even go as far as saying that if you get the entry right, you have taken care of 85 percent of the entire trade. The other 15 percent is nothing more than trade management and profit-taking skills, which we cover in detail in the following chapters.

Each time you take a trade, you are putting your hard-earned capital on the line. You will want to make sure that you put that money of yours on the line in the proper way. It should be realized that every sound trading strategy or plan is comprised of three components: one entry, and two exits. One exit below your entry price, better known as an *initial stop loss*, and one exit above your entry price, better known as the *price objective*. However, if you get the entry wrong, you run the risk of ruining the entire trade. This calls for a clear understanding of exactly when, where, and how to strike (enter). Let us now delve into this all-important world of entering stocks the proper way.

We have devised three entry techniques that have served us very well for many years. These three entry methods have been taught to scores of traders all over the world, and we are certain that, once digested, they will elevate your timing and trading skill to that of a master. Without any delay, let's look at all three entry techniques now.

ENTRY TECHNIQUE #1: KEY BUY

KEY BUY DESCRIPTION

Successful trading calls for the ability to find two groups of ill-informed individuals: (1) Those gripped by fear and anxious to give up their merchandise (stock) to you too inexpensively and (2) those led by greed, willing to take your merchandise (stock) too expensively. The key buy setup was designed to help the master trader come into the market as a buyer, precisely when the group gripped by fear and fright is anxious to leave the game. This simple entry technique is one of the most powerful concepts in our trading arsenal. In fact, it is so powerful that it can often be used as a stand-alone trading technique. If you truly understand it and use it properly, we are certain it will elevate your level of skill in the market substantially.

The key buy setup involves three simple steps: two basic setup criteria and one action. Let's go over what those two criteria and one action step are.

THE KEY BUY SETUP

1. *New high.* This criterion calls for a stock that has recently made a higher high than its prior rally. This is not to be confused with an all-time new high, or a 52-week high. We are simply interested in stocks that have recently experienced a robust rally to ensure that we are dealing with those being bought aggressively. One general guideline we use is this: the stock should have made a new high no longer than 8 bars (days if looking at daily charts) ago.

2. *Three or more consecutive lower highs.* This criterion calls for a stock to have experienced a 3-bar decline or more. This is similar to our 3 to 5 bar drop strategy described in a prior chapter. But in this case, any 3-bar decline is not good enough. It must be a 3- or more bar decline that is also accompanied by 3 or more consecutive lower highs. In other words, the high of each down bar must be lower than the prior bar's high.

Note that we consciously use the term "bar," as opposed to the term "day" in these criteria. That is because this concept is applicable in intraday time frames, as well as daily and weekly time frames. Once a stock has met these criteria, the master trader is ready for step 3, the action.

The Action

3. Buy the stock whenever it trades $\frac{1}{16}$ to $\frac{1}{8}$ above a prior bar's high.

Let's look at Figure 14.1, a diagram of the key buy setup.

Criterion 1: Recent new high

Criterion 2: Three or more lower highs.

Criterion 3: Buy $\frac{1}{16}$ to $\frac{1}{8}$ above prior high

Now let's look at a few real examples (Figures 14.2 and 14.3).

Now, a word about gaps. Let's say the stock you intend to buy, after the first two criteria are met, gaps up (or down in the case of a short) excessively at the open. How should you handle this scenario? Should you buy immediately at the open? Should you buy later? Or is the correct action to disregard the trade? We will now move to educating you on the

---

F I G U R E   14.1

The key buy setup.

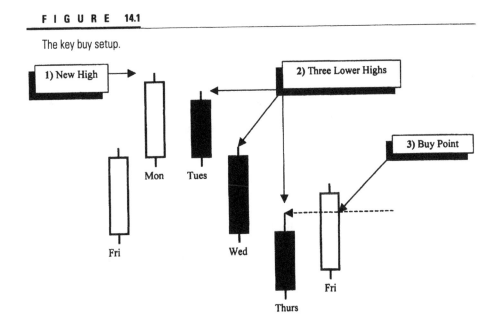

F I G U R E   14.2

This daily chart of BGEN shows a near-perfect key buy setup. After making a new high (criterion 1), BGEN experiences five consecutive lower highs (criterion 2). Note that the decline ended with a bullish reversal bar, accentuated with a bottoming tail. At this point, the key buy setup calls for step 3—a buy above the high of the bullish RB. That is the first time BGEN was able to trade above a prior bar's high. As you can see, a very sharp rally ensued. *Tip:* Aggressive master traders could buy (near the close) on any bullish RB following a 3 to 5 bar drop.

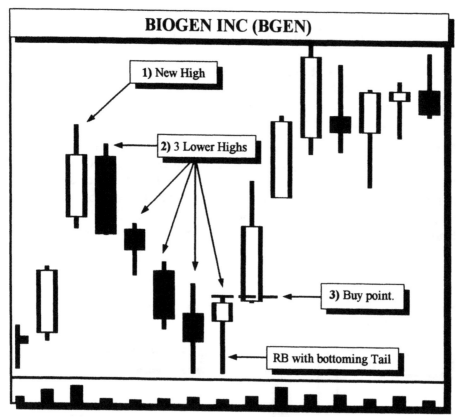

Chart by The Executioner.com

proper way to handle stocks that gap up (or down if shorting) at the open, after they have met the first two criteria of the key buy setup. Keep in mind that in today's volatile markets, gaps are very common occurrences. And the trader who lacks the ability to deal with them is playing at a distinct disadvantage. Your ability to play gaps like a professional will make gaps a good friend, not an enemy. You are about to learn just how to handle them as we move into another entry technique, namely, the 30-minute buy technique.

FIGURE   14.3

This daily chart of LXX shows two 3 to 5 bar drops. It's the second decline that set ups a perfect key buy. Shortly after a new high (criterion 1), LXK experiences a decline accompanied by three or more consecutive highs (criterion 2). Step 3 calls for a buy once LXK trades above a prior bar's high. Note the sharp rally that followed. Easy as 1-2-3.

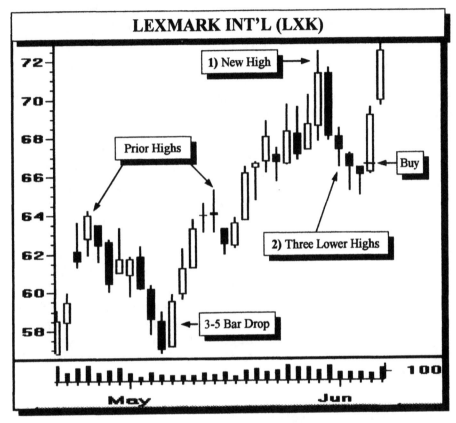

Chart by The Executioner.com

ENTRY TECHNIQUE #2: 30-MINUTE BUY

30-MINUTE BUY DESCRIPTION

The master trader must be aware that the first 20 to 30 minutes of trading is perhaps the trickiest time period of the day, particularly when the market is poised to open up very strongly. Why? Because buy orders that have accumulated over night and just before the open provide professional market makers and specialists with an extra advantage that they simply don't enjoy during any other part of the trading day. These accumulated market orders provide them with advanced or, shall we say, inside information on the abundant demand for a stock, which gives them a much greater ability to influence the opening price of the stock. This is what causes stocks to gap up, large numbers of accumulated buy orders placed before the market opens. But here is the key, a very important key. In many cases, the amount which the professional market maker or specialist opens the stock up is often excessive, setting up what we call a *bull trap*. In other words, the stock is opened up artificially high to sucker in novice buyers (those who buy simply because a stock has good news or looks strong) so that they, the pros, can get out. Remember, for every buy order, there is someone on the other side with a matching sell order. The question is who's smarter in this case? The buyer or the seller? Well, when a stock gaps up excessively, it is usually the seller who is the smart one. This is why many stocks that gap up tend to pull back rather sharply after the first 10 to 20 minutes of trading. Once the abundant premarket buy orders have all been satisfied, the demand is gone, and the stock tends to give way to "professional" selling and a lack of demand. But there is an exception, and it is this exception that sets the stage for one of our most powerful intraday trading tactics. *Our studies have shown that if a stock that has gapped up and is able to trade to a new daily high after 30 minutes of trading, the strength demonstrated at the open was not artificial, but real.* The strength in this case is real because it is being confirmed by continued buying *after* the early morning rush (the first 20 minutes or so of trading). This one simple discovery encouraged us to design a simple, yet powerful way for the trader to capitalize on the stocks that are truly strong. It's called the 30-minute gap buy rule. Here's how it works.

The 30-Minute Buy Setup

1. The stock must gap up at the open by $\frac{5}{8}$ or more. In most cases, a gap up much greater than $1 will be news related (positive earnings, brokerage upgrade, etc.), which is fine. *Note:* It is best if the stock does not rally much from its opening price. While this is not absolutely crucial, we have found that those stocks which gap and stall immediately make the very best candidate for this strategy.

The 30-Minute Buy Action

2. Once the stock has gapped open, the master trader must let it trade for a full 30-minutes. No action other than watching the

stock is required during this time. Often the trader will be watching and monitoring several stocks that have met the preceding setup criterion.

3. Once 30 minutes has transpired, the master trader sets an alert $\frac{1}{16}$ above the high of the day, which in many cases will not be too far away from the current price.

4. Once the alert is triggered (the stock breaks to a new daily high), the trader buys with a protective stop $\frac{1}{16}$ below the day's low. This often makes the play low risk. *Note:* The ideal situation occurs when the stock breaks to a new daily high an hour or so after the first half hour of trading. But we don't let the lack of the ideal situation hinder our action. The play can be taken any time the stock breaks to a new daily high after 30 minutes of trading. It's just that our studies show bigger moves occur when the stock breaks out after several hours of trading have transpired.

5. Once in, the master trader would use the trade management and profit-taking steps explained in the chapters that follow.

Let's look at a real example (Figure 14.4). There you have it. A simple, yet powerful way to capitalize on gaps. This strategy has above-average profit potential, as well as an inherent safety measure, better known as a *protective stop*. It also automatically helps the trader to distinguish between those stocks that open up artificially strong and those that are genuinely explosive. It is a powerful strategy, and as a student of the market, you will be served well by its proper use. We take this moment to welcome you into the circle of champions. You now have the ability to read and play gaps like a professional.

Now it is necessary for us to cover our last entry technique. It is our main method of entry for those intraday scalping (micro) trades that so many of the more active day traders like. We are sure you will find this last entry technique enlightening, as it is the basis for an intelligent intraday (micro) trading style that has earned us daily profits in the market for many years. Let's quickly move on so that we can uncover the wonderful possibilities that the late-day breakout technique has to offer.

ENTRY TECHNIQUE #3: LATE-DAY BREAKOUT

LATE-DAY BREAKOUT BUY INTRODUCTION

True master traders are not one-dimensional in approach. The seasoned traders, who have moved into that realm we call mastery, know how to

F I G U R E   14.4

This 5-minute chart of RNWK shows how viable the key buy setup is in all time frames. This RNWK example shows two buy opportunities. The highs or peaks come first (1), followed by three or more lower individual highs (2). Once RNWK trades above a prior bar's high, the master intraday trader strikes (buys). Note how robust the rallies were that followed.

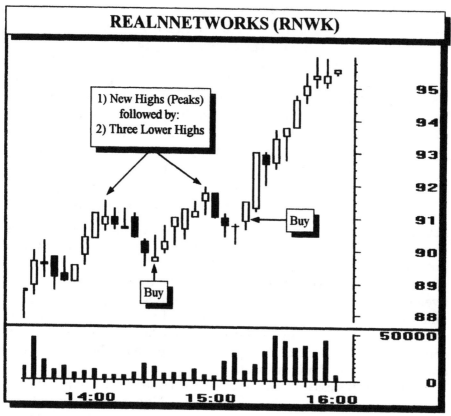

Chart by The Executioner.com

handle themselves in various dimensions, in various time frames, and with various trading styles. The intraday trade (or microtrade) is the most demanding of all trades, and it often requires the greatest degree of skill and, without a doubt, the greatest degree of emotional and psychological stability. The intraday trading entry technique we are about to show you forms the foundation upon which a big part of our microtrading style is built.

The late-day breakout technique will provide the first and most important tool that every microtrader needs in order to have long-term success as an agile scalper. If you have a true desire to be able to microtrade the market with dexterity and great skill, we strongly encourage that you delve deeply into the following section. If you do, you may just walk away with a skill that has the power to reward you for a lifetime. It certainly has rewarded us. So without further delay, let's take a look at this all-important intraday entry technique called the late-day breakout.

LATE-DAY BREAKOUT DESCRIPTION

The latter part of the trading day offers the master trader one of the best opportunities for picking up robust microtrading gains. We teach our private students and in-house traders to divide each trading day into three parts: the beginning, the middle, and the end. Now we realize this sounds obvious, but as explained in an earlier chapter, it is often the middle part of the day that robs many traders of the hard-earned gains that may have come in the morning from overnight trades and early morning microtrades. We call this middle part of the day, which starts around 11:15 a.m. and ends 2:15 p.m. EST, the mid-day doldrums (see Chapter 7 for more details), and it often serves as a dangerous black hole for microtraders. But this 3-hour period of lackluster activity also serves as the incubator or breeding grounds for one of the best trading periods of the day, namely, the late-day breakout period.

Why is this period so good for microtraders? Because the market often continues where it left off before the start of the mid-day doldrums, providing the master microtrader with a brand new batch of trading possibilities. It's almost like the 2:15 – 4:00 p.m. EST period is a separate day in and of itself, complete with its own set of unique trading opportunities. The traders who acquire the tools and techniques necessary to master this time period will find that the majority of their microtrading gains will come during this short time zone. In fact, if we had to teach traders only one microtrading style, it would call for trading only one specific price pattern after 2:15 EST. We will now delve into the setup and the method we call late-day breakout trading. It is important to note here that we use 5-minute charts for the late-day breakout technique.

Late-Day Breakout Setup

1. The stock must be up on the day (trading higher than the prior day's close).
2. The stock must be trading at or above its opening price.

3. The stock must be currently basing sideways at or near the day's high.

4. The sideways base must be at least 1½ hour in length (use 5-minute charts).

Once the master microtraders have found a list of stocks that meet these criteria, they look to take the following action. Keep in mind, all of this is taking place by viewing 5-minute charts.

Late-Day Breakout Action

5. Looking at a 5-minute price chart, the master trader looks to buy ¹⁄₁₆ above the most recent series of equal highs. *Note:* This entry point will often be below the day's high, which is preferable. Most traders are taught to buy new daily highs. We teach traders trading techniques that often get them in just before a new daily high, allowing for the rush of those late buyers to help lift their shares higher.

6. Once in, the master trader places a protective stop just below the sideways base, or below the low of the 5-minute breakout (entry) bar. See Chapter 15 for a more detailed discussion of protective stops.

7. Look to sell incrementally as the stock moves higher. See Chapter 15 for a more detailed discussion of selling.

Let's look at a late-day breakout example (Figure 14.5). The late-day breakout technique can be applied to daily charts as well, although the term late day would not apply in this case. It should be noted that the most important item is the chart pattern, not the time frame. If a specific price pattern works in a 5-minute time frame, it should work in a daily, weekly, or hourly time frame. Remember, charts are nothing more than the footprints of money. They reveal the fear, greed, and uncertainty of the players. Those fears, greed, and uncertainties are the same in all time frames. Here's an interesting example of a daily breakout buy, played just as if it were a late-day breakout play in a 5-minute time frame. Pay particular attention to how similar the charts of POST and SSCC are, despite their vastly different time frames (Figure 14.6).

Well, there you have it. Three unique ways to enter stocks like a professional. As we've stated earlier, the entry is by far the most critical part of the trade. Get it right, and you have solved 85 percent of the trading

F I G U R E   14.5

This 5-minute chart of SSCC shows a near-perfect 30-minute buy setup. On the morning of October 11, SSCC gapped up ⅝ at the open, satisfying the initial gap up criterion (see criterion 1). After SSCC trades for a full 30 minutes, the master trader marks the high of the day (see criterion 2) using an alert. At point 3, the master trader buys SSCC as the stock trades to a new daily high later in the day, placing a protective stop ¹⁄₁₆ below the low of the day. As you can see, a nice intraday run ensued after the breakout. The strength from this late-day breakout even spilled over into the following day (October 12).

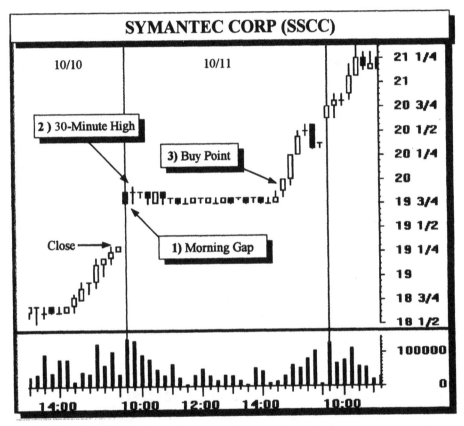

SYMANTEC CORP (SSCC)

Chart by The Executioner.com

equation. But despite its great importance, the master trader's plan is still incomplete without a well-put together trade management plan. That is what we cover next.

F I G U R E   14.6

This 15-minute chart of IMNX shows another 30-minute buy setup. On the morning of October 18, IMNX gapped up over $2½ at the open, satisfying the initial gap up criterion (see criterion 1). IMNX moved down during the first 15-minute period and stabilized during the following 15-minute period. The high during this 30-minute time frame was established at the open. The master trader marks this high of the day (see criterion 2) using an alert. At point 3, the master trader buys IMNX, as the stock trades to a new daily high, placing a protective stop $\frac{1}{16}$ below the low of the day. As you can see, a very robust intraday run ensued after the breakout. In this case, the gap was an indication of real strength.

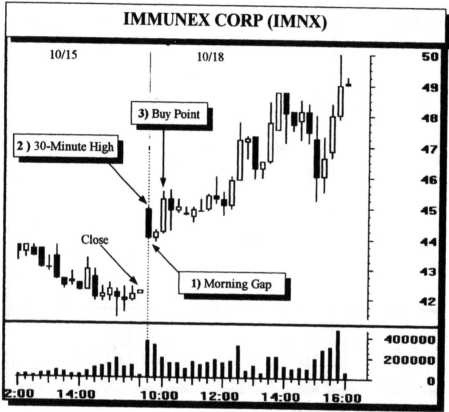

Chart by The Executioner.com

15
C H A P T E R

TRADE MANAGEMENT TOOLS AND TACTICS

A Step-by-Step Guide to Managing Your Trades Like a Pro

We would love to be able to say that life is perfect and every single trade you take will work out. We'd also like to be able to say that you'll never have to experience the pain of loss, only the joys of filling out bank deposit slips. But needless to say, this is not the case. Loss is, and always will be, a permanent part of every trader's life. One of the key differences between a winning trader and a losing trader is that the winner knows how to *manage* his losses, to keep them small and contained. The losing trader allows his losses to fester and grow, until they start to manage and control *him* or *her*.

Trading is a business. And like every other business concern, it requires insurance to protect itself from unexpected catastrophe. The trader's main insurance vehicle is none other than the almighty *stop loss*. At Pristine, we call it the insurance policy. Let's take a closer look at this invaluable money management tool.

TOOL #1: THE INITIAL STOP: YOUR INSURANCE POLICY

INITIAL STOP DESCRIPTION

Before you enter each trade, you must already have a price at which you will cut your losses and call it quits. That price point is your initial (protective) stop. This price represents where you will draw the line in the sand. It is the point at which you will entirely eliminate the stock from you life. This protective stop can be an actual stop placed on the books of, say, the NYSE (the NASDAQ does not except stops), or it can be a mental one. The manner in which it is placed does not matter, as long as action is taken immediately when it's violated. If and when a stock that you are in triggers your stop, you must have the discipline to get out of the position *immediately*. No hesitation. No ifs, ands, or buts. Just get out! Sure there will be times when the stock will rebound shortly after your exit. And yes, those times will be frustrating. But over time, you will find that this strict course of action will save your financial life.

Let's look at it this way. Each time you buy a stock, you are, in a sense, hiring an employee. This employee (the stock) has one job and one job only: *to work hard at making you money.* Like all employees, the stock should be given some time and some leeway to perform. That leeway, my friends, is the distance between your entry price and the initial stop. *This is the only insurance you have to protect yourself from a bad and/or destructive employee.* And it must be adhered to religiously. As mentioned here, there will be times when you will sell the stock (fire the employee) only to find out later that the stock (the employee) has regained its luster and earning ability. Nothing's perfect. But as mentioned earlier, trading is a business. And all smart business people know that they must draw the line in the sand somewhere. They know that they must cut their losses short at some point. To operate without insurance (an initial stop) is to flirt with disaster. And continued failure to adhere to your initial stops will *eventually* bring about your demise. Following are some guidelines that we use to place our initial stops.

HOW THE MASTER TRADER PLACES INITIAL STOPS

- When entering a trade above the high of the previous bar, the master trader has two stop methods to choose from. The first is called the *prior bar stop method.* This method calls for placing the initial stop $\frac{1}{16}$ to $\frac{1}{8}$ *below* the previous bar's low. Here's an example (see Figure 15.1). Let's assume XYZ traded on Wednesday between a high of $30 and a low of $29. On Thursday, the master trader buys XYZ at 30\frac{1}{16}$ ($\frac{1}{16}$ of a point above Wednesday's high). Once the purchase of XYZ is complete, the master trader would place an initial stop at 28\frac{15}{16}$ ($\frac{1}{16}$ of a point below Wednesday's low).

FIGURE   15.1

The master trader enters XYZ at $30 1/16, with an initial stop of $28 15/16, making the downside risk $1 1/8.

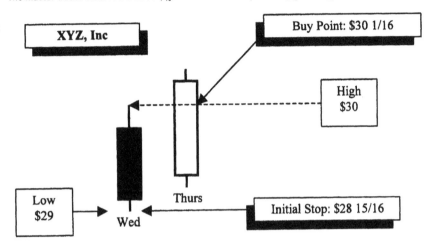

- If the prior bar stop method described previously places too much capital at risk, the master trader can opt to use the second stop option called the *current bar stop method*. This method entails placing the initial stop $1/16$ to $1/8$ *below* the low of the *current* (entry) bar. Let's take a look at another example (Figure 15.2). ABC, Inc., traded on Wednesday between a high of $40 1/2$ and a low of $38 1/2$, a $2 range. On Thursday, the master trader buys ABC at $40 9/16$ ($1/16$ of a point above Wednesday's high). Once the purchase of ABC is complete, the master trader, using the current bar stop method, would place an initial stop at $39 7/16$, risking $1 1/8$. Under the prior bar stop method, the stop would be placed at $38 7/16$, increasing the risk to an unacceptable $2 1/8$. Many traders, including Pristine's well-trained in-house traders, would opt for the current bar stop method. *Tip:* Keep in mind that using the prior bar stop method or the current bar stop method is totally a matter of personal choice. Each has its advantages and disadvantages. The prior bar stop method will tend to produce fewer shakeouts as the stock is given more wiggle room. The current bar stop method, while rendering more frequent shakeouts, will often result in smaller losses when they occur.
- When entering a trade on the breakout of a sideways base, the master trader also has two stop methods to choose from. The

F I G U R E   15.2

The master trader enters ABC at $40\%_{16}$, with initial stop choices of $38\%_{16}$ or $39\%_{16}$. Because the initial stop of $38\%_{16}$ would render a loss of $2\frac{1}{8}$, the master trader is justified in using $39\%_{16}$ as the stop, which would only render a $1\frac{1}{8}$ loss.

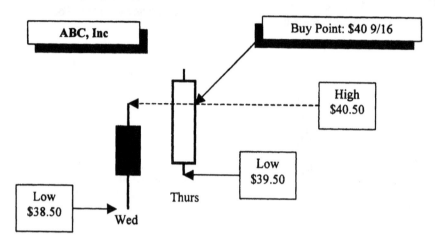

first is called the *base stop method*. This method calls for placing the initial stop $\frac{1}{16}$ to $\frac{1}{8}$ *below* the entire sideways base. Here's an example (Figure 15.3). POST traded in a tight sideways range for weeks, vacillating between $4\frac{5}{8}$ and $4\frac{3}{8}$. The master trader buys on the breakout above $4\frac{5}{8}$, with a stop at $4\frac{5}{16}$ ($\frac{1}{16}$ below $4\frac{3}{8}$, the lower level of the sideways base).

- If the base stop method described previously places too much capital at risk, the master trader can opt to use the second stop option called the *breakout bar method*. This is similar, if not identical, to the current bar method, which entails placing the initial stop $\frac{1}{16}$ to $\frac{1}{8}$ *below* the low of the breakout or entry bar. In other words, when buying breakouts, the master trader can either place the initial stop just below the entire sideways base or just below the bar that produced the breakout.

A FINAL NOTE ON INITIAL STOPS

The following point should never be forgotten. *Winning tends to take care of itself. It's losing properly that requires great skill, rigid discipline, and deep maturity.* We at Pristine.com can always spot novice traders by how diffi-

FIGURE   15.3

The master trader buys POST above $4⅝, with an initial stop just below $4⅜, making it a low-risk, high-reward play.

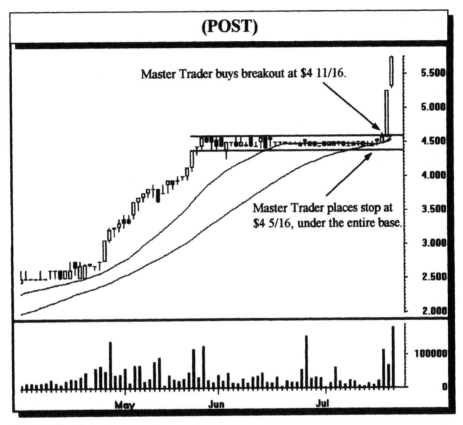

Chart by The Executioner.com

cult it is for them to cut their losses short. The experienced traders have learned that their most precious commodity is their initial capital, and the only tool they have to keep it intact is the initial stop. Therefore, the seasoned traders take their stops at the speed of light and move on, knowing that tomorrow is another day and another trade. Life *always* goes on for traders who adhere to their initial stops. But life can, and often does, end abruptly for those who are not disciplined enough to do so. Don't be cheap, my friends. Instead we urge you to be smart. Pay your insurance premiums. In other words, adhere to your initial stops. One day, they will save your life, and you'll thank us.

TOOL #2: THE BREAK-EVEN STOP: PLAYING WITH THE MARKET'S MONEY

BREAK-EVEN STOP DESCRIPTION

Once you have entered a trade and placed your initial stop, your first goal is to get to the point at which you are not risking *your* money, but are playing with the market's money. In the first stage of each trade, it is your money that will be at risk. If something goes wrong with the trade immediately, your initial stop will be triggered resulting in a loss of capital, albeit a small one (see Initial Stop section earlier in this chapter). While this will happen at times, on many occasions your stock will rise enough (or fall enough if short) for you to move your stop to your entry price. Let's look at an example. You buy XYZ at $20 with the objective of capturing a $1.75 to $2 gain. Your initial stop is at $19.25, making your risk 75 cents. That's what it may cost you for the right, or the chance, to go after the potential $1.75 to $2 gain. Not a bad ratio. If the trade goes sour right away, you'll lose 75 cents. However, if the stock advances enough, you will quickly want to raise your initial stop from $19.25 to your entry price of $20. Raising your stop to the price at which you entered the stock accomplishes two things. First of all, it nearly eliminates your risk. At that point, you are playing with the market's money. Not yours. The worst that can happen, barring any negative news item overnight, is that you have to exit the trade at or near your entry price. Yes, you will lose the amount of your commissions, but that should be viewed as the cost of doing business as a trader, not as an actual loss. Commissions are like the supplies, rent, and utilities paid for by other businesses. They are necessary in order to conduct business, and there is nothing we can do about them. Secondly, raising your stop to break even creates a psychological advantage. Because you are no longer in danger, you can figuratively sit back, put your feet on the coffee table, and relax. At this point you know the stock has to either make you money or get eliminated, at virtually no cost to you. It's all on the market. And you've got to like that. But here is the caveat. You must know *when* to raise your stop to break even. Do it too prematurely, and you will be asking to get taken out of good trades prematurely. Do it too late, and you will lose your hard-earned gains unnecessarily. So when is the correct time? That's next.

THE $1 RULE: ONCE A WINNER, ALWAYS A WINNER

Once a stock (your employee) has moved favorably by $1, you should immediately adjust your initial stop to your break-even price. Now note that we did not say, "Once you have a $1 gain . . . " No. You will move your stop to break even once the stock itself has risen (fallen if short) $1 above the ideal entry price. It sounds the same, but there is a major difference. Continuing with the previous example, you have bought XYZ at $20. Your initial stop is at $19.25, and you are looking for a $1.75 to $2 gain. The stock moves to $21, making for a $1 rise. If you were to sell at this point, you may not be able to get $21. A rise of $1 does not always equal a profit of $1. But that's not the point. Because it has risen $1, your action should be to raise your stop from $19.25 to $20, your break-even point. At this point, it's all smooth sailing. You can sit back, and relax in the comfort that you will make money at best, or break even at worst. The market is now paying for your trade. And as we've mentioned, you've got to like that. *Tip:* Our in-house traders use a 75-cents rule when trading stocks under $12. We encourage you to do the same.

A FINAL NOTE ON BREAK-EVEN STOPS

Keep in mind that the $1 rule is only intended for swing trades (trades intended to be held overnight). A much smaller increment, such as $\frac{1}{4}$ or $\frac{3}{8}$ should be used for intraday trades.

TOOL #3: TRAILING-STOP METHOD: YOUR STAIRWAY TO PROFITS

TRAILING-STOP DESCRIPTION

There is no doubt about it. Your most precious commodity is your starting capital. Your next most cherished commodity is your hard-earned profit. Master traders must never allow themselves to lose their profits or give them back. It is hard enough earning consistent profits in the market. The last thing you want to do is earn a nice profit, then let it slip away. This is why we have designed the *trailing-stop method*, a technique that helps traders ride a winning stock for potentially huge gains, while safeguarding the profits earned. Its application is simple, yet powerful, basic yet very effective. Here's how it works.

You have bought XYZ at $20, with an initial stop at $19.25. The day you entered the stock is considered to be the stock's first day of employment. You have hired XYZ to do a job for you, and it had better work hard, or it will get eliminated. We know that if XYZ rises by $1, the $1 rule will have us move our stop to break even. But let's say that at the end of XYZ's first day, it rises by only ½, at the high, and closes at $20⅜. If this is the case, our stop must stay at $19¼. On day two, let's say XYZ manages to reach a high of $20⅝, but closes at the same $20⅜ price. Now we start applying our trailing-stop technique. At the close of trading on day 2, we must move our initial stop to ¹⁄₁₆ below the low (or above the high if short) of that trading day. So, in other words, if on day 2 XYZ had a high of $20⅝, a low of $19⅞ and a closing price of $20⅜, your stop would be moved from $19¼ to $19¹³⁄₁₆ (¹⁄₁₆ below the day's low). And, after the close of each subsequent day, the trader would simply repeat, raising his stop to ¹⁄₁₆ under the low of that day. *This is called tracking the lows.* Let's continue the previous example. On day 1, your entry day, the initial stop is at $19¼. At the close of trading on day 2 your stop is moved up to $19¾ (see earlier). Now, let's say during day 3, XYZ rises to $21. At this point, you would quickly move your stop to break even, or $20, based on the $1 rule we mentioned before. You must not forget this. But let's say after the close of trading on that day (day 3), XYZ had a high of $21⅜, a low of $20⅜, and a closing price of $21¼. You would then move your stop to $20 ⁵⁄₁₆, ¹⁄₁₆ under the current day's low. Now remember. During day 3, you moved your stop to break even, based on the $1 rule. That was a temporary measure that transferred the risk from you to the market. But now, with the market closed, you will want to continue utilizing our trailing-stop method. You have a $1⅜ profit ($21⅜ close − $20 entry = $1⅜ gain), and will want to start protecting some of it. On day 4 if XYZ reaches $21¾ to $22, you will sell, given the fact that it has worked hard enough to meet your $1.75 to $2 profit objective. If it has not reached your objective by the close of trading on day 4, you will raise your stop to ⅛ under the low of that day. And on and on it goes until you get stopped out, or you reach your profit objective, or . . . Yes. There is another consideration. Now let's go over that.

TOOL #4: TIME-STOP METHOD: TIME IS MONEY

TIME-STOP DESCRIPTION

Trading is a game of money. And time is the stuff money is made of, so it is crucial that we don't waste it. We teach all of our in-house traders to utilize what we call time stops. Like all of our tactics, it is simple, yet very effective. The time stop prevents us from tying up our money too long in nonperforming stocks. It keeps our money flowing, searching, and seeking for opportunity. As a short-term trader, you never want your money lingering too long without getting rewarded. This is not investing. It's trading. And you are not Warren Buffet when trading. Your goal is to stick and jab, not stick and stay. So the rule goes like this.

Time-Stop Rule

If a stock has neither reached your profit objective nor stopped you out by day 5, sell it. Fire the stock and move on, no matter where it is or what your profit or loss is. Consider each stock as your employee that is hired to perform a specific job (hit a price target) within a specific time frame (5 days). If by day 5, the employee has failed, fire it. Time is money. The swing-trading tactics explained in this book are designed to reach their price objectives in 1 to 3 days. If by the fifth day (your entry day counts as day 1), the objective has not been reached, what we expected to happen has *not* happened, and the play should be eliminated. Again time is money, and the master trader doesn't waste it!

Important Note: For intraday trades, the time stop is much different. We are often willing to give an intraday trade as much as 1 to 2 hours to work out. But anything beyond that puts the master trader in what we call "hope mode." And hope, when it comes to the market, is a dangerous thing. Remember this.

16

EXIT TOOLS AND TACTICS

A Step-by-Step Guide to Exiting Your Trades Like a Pro

Taking profits is an art that, once mastered, represents the crowning jewel of professionalism. While getting into a play properly is critical to the master trader's success, knowing when and how to take profits maximizes the benefits derived from knowing when to get in. Too many traders don't know when enough is enough, and through greed, invite disaster by overstaying their welcome in a stock. One must never forget that the last ⅛ in a trade is the most expensive ⅛ of all, and the price one has to pay to go after that last ⅛ is often the entire, hard-earned gain. Furthermore, the truly astute master trader wants to be gone long before the stock reaches its climax. Why? Because the top of each short-term move is saturated with novice traders. It is where the wannabes are. It's where those who do not know hang out, and master traders avoid the hangouts of novice players like the plague. Most master traders fully understand that winning at the game of trading entails being a master at taking the middle out of each move. Attempts to grab the very bottom and top of a move are often futile and always unnecessary. The only traders who consistently buy the bottom and sell the top are liars anyway.

We will now delve into the sparsely populated world of proper profit taking. I use the term "sparsely populated" because after 13 years of trading, I have fully realized that few market players have a trading plan, much less a profit-taking plan. Long-term traders and investors, devoid of intelligent profit-taking guidelines, hide behind the vague notion of retirement. Their assumption is that "time" will compensate them for their lack of a game plan. But the length of one's trade is no excuse for a vague plan of action. Short-term traders have their problems too. Many microtraders or intraday traders, preoccupied with trying to protect themselves from yet another loss, often snatch at anything even resembling a gain. With each passing second, the level of fear for these traders intensifies, preventing them from capitalizing on the very robust gains that are there at times just for the asking. Having a sound entry game is critical. Knowing how to professionally manage your trade is also a key element of market success. We have covered these two important parts at length in prior chapters. Now, let us delve into the last part, which deals with the art of exiting your trades like a professional.

THE INCREMENTAL SALE

One of your entry methods got you into a nice trade. Your well-developed ability to manage the trade has kept you cool, calm, and mostly collective throughout the stock's entire move. Now, the merchandise you bought just a short while ago is worth significantly more than you paid for it. For a brief moment, you pity the uninformed person who gave up their stock to you, obviously too cheaply. But a quick review of the gain you now have cures any feelings of guilt and inadequacy. Now you realize that the third aspect of the trade must come into the play: Taking your profit or, taking the salad, as some real-time trading members call it. *When* do you take it? *Where* do you take it? Here is an important key. *The very best market players almost never sell all of their inventory (stock) in one spot or price.* They realize that this would be akin to a sidewalk merchant selling an entire lot of wares on the very first offer without allowing other potential buyers a chance to bid higher. What if your profitable stock (merchandise) can fetch a higher price? Sure the price right now is nice, but if and when you have the right stock, the price can get much nicer. And if the stock is up, isn't that proof enough that you have the right merchandise? But then again, how many times have you tried to hold out for a sweeter, richer price, only to see the price you could have had with ease vanish like the wind? Is the urge to take the money right now nervousness or is it prudence? Is the desire for a bigger gain greed or is it intelligence? How is one to solve this dilemma? Answer: *the incremental sale.* We have always found selling a stock in two or more pieces to be the very best way to take profits. This not only solves the dilemma of whether the trader should take a profit, it also gives the trader a chance to capture even bigger gains. In short, the *incremental sale* is the answer that puts an end to the civil war that is constantly being waged when the trader has a profit. To sell or *not* to sell is the minute-by-minute question. Our view is that the answer to this eternal question is almost always "to sell," but only part of the position. Here's an example. Let's assume a master trader, let's call him Mr. Velez, has a $1 paper profit on 1000 shares. He has moved his initial stop to the break-even point, in accordance with our break-even rule. Now, the $1 paper gain is starting to eat a whole in his pocket. Mr. Velez, knowing that a profit in hand is worth two on paper, decides to sell half his position, locking in a $500 gain. By doing this one simple thing, Mr. Velez has satisfied his urge to take the gain. The anxiety of losing all his paper profit has been completely eliminated, yet he has still left himself with the possibility of a bigger score. A cool sense of power starts to reemerge for Mr. Velez. Why? Because the psychological demons who were playing tug of war with his emotions have been beaten back. And once again, clarity and that ever-so-important sense of calm has returned. Mr. Velez is now ready for the next phase of his profitable trip: maximizing his gains. *Tip:* Despite the importance of this subject, calming and dealing with the psychological demons that frequently plague the trader is an area that has gotten very little attention. Mark Douglas' book entitled *The Disciplined Trader* is the best work we've seen on this topic. Visit *www.pristine.com/ books* to get more information on this and several more books we regard as invaluable. There are few good books that offer real meat for the active trader. This is one of them.

A PERSONAL NOTE FROM OLIVER L. VELEZ

I have always been plagued by the dilemma described earlier. During my developmental years as a trader, I'd find myself frequently missing the really big gains as a result of selling too quickly. My problem lay in the fact that I love to "ring the cash register." Whenever I tried to correct this problem by holding on to my stocks longer, that's when they would invariably lose steam, and the gains I could have had vanished. This inconsistent whipsawlike action in my stocks and my performance kept me perpetually confused and constantly frustrated. *That is, until I stopped fighting the two urges, and started trying to satisfy them both.* That was the answer for me. That was the breakthrough. For years I was trying to take sides, to force myself into one mode or the other. At first, it did not dawn on me that choosing one way or the other was not necessary. Then I quickly realized I could do both. I could satisfy both demons (the nervous one and the greedy one) and on balance come out better. That is when I started using the incremental sale method. And let me tell you, it works. To this very day, I'm an ardent user of the incremental sell. Not only that, it remains a potent part of our rigorous in-house training program. All our in-house traders are carefully schooled in its proper use, whether they are microtraders or swing traders.

Selling right is the last rung on the ladder that leads to trading mastery, and when you've got more than one shot to get it right, the odds of handling it like a professional increase exponentially. So use it. Practice this incremental sale method. You won't be sorry. The very next time you find yourself in profitable territory, and those two demons I just spoke about rear their ugly heads, shut both of them up by selling half your stock. In other words, toss them both a bone. Once you have taken some profits off the table, cast your full attention on maximizing your remaining gain to the fullest. How do you go about doing that? That is next. Let's move on.

MAXIMIZING YOUR GAIN

OK. You entered your trade just as smoothly and confidently as any seasoned master trader. After setting your insurance policy (initial stop), you start using your well-honed trade management skills. You begin trailing your stop step by easy step, with a calm precision that would evoke awe from even the most astute Wall Street market professional. After a brief time, you find yourself boldly in profitable territory by $1.50. Your stop has been swiftly moved to your break-even point, eliminating any chance of a damaging loss. At this point, a wide smile slowly breaks open across your entire face as you ponder how difficult you once found these relatively simple, but potent, actions. *Tip:* The trader who knows what to do at every step acts with a confidence and certainty that evokes the winner's attitude.

The smile, now at its widest point, gives birth to a babylike drool. Your growing paper gain has evoked a now familiar glandular response, and you begin to actively salivate. The more you monitor your open position, the more you salivate. After wiping your mouth with the back of your hand, you decide to lock in some of your tasty gains. In the time it takes to say Pristine.com, you immediately offer out for sale 500 shares of your 1000-share lot. Bang! Someone who wasn't smart enough to spot the opportunity you did when it was almost being given away just took the bait. Ah! One-half is now in the bag. Your chest begins to protrude.

You find your shoulders being automatically forced back by some secret but powerful force. You realize this sensation to be none other than pride. But not that foolish pride so often possessed by the slow and the ignorant. The pride which you feel at this moment is the result of pulling off a series of complex actions, seamlessly and flawlessly. This pride is the mark of professionalism, the badge of excellence. And your veins are now pumped and saturated with it. After a brief pause to experience the full ecstasy of our success, you direct your attention to maximizing the gain you have left. These are the steps you take to ride the winning wave you have caught.

RIDING THE WINNING WAVE IN THREE EASY STEPS

1. *You maintain your break-even stop for the remainder of the trading session.* Remember that you sold half your position during market hours. The day is not yet complete. You are relaxed, knowing that the worst-case scenario is that you make money on the lot you sold, and break even on the lot you hold. At this point, no one can take your gain or your serenity away from you.

2. *The following day, you use the prior bar stop method as your new stop.* Note: If this new stop is *below* your break-even stop, you will keep the break-even stop. If the new stop at the prior day's low is only slightly higher than your break-even point, you can also opt to keep the break-even stop. This is a matter of choice. Of course, if the prior day's low is significantly higher than your break-even point, you should go with it.

3. *Each day after, you will use the trailing stop approach until any one of the following sellable events occurs:.*

KNOWING THE SELLABLE EVENTS

1. *You will sell the remainder of your position if the stock gaps up at the open by half or more.* It should be noted that market makers and specialists gap stocks up to sell, not to buy. They also gap stocks down to buy, not to sell.

2. *You will sell the remainder of your position if in the last 30 minutes of the day the stock is trading at or near the day's low.* This is the

first warning sign (in a rising stock) that sellers have started to overpower the buyers.

3. *You will sell the remainder of your position if,* after being up significantly on the day, *the stock drops back below its opening price.* The opening price is like the starting line of a race. As long as the stock is above its opening price, the bulls (buyers) are winning the race. If the stock is trading below its open, the bears (sellers) are winning that day's race. Don't get events 2 and 3 confused. There is a difference.

4. *You will sell the remainder of your position if the stock gaps down more than half, then proceeds to break the low of the day* after 30 *minutes have transpired.* A new daily low made 30 minutes after a gap down is bearish.

Note: All that we've discussed assumes a long trade and not a short. Simply reversing the criteria for short plays will provide you with the right guidance.

WHEN DISASTER STRIKES

I have spent a great deal of time talking about how to handle winning trades. But as we all know, the life of the master trader is not always full of roses. Active traders, more so than any other type of market player, have got to know how to handle the times when disaster strikes. When traders find that the most unimaginable nightmare has become a hard cold reality, they must know precisely what to do. They can't know in 5 minutes or 10 minutes. They've got to know precisely what steps to take at that moment, in that instant. Keep in mind that today's active traders are totally devoid of that luxury we call time. They cannot afford to freeze up, fall apart, or wimp out when stormy clouds start to hover. An angry market allows not even a moment of weakness. If there ever was a time when victory or survival goes to the swift, it is when the market has hand delivered you a ticking bomb. Only a well-thought out contingency plan can evoke the type of immediate action and professional handling I speak of. There is nothing more beautiful than watching a seasoned master trader trapped in the jaws of a furious stock. True professionals become even more astute when danger strikes. Like lion tamers who stick their heads in the mouth of a lion, their senses become more acute, their nerves more sensitive, their actions more deliberate and certain. When you look closely, you will notice that the master traders' awareness, already sharpened through years of grueling experience, actually heightens. Each thought and action exudes a confidence that would seem more appropriately matched with a winning situation. But all the great traders know that it is that type of control that traders must maintain in the face of adversity. Otherwise, that great white shark we call the bear markets will completely rip you to shreds.

You see, my friends, the market is both friend and foe. Those who have mastered the game simply know how to deal with the market in both states. With only a few simple yet powerful actions, which we will detail here, you will too. We want every one of our readers to know what greatness is. And you cannot be considered great until you know, beyond a shadow of a doubt, how to handle yourself in the face of major disasters. Here's how we do it.

HOW TO HANDLE THE MONSTER GAP DOWN

It is an inescapable fact that we live in a news-driven world. As active traders, we do our very best to take advantage of this fact, to use it for our benefit. But every now and then, an unexpected news item announced after the closing bell or shortly before the opening bell will cause a stock that we are in to open down significantly below our purchase price. Of course, extended market hours, which will soon move to 24-hour trading, will help diminish this type of overnight risk. But until these much needed moves happen in full force, the only course of action traders have is to try to minimize the damage, to control it as best they can. Ideas of getting the money back by holding the stock long term should not even come close to the master trader's mind. This occasional disaster is considered the cost of being an active trader and it is dealt with in the most professional manner possible. Should you find yourself in this unwelcome scene, the steps you should take are as follows.

STEPS TO TAKE WHEN DISASTER STRIKES

1. *When the stock opens, monitor its trading activity for a full 5 minutes.* During this time, you are to do nothing. You are not to sell. You are not to buy more. Your only action is the watch your sad stock trade. *Tip:* Because market makers and specialists tend to gap stocks down too excessively so that they can buy cheap stock, giving your shares up during the

first 5 minutes of trading is statistically unwise. Now this is not to say that the stock can't or won't trade lower. This action simply prevents the trader from jumping on the sell side with the rest of the herd. Panic, which is typically at its peak in the first 5 minutes of trading, is not the state of mind in which a trader wants to do anything, much less give up. *Rule: Never give up your shares in a state of panic.* There are times when giving up is the right thing to do. We simply can't and won't win them all. But you must only give up while thinking clearly and while in a calm, controlled state. Waiting for 5 minutes to transpire *before* you act will help accomplish this. Look at it this way. You are already crushed. Unless you are trading a high-priced Internet stock, an extra 5 minutes won't make or break you much more.

2. *After 5 minutes have gone by, mark off the day's low* (the lowest price the stock traded during the first 5 minutes). This will be the most important price of your life for the next 30 minutes.

4. *Sell at* least *half your stock if and when the stock breaks below the 5-minute low* (the day's low established after the first 5 minutes). Why is selling only half acceptable at times? Because the 30-minute low (not the 5-minute low) is the really significant one. Until we let the stock trade for a full 30 minutes, we have not really given it a full chance to rebound. Then why sell half on the break of the 5-minute low? Just in case the stock continues to drop furiously during the first 30 minutes of trading. Keep in mind that these are just guidelines. We don't want to be stupid. The truth of the matter is that we have a problem, and these actions are nothing more than damage control. Selling half your problem always provides for more clarity. The less burdened we are, the better. This is why giving up half of our headache is the best course of action, *if the stock breaks to a new daily low after 5-minutes have past. Note:* It should not be missed that many traders will be best served selling the whole lot at this point. The half option should only appeal to those gap downs that are not overly monstrous.

4. *After 30 minutes of trading, mark the day's low again.* Now keep in mind that this 30-minute low will either be lower than the 5-minute low, or the same. If the stock breaks below its 5-minute low *before* 30 minutes have gone by, the low the trader will use after the 30-minute mark will be lower. If the 5-

minute low is never violated during the first half hour, the 5-minute low will be the same as the 30-minute low. Understanding this point is crucial.

5. *Sell* all *your stock if and when the stock breaks below the 30-minute low* (established during the first 30 minutes of trading). Keep in mind that this is the real line in the sand that must be drawn. Just as we explained in the gap buy and gap sell sections of this book, what happens *after* the first 30 minutes of trading tells it all. If the stock moves to a new daily high after its first half hour of trading, the strength is real and should be respected. If the stock breaks to a new daily low after the first half hour of trading, watch out. This is a very weak stock that has further downside to go. The stock must be eliminated. No ifs, ands, or buts about it. Gone!

6. Use *The Trailing-Stop Method*. This is the action the trader would take if the stock managed to remain above its 30-minute low throughout the whole day. *Note:* Some traders we have taught opt to keep their stop at the low of the disaster day. In other words, they don't use a trailing-stop method. Their view is that as long as the stock remains above the low of the gap down day, it can be considered to have bottomed. Sometimes this approach improves the outcome. But the trader's risk of doing this is possibly losing the opportunity to narrow the loss forever. I have found this alternative approach to be most useful on leading technology stocks that gap down, such as an Intel, a Dell, or a Microsoft.

AN AGGRESSIVE APPROACH

Some of our most aggressive traders will use the 5-minute rule on the upside to add to their crushed position. In other words, if the stock breaks above the high established during the first 5 minutes of trading, they buy more stock with the idea of flipping it (selling the new lot quickly) several levels higher. This aggressive strategy which we teach in our seminars is called the *bullet play*, and it often helps astute traders to further narrow their losses. However, it must be realized that the same 5-minute sell rule stays intact. The only difference here is the additional buy. Nothing on the sell side of the equation changes. This is just a note for those who consider themselves to be aggressive.

SIGNS OF IMPENDING DANGER

While we can never prevent disasters from taking place, there are times when clear signs of impending danger can alert us before a debacle occurs. Knowing what those signs are can save the master trader thousands, if not tens of thousands, of dollars over a lifetime. Not only that, under the right scenario, the astute trader can even use some of these warning signs as a way to profit in reverse. Let's face it. Sometimes bad things happen to good traders, but knowing and watching for the warnings signs listed here will ensure that those bad things happen to you a lot less than they will to others. Become intimate with each sign, for they will literally save your financial life. And I'm willing to bet they save it more than once.

Signs that danger may be close at hand are:

- The stock gives back most of its gains during the last 2 hours of trading.
- The stock closes at or near its low, after initially being up decently.
- The stock produces little to no gain on above average daily volume.
- The stock gaps up excessively at the open, then trades below the prior bar's high.
- The stock is struggling in the same price area that kicked off a previous decline.
- A major market maker such as GSCO, SBSH, or MLCO is selling the stock blatantly and steadily throughout the day.

These are some of the signs that often precede danger. Be out on the lookout for them. For short play, simply reverse them.

PART THREE

LOOKING AHEAD

17
C H A P T E R

HOW TO PUT IT ALL TOGETHER

HOW TO PUT IT ALL TOGETHER USING DAILY CHARTS

AVNET, INC. (AVT)

This daily chart of Avnet, Inc. (AVT) (Figure 17.1) shows the power of the 200 SMA combined with several other events:

1. The 200 SMA serves as resistance. The bearish RB with a topping tail reveals big sellers.
2. An NRB that closes above its open puts an end to AVT's decline in the area of a prior gap. *Tip:* An NRB that closes above its opening price is exceptionally potent. It should also not be forgotten that gaps often serve as areas of support and/ or resistance.
3. After making a new high, AVT's pullback abruptly ends with a gap down to the 200 SMA on climactic volume.

BROADCAST.COM (BRCM)

1. BRCM (Figure 17.2) tops out and proceeds to decline in a very big way. *Tip:* Tops followed by big declines typically serve as very significant points of resistance when they are retested.
2. BRCM forms a bullish RB with a bottoming tail, revealing big buying. This area becomes a key reference point on a retest.
3. BRCM retests its prior low on climactic volume, confirming major price support. Note that the prior advance marked as "A"

F I G U R E   17.1

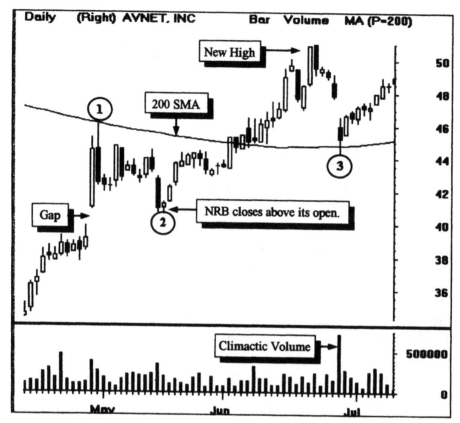

Chart by The Executioner.com

was a near 100 percent retracement of the prior decline. This increased the odds that BRCM would hold at the prior low.

4. A bearish RB with a topping tail at the prior high reveals heavy selling. *Tip:* Aggressive traders often buy on RBs that form at major support and sell short on RBs that form at major resistance.

BMC SOFTWARE (BMCS)

1. BMCS's explosive rally (Figure 17.3), which is kicked off by a professional gap, halts dead in its tracks at the flat 200 SMA.

F I G U R E   17.2

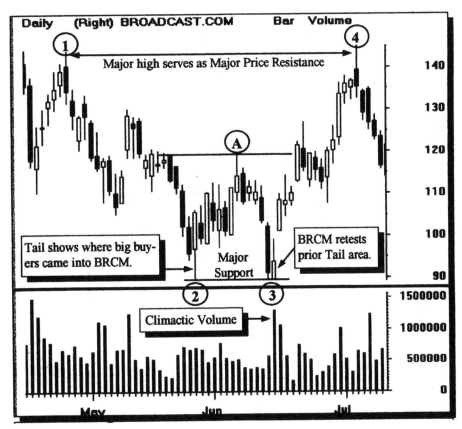

Chart by The Executioner.com

2. BMCS bottoms after experiencing a 50 percent retracement, a 3 to 5 bar drop, and a bullish RB with a bottoming tail. All of these charting events occurring simultaneously represent a very compelling buy point.

3. After another 3 to 5 bar drop, BMCS simultaneously finds major support at its prior low and on its 200 SMA.

4. The bullish RB with a bottoming tail is followed by two NRBs which are also on the 200 SMA. The second NRB which closes above its opening price is the key sign that BMCS is ready to blast off.

F I G U R E   17.3

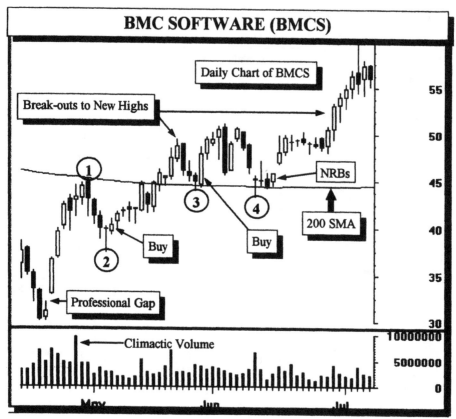

Chart by The Executioner.com

ADVANCED FIBER COMMUNICATIONS (AFCI)

AFCI (Figure 17.4) demonstrates how potent minor price support combined with other events can be:

1. AFCI pulls back to minor price support and its rising 20 SMA, and lifts. The bottoming tail suggests big buying.
2. After making a new high, AFCI pulls back again to minor price support and its rising 20 SMA to form a bullish RB with a bottoming tail. *Tip:* The first pullback from a new high is typically buyable.

F I G U R E   17.4

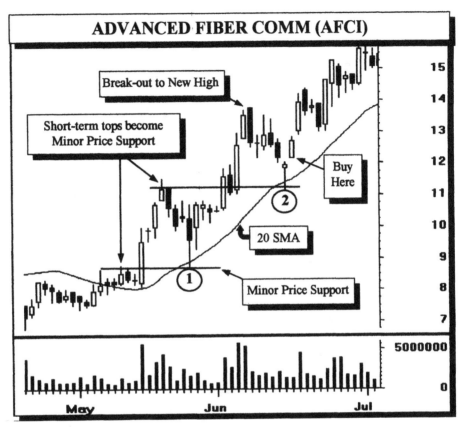

Chart by The Executioner.com

BIOGEN INC. (BGEN)

In mid-June, BGEN (Figure 17.5) presented a very interesting buying opportunity to the alert master trader. At point 1, BGEN pulls back to test its prior low at point A. *Tip:* Prior lows serve as major price support, particularly if they are followed by breakouts to new highs. What is most compelling is the fact that BGEN forms a bullish RB that closes above its open with a bottoming tail. The master trader buys either on the bullish RB or on the following day at point B.

F I G U R E   17.5

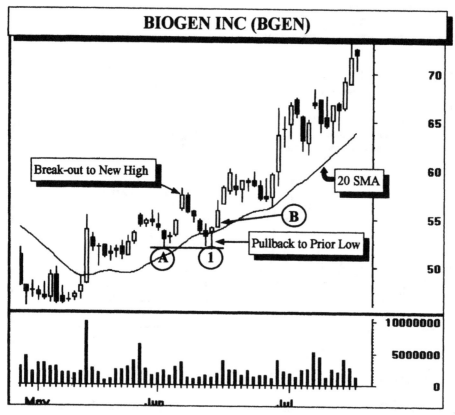

BIOGEN INC (BGEN)

Break-out to New High

20 SMA

B

Pullback to Prior Low

A

1

Chart by The Executioner.com

COMPUTER ASSOCIATES INTERNATIONAL (CA)

1. CA (Figure 17.6) rebounds off its rising 20 SMA, right after forming two NRBs. *Tip:* Master traders will often buy on an NRB that closes above its open. See Figure 17.6.

2. After moving to a new high, CA pulls back to its rising 20 SMA again, forms another NRB that closes above its opening price, and then rallies.

3. CA rallies to retest its prior high, forming a Doji-like NRB that quickly leads to a $2 plus decline. *Tip:* Keep in mind that a new game begins with each new high. After each new high,

FIGURE 17.6

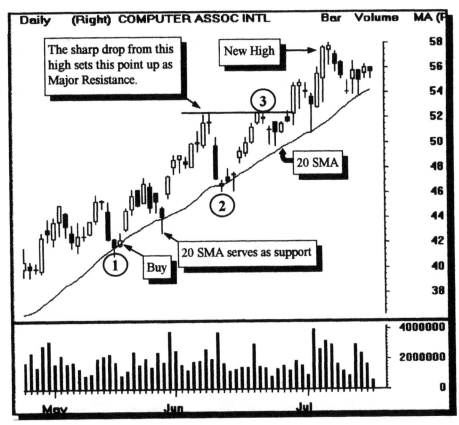

Chart by The Executioner.com

the master trader looks to buy the next decline, provided any one or more of the events takes place.

CONCORD EFS (CEFT)

This daily chart of CEFT (Figure 17.7) presented a near perfect key buy setup.

1. CEFT rallies strongly to a new high. This robust rally tells the master trader that the next pullback is buyable, provided one or more event takes place.
2. CEFT experiences a 3 to 5 bar drop to minor price support. Two NRBs with small tails materialize near the 20 SMA. All of

F I G U R E   17.7

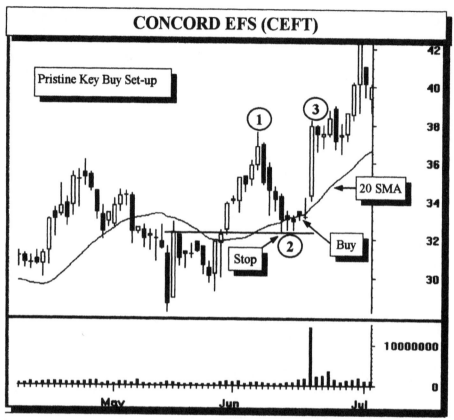

Chart by The Executioner.com

these events lining up at the same point present a very
compelling buy opportunity. The master trader buys CEFT
the very next time CEFT trades above a prior high, then places
a stop $\frac{1}{16}$ to $\frac{1}{8}$ below the lowest low of the 3 to 5 bar drop.

3. A 5-point move to the upside follows. *Tip:* The bigger the
number of events, the bigger the expected move.

COMPUTER SCIENCES (CSC)

CSC (Figure 17.8) shows three events, all of which are tradeable:

FIGURE 17.8

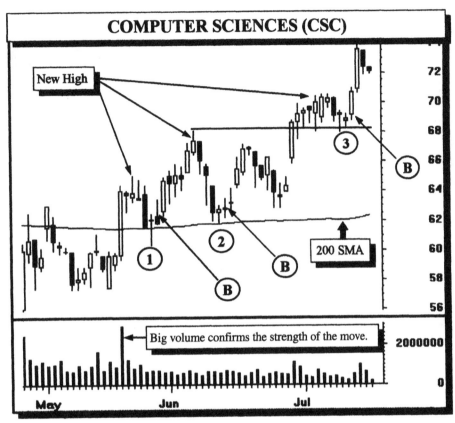

COMPUTER SCIENCES (CSC)

Chart by The Executioner.com

1. After CSC makes a new high, a bullish tail halts the pull back at its 200 SMA. The master trader buys above the high of the bar with the tail.
2. After another high, CSC experiences a 3 to 5 bar drop to retest its prior low and its 200 SMA. This forms a near perfect buy setup. The master trader buys as soon as CSC trades above a prior bar's high.
3. After a new high, CSC pulls back to minor support and forms an NRB. The master trader buys above the NRB.

F I G U R E   17.9

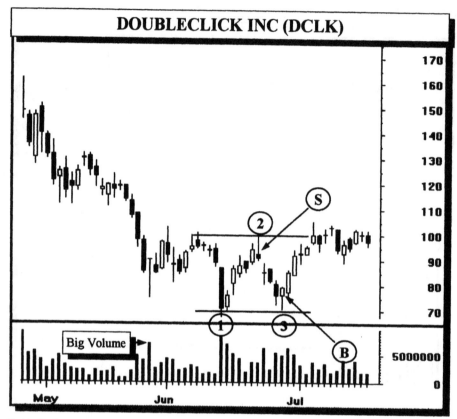

Chart by The Executioner.com

DOUBLECLICK (DCLK)

DCLK (Figure 17.9) shows the power of major support and resistance combined with other events:

1. DCLK drops on climactic volume to end its decline. This is not a playable event, but does serve as an attention grabber, particularly after the prior surge in volume which provided the first sign that big buyers were stepping up to the plate.
2. DCLK rallies back to its prior, which serves as major resistance. The formation of the bearish RB at major resistance

sets up a shorting opportunity. *Tip:* Master traders often enter on RBs near the end of the day.

3. DCLK experiences a 100 percent retracement. The formation of a bullish RB right off major support sets up a perfect buy. The master trader buys either on the RB or above the high of the RB on the following day. *Note:* The master trader would look to sell into major resistance.

IMMUNEX CORP. (IMNX)

This daily chart of IMNX (Figure 17.10) shows a number of powerful events that would have served as key signs or signals for the master trader:

1. The Doji-like topping bar kicked off a very severe decline for IMNX. *Tip:* Tops that kick off sharp declines tend to serve as major resistance on retests.
2. IMNX halts its decline after filling the gap it formed 1 month earlier. *Tip:* Gaps serve as areas of support and resistance.
3. IMNX retests its prior top, which now serves as major resistance.
4. IMNX experiences a 3 to 5 bar drop to its prior low which serves as major support. Note that on this pullback, IMNX forms a perfect bullish RB with a tail. The master trader buys on the RB day or above the high of the RB on the following day.

HOW TO PUT IT ALL TOGETHER USING INTRADAY CHARTS

BROADCOM CORPORATION (BRCM)

The 15-minute chart of BRCM (Figure 17.11) demonstrates the power of the 200 SMA, combined with key reversal times. Even a quick glance will show that the 200 SMA served as resistance at four different points:

1. Shortly after touching the 200 SMA, BRCM gaps to the down side and declines 4 points.
2. After gapping back up to the 200 SMA at the open on the following day, BRCM begins another big decline that bottoms out with a tail in the 10:30 a.m. reversal time period.

F I G U R E   17.10

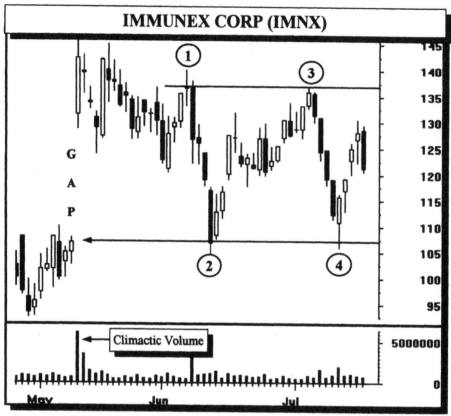

Chart by The Executioner.com

3. A rebound back to the flat 200 SMA peters out again, with the topping bar closing below its open. *Tip:* A flat overhead 200 SMA will serve as greater resistance than a sloping SMA.

4. A shallow 40 percent retracement bottoms around the 1:30 p.m. reversal time, and an NRB, which closes above its open, kicks off another rebound back to the 200 SMA.

5. BRCM opens up the following day near the 200 SMA, and a new decline ensues in the area of the 10:00 a.m. reversal time.

FIGURE   17.11

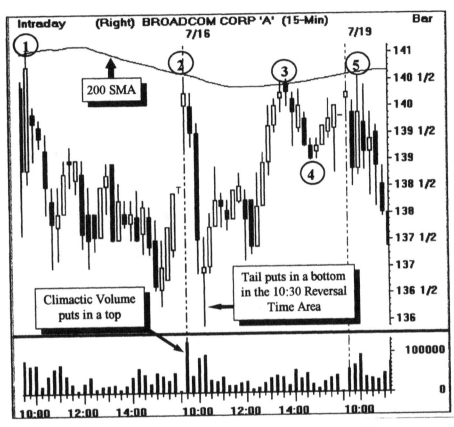

Chart by The Executioner.com

HOW TO PUT IT ALL TOGETHER USING MULTIPLE TIME FRAMES

CYBERCASH, INC. (CYCH): USING THE DAILY CHART TO DETERMINE WHAT ACTION TO TAKE

A look at the 15-minute chart of CYCH (Figure 17.12) reveals a multiday sideways base. *Tip:* Buying breakouts from intraday sideways bases is a low-risk trading strategy. Keep in mind that the master trader is now looking at a more detailed picture of CYCH's last 2 days of trading.

F I G U R E   17.12

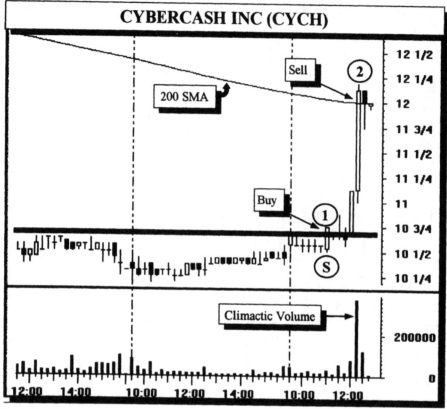

Chart by The Executioner.com

1. The master trader buys CYCH on the breakout of the
   sideways base. It must not be forgotten that part of this base is
   the NRB viewed on the daily chart. Once bought, the master
   intraday trader sets a mental stop under the breakout bar. See
   "S" in Figure 17.12. *Tip:* Stocks that move to a new daily high
   after 30 minutes of trading tend to be strong throughout the
   day. Refer to the 30-minute buy rule in Chapter 14.

2. As CYCH explodes to the upside, the master trader is aware of
   the 200 SMA overhead. Climactic volume ends the move right
   near the 200 SMA which is where the master intraday trader

FIGURE   17.13

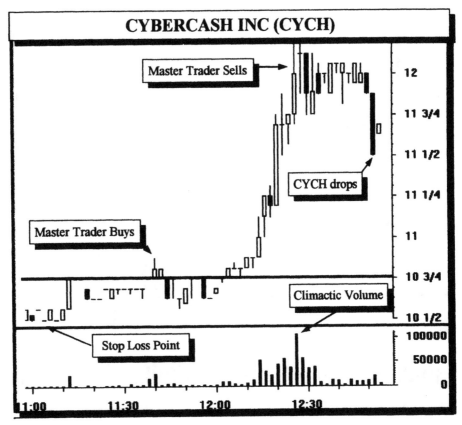

Chart by The Executioner.com

looks to offer out (sell) the stock, effectively locking in a $1.25 gain. *Tip:* An overhead 200 SMA will typically stop an intraday rally dead in its tracks. Figure 17.13 tells the story.

CYBERCASH INC. (CYCH): USING THE 15-MINUTE CHART TO DETERMINE WHEN TO TAKE IT

This 2-minute chart of CYCH (Figure 17.13) demonstrates the effect the 200 SMA on the 15-minute chart has on the stock's intraday rally. Not surprisingly, CYCH drops sharply. *Tip:* The overhead 200 SMA is an ex-

F I G U R E   17.14

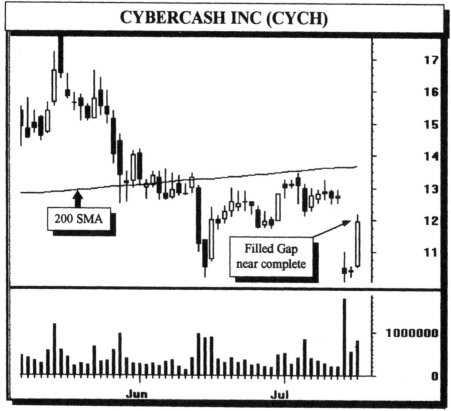

Chart by The Executioner.com

cellent profit-taking guideline for master intraday traders. Keep in mind
that this tactic also works well in reverse.

CYBERCASH, INC. (CYCH): USING THE 2-MINUTE CHART
FOR GREATER PRECISION

This resulting daily chart of CYCH (Figure 17.14) shows a filling of the
gap, which is another powerful selling reason for the master trader. *Tip:*
Gaps serve as areas of support and resistance. In this case, the downside
gap area is a form of resistance.

FIGURE 17.15

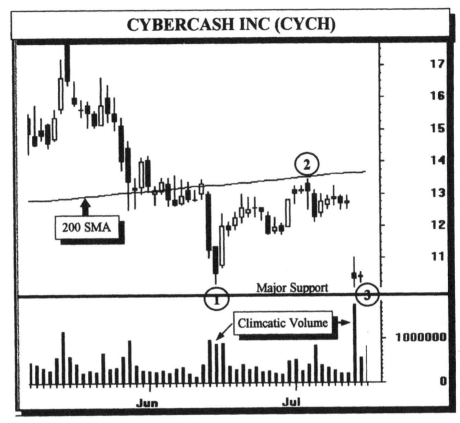

Chart by The Executioner.com

CYBERCASH, INC. (CYCH): USING THE DAILY CHART
TO DETERMINE THE SELL POINT

This daily chart of CYCH (Figure 17.15) demonstrates how a master
trader might capitalize on the concept of climactic volume combined
with major support. We will also show how the master trader utilizes
multiple time frames to make more intelligent decisions.

1. CYCH drops from the area of its 200 SMA. The drop ends
   with a large pickup in volume. The master trader makes a
   mental note of the strong rally that follows. *Tip:* A prior low

from which a sharp rally ensues will always serve as a key area of major support on a retest.

2. The 200 SMA serves as resistance and eventually kicks off another sharp decline.

3. CYCH gaps down on climactic volume and holds at major price support. The day after the gap is down, an NRB forms, signaling that a strong rebound may be close at hand. The master trader decides to buy above the high of the NRB, but first flips to the 5- and/or 15-minute chart to get a closer view.

CYBERCASH, INC. (CYCH): USING THE DAILY CHART TO SEE THE RESULT

This final daily chart of CHCH (Figure 17.16) shows just how significant gaps can be as areas of resistance. Note how sharp the decline was.

THREE EXAMS FOR THE MASTER TRADER

TEST 1. LEXMARK INTERNATIONAL (LXK): NAME THE FOUR TRADABLE EVENTS

Quiz

This daily chart of LXK (Figure 17.17) contains four key events. Can you name them?

1. _____
2. _____
3. _____
4. _____

Answers

1. *Key buy setup accentuated by a narrow-range bar (NRB).* The master trader buys LXK above the high of the NRB, with an initial stop $\frac{1}{16}$ below the low of the NRB. The master trader sells on the reversal bar some $13 higher. *Note:* All sells are marked by S on the chart.

2. *Key buy setup off the rising 20 MA.* The master trader buys at 2, with an initial stop below the prior or current bar's low. The

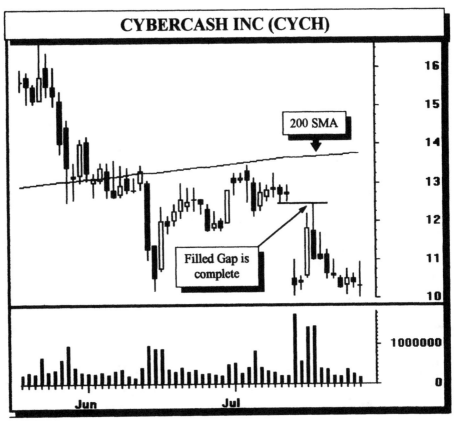

FIGURE 17.16

CYBERCASH INC (CYCH)

Chart by The Executioner.com

master trader gets stopped out the next day for a several point loss.

3. *Key buy setup right off the rising 20 MA.* The master trader buys at 3, with an initial stop below the prior bar's low. The master trader sells near prior high on the deadly Doji setup for a near $6 gain. *Tip:* The master trader protects profits in each trade by utilizing the $1 rule and the trailing-stop method.

4. *Key buy setup accentuated by a bullish tail, right off the rising 20 MA and minor price support.* The master trader buys at 4, with an initial stop below the prior bar's low. The master trader sells near the prior high for a $4 to $5 gain.

F I G U R E   17.17

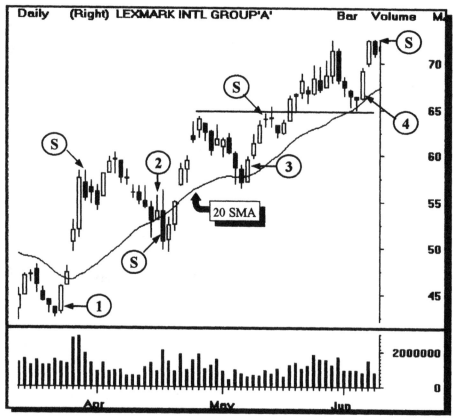

Chart by The Executioner.com

TEST 2. CONCENTRIC NETWORK (CNCX): NAME THE SIX TRADABLE EVENTS

Quiz

This daily chart of CNCX (Figure 17.18) contains at least six key events. Can you name them?

1. _____

2. _____

3. _____

4. _____

FIGURE 17.18

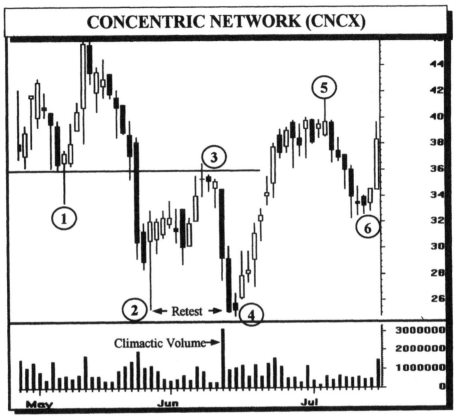

CONCENTRIC NETWORK (CNCX)

Chart by The Executioner.com

5. _____

6. _____

Answers

1. *Key buy setup, accentuated by a bullish reversal bar (RB) with a tail.* The master trader buys on or above RB.

2. *Bullish reversal bar with a tail.* This suggests that buyers are very active in the $26 to $28 price area. Keep in mind that this is not a playable event. It only serves as a sign of where the buyers are active. *Tip:* Buying on or above a bullish RB should only be done on a pullback from a new high. CNCX has actually

broken below its prior low, qualifying it as a stock in a downtrend.

3. *Key Sell setup at minor price support.* This sell setup is accentuated by a narrow-range bar (NRB). The master trader shorts CNCX below the low of the NRB.

4. *Narrow range bar (NRB) on major price support shortly after climactic volume.* The master trader aggressively buys above the NRB.

5. *New high with a tail.* This is not a playable event. The new high only indicates that CNCX can be bought on the next pullback, provided one or more events materialize.

6. *Fifty percent retracement, setting up a near perfect key buy setup, accentuated by a narrow range bar (NRB).* The master trader buys above the NRB.

COSTCO COMPANIES (COST): NAME THE SIX TRADABLE EVENTS
Quiz

This daily chart of COST (Figure 17.19) contains six key events. Can you name them?

1. _____

2. _____

3. _____

4. _____

5. _____

6. _____

Answers

1. *Climactic volume halts COST's decline, setting up a potential area of price support.* This is not a playable event.

2. *Key sell setup accentuated by a narrow range bar (NRB).* The master trader sells COST short below the NRB.

3. *Key buy setup right on major price support and the 200 SMA.* It should be noted that this retest of the prior low can also be viewed as a 100 percent retracement. The master trader buys the very next time COST trades above a prior day's high.

FIGURE 17.19

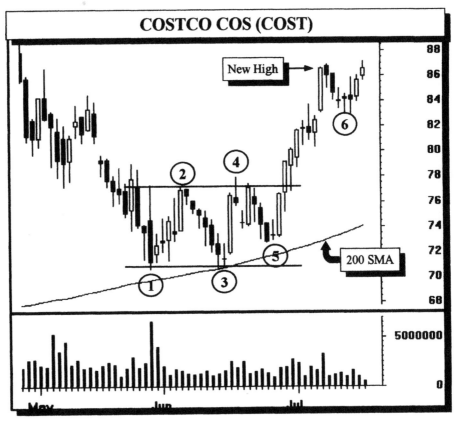

Chart by The Executioner.com

4. *Reversal bar (RB) with a negative tail at major price resistance.* Note that COST gapped down over 2 points the following day.

5. *Key buy setup.* While this setup did not correspond with another event, the Doji-like bar that marked the bottom was a key indication that a rally would likely materialize. Aggressive traders would buy above the Doji-like bar.

6. *Key buy setup with a series of bullish tails. Tip:* The first pullback after a new high is buyable, proving one or more of the events materialize.

18

C H A P T E R

ESP

The Future of Electronic Trading Software

A NEXT-GENERATION TRADING TOOL

The master trader who has worked hard to acquire the necessary skills of successful market play realizes that a key challenge in short-term trading is finding quality trading opportunities, or setups, *at the very moment when action should be taken.* While longer-term traders often trade at the open based on daily and weekly charts, the professional short-term trader often makes trading decisions based on rapidly moving intraday charts. Because of this, the short-term trader must be able to quickly and efficiently identify trading opportunities *as they occur during the market day.*

The developing short-term trader is often able to identify quality trade opportunities, but only *after* it is too late to take action on most of them. While reviewing hundreds or even thousands of intraday stock charts, the trader will see many profitable opportunities that were missed minutes or even hours earlier. The inescapable reality is that only a very few quality opportunities will be found at the appropriate time to take action and initiate a successful trade. Worse yet, many developing traders weaken their entry criteria in order to "create" opportunities, which of course tends to further deteriorate their trading performance. This is where technological advancements can deliver big.

The master traders take advantage of every tool that technology offers to improve their trade selection and timing. Keep in mind that master traders do not rely solely on technology as a crutch, hoping to benefit without gaining the necessary knowledge. That can never happen, no matter how advanced the technology. Rather the master traders use technology to further enhance their already earned ability to profit from the market. We hope you get this important point, because financial grave sites are filled with traders who mistakenly believed that a technological edge was all they needed to become successful traders. Nothing will ever replace knowledge and skill. The main purpose of technology is to utilize that knowledge and skill more efficiently.

With that being said, the advent of powerful computer systems and artificial intelligence technology have recently enabled the development of exciting new tools to aid the knowledgeable short-term trader, and Pristine.com has moved to the forefront of these dynamic new changes with a revolutionary product called Pristine ESP.

AUTOMATED TRADE IDENTIFICATION AND ALERTING

Students of our 1- and 3-day seminars and our advisory services have long recognized the value of the trading setups, many of which are outlined in this book. However, with a universe of over 10,000 stocks, it is very difficult to quickly identify stocks meeting the Pristine criteria at the precise moments when the trading opportunities present themselves. Fortunately, computing power and artificial intelligence technology has enabled us to monitor thousands of stocks against dozens of trading setups and systems on a real-time basis, providing instantaneous alerting when any Pristine opportunity is identified in any stock.

The ESP product (*sales@pristine.com*) uses these new technologies to aid master traders by alerting them to potential trading opportunities for every trading setup. These systems range from the longer-term (2- to 5-day) methods such as the swing buy and sell setups to the shorter-term (1- to 2-hour) day trading methods such as the intraday breakout plays. There are currently over 20 different trading setups programmed into ESP, and more are continuously being added. ESP also alerts the trader to stocks meeting other, more generic criteria, which are always of interest to the master trader. These additional alerts include notifying the trader the moment a stock hits a new 52-week high/low, or the moment a stock, with a sudden increase in volume, is accompanied by a sharp price movement.

AUTOMATED STOCK SCANNING AND SCREENING

Another powerful feature of ESP is its scanning and screen capability. ESP continuously screens all stocks based on key criteria such as:

- Percent gainers and losers
- Point gainers and losers
- Most active stocks based on volume
- Most active stocks based on trades in the past 1 minute
- Stocks hitting new highs or lows during the day
- Stocks nearing the trigger point for a trade opportunity
- Many other screens are also available in ESP

These lists are easily integrated directly into the market minder displays of such direct access systems like the Executioner to enable the trader to quickly review the intraday charts and Level 2 status of these candidate stocks. The lists are continuously updated to provide the trader with accurate information on which to make trading decisions.

HOW IT WORKS

The ESP product has been programmed to identify key setups occurring daily in the marketplace. A powerful computer and satellite data feed are combined with an artificial intelligence engine to comb through and find tradable opportunities. Every movement and change that occurs in every stock is continuously monitored. Using client/server technology and the Internet, ESP alerts and scans are instantaneously broadcast to the trader's computer at the moment, the instant they occur throughout the day. It is important to note that the extensive computing power, software systems and data feed are maintained on internal Pristine computers. The Internet is used only to transmit the results, namely, the alerts and scans processed by the system. Therefore, the computing power and bandwidth requirement needed for the trader's computer to support ESP is negligible.

It is our view that artificial intelligence technology will begin to play a bigger role in the financial market going forward, and ESP is one of the first products to fully utilize this technology to benefit the active trader. ESP will improve the trading performance of master traders by enabling them to narrow their attention to a smaller list of stocks that present potential trading opportunities. Using the intelligence of ESP, the master traders are able to quickly and efficiently make trading decisions without being bogged down with the difficult and time-consuming process of sorting through the thousands of available stocks to find the quality setups described in this book. As a result, the master traders are able to improve their trading results quite dramatically. Pristine in a box. What a wonderful thing.

19 CHAPTER

CONCLUSION

YOU ARE A LEADER

Because of our decade-long commitment to the education of active, self-directed traders, and our relentless fight for equality on Wall Street, many people all over the world have looked to us as their leaders. The responsibility that comes with thousands of followers relying on your teaching and guidance is no doubt a heavy one. I remember feeling overwhelmed shortly after being thrust in the limelight of the day trading community. The most dominant thought I had at the time dealt with my own level of progress as a trader. "Who was I to be giving advice and suggestions?" "Wasn't I still a growing and developing trader myself?" "Didn't I still succumb to some of the most obvious errors that haunt and plague day traders young and old?" Of course I did. But the requests for my leadership, my knowledge, and my experience did not stop, and as our following grew, so did my desire to make myself more worthy of this worldwide respect.

It was only after researching the word "leader" that I completely threw myself to the task of leading. Leader is a word that has special meaning in every language. According to history, it can be traced back at least as far as ancient Egypt. In English, the word leader is more than a thousand years old, and little has changed from its Anglo-Saxon root *laedere*, which means "people on a journey."

Think about this meaning for a moment. Leader is actually plural, meaning *people on a journey*. Not person or individual, but *people* on a journey. This epiphany is what made me feel much better about being regarded as a leader. As a growing trader, I felt that I, too, was still on the journey, and, yes, that did make me a leader. But according to the definition, we are *all* leaders. We are all people on a journey. So in reality, I am no more a leader than you are. Each individual reading this book today has the right to say out loud, "I am a leader," as long as that individual is on the path. While it is true that there are few, if any, universal paths to trading mastery, we have to say thank you for taking the time to study ours.

TIME WELL SPENT

We believe with all our heart and soul that the time you've chosen to spend on this book will prove to be time well spent. Not only will the wisdom, the lessons, the skills, and the techniques in this book aid you in reaching that state we so affectionately call trading mastery, they will help you in just about every other walk of life. Little do people know that what calls for living a successful trading life is exactly what calls for living a successful life, in general.

It is our hope and dream that this book will, in some small way, keep today from being another sporadic, orphaned instance in Wall Street's history in which the individual had equal footing with the powerful insiders. We recognize that one of the best ways of underwriting the future of this industry is sharing the lessons, the skills, the powers, the attitudes, and the hard-won advances that we so diligently sought after over a decade ago.

It is our passionate desire to both protect and share the progress and advancements we have made, and we want to be sure that those who come after us have shoulders to stand upon. With this book, I hope we have in some measure accomplished this.

YOU "WILL" SUCCEED

In closing I'd like you to know that we agree wholeheartedly with the philosopher who said, "There are three types of individuals in this world: the *wills*, the *wont's*, and the *cant's*. The first *accomplish* everything. The second *oppose* everything. And the third *fail* at everything." Your purchase and completion of this book stands as a living testament that you are neither a "won't" or a "can't," but rather a permanent member of that group called the "wills." And with a little bit of patience and a lot of study and dedication, you *will* accomplish what you set out to do.

THE REST IS UP TO YOU

Just keep in mind that while we have conferred the knowledge, experience is no person's to give. Experienced traders cannot share their seasoning with those who desire advancement. Their only option is to give them the knowledge and the opportunities for developing their own experiences. This book gives the knowledge *and* the opportunity. The rest, my friends, is up to you. Good luck.

STOCK INDEXES

NASDAQ 100 Stock Index (Symbol: NDX)

Symbol	Name	Symbol	Name
COMS	3COM CORP	DLTR	DOLLAR TREE STOR
ADPT	ADAPTEC INC	EBAY	EBAY INC
ADCT	ADC TELECOM INC	ERTS	ELEC ARTS INC
ADBE	ADOBE SYS INC	EFII	ELEC FOR IMAGING
ALTR	ALTERA CORP	ERICY	ERICSSON LM-ADR
AMZN	AMAZON.COM INC	FAST	FASTENAL CO
APCC	AMER POWER CONV	FHCC	FIRST HEALTH GRP
AMGN	AMGEN INC	FISV	FISERV INC
ANDW	ANDREW CORP	GENZ	GENZYME-GENL DIV
APOL	APOLLO GROUP-A	GBLX	GLOBAL CORSSING
AAPL	APPLE COMPUTER	IMNX	IMMUNEX CORP
AMAT	APPLIED MATERIAL	INTC	INTEL CORP
ATHM	AT HOME CORP	INTU	INTUIT INC
ATML	ATMEL CORP	JDSU	JDS UNIPHASE
ADSK	AUTODESK INC	KLAC	KLA-TENCOR CORP
BBBY	BED BATH & BEYOND	LVLT	LEVEL 3 COMM INC
BGEN	BIOGEN INC	LNCR	LINCARE HOLDINGS
BMET	BIOMET INC	LLTC	LINEAR TECH CORP
BMCS	BMC SOFTWARE INC	LCOS	LYCOS INC
CATP	CAMBRIDGE TECH	MXIM	MAXIM INTEGRATED
CBRL	CBRL GROUP INC	WCOM	MCI WORLDCOM INC
CHIR	CHIRON CORP	MCLD	MCLEODUSA INC-A
CIEN	CIENA CORP	MCHP	MICROCHIP TECH
CTAS	CINTAS CORP	MUEI	MICRON ELECTRON
CSCO	CISCO SYSTEMS	MSFT	MICROSOFT CORP
CTXS	CITRIX SYSTEMS	MLHR	MILLER (HERMAN)
CMGI	CMGI INC	MOLX	MOLEX INC
CNET	CNET INC	NETA	NETWORK ASSOC
COMR	COMAIR HOLDGS INC	NXTL	NEXTEL COMM-A
CMCSK	COMCAST CORP-SPL	NWAC	NORTHWEST AIRLIN
CPWR	COMPUWARE CORP	NOVL	NOVELL INC
CMVT	COMVERSE TECH	NTLI	NTL INC
CEFT	CONCORD EFS	ORCL	ORACLE CORP
CNXT	CONEXANT SYS	PCAR	PACCAR INC
CEXP	CORP EXPRESS INC	PHSY	PACIFICARE HLTH
COST	COSTCO WHOLESALE	SPOT	PANAMSAT CORP
DELL	DELL COMPUTER	PMTC	PARAMETRIC TECH

NASDAQ 100 Stock Index (Symbol: NDX) (Cont.)

Symbol	Name	Symbol	Name
PAYX	PAYCHEX INC	SBUX	STARBUCKS CORP
PSFT	PEOPLESOFT INC	STEI	STEWART ENTERPR
QCOM	QUALCOMM INC	SUNW	SUN MICROSYSTEMS
QTRN	AUINTILES TRANS	SNPA	SYNOPSYS INC
QWST	QWEST COMMUNICAT	TECD	TECH DATA CORP
RTRSY	REUTERS GRP-ADR	TLAB	TELLABS INC
RXSD	REXALL SUNDOWN	USAI	USA NETWORKS INC
ROST	ROSS STORES INC	VRTS	VERITAS SOFTWARD
SANM	SANMINA CORP	VISX	VISX INC
SEBL	STEBEL SYSTEMS	VTSS	VITESSE SEMICOND
SIAL	SIGMA-ALDRICH	WTHG	WORTHINGTON INDS
SSCC	SMURFIT-STONE CO	XLNX	XILINX INC
SPLS	STAPLES INC	YHOO	YAHOO INC

Merrill Lynch 100 Tech (Symbol: MLO)

Symbol	Name	Symbol	Name
COMS	3 COM CORP	CPQ	COMPAQ COMPUTER
ADPT	ADAPTEC INC	CA	COMPUTER ASSOC
ADCT	ADC TELECOM INC	CSC	COMPUTER SCIENCE
ADBE	ADOBE SYS INC	CPWR	COMPUWARE CORP
AMD	ADV MICRO DEVICE	DELL	DELL COMPUTER
ALA	ALCATEL SA - ADR	EGRP	E*TRADE GROUP
ALTR	ALTERA CORP	EBAY	EBAY INC
AMZN	AMAZON.COM INC	ECIL	ECI TELECOM
APCC	AMER POWER CONV	ERTS	ELEC ARTS INC
AOL	AMERICA ONLINE	EDS	ELEC DATA SYSTEM
ADI	ANALOG DEVICES	EMC	EMC CORP/MASS
AAPL	APPLE COMPUTER	ERICY	ERICSSON LM-ADR
AMAT	APPLIED MATERIAL	FDC	FIRST DATA CORP
ASML	ASM LITHOGRAPHY	FISV	FISERV INC
ATHM	AT HOME CORP	IT	GARTNER GROUP-A
ADSK	AUTODESK INC	GTW	GATEWAY INC
AUD	AUTOMAIC DATA	GIC	GEN INSTRUMENT
BANF	BAAN COMPANY NV	HWP	HEWLETT-PACKARD
BMCS	BMC SOFTWARE INC	INKT	INKTOMI CORP
BRCM	BROADCOM CORP-A	INTC	INTEL CORP
CDN	CADENCE DESIGN	IBM	INTL BUS MACHINE
CEN	CERIDIAN CORP	INTU	INTUIT INC
CSCO	CISCO SYSTEMS	IOM	IOMEGA CORP
CTXS	CITRIX SYSTEMS	JBL	JABIL CIRCUIT

Merrill Lynch 100 Tech (Symbol: MLO) (Cont.)

Symbol	Name	Symbol	Name
JDEC	JD EDWARDS & CO	QCOM	QUALCOMM INC
JDSU	JDS UNIPHASE	DSS	QUANTUM CO - DSSG
KEA	KEANE INC	RATL	RATIONAL SOFTWAR
KLAC	KLA-TENCOR CORP	RNWK	REALNETWORKS INC
LXK	LEXMARK INTL-A	SANM	SANMINA CORP
LLTC	LINEAR TECH CORP	SAP	SAP AG-SPONS ADR
LSI	LSI LOGIC CORP	SCI	SCI SYSTEMS INC
LU	LUCENT TECH INC	SEG	SEAGATE TECH INC
MXIM	MAXIM INTEGRATED	SEBL	SIEBEL SYSTEMS
MU	MICRON TECH	SGI	SILICON GRAPHICS
MSFT	MICROSOFT CORP	SLR	SOLECTRON CORP
MOLX	MOLEX INC	SE	STERLING COMMERC
MOT	MOTOROLA INC	STM	STMICROELECTRONT
NSM	NATL SEMICONDUCT	STK	STORAGE TECH
NTAP	NETWORK APPLIANC	SUNW	SUN MICROSYSTEMS
NETA	NETWORK ASSOC	SNPS	SYNOPSYS INC
NN	NEWBRIDGE NETWRK	TECD	TECH DATA CORP
NXTL	NEXTEL COMM-A	TLAB	TELLABS INC
NOK	NOKIA CORP -ADR	TER	TERADYNE INC
NT	NORTEL NETWORKS	TXN	TEXAS INSTRUMENT
NOVL	NOVELL INC	UIS	UNISYS CORP
ORCL	ORACLE CORP	VRTS	VERITAS SOFTWARE
PMTC	PARAMETRIC TECH	VTSS	VITESSE SEMICOND
PAYX	PAYCHEX INC	XRX	XEROX CORP
PSFT	PEOPLESOFT INC	XLNX	XILINX INC
PHG	PHILIPS ELEC - NY	YHOO	YAHOO INC

AMEX Oil Index (Symbol: XOI)

Symbol	Name	Symbol	Name
AHC	AMERADA HESS CP	OXY	OCCIDENTAL PETE
ARC	ATLANTIC RICH CO	P	PHILLIPS PETE
BPA	BP AMOCO PLC-ADR	RD	ROYAL DUT PE-NYS
CHV	CHEVRON CORP	SUN	SUNOCO INC
COC/A	CONOCO INC-A	TX	TEXACO INC
XON	EXXON CORP	TOT	TOTAL FINA -ADR
KMG	KERR-MCGEE CORP	UCL	UNOCAL CORP
MOB	MOBIL CORP	MRO	USX-MARATHON GRP

AMEX Biotech Index (Symbol: BTK)

Symbol	Name	Symbol	Name
AMGN	AMGEN INC	IDPH	IDEC PHARMACEUT
BTGC	BIO-TECH GENERAL	IMNX	IMMUNEX CORP
BGEN	BIOGEN INC	MEDI	MEDIMMUNE INC
CEPH	CEPHALON INC	MLNM	MILLENNIUM PHARM
CHIR	CHIRON CORP	ORG	ORGANOGENESIS
CORR	COR THERAPEUTICS	PDLI	PROTEIN DESIGN
GENZ	GENZYME-GENL DIV	VRTX	VERTEX PHARM
GILD	GILEAD SCIENCES		

AMEX The Street.com Index (Symbol: ICX)

Symbol	Name	Symbol	Name
AMZN	AMAZON.COM INC	ETV	E4L INC
AMTD	AMERITRADE HLDNG	EBAY	EBAY INC
BYND	BEYONG.COM CORP	EGGS	EGGHEAD.COM INC
BVSN	BROADVISION INC	ONSL	ONSALE INC
CDNW	CDNOW INC	POD	PEAPOD INC
COOL	CYBERIAN OUTPOST	PTVL	PREVIEW TRAVEL
DRIV	DIGITAL RIVER	UBID	UBID INC
EGRP	E*TRADE GROUP		

CBOE Technology Index (Symbol: TXX)

Symbol	Name	Symbol	Name
COMS	3 COM CORP	LLTC	LINEAR TECH CORP
ADCT	ADC TELECOM INC	LU	LUCENT TECH INC
ADBE	ADOBE SYS INC	MU	MICRON TECH
AOL	UN AMERICA ONLINE	MSFT	MICROSOFT CORP
AAPL	APPLE COMPUTER	MOT	MOTOROLA INC
AMAT	APPLIED MATERIAL	ORCL	ORACLE CORP
CSCO	CISCO SYSTEMS	PMTC	PARAMETRIC TECH
CPQ	COMPAQ COMPUTER	QCOM	QUALCOMM INC
CA	COMPUTER ASSOC	SEG	SEAGATE TECH INC
CSC	COMPUTER SCIENCE	SUNW	SUN MICROSYSTEMS
DELL	DELL COMPUTER	SNPS	SYNOPSYS INC
GTW	GATEWAY INC	TLAB	TELLABS INC
HWP	HEWLETT-PACKARD	TXN	TEXAS INSTRUMENT
INTC	INTEL CORP	XLNX	XILINX INC
IBM	INTL BUS MACHINE	YHOO	YAHOO INC

The Street.com Net Index (Symbol: DOT)

Symbol	Name	Symbol	Name
AMZN	AMAZON.COM INC	MACR	MACROMEDIA INC
AOL	AMERICA ONLINE	MSPG	MINDSPRING ENTER
ATHM	AT HOM CORP	NETA	NETWORK ASSOC
BVSN	BROADVISION INC	ONSL	ONSALE INC
CHKP	CHECK POINT SOFT	OMKT	OPEN MARKET INC
CMGI	CMGI INC	RNWK	REALNETWORKS INC
EGRP	E*TRADE GROUP	RSAS	RSA SECURITY INC
EBAY	EBAY INC	SEEK	INFOSEEK
INKT	INKTOMI CORP	USWB	USWEB CORP
LCOS	LYCOS INC	YHOO	YAHOO INC

Morgan Stanley High Tech (Symbol: MSH)

Symbol	Name	Symbol	Name
COMS	3 COM CORP	INTU	INTUIT INC
AMZN	AMAZON.COM INC	LU	LUCENT TECH INC
AOL	AMERICA ONLINE	MU	MICRON TECH
AMAT	APPLIED MATERIAL	MSFT	MICROSOFT CORP
AUD	AUTOMATIC DATA	MOT	MOTOROLA INC
BRCM	BROADCOM CORP-A	NT	NORTEL NETWORKS
CSCO	CISCO SYSTEMS	ORCL	ORACLE CORP
CPQ	COMPAQ COMPUTER	PMTC	PARAMETRIC TECH
CA	COMPUTER ASSOC	PSFT	PEOPLESOFT INC
CSC	COMPUTER SCIENCE	SEG	SEAGATE TECH INC
DELL	DELL COMPUTER	SLR	SOLECTRON CORP
ERTS	ELEC ARTS INC	STM	STMICROELECTRONI
EDS	ELEC DATA SYSTEM	SUNW	SUN MICROSYSTEMS
EMC	EMC CORP/MASS	T LAB	TELLABS INC
FDC	FIRST DATA CORP	TXN	TEXAS INSTRUMENT
HWP	HEWLETT-PACKARD	XLNX	XILINX INC
INTC	INTEL CORP	YHOO	YAHOO INC
IBM	INTL BUS MACHINE		

Dow Jones Industrial Average (Symbol: INDU)

Symbol	Name	Symbol	Name
AA	ALCOA INC	GT	GOODYEAR TIRE
ALD	ALLIEDSIGNAL INC	HWP	HEWLETT-PACKARD
AXP	AMER EXPRESS	IBM	INTL BUS MACHINE
T	AT&T CORP	IP	INTL PAPER CO
BA	BOEING CO	JNJ	JOHNSON & JOHNSON
CAT	CATERPILLAR INC	MCD	MCDONALS CORP
CHV	CHEVRON CORP	MRK	MERCK & CO
C	CITIGROUP INC	MMM	MINNESOTA MINING
KO	COCA-COLA CO	JPM	MORGAN (J.P)
DIS	DISNEY (WALT) CO	MO	PHILIP MORRIS CO
DD	DU PONT (EI)	PG	PROCTR & GAMBLE
EK	EASTMAN KODAK	S	SEARS ROEBUCK
XON	EXXON CORP	UK	UNION CARBIDE
GE	GEN ELECTRIC	UTX	UNITED TECH CORP
GM	GEN MOTORS	WMT	WMT

Dow Jones Transportation Average (Symbol: TRAN)

Symbol	Name	Symbol	Name
ABF	AIRBORNE FREIGHT	NSC	NORFOLK SOUTHERN
ALEX	ALEXANDER & BALD	NWAC	NORTHWEST AIRLIN
AMR	AMR CORP	ROAD	ROADWAY EXPRESS
BNI	BURLINGTON/SANTA	R	RYDER SYSTEM INC
CNF	CNF TRANSPORTATI	LUV	SOUTHWEST AIR
CSX	CSX CORP	UAL	UAL CORP
DAL	DELTA AIR LINES	UNP	UNION PAC CORP
FDX	FDX CORP	U	US AIRWAYS GROUP
GMT	GATX CORP	USFC	USFREIGHTWAYS CP
JBHT	HUNT (JB) TRANS	YELL	YELLOW CORP

Dow Jones Utilities Average (Symbol: UTIL)

Symbol	Name	Symbol	Name
AEP	AMER ELEC PWR	PCG	PG&E CORP
CG	COLUMBIA ENERGY	PEG	PUB SERV ENTERP
ED	CONS EDISON INC	REI	RELIANT ENERGY
CNG	CONS NATURAL GAS	SO	SOUTHERN CO
DUK	DUKE ENERGY CORP	TXU	TEXAS UTIL
EIX	EDISON INTL	UCM	UNICOM CORP
ENE	ENRON CORP	WMB	WILLIAMS COS INC
PE	PECO ENERGY CO		

AMEX Airline Index (Symbol: XAL)

Symbol	Name	Symbol	Name
ALK	ALASKA AIRGROUP	KLM	KLM-NY SHARES
AMR	AMR CORP	NWAC	NORTHWEST AIRLINE
COMR	COMAIR HLDGS INC	LUV	SOUTHWEST AIR
CAL	CONTL AIR-B	UAL	UAL CORP
DAL	DELTA AIR LINES	U	US AIRWAYS GROUP

Interactive WK Internet (Symbol: IIX)

Symbol	Name	Symbol	Name
COMS	3COM CORP	EXDS	EXODUS COMM INC
AMZN	AMAZON.COM INC	HRBC	HARBINGER CORP
AOL	AMERICA ONLINE	SEEK	INFOSEEK CORP
ARBA	ARIBA INC	INKT	INKTOMI CORP
ATHM	AT HOME CORP	INTU	INTUIT INC
BRCM	BROADCOM CORP-A	LVLT	LEVEL 3 COMM INC
BVSN	BROADVISION INC	MSPG	MINDSPRING ENTER
CDNW	CDNOW INC	NETA	NETWORK ASSOC
CHKP	CHECKPOINT SOFT	NSOL	NETWORK SOLUTION
CKFR	CHECKFREE HLDGS	NOVL	NOVELL INC
CSCO	CISCO SYSTEMS	ONSL	ONSALE INC
CMGI	CMGT INC	OMKT	OPEN MARKET INC
CNET	CNET INC	PAIR	PARGAIN TECH
CPTH	CRITICAL PATH	PCLN	PRICELINE.COM
CYCH	CYBERCASH INC	PSIX	PSINET INC
DCLK	DOUBLECLICK INC	QCOM	QUALCOMM INC
EGRP	E*TRADE GROUP	QWST	QWEST COMMUNICAT
EELN	E-LOAN INC	RNWK	REALNETWORKS INC
ELNK	EARTHLINK NETWORK	RTHM	RHYTHMS NETCONNE
EBAY	EBAY INC	RSAS	RSA SECURITY INC

GLOSSARY

COMMONLY USED MARKET TERMS

Accumulation   Term usually applied to the transfer of stocks into the institutional sector, or buying pressure resulting in increased stock values.

Advance-decline line   Each day's number of declining issues is subtracted from the number of advancing issues. The net difference is added to a running sum if the difference is positive or subtracted from the running sum if the difference is negative.

American Depositary Receipts (ADRs)   Receipts held by an American bank that represent shares in a foreign company.

Arbitrage   Technique of buying and selling securities to take advantage of small differences in price.

Auction market   Trading securities on a stock exchange where buyers compete with other buyers and sellers compete with other sellers for the best stock price. Trading in individual stocks is managed and kept orderly by a specialist.

Bear   A person who thinks that prices, the market, an industry, etc., will decline.

Bear market   Generally a time period when security prices decline 15 percent or more.

Big Board   Another name for the New York Stock Exchange.

Block trade   Buying or selling 10,000 shares of stock or $200,000 or more worth of bonds.

Bloomberg-BTRD   An ECN that is targeted toward larger institutions that is part of the Bloomberg financial family.

Blue chip stocks   Stocks of companies known for their long-established record of earning profits and paying dividends.

Bollinger bands   Fixed lines above and below a security's average price. As volatility increases, the bands widen.

Bottom fishing   Buying stocks whose prices have bottomed out or fallen to low levels.

Breakaway/runaway gap   When a tradable stock exits in a range by trading at price levels that leave a price area where no trading occurs on a bar chart. These gaps appear at the completion of important chart formations.

Broker-dealer   A securities firm that sells mutual funds or other securities to the public. The broker-dealer is responsible for oversight of their affiliated brokers.

Bull market   A time period when security prices increase.

Call option   Agreement that gives an investor the right, but not the obligation, to buy a stock, bond, commodity, or other instrument at a specified prices within a specific time period.

Candlestick charts Price activity is aggregated and displayed for specific periods of time and coded in the form of candlesticks. The convention of candlesticks visually posts the open, high, and low price of the period.

Cash market The trading of securities according to their current or spot price, as opposed to trading in a security for future delivery.

Channel In charting, a price channel contains prices throughout a trend. There are three basic ways to draw channels: parallel, rounded, and channels that connect lows or highs.

Chicago Board of Trade (CBOT) A commodity trading market.

Chicago Board Options Exchange (CBOE) An exchange set up by the Chicago Board of Trade to trade stock options.

Circuit breakers Measuring used by some major stock and commodities exchanges to restrict trading temporarily when markets rise or fall too far and/or too fast.

Closing price The last trading price of a stock when the market closes.

Composite trading Total amount of trading across all markets in a share that is listed on the New York Stock Exchange or American Stock Exchange. This includes transactions on those exchanges, the five regional exchanges, and on the NASDAQ Stock Market.

Congestion area or pattern Series of trading days in which there is no visible progress in price.

Consolidation A pause that allows market participants to reevaluate the market and sets the stage for the next price move.

Consumer price index (CPI) A gauge of inflation that measures changes in the prices of consumer goods. The index is based on a list of specific goods and services purchased in urban areas, and is released monthly by the Labor Department.

Correction A reverse movement, usually downward, in the price of an individual stock, bond, commodity, index, or the stock market as a whole.

"Curbs in" An indication that trading curbs have been installed on the New York Stock Exchange.

Cyclical stocks Shares that tend to rise during an upturn in the economy and fall during a downturn.

Crossed market A situation in which one broker's bid exceeds the lowest offer of another or vise versa. NASD rules prohibit a broker from intentionally entering such bids or offers.

Cup and handle Accumulation pattern observed on bar charts that generally lasts from 7 to 65 weeks. The cup is in the shape of a "U" and the handle is usually more than 1 or 2 weeks in duration. The handle is a downward drift with low trading volume from the right side.

Daily chart This is a chart where the periods are set to equal 1-day periods. The value that is charted is typically the closing price for each day.

Day order   An investor's order to buy or sell stock that will be canceled by the end of the day if not filled.

Day trading   Day trading is a mentality that traders follow to take advantage of the liquidity and execution available through real-time trading systems like The Executioner. Traders enter the day flat (with no inventory or predispositions) and trade on intraday moves and exit the day with no open positions.

Dead-cat bounce   Market rebound that sees prices recover and come back up.

Defensive securities   Stocks with investment returns that do not tend to decline as much as the market in general in times when stock prices are falling. Those include companies with earnings that tend to grow despite the business cycle, such as food and drug firms, or companies that pay relatively high dividends like utilities.

Delayed opening   The postponement of trading of an issue on a exchange beyond the normal opening because of market conditions that have been judged by exchange officials to warrant such a delay (that is, an influx or imbalance of buy or sell orders and/or pending corporate news).

Dip   A slight decline in securities prices followed by a rise.

Discount rate   The interest rate charged by the Federal Reserve on loans to banks and other financial institutions. This rate influences the rates these financial institutions can charge their customers.

Double bottom/top   Price action of a security or market average where it has declined (advanced) two times to the same approximate level, indicating the existence of a support (resistance) level and a possibility that the downward (upward) trend has ended.

Dow Jones Average   There are four Dow Jones averages that track price changes in various sectors. The Dow Jones Industrial Average tracks the price changes of the stock of 30 industrial companies. The Dow Jones Transportation Average monitors the price changes of the stocks of 20 airlines, railroads, and trucking companies. The Dow Jones Utility Average measures the performance of the stock of 15 gas, electric, and power companies. The Dow Jones 65 Composite Average monitors the stock of all 65 companies that make up the other three averages.

Dow Jones Industrial Average (DJIA)   Often referred to as the Dow, it is the best know and most widely reported indicator of the stock market' s performance. The Dow tracks the price changes of 30 significant industrial stocks traded on the New York Stock Exchange. Their combined market value is equal to roughly 20 percent of the market value of all stocks listed on the New York Stock Exchange.

Earnings   Income after a company's taxes and all other expenses have been paid. Also called profit or net income.

Earnings per share   Calculated by dividing the number of outstanding shares into earnings.

Economic indicators   Key statistics used to analyze business conditions and to make forecasts.

Elliot wave theory   Originally published by Nelson Elliot in 1939, it is a pattern-recognition technique based on the thesis that stock markets follow a pattern or rhythm of five waves up and three waves down to form a complete cycle of eight waves. The down waves are referred to as "correction" waves.

Emerging markets   Financial markets in nations that are developing market-based economies and have become popular with U.S. investors, such as China and Peru.

Exchange   A centralized place for trading securities and commodities, usually involving an auction process.

Fade   Selling a rising price or buying a falling price.

Fair value   A mathematical relationship between the S&P 500 cash and futures index.

Federal funds rate   The interest rate banks charge on overnight loans to banks that need more cash to meet bank reserve requirements. The Federal Reserve sets the interest rate.

Federal Open Market Committee (FOMC)   The policy-making arm of the Federal Reserve Board. It sets monetary policy to meet the Fed's objectives of regulating the money supply and credit. The FOMC's chief tool is the purchase and sale of government securities, which increase or decrease the money supply, respectively. It also sets key interest rates, such as the discount rate.

Federal Reserve   The central bank of the United States that sets monetary policy. The Federal Reserve oversees money supply, interest rates, and credit with the goal of keeping the U.S. economy and currency stable. Governed by a seven-member board, the system includes 12 regional federal banks, 25 branches, and all national and state banks that are part of the system.

Fibonacci numbers   Fibonacci numbers are a sequence of numbers in which each successive number is the sum of the two previous numbers: 1, 2, 3, 5, 8, 13, 21, 34, 55, 89, 144, 610, etc. There are four popular Fibonacci studies: arcs, fans, retracements, and time zones. The interpretation of these studies involves anticipating changes in trends as prices near the lines created by the Fibonacci studies.

Flag   A sharp price spike followed with a sideways consolidation with a bias counter to the rally. Prices usually break out of this consolidation pattern with an objective equal to the mast preceding the flag.

Float   The number of outstanding shares in a corporation available for trading by the public.

Fundamental analysis   Analysis technique that looks at a company's financial condition, management, and place in its industry to predict a company's stock price movement.

Hedging   Buying or selling a product or a security to offset a possible loss from price changes on a future corresponding purchase or sale.

Index fund   A mutual fund that seeks to produce the same return that investors would get if they owned all the stocks in a particular stock index, often the Standard and Poor's 500 stock index.

Index arbitrage   Buying or selling baskets of stocks while at the same time executing offsetting trades in stock-index futures. For example, if stocks are temporarily cheaper than futures, an arbitrager will buy stocks and sell futures to capture a profit on the difference or spread between the two prices.

Indexing Buying and holding a mix of stocks that match the performance of a broad stock market barometer such as the Standard & Poor's 500 stock index.

Initial public offering (IPO) The first time a company issues stock to the public.

Insider A person, such as an executive or director, who has information about a company before the information is available to the public.

Inside trading In one respect, it refers to the legal trading of a security by corporate officers based on information available to the public. In another respect, it refers to the illegal trading of securities by any investor based on information not available to the public.

Intermarket trading An electronic communications network linking the intermarket trading systems (ITS) floors of the seven registered exchanges to forster competition among them in stocks listed on either the NYSE or AMEX and one or more of the regional exchanges.

Lagging economic indicators A composite of seven economic measurements that tend to trail developments in the economy as a whole. Those indicators are duration of unemployment, ratio of inventories to sales, index of labor costs per unit of output, average prime rate, outstanding commercial and industrial loans, ratio of outstanding consumer installment credit to personal income, and consumer price index for services.

Leading economic indicators A composite of 11 economic measurements developed to help forecast likely changes in the economy as a whole. The components are average work, unemployment claims, orders for consumer goods, slower deliveries, plant and equipment orders, building permits, durable order backlog, material prices, stock prices, M2 money supply, and consumer expectations.

Long-term equity anticipation securities (LEAPS) Options that won't expire for up to three years.

Level I Level I (sometimes called quick quote) is trade and quote data that only shows current bid, ask, last trade value and volume, and some daily summary information. You do not see who is buying and selling nor do you know the number of shares for sale at all price levels.

Listed stock The stock of a company which is traded on a securities exchange.

Long bond Slang for a 30-year bond issued by the U.S. Treasury. It is considered a key indicator, or benchmark, of trends in long-term interest rates.

Margin call A demand upon a customer to deposit money or securities with a broker. Margin calls are made in accordance with Regulation T which governs the amount of credit that may be advanced by brokers to customers for the purchase of securities.

Market capitalization The total market value of a company or stock, which equals the number of shares times the current market price of the shares.

Market minder A customizable table that allows you to isolate and display key information fields on a list of stocks or indexes. You set the list and develop column layout of the market minder.

Market sentiment   A measurement of the bullish or bearish attitude of the crowd.

Market timing   Shifting money in and out of investment markets in an effort to take advantage of rising and falling prices.

Momentum   Momentum is the most basic concept in oscillator analysis. Momentum is the rate of change at which the market is rising or falling.

NASDAQ   An electronic stock market run by the National Association of Securities Dealers. Brokers get price quotes through a computer network and trade via telephone or computer network.

NASDAQ Composite Index   An index that covers the price movements of all stocks traded on the NASDAQ Stock Market.

NASDAQ National Market   A subdivision of the NASDAQ Stock Market that contains the largest and most actively traded stocks on NASDAQ. Companies must meet more stringent standards to be included in this section than they do to be included in the other major subdivision, the NASDAQ small-cap market.

National Association of Securities Dealers (NASD)   A membership organization for securities-brokerage firms and underwriters in the United States that promise to abide by association rules. It sets guidelines for ethics and standardized industry practices, and has a disciplinary structure for looking into allegations of violations. The NASD also operates the NASDAQ Stock Market.

New York Stock Exchange   Founded in 1792, it is the roughly 23,000 companies whose shares are listed there totaling about $5 trillion.

NYSE Composite Index   An index that covers the price movements of all stocks listed on the New York Stock Exchange.

Odd lot   Order to buy or sell less than 100 shares of stock.

Offer   Same as the ask price. *See* Ask under Commonly Used Technical Terms.

Open order   A buy or sell order that has not yet been executed or canceled.

Options   An agreement allowing an investor to buy or sell stock during a specific time for a specific price. Options are traded on several exchanges, including the Chicago Board of Options Exchange, the American Stock Exchange, the Philadelphia Stock Exchange, the Pacific Stock Exchange, and the New York Stock Exchange.

Over the Counter (OTC)   Market where transactions are conducted over the telephone and computer network of dealers rather than on the floor of an exchange.

Penny stocks   While many legitimate companies have share prices that low, the term "penny stocks" includes stocks that are priced at $5 and below and usually refers to speculative companies with little or no real business that are heavily promoted by hard-selling brokerage firms.

Pink sheets   The printed quotations of the bid and ask prices of over-the-counter stocks, published by National Quotation Bureaus, Inc.

Point   A change of $1 in the market price of a stock is equal to one point.

Portfolio   A collection of securities held by an investor.

Private Placement   The sale of stocks or other investments directly to an investor. The securities in a private placement don't have to be registered with the Securities and Exchange Commission.

Producer price index (PPI)   A group of statistics compiled by the Labor Department that are used as a gauge of inflation at the wholesale level. The index for finished goods—which tracks commodities that will not undergo further processing and are ready for sale to the ultimate user—is the most prominently reported of the statistics.

Profit taking   Selling securities after a recent, often rapid price increase.

Program trading   Stock trades involving the purchase or sale of a basket including 15 or more stocks with a total market value of $1 million or more. Most program trades are executed on the New York Stock Exchange, using computerized trading systems. Index arbitrage is the most prominently reported type of program trading.

Put option   An agreement that gives an investor the right but not the obligation to sell a stock, bond, commodity, or other instrument of a specified price within a specific time period.

Put/call volume ratio   The volume of trading in puts—options to sell—divided by the total calls—options to buy—for a security or an index.

Quote   A bid to buy a security or an offer to sell a security in a given market at a given time.

Reversal gap   Chart formation where the low of the day is above the previous day's range and the close is above the day's open.

Reversal stop   An order to reverse position when a specific price is hit.

Round lot   A unit of trading or a multiple thereof, generally consisting of 100 shares of stock.

Russell 2000   A small-capitalization stock index. It consists of the 2000 smallest securities in the Russell 3000 ($RUT.X).

Secondary market   Market for issues that were previously offered or sold.

Secondary offering   The sale to the public of a usually large block of stock that is owned by an existing shareholder.

Sector funds   Mutual funds that invest in a single-industry sector such as biotechnology, gold, or regional banks. Sector funds tend to generate erratic performance, and they often dominate both the top and bottom of the annual mutual fund performance charts.

Securities and Exchange Commission (SEC)   The federal agency that enforces securities laws and sets standards for disclosure about publicly traded securities, including mutual funds. It was created in 1934 and consists of five commissioners appointed by the president and confirmed by the Senate to staggered terms.

Secular   Long term as opposed to seasonal or cyclical.

Security   A financial instrument that indicates the holder owns a share or shares of a company (stock) or has loaned money to a company or government organization (bond).

Share   An investment that represents part ownership of a company or a mutual fund. *See also* Stock.

Short covering   Trades that reverse, or close out, short-sale positions. In the stock market, for instance, shares are purchased to replace the shares previously borrowed.

Short interest   Total number of shares of a given stock that have been sold short and not yet repurchased.

Small cap stocks   Shares of relatively small publicly traded corporations, typically with a total market value, or capitalization, of less than $600 million.

Stock   An investment that represents part ownership of a company. There are two different types of stock: common and preferred. *Common stocks* provide voting rights but no guarantee of dividend payments. *Preferred stocks* provide no voting rights but have a set, guaranteed dividend payment. *See also* Share.

Stock index futures   A contract to buy or sell the cash value of a stock index by a specified date.

Stock option   An agreement allowing an investor to buy or sell shares of stock within a stipulated time and for a certain price.

Stock split   A change in a company's number of shares outstanding that doesn't change a company's total market value, or each shareholder's percentage stake in the company. Additional shares are issued to existing shareholders, at a rate expressed as a ratio. A 2-for-1 stock split, for instance, doubles the number of shares outstanding. Investors will own two shares after the split for each share they owned before the split. Stock splits are typically viewed by investors as bullish.

Stop limit order   A stop order that becomes a limit order after the specified price has been reached.

Technical analysis   Research of a security or market sector that uses trading data, such as volume and price trends, to make predictions on stock movements.

Third-market trading   Over-the-counter trading in stocks that are listed on an exchange.

Ticker   In trading systems like the Executioner, tickers can be set to display market maker positioning and/or trade details and are color coded in order to easily recognize market direction.

Ticker symbol   Letters that identify a security for trading purposes. A security's ticker symbol also may be used in news and price-quotation services to identify the security.

Time and sales   Time and sales ticker displays information about specific trades as they go off. The selling institution is responsible for posting the trade (within 90 seconds) and traders use this to see where the market sentiment is at a certain time.

Timed out   After you place an order, whether on SOES or on an ECN, the order will only be "live" for a specified amount of time. Then your order has "timed out" which means that it has run out of time and it will be automatically canceled by the proper exchange. Time constraints vary for each type of order.

Townsend Analytics Townsend Analytics is the software developer who developed Real Tick III and the Executioner.

Trade date The actual date on which your shares are purchased or sold. The transaction price is determined by the closing net asset value on that date. This date also determines the eligibility for dividends.

Traders People who negotiate prices and execute buy and sell orders, either on behalf of an investor or for their own account.

Trading curbs One of several "circuit breakers" adopted by the NYSE and approved by the Securities and Exchange Commission in response to the October 1987 stock market crash.

Triple witching Slang for the quarterly expiration of stock index futures, stock index options, and options on individual stocks. Trading associated with the expirations inflates stock market volume and can cause volatility in prices. It occurs on the third Friday of March, June, September, and December.

Unlisted stock A security not listed on a stock exchange and generally traded in the OTC market.

Up to bid This happens when a market maker moves his or her current bid to the highest bid. This is a bullish sign because the market maker will now pay a higher price to buy a stock than any other market maker at that time.

Volatility The characteristic of a security or market to fall or rise sharply in price in a short-term period.

VIX The CBOE's volatility index.

Volume Number of shares traded in a company or an entire market during a given period.

Wedge Technical pattern where two converging lines connect a group of price peaks and troughs.

Whipsaw Losing money on both sides of a price swing.

GLOSSARY OF COMMONLY USED TECHNICAL TERMS

The following are commonly used technical terms. Please read and become very familiar with them as this will maximize your learning growth to trading mastery.

Ask Low ask (offer) is the lowest price that someone is willing to accept for a security.

Bid High bid is the highest price that someone is willing to pay for a security. "Hit the bid" means to sell a stock on the current bid price.

Breakout Point when the market price moves out of the trend channel.

Day trade *See* Appendix 3 for definition.

Doji A candlestick in which the open and close of the stock price are the same, or substantially the same.

Downtick   A sale of a listed security that occurs at a lower price than the previous transaction.

Electronic Communication Network (ECN)   Electronic Communication Newwork consists of ARCA (Archipelago), BTRD (Bloomberg), INCA (Instinet), ISLD (Island), SelectNet (NASD), and REDI (Spear Leads). ECNs work as order-matching systems and allow traders to advertise a price better than the current bid or offer. By using ECNs, traders can bypass the SOES network and can make markets by playing or splitting the spread.

Futures   An agreement to purchase or sell a given quantity of a commodity, security, or currency at a specified date in the future. Also called a *futures contract*. We use the governing S&P 500 futures contract (changes each quarter) as the key leading indicator of the equity market. *See also* Index Arbitrage under Commonly Used Market Terms.

Inside day   Day in which the price range is within the previous day's price range.

Inside market/price   The highest bid and the lowest ask (offer) at any given time for an issue.

Instinet   A method by which large institutional clients can trade stocks during nonmarket hours.

Intraday   Price and volume information that occurs during a single trading day as opposed to daily information, which summarizes trades on a day-by-day basis.

Island (ISLD)   Island is an Electronic Communication Network (ECN).

Level II   Level II data is a real-time display of market maker or ECN bids and offers. Studying this data allows a trader insight into the intentions of the market makers and into the intentions of the market makers and the propensity that the stock has to move multiple levels.

Limit order   An order to buy or sell a stock when it reaches a certain price.

Market internal   Market internals are used to gauge market strength or weakness. Pristine follows the governing S&P 500 futures contract, the tick, trin, bond futures, and the strength or weakness of particular sectors.

Market maker   In a stock market, a trader responsible for maintaining an orderly market in an individual stock by standing ready to buy or sell shares. On a stock exchange, a market is known as a specialist.

Market order   Order to buy or sell at the best available price.

Mid-day doldrums   We refer to this as the 11:15 a.m. – 2:15 p.m. period. This is the time when breakouts often fail. This is typically a slow time, when many Wall Street market makers are off at lunch and doing other things besides trading. Pristine suggests that only experienced traders trade during this period, if at all. Pristine uses the mid-day doldrums to search for stocks that have favorable setups for possible afternoon scalping plays or swing trade opportunities.

Momentum trading   A style of trading where a trader attempts to identify short bursts of buying or selling pressure in order to quickly enter and exit stocks.

Moving average Moving averages are one way to view historic price levels. Moving average takes into account some number of price periods (a new period is added and the oldest is dropped from the calculation) to show average price over time. It is possible to weight more recent prices by linearly or exponentially recent prices smoothing the average lines. The longer the averaging period, the more lag you will see between the average and the most recent prices. Pristine uses the following simple moving averages on its charts in making trading decisions:

Chart duration	Period moving averages used
Daily	10, 20, 50, 100, and 200
Weekly	20, 50, 100, and 200
Hourly	20 and 200
15-Minute	20 and 200
5-Minute	20 and 200
1 or 2-Minute	10 and 20

NOTE: Also see Pristine's Educational Report, "The Mighty 50-Period Moving Average" at *www.pristine.com*.

Offer out Price at which a market maker sells his or her stock and the general public buys. When you "offer out," you are in essence taking the role of a market maker by offering to sell your stock on the offer, typically on an ECN, SelectNet, or ARCA.

Refreshes Essentially the same as "he stays." Used when a market maker has filled someone at the bid or offer and the market maker remains, continuing to buy or sell stock at the quoted price.

Reversal times Over the many years of trading and study of the markets, Pristine has noted and used profitably various "reversal periods." These are the times during which the direction of the market often changes course. The morning reversal periods are 9:50 – 10:10 a.m. and 10:25 – 10:30 a.m. EST. For example, if the market is showing great strength at the market open, we have experienced that the buying pressure typically ceases and reverses in the first reversal period. Then, for example, if the market continues to sell off, we often find that the selling pressure ceases and often rallies in the 10:25 – 10:30 a.m. reversal period. Trading can be very profitable through 11:15 a.m. or so, which leads us to the next reversal period to watch. We refer to the 11:15 a.m. – 2:15 p.m. period as the midday doldrums. Then 2:15 p.m. is our first afternoon reversal period when traders are back getting ready for the afternoon session. When market internals are very positive, it is even possible to take half-lot anticipatory swing trades after this time that are breaking out of consolidation and support on the 15-minute chart. Then, the closing of the bond market at 3:00 p.m. provides the next reversal period. It seems that the closing of bond market gives traders one less thing to worry about, so the market typically picks up steam in one direction or another at this time. Then, the final reversal period is around 3:30 p.m. As Pristine traders are well aware, just because a stock looks good in the morning or early afternoon does not mean that it will close that way. The last 30 minutes of trading can be extremely profitable for scalping or day or swing trades. It is during this time that many buyers wait to commit and robust rallies occur into the close. Based on these principles, Pristine believes that the lowest risk trading occurs between 9:35 – 11:15 a.m. and 2:15 – 4:00 p.m.

Scalp trade (scalping)   *See* Appendix 3 for definition.

SelectNet   SelectNet is an ECN that crosses orders and is supported by the NASD. SelectNet orders must be at or between the spread.

Sell off   A period of intensified selling in a market that pushes prices sharply lower.

Short covering   Trades that reverse, or close out, short-sale positions. In the stock market, for instance, shares are purchased to replace the shares previously borrowed.

Short selling   A trading strategy that anticipates a drop in a share's price. Stock or another financial instrument is borrowed from a broker and then sold, creating a short position. That position is reversed, or covered, when the stock is repurchased to repay to loan. The short seller profits by repurchasing the stock at a lower price than sold for in creating the short positions. An "uptick" (the most recent sale occurred at the offer) is required to sell short.

Specialist   A stock exchange member who is designated to maintain a fair and orderly market in a specific stock. They are required to buy and sell for their own account to counteract temporary imbalances in supply and demand.

Spread   The difference between the bid and asked prices.

Small order execution system (SOES)   SOES was developed in 1984, but made mandatory in 1988 in response to the stock market crash of 1987. It is a non-negotiated exchange where market makers place offers and bids and are required to met certain fill requirements set forth in their participation agreement with the NASD.

Standard & Poor's 500 Stock Index   A benchmark index of 500 large stocks, maintained by Standard & Poor's, a division of The McGraw-Hill Companies.

Stop (protective stop)   The price at which a trader will close out an existing position to cut losses in the event the trade does not move in the intended direction. A trailing, or progressive stop, is a technique that trails the price of a stock up with a stop right behind it.

Swing trading   *See* Appendix 3 for definition.

Teenie   One-sixth of one point.

Ticks   Upward or downward price movements in a security or index. A downtick is the sale of a security at a price below the preceding sale. An uptick is a sale executed at a price higher than the preceding sale.

Tick spread   The difference between the high and low of the NYSE tick indicator of each trading day. For intraday trading, Pristine views the tick of under 1000 as oversold and over 1000 as overbought, and looks for intraday reversals (bounces) when such levels correspond with other extreme levels in the S&P futures and TRIN.

TRIN   The short-term trading index (or "ARMS index") measures the breadth of the market while taking volume into account. The index measures the concentration of the volume in advancing and declining stocks. TRIN is a ratio of the advance/decline ratio to the up volume/down volume ratio, or

$$TRIN = \frac{\text{\# of advancing issues}/\text{\# of declining issues}}{\text{advancing volume}/\text{declining volume}}$$

TRIN readings above 1.0 indicate oversold conditions or more relative volume in declining issues, while values below 1.0 indicate overbought conditions, or more relative volume in advancing issues. For intraday trading, Pristine views a TRIN reading of over 1.5 as very oversold and under 0.35 as very overbought, and looks for intraday reversals (bounces) when such levels correspond with other extreme levels in the S&P futures and tick.

Uptick A sale of a listed security that occurs at a higher price than the previous transaction.

ECONOMIC DATA DEFINITIONS

Capacity utilization Percentage of industrial capacity in use, monthly, from the Federal Reserve.

CPI Percentage change in consumer price index, monthly, from the Labor Department.

CPI core Percentage change in the CPI, excluding food and energy, monthly, from the Labor Department.

CRB Index Index of commodity prices, end of month reading, from the Commodity Research Bureau.

Employment costs Change in the employment cost index at an annual percentage rate, quarterly, from the Labor Department.

Existing home sales Sales of previously owned houses at an annual rate, in millions, from the National Association of Realtors.

Factory orders Percentage change in orders for factory goods, monthly, from the Commerce Department.

GDP Real change in gross domestic product at annual percentage rate, quarterly, from the Commerce Department.

Hourly earnings Percentage change in hourly earnings in the private sector, monthly, from the Labor Department.

Housing starts Starts of housing units at an annual rate, in thousands, monthly, from the Commerce Department.

Industrial production Percentage change in industrial output, monthly, from the Federal Reserve.

Inventory change Change in business inventories, in billions of dollars, quarterly, from the Commerce Department.

Jobless rate Percentage of unemployed adults in the workforce, monthly, from the Labor Department.

NAPM Index Diffusion index of current business conditions in manufacturing, monthly, from the National Association of Purchasing Management.

NAPM prices paid   Diffusion index of companies paying higher prices, monthly, from the National Association of Purchasing Management.

Payrolls   Change in nonfarm payrolls, in thousands, monthly, from the Labor Department.

Personal income   Percentage change in household income, monthly, from the Commerce Department.

Personal spending   Percentage change in personal consumption expenditures, monthly, from the Commerce Department.

PPI   Percentage change in producer price index for finished goods, monthly, from the Labor Department.

PPI core   Percentage change in the PPI for finished goods, excluding food and energy, monthly, from the Labor Department.

Producers' durables   Percentage change in investment of producers' durable equipment, quarterly, from the Commerce Department.

Productivity   Change in nonfarm business productivity at annual percentage rate, quarterly, from the Labor Department.

Purchases deflator   Change in gross domestic purchase price deflator at an annual percentage rate, quarterly, from the Commerce Department.

Retail sales   Percentage change of sales at retail establishments, monthly, from the Commerce Department.

S&P 500   S&P 500 stock index, end of month reading, from Standard & Poor's.

Ten-year T-note   Yield on 10-year treasury notes, monthly average of daily close, from the Federal Reserve.

Thirty-year T-bond   Yield on 30-year treasury bonds, monthly average of daily close, from the Federal Reserve.

Three-month T-bill   Yield on three-month treasury bills, monthly average of daily close, from the Federal Reserve.

Trade gap   Balance of international trade in goods and services, in billions of dollars, monthly, from the Commerce Department.

US$-Euro   Dollars per euro, monthly average of daily noon price, from the Federal Reserve.

Yen-US$ Yen per dollar, monthly average of daily noon price, from the Federal Reserve.

TRADE TYPES

The following is a list of the most common trade types complete with a brief description of each style of trade. These trade types should not be confused with the many specific, proprietary trading strategies and tactics taught in Pristine's 1- and 3-day advanced trading seminars.

Scalp trade: A style of trading that is designed to capitalize on small moves, using price setups that present exceptionally low-risk opportunities. The typical objective for a scalp trade is ¼ to a ⅝ or more. Scalping demands a familiarity with Level II as well as the use of a direct access system such as The Executioner (*www.executioner.com*) for instant order execution. The best scalping opportunities are found in liquid stocks (trading 500,000 or more shares a day) with quality market maker representation. Pristine's scalp setups are typically found using charts in smaller intraday timeframes such as a 2, 5, and 15 minutes.

Day trade: Conventionally speaking, a day trade is a position initiated and closed out in the same trading session. In Pristine's real-time trading room, a day trade is an opportunity with the potential to become an overnight (O/N) and/or develop into a swing trade, but because it occurs early in the day, it is typically treated more aggressively in terms of locking in partial or complete profits. Day trades also typically employ tighter stops than the average swing trade does. We have found that the best day trades usually have "room to run," with resistance being far enough away to warrant holding through a brief pullback or period of consolidation if necessary. Day trades are typically found using intraday charts with medium length time frames such as a 15-minute or hourly chart.

Overnight trade: An overnight trade is typically a position entered late in the day in a stock which is closing at or near its high (or low, for shorts) with the potential to gap up or see follow-through the next morning. As mentioned earlier, an overnight can also start as a day trade that closes strong enough to warrant holding past the close and into the following day. Overnights are frequently closed out in the early going of the following morning (if not right at or before the open) with some traders opting to sell only half, with the remaining half held for a longer period and a potentially larger price gain.

Swing trade: A swing trade is one that is entered with the idea of profiting from the natural ebb and flow of a stock's daily movements. Swing trades are usually initiated in an area of significant support (or resistance, for shorts), and seek to capture between $1 to $4 in profits, depending on the situation. Typically held for a period of 2 to 5 (or more) days, swing trades take advantage of a very profitable market niche overlooked by most active investors. Too brief for large institutional concerns to take advantage of and, at the same time, too lengthy for floor traders (who typically don't hold positions overnight) to be comfortable with, this time frame offers the perfect opportunity for independent traders who possess the expertise necessary to profitably exploit it. Swing trades are found primarily using daily (and weekly) charts, with occasional reference to a 15-minute chart as well.

POPULAR WEB SITES AND CHAT ROOMS
FOR THE DAY TRADING ENTHUSIST

.COM-ING THE DAY TRADING INDUSTRY

Active Traders Network: *www.activetraders.net*
Avid Trading Company: *avidtrader.com*
The Daily Trader: *www.dailytrader.com*
Dayinvestor: *www.dayinvestor.com*
Daypicks: *www.daypicks*
Daytrader's Bulletin: *www.daytradersbulletin.com*
Daytraders On-line: *www.daytraders.com*
The Daytrader Toad: *members.tripod.com/daytrader/index.html*
Day Trading International: *www.daytradingintl.com*
Daytradingstocks.com: *www.daytradingstocks.com*
Dynamic Daytrader: *www.dynamicdaytrader.com*
Elite Trader: *www.elitetrader.com*
Intelligent Speculator: *intelligentspeculator.com*
The Hard Right Edge: *www.hardrightedge.com*
Mkt Traders: *www.dtrades.com*
Momentum Trader: *www.mtrader.com*
MonyWolff: *www.monywolff.com*
Online Daytraders: *www.onlinedaytraders.com*
PC Trader: *www.pctrader.com*
Pristine Day Trader: *www.pristine.com*
The Rookie Day Trader; *www.rookiedaytrader.com*
TradeHard: *www.tradehard.com*
Trading Systems Network: *www.tradingsystems.net*
Trading Tactics: *www.tradingtactics.com*
The Underground Trader: *www.undergroundtrader.com*

CHATS AND BOARDS

BrowseMaster.com: *www.browsemaster.com*
MarketForum: *www.marketforum.com*

ECooler Network: *www.ecooler.net*
Silicon Investor: *www.techstocks.com*
Stock-Talk: *www.stock-talk.com*

INDEX

ABOUT THE AUTHORS

Oliver Velez and **Greg Capra** are co-founders of Pristine Capital Management, Inc., and its top-rated website Pristine.com. When they aren't conducting detailed technical analysis of the markets, delivering trading insights to their website subscribers, or locking horns with other traders on the electronic battlefield (as they have done for over a decade), Velez and Capra are two of the electronic trading industry's most sought-after speakers.

Printed in the USA
CPSIA information can be obtained
at www.ICGtesting.com
CBHW080246091224
18589CB00016B/70

9 781265 802370